Nag Hammadi and Manichaean Studies

VOLUME 57

Mediaeval
Manichaean Book Art

A Codicological Study of Iranian and Turkic
Illuminated Book Fragments from 8th–11th
Century East Central Asia

by

Zsuzsanna Gulácsi

BRILL
LEIDEN · BOSTON
2005

Despite our efforts we have not been able to trace all rights holders to some copyrighted material. The publisher welcomes communications from copyrights holders, so that the appropriate acknowledgements can be made in future editions, and to settle other permission matters.

This book is printed on acid-free paper.

Library of Congress Cataloging-in-Publication Data

Gulácsi, Zsuzsanna.
   Mediaeval Manichaean book art : a codicological study of Iranian and Turkic illuminated book fragments from 8th-11th century east Cenral Asia / by Zsuzanna Gulácsi.
      p. cm. — (Nag Hammadi and Manichaean studies, ISSN 0929-2470 ; v. 57)
   Includes bibliographical references and index.
   ISBN 90-04-13994-X (hardback : alk. paper)
   1. Illumination of books and manuscripts, Manichaean—Asia, Central. 2. Illumination of books and manuscripts, Medieval—Asia, Central. I. Title. II. Series.

ND2932.G85 2005
745.6'7'0958—dc22

                                                            2005047119

ISSN   0929-2470
ISBN   90 04 13994 X

Dedicated to Prof. Dr. Marianne Yaldiz

CONTENTS

List of Tables. ix
List of Figures xi
List of Color Plates xiii
Acknowledgments xv

Introduction: A Codicological Approach to a Unique Group of Objects 1
    History of the Manichaean Religion 1
    History of Research 4
    The Codicological Approach 8
    Practical Steps of Research 10
    Terminology 12

I.   Identifying the Corpus of Manichaean Book Art 15
    Criteria of Identification 19
    Conclusion 34

II.   Dating the Remains: Scientific, Textual, and Artistic Evidence 39
    Wide Horizon (ca. 270 Years) 40
    Medium Horizon (126 Years) 45
    Narrow Horizons (19 and 17, and ca. 40 Years) 52
    Conclusion 57

    Color plates

III. Codicological Characteristics: Artisanship of Bookmakers and Scribes in Manichaean Turfan 59
    The Making of Illuminated Codices 60
    The Making of Illuminated Hand Scrolls and Pustakas 88
    The Work of the Scribes 93
    Conclusion 103

IV. The Work of the Illuminator: The Four Basic Painting Styles of Turfan Manichaean
    Book Illumination 105
    The West Asian Fully Painted Style 106
    The West Asian Outline Drawing Style 116
    The Chinese Fully Painted and Outline Drawing Styles 123
    Conclusions 131

V.   Patterns of Page Arrangement: Integration of Text and Image 133
    Reconstructible Codex Fragments with Decorative Designs 138
    Reconstructible Codex Fragments with Figural Scenes 141

Interpretation of Non-reconstructible Illuminated Codex Fragments 162
Layouts of Illuminated Codex Fragments 169
Layouts of Illuminated Hand Scroll and Pustaka Fragments 177
Conclusion 191

VI. The Written and the Painted Message: Contextual Cohesion of Text and Image 195
Survey of Identifiable Texts 196
Survey of Identifiable Figural Scenes 203
Identifiable Texts and Their Illuminations 206
Conclusion 218

Postscript 221
Bibliography 223

Index 235

LIST OF TABLES

1/1 Illuminated Book Fragments Attributed to the Manichaean Corpus from the two Berlin Collections between 1913 and 2001 (84 illuminated book fragments)

1/2 Provenance of Berlin Artifacts Attributed to the Corpus of Manichaean Illuminated Book Fragments (79 examples)

1/3 Provenance of non-Berlin Artifacts Attributed to the Corpus of Manichaean Illuminated Book Fragments (9 examples)

1/4 The Reference Group: Manichaean Illuminated Book Fragments Identified by Script and Textual Content (63 examples)

1/5 Book Fragments Identified through Elects in Figural Scenes (4 examples)

1/6 Book Fragments Identified through Decorative Designs (10 examples)

1/7 Book Fragments Identified by Motifs Common in Reference Group (9 examples)

1/8 Berlin Fragments Identified through Documentary Evidence (3 examples)

1/9 Regrouping of Fragments Attributed to the Manichaean Corpus (20 examples)

1/10 Manichaean Illuminated Book Fragments in the Museum of Indian Art, Berlin (57 examples)

1/11 Manichaean Illuminated Book Fragments in the State Library, Berlin (23 examples)

1/12 Manichaean Illuminated Book Fragments in Four Other Collections (9 examples)

2/1 Compared Epithets

3/1 Comparison of Manichaean Quire Numbers and Thicknesses

3/2 Sample Distribution of Binding Holes on non-Illuminated Codices (5 examples)

3/3 Distribution of Binding Holes on Illuminated Codex Fragments (6 examples)

3/4 Summary of Size Data on Manichaean Codices

3/5 Examples of Extra Small non-Illuminated Codices (5 examples)

3/6 Examples of Extra Large non-Illuminated Codices (2 examples)

3/7 Remnants of Small-size Illuminated Codices (8 examples)

3/8 Remnants of Medium-size Illuminated Codices (11 examples)

3/9 Remnants of Large-size Illuminated Codices (4 examples)

3/10 Summary of Size Data on Manichaean Pictorial and Illuminated Scrolls

4/1 West Asian Fully Painted Illuminations in Codex Format (66 examples)

4/2 Examples of the West Asian Outline-drawing Style (32 examples)

4/3 Examples of the Chinese Fully Painted Styles (12 examples)

4/4 Examples of the Chinese Outline Drawing Styles (3 examples)

5/1 Page Elements of two Reconstructable Codex Fragments with Decorative Designs (8 examples)

5/2 Page Elements of 11 Reconstructable Codex Fragments with Figural Scenes (20 examples)

5/3 Decorative Design within Text Area (2 examples)

5/4 Decorative Design along the Upper Margin (33 examples)

5/5 Decorative Design along the Upper and Outer Margins (21 examples)

5/6 Decorative Design along Upper, Outer, and Lower Margins (4 examples)

5/7   Decorative Designs at Unidentifiable Marginal Location (18 examples)
5/8   Figural Scenes along the Outer Margins (12 examples)
5/9   Figural Scenes along the Bottom Margin (4 examples)
5/10   Intratextual Figural Scenes Preserved from Manichaean Books (17 examples)
5/11   Full-page Figural Scenes Preserved from Manichaean Books (8 examples)
5/12   Full-page or Intratextual Figural Scenes Preserved from Manichaean Books (18 examples)
5/13   Fragments of Illuminated Hand Scrolls (6 examples)
5/14   Fragments of the Illuminated Pustaka Book (38 examples)

6/1   Overview of Literary Genres and Types of Illumination in Identifiable Texts (39 examples)
6/2   Hymns Preserved from Manichaean Illuminated Books (21 examples)
6/3   Religious Prose Preserved from Manichaean Illuminated Books (8 examples)
6/4   Benedictions Preserved from Manichaean Illuminated Books (6 examples)
6/5   Colophons Preserved from Manichaean Illuminated Books (2 examples)
6/6   Overview of Pictorial Subjects in Identifiable Figural Scenes of Manichaean Illuminated Book Fragments (25 examples)
6/7   Degrees of Contextual Cohesion between Identifiable Texts and Identifiable Illuminations (34 examples)

LIST OF FIGURES

0/1   Map of the Silk Roads and the Historical Sites of the Turfan Region
0/2   Terminology of Manichaean Book Design

1/1   Scope of Primary Sources Narrowed for this Study
1/2   Books in Turfan Manichaean Paintings
1/3   Fragment of Parchment Folio with Intratextual Figural Scene
1/4   Fragment of Codex Folio with Illuminated Header

2/1   Radiocarbon Analysis of MIK III 8259
2/2   Carbon-dated Codex Fragment
2/3   Three Book paintings by the Same Carbon-dated Illuminator
2/4   Correlating Details of the Three Book paintings
2/5   Book Paintings in a Style Similar to that of the Carbon-dated Painter
2/6   The Elect named *Ram-Frazend* Identified in Two Book Paintings
2/7   Correlating Details of Paintings by the Carbon-dated Illuminator and MIK III 4979
2/8   Timeline of Dated Manichaean Illuminated Manuscripts

3/1   Reconstructed Quire of a Turfan Manichaean Codex
3/2   Remnants of a Bema Hymnbook
3/3   Bindings Holes of Manichaean Codices
3/4   Strengthened Binding Holes
3/5   Horizontally Spliced Bifolia
3/6   Vertically Spliced Bifolia
3/7   Remnants of a Paper-reinforced Silk Codex Folio
3/8   Measurements of Page Elements on a Codex Folio Fragment
3/9   Documented Size Range of Turfan Manichaean Codices
3/10   Documented Proportion Range of Turfan Manichaean Codices
3/11   Sizes and Proportions of Turfan Manichaean Codices
3/12   Codex Cover with Flap Closure
3/13   Leather Wrappers
3/14   Techniques of Leather Decoration Documented on Manichaean Codex Cover Fragments
3/15   Documented Sizes of Turfan Manichaean Illuminated Scrolls
3/16   Ruling Documented on Turfan Manichaean Book Fragments
3/17   Examples of Calligraphy and Scribal decoration
3/18   Examples of Scribal Decoration

4/1   West Asian Fully Painted Style of Uygur Manichaean Art: Samples of Reoccurring Motifs (I)
4/2   West Asian Fully Painted Style of Uygur Manichaean Art: Samples of Reoccurring Motifs (II)
4/3   West Asian Comparative Examples from the early 13th centuries
4/4   Examples of the West Asian Outline Drawing Style of Turfan Manichaean Art
4/5   Examples of Draftsmanship in the two West Asian Styles of Turfan Manichaean Art

4/6   West Asian Fully Painted & Line Drawing Styles of Turfan Manichaean Art: Samples of
         Reoccurring Motifs
4/7   West Asian Comparative Examples from the mid 10th and the early 15th Centuries
4/8   Examples of Manichaean Wall and Textile Paintings in Chinese Fully Painted Style
4/9   Comparative Examples from Chinese Imperial Paintings from the 7th–9th Centuries
4/10   Comparative Examples of Chinese Paintings from Dunhuang from the early 11th Century
4/11   Likelihood of Manichaean Art Production in the Turfan Region

5/1   Orientation Experiment with a Fragmentary Illuminated Folio (MIK III 4959, recto)
5/2   The Picture-viewing Direction of a Fragmentary Illuminated Folio (MIK III 6368)
5/3   The Text-reading Direction of a Fragmentary Illuminated Folio (MIK III 6368)
5/4   Symbols of Figures Painted on Blue Background
5/5   Reconstruction of an Illuminated Bifolio (M 171)
5/6   Reconstruction of an Illuminated Bifolio (M 797)
5/7   Reconstruction of an Illuminated Bifolio (MIK III 8259)
5/8   Reconstruction of an Illuminated Folio (MIK III 4974)
5/9   Reconstruction of an Illuminated Folio (MIK III 4979a–d)
5/10   Reconstruction of an Illuminated Folio (Or 8218-1692)
5/11   Reconstruction of an Illuminated Folio (MIK III 36)
5/12   Reconstruction of an Illuminated Folio (M 576)
5/13   Reconstruction of an Illuminated Folio (MIK III 6368)
5/14   Reconstruction of an Illuminated Folio (So 18700 and 17501 c)
5/15   Interpretation of an Illuminated Folio Fragment (Or 12452/3)
5/16   Interpretation of an Illuminated Folio Fragment (MIK III 4959)
5/17   Interpretation of Four Fragments of two Illuminated Folia (MIK III 4971 a–d)
5/18   Interpretation of an Illuminated Folio Fragment (M 559)
5/19   Interpretation of Text and Decorative Design on the Turfan Manichaean Codex Page
5/20   Interpretation of Four Illuminated Folio Fragments (MIK III 4976 a, b and S 49)
5/21   Integration of Text and Figural Scene on the Turfan Manichaean Codex Page
5/22   Textual Scroll with a Graffito (Ch 0015)
5/23   Reconstruction of an Illuminated Letter Scroll (81 TB 65:01)
5/24   Interpretation of an Illuminated Letter Scroll Fragment (MIK III 4614)
5/25   Interpretation of a Pictorial Scroll Fragment (MIK III 4975)
5/26   Interpretation of two Matched Fragments from a Pictorial Scroll (MIK III 4947 and III 5d)
5/27   Interpretation of a Pictorial Scroll Fragment (MIK III 6989a)
5/28   Illuminated Manichaean Pustaka Book

6/1   Example of Interrelated Text and Illumination (M 556 verso [?])
6/2   Example of Unrelated Text and Illumination (MIK III 36)
6/3   Example of Unrelated Text and Illumination (MIK III 4974)
6/4   Example of Unrelated Text and Illumination (So 18700 and M 501e)
6/5   Pictorial Inserts of Illuminated Letters (81 TB 65:01 and MIK III 4614)

LIST OF COLOR PLATES

Plate 1   Non-illuminated Parchment Bifolio
Plate 2   Fragments of Silk Codex Folia
Plate 3   Elects in Scribal Duty
Plate 4   Writing in Gold and Multicolored Outline Writing
Plate 5   Illuminated Folio with Sideways Image
Plate 6   The Four Book Painting Styles of Turfan Manichaean Art
Plate 7   Identifiable Pictorial Subjects (I)
Plate 8   Identifiable Pictorial Subjects (II)

ACKNOWLEDGMENTS

The world's most extensive museum and archival collection of Manichaean works of art is found in Berlin, where as part of this research I had the fortune to work with these treasures. The excitement of new discoveries became a daily experience while working in the study collection of the *Museum für Indische Kunst* (Staatliche Museen zu Berlin, Preußischer Kulturbesitz). Under the care of Prof. Dr. Marianne Yaldiz, the experience of my Ph. D. research was complemented by seeing museum work handled with efficient professionalism, sophisticated warmth, and a cosmopolitan humor—qualities of conduct that would inspire any young woman at the beginning of her academic career. On the more practical size, Prof. Dr. Yaldiz also helped my work in numerous ways. Most importantly, she allowed me to survey the entire Turfan collection in order to be able to work out a strategy for the secure identification of Manichaean works of art; she authorized the carbon dating of a illuminated folio fragment that resulted in the possibility to reassess the dates associated with the Manichaean artistic corpus; and supplied me with research slides that facilitated my off-sight work for many years to come. For her long-lasting, ever so generous support of this research project, I would like to extend my gratitude by dedicating this book to Prof. Dr. Marianne Yaldiz.

The research for this project builds on a study of the Turfan remains located in six collections world-wide. Especially in Berlin, numerous scholars aided my extensive field study. I would like to thank Prof. Dr. Werner Sundermann (Turfanforschung, Berlin-Brandenburgische Akademie der Wissenschaften) and Dr. Hartmut-Ortwin Feistel (Orientabteilung, Staatsbibliothek zu Berlin, Preußischer Kulturbesitz) for their kind scholarly and personal support. For aiding my daily work in academic and practical ways, I would also like to thank Dr. Lore Sander (Museum für Indische Kunst), Dr. Simone-Christiane Raschmann and Dr. Christiane Reck (KoHD, Akademie der Wissenschaften zu Göttingen), Dr. Peter Zieme and Dr. Ingrid Warnke (Turfanforschung, Berlin-Brandenburgische Akademie der Wissenschaften), and Dr. Chhaya Bhattacharya-Haesner (Museum für Indische Kunst). For her superb photography and long hours of careful collaboration, I also wish to thank Ms. Iris Papadopoulos (Museum für Indische Kunst). In addition to Berlin, I had a chance to work extensively in the British Library, London, where Dr. Susan Whitfield (International Dunhuang Project) aided my research. I also visited in the Manuscript Collection of the Ryukoku University, Kyoto; Oriental Institute, St. Petersburg, and Turfan Museum in Turfan, Xinjiang Uygur Autonomous Region, PRC.

This study was also aided by a supportive and fertile academic atmosphere established by my professors at Indiana University, Bloomington. First and foremost, I would like to thank Prof. Larry Clark, who, in his methods classes offered at the Department of Central Eurasian Studies, taught me the rules and techniques of research and argument, and the importance of clear written and oral communication. Prof. Clark guided my studies in Turkology and was my main academic advisor during my graduate years at this institution. My interest in the arts and religions of pre-Islamic Central Asia began in a course of Prof. Michael Walter (Department of Central Eurasian Studies) on Buddhism in Central Asia. Prof. Walter directed my attention to the Buddhist art and texts discovered there, which ultimately led me to devote a significant segment of my graduate class work on this and overlapping fields. I am grateful to Prof. Jan Nattier (Department of Religious Studies), under whose guidance I surveyed the basics of Buddhist history, and the vast literature on Central Asian Buddhism. Also, I would like to thank Prof. Larry Moses (Department of Central Eurasian Studies), whose classes introduced me to the details of Mongolian history and Siberian art and archaeology. Furthermore, I am indebted to Prof. Christopher Beckwith (Department of Central Eurasian Studies), with whom I studied Tibetan history. Prof. Henry Glassie (Departments of Folklore and Central Eurasian Studies) drew my attention to the vastness of Turkish art and, more importantly, reminded me of the importance of Folklore methodology for understanding art and its context. Through the Mid-West University Exchange Program, I had a chance to spend an intense and productive semester studying Indian art under Prof. Susan Huntington at Ohio State University in Columbus. From among the members of the faculty at the Art History Program at Indiana University, I am grateful to Prof. Elizabeth Pastan (now at Emory University), with whom I worked on Islamic art. As my academic advisor in art history, Prof. Eugene Kleinbauer supervised my doctoral research and greatly aided my work with his insight. Also, I would like to thank Prof. Susan Nelson, who taught not only Chinese art, but helped me to develop my teaching skills in art history.

Both the direction and presentation of my research were influenced by a variety of scholars, who discussed and critiqued my work throughout the past several years. In the process of researching and writing the dissertation version of this research, the scholarship of Dr. John Lowden (Courtauld Institute of Art, University of London), and Dr. Jason D. BeDuhn (Department of Humanities, University of Northern Arizona) were most influential. Dr. Lowden's articles and books on early Christian art, and Byzantine illuminated manuscripts helped me to find a method for researching my sources and introduced a way to think about illuminated books. Similarly, Dr. BeDuhn's knowledge on the Manichaean religion aided my understanding of religious studies essential for pursuing my research. Together with Dr. Lowden and Dr. BeDuhn, I would like to extend special thanks for a group of scholars who read and critiqued my manuscript at various stages, including Dr. Geoff Childs (Washington University, St. Louis), Dr. Brian Schmidt (University of Michigan), Dr. Yutaka Yoshida (Kobe City University, Japan), Dr. Takao Moriyasu (Osaka University, Japan), Prof. Dr. Johannes van Oort (University of Utrecht), Dr. Larry Clark (Independent Scholar), and Prof. Dr. Werner Sundermann.

The computer images form an integral part of this project, since they enhance the presentation of the research findings. Therefore, I would like to extend my gratitude for a variety of specialists, starting with William Yang (Indiana University, Bloomington), who himself as a fellow graduate student at that time, worked with me in creating circa half of the codex-diagrams in 1998. The remaining half of the computer imaging was done at Northern Arizona University, Flagstaff, between 2002 and 2005, where I had the pleasure to work with the superb staff of the Bilby Research Center. Special thanks to Ronald Redsteer, Daniel Boone, and Patrick McDonald (Illustration Services), as well as Louella Holter (Editorial Services). The precision, professionalism, and joy of work exhibited by these colleagues became a source of inspiration.

Last, but not least, I must mention the sources of financial support of this complex research project that I received throughout the past 10 years. Firstly, I am grateful to the Indiana University Graduate School in Bloomington, Indiana (USA), and the Free University of Berlin (Germany), that supported my initial fieldwork in Berlin during 1995 and 1996. Further research trips in 2001 and 2002 were made possible through a generous travel grant of the *Young Scholar Fellowship* issued by the Cultural Ministry of Japan, which I received while working at Sophia University in Tokyo (Japan). During the final stages of this project, in 2003 and 2004, the Intramural Grant Program of Northern Arizona University aided my work, as I was teaching and writing in Flagstaff, Arizona.

A CODICOLOGICAL APPROACH TO A UNIQUE GROUP OF OBJECTS

This study explores an important body of illuminated manuscript fragments from around the tenth century that were previously considered lost to art historical research due to their badly damaged condition and little understood religious and cultural contexts. Approximately 100 codex folio and scroll fragments provide rich sources of information when investigated using a specific methodology that considers the whole manuscript as a work of art, and not just its components (miniatures, calligraphy, decorated covers) in arbitrary isolation. By systematically accumulating evidence on artistry, design, and content according to this methodology, the silhouette of a sophisticated book culture emerges, urging us to further explore the formation of manuscript illumination in mediaeval West and Central Asia in light of one of its essential, newly reassessed components—Manichaean book art.

The material considered here originated in the context of the East Central Asian epoch of the Manichaean religion. Between the eighth and eleventh centuries, Manichaeism was adopted by the leading elite of the Turkic-speaking Uygurs, who established their winter capital along the Silk Road in Kocho near to what is today the Turfan oasis (in northwest China). Under local imperial sponsorship, this highly literate religion introduced a West Asiatic book culture to the Turfan region. During a nearly 300-year period, the faithful maintenance of the tradition's roots, together with local innovations, developed into what is called today Turfan Manichaean book art.

The methods and the overall scheme of research manifested in the so-called codicological approach of this study allow us, for the first time, to gain a basic understanding of this splendid book art. Due to the highly specialized nature of both the cultural setting of the material and the method by which its artistic history can be elicited, it is necessary before starting the actual analysis and interpretation of the sources to briefly provide some basic background on the history of Manichaeism, the discovery of the sources and their previous art historical study, as well as the codicological method and terminology used in this project.

History of the Manichaean Religion

Manichaeism is an extinct world religion that existed between the third and the fifteenth centuries CE.[1] Its origin is tied to the international milieu of late antique Mesopotamia, where Mani, the founder of this religion, lived most of his life. In 216, Mani was born to a family distantly related to the Parthian Arsacid royal lineage. Just before Mani's birth, his father gave up worldly life and joined the Elchasaite community near Babylon (Figure 1).[2] From the age of four, Mani was brought up in this community. According to a primary source that includes sections from his biography, Mani had his first religious experience as a twelve-year-old boy.[3] His heavenly "twin" came to announce that Mani was special and that his life

---

[1] The last evidence for Manichaean presence is documented in Fukien Province of South China (Lieu 1992, 302–304).
[2] Asmussen 1965, 9–10; Lieu 1992, 36. On the Elchasaite community, see Henrichs 1973.
[3] *Cologne Mani Codex* 11.1–12.15 (Cameron and Dewey 1979, 15).

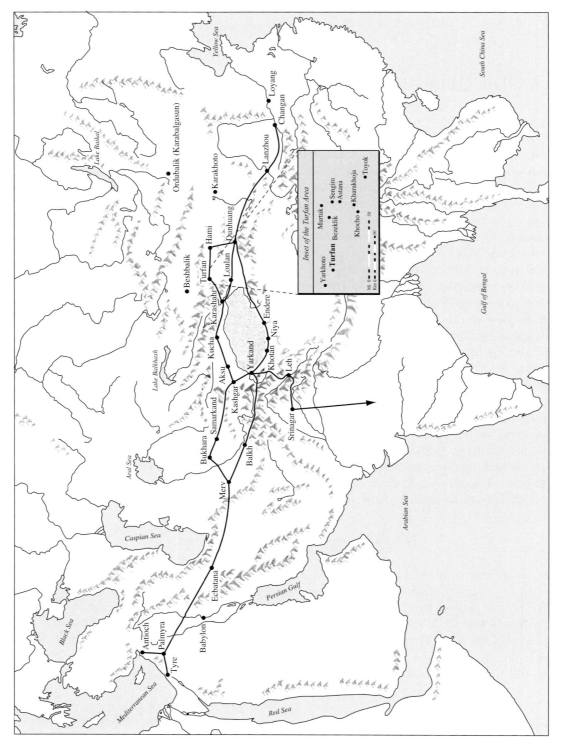

Figure 0/1. Map of the Silk Roads and the Historical Sites of the Turfan Region

was being watched.[4] After this revelation, Mani began to live a life unusually sensitive to the silent cries of pain around him. He could hear the rivers protest as they were soiled by dirt washed into them,[5] and could see blood seeping from the flesh of freshly cut fruits and vegetables.[6] These visions indicated for him that human action collaborated with evil in causing harm. Exposure to Zoroastrian, Christian, and Buddhist teachings convinced Mani that his insights agreed with those of the great prophets of the past, and he began to form his own philosophy. At age twenty-four, he was ready to answer a second call, to found a new religion.[7]

Mani designed a comprehensive and coherent religious system, whose rituals would undertake the job of gradually bringing an end to the suffering of the world by liberating, particle by particle, the trapped forces of good, light, and life from the forces of evil, darkness, and death. Since the good forces could be found even in food, meals became daily rituals to accomplish the work of the religion: the liberation of light from darkness.[8] For this Mani needed a special group of men and women, the *elect* who, as he did, dedicated their own bodies as instruments of liberation. In addition, the envisioned work needed a supporting group of generous laity, the *auditors*, to facilitate the process by answering the needs of the elects. In return for their services to the religion, the elects secured their own place in heaven and the auditors gained merit toward a better rebirth.[9] Manichaean cosmology described the world as a combat between the forces of light and darkness, good and evil, and life and death. The eschatology revealed that humans are judged on the basis of which side they take in this cosmic battle.[10]

The *Religion of Light*, as it is referred to in Manichaean sources, was spread through a missionary program by Mani and his disciples first in Mesopotamia and then in its immediately neighboring territories: across the frontiers into the Roman Empire, to northern India, and into West Central Asia. Various didactic means were employed to disseminate the teachings and translations.[11] Multilingual missionaries were accompanied by scribes to assure the accurate transmission of doctrine. These efforts accorded with the practice of Mani, who himself preached and composed in Syriac, Middle Persian, and Parthian, and painted pictures to illustrate his philosophy for those who could not read.[12]

After enjoying an initial period of success in Persia, the Manichaean church mostly experienced profound persecution during the rest of its history. Following the royal support of Shapur I (240–272) and Hormizd I (272–273), Bahram I (273–276) banned the mission in 276 and threw Mani into prison, where he died.[13] The dispersal of the community from Mesopotamia only furthered the spread of Mani's teachings to the east into Central and East Asia, as well as to the west into the Mediterranean world.[14] The hostility that confronted the Manichaeans did not necessarily result from opposition to their radical ideas; it was mainly due to the antagonism of state-endorsed faiths that were intolerant of any religious views different from their own. Much of our knowledge about Manichaeism therefore comes from polemical accounts written

---

[4] *Cologne Mani Codex* 2.2–4.6 (Cameron and Dewey 1979, 9).

[5] *Cologne Mani Codex* 94.10–96.17 (Cameron and Dewey 1979, 77).

[6] *Cologne Mani Codex* 7.2–8.14, and 10.1–10.14 (Cameron and Dewey 1979, 11–13 and 13–15).

[7] *Cologne Mani Codex* 18.1–24.15 (Cameron and Dewey 1979, 19–25).

[8] Asmussen 1975, 59–60; BeDuhn 1995.

[9] In modern scholarship the two orders are traditionally referred to by Latin terms *electus/electa* (pl. *electi/electae*) and *auditor* (pl. *auditores*). Recently, English forms are seen more often with cropped endings: elect(s) and auditor(s).

[10] Lieu 1992, 10–32.

[11] Regarding the history of the Manichaean mission prior to Mani's death, and Mani's views of the mission, see Asmussen 1975, 17–25 and Lieu 1992, 70–105.

[12] Ephrem's *Prose Refutations* 126.31–127.11 (Reeves 1997, 262–263).

[13] Asmussen 1975, 52–59; Lieu 1992, 107–109.

[14] On the eastward and westward spread of Manichaeism after Mani's death, see Lieu 1992, 106–120. On the diffusion of Manichaeism into the eastern Roman Empire, see Lieu 1994, 22–131.

from the viewpoints of these official religions. Such writings preserved the details of the vanishing Manichaean world by recording heated theological debates, forced conversions, physical destruction of scriptures and Mani portraits, and martyrdom.[15]

An exception to this sad tale occurred when, remarkably, Manichaeism became the faith of the ruling elite of the powerful Uygur Steppe Empire in central and northeast Asia. Mani's teachings enjoyed the support of the Turkic-speaking Uygurs who ruled the steppe from its center at Ordubalik (the later Karabalgasun of the Mongols) from 744 until 840.[16] The position of the Uygurs not only assured potential success for the religion in the Uygur homeland and the areas it controlled along the northern branch of the Silk Road, but also pressured Tang China into an official tolerance toward the missionary activities of this foreign church. After 840, the dissolution of the Steppe Empire resulted in the transfer of the Uygur sphere of power to the cities of Beshbalik north of the Tian Shan and Kocho in the northern Tarim Basin, and to the Dunhuang region of what is now Gansu province.[17] Their continuing affiliation with the faith is documented in textual sources until the early decades of the eleventh century. In the history of the Manichaean church, the era of Uygur royal patronage represents a highpoint reflected in the luxuriant quality of the Turfan Manichaean remains.

The Uygur leadership gave up its Manichaean faith and switched its support to Buddhism during the first half of the eleventh century. Although this process must have been devastating for some, it was not accompanied by the excessive violence experienced by Manichaeans elsewhere. The replacement of Manichaean monastic buildings by Buddhist monasteries is well documented.[18] The details of what actually happened to the Manichaean community and its religious objects, however, remain blurry. Certain similarities between the format, techniques, and aesthetics of Manichaean and Buddhist illuminated manuscripts suggest a degree of influence of the former on the latter.[19] Likewise, the presence of Manichaean manuscripts and textiles at Buddhist sites indicates that the Buddhists took control of Manichaean property and often reused the paper and silk in the service of their own faith. After the buildings of Kocho were probably abandoned as the city became less important for the Uygur court during the late thirteenth century,[20] and the Buddhist structures of Turfan became deserted by the complete Islamization of the region in the sixteenth century,[21] the remoteness of the forsaken sites and the arid climate of the Taklamakan desert preserved these artifacts.

HISTORY OF RESEARCH

The first primary Manichaean sources known to scholars derived from the Turfan region of East Central Asia, which turned out to be the richest source of Manichaean texts and art. Buried under sand in the ruins of mud-brick buildings, or deposited in sealed storage areas built into cave walls or stupas, these artifacts lay in wait for centuries. Following the returns of each of the four Prussian expeditions between 1904 and 1914, German scholars secured and organized the remains, and then started work on publishing their findings. Already in 1904, the great orientalist Friedrich Wilhelm Karl Müller recognized that the unusual

---

[15] E.g., Mez 1939, 175; Lieu 1992, 203–205, 238.
[16] Mackerras 1973, 1990.
[17] Czeglédy 1984; Abe 1954.
[18] *Käd Ogul Koštir's Memoir* (Geng and Klimkeit 1985; Moriyasu 1991, 147–160); and Clark 1997, 103 and 132, row 106.
[19] Note the blue background, and certain iconographic elements (e.g., the white scarfed headgear of the kneeling figure) in the book painting of a Buddhist manuscript, MIK III 10, published by Härtel and Yaldiz 1982, No. 120.
[20] Abe 1954, 436.
[21] Ross 1972, 97; Clark 1975, 27–28.

version of the Syriac script on thousands of the newly found manuscripts was used by the Manichaeans.[22] This discovery led Albert von Le Coq, a Turkologist who became an art historian, to focus the activities of the second expedition on the excavation of buildings in Kocho likely to contain more Manichaean remains.[23] His success yielded the majority of Manichaean items currently known.

The art brought back by the Prussian expeditions is housed in two Turfan collections in Berlin, as a result of the divergent routing of textual and artistic material within the German museum establishment. Today the artistic material belongs to the collection of the Berlin State Museums of the Prussian Cultural Heritage Foundation (Staatliche Museen zu Berlin, Preußischer Kulturbesitz) and is housed in the Museum of Indian Art (Museum für Indische Kunst). The texts are possessed by the Berlin-Brandenburg Academy (Berlin-Brandenburgische Akademie der Wissenschaften). Some of the Manichaean objects owned by the Museum of Indian Art are displayed in its permanent exhibition, and occasionally in international exhibitions, and they often are featured in museum art publications. The Academy's Turfan collection functions as an archival resource for textual studies, and the numerous philological publications of these texts occasionally contain pieces of art interest.

The British, the Japanese, and the Russians also led expeditions to East Central Asia at the turn of the century. Their excavations and purchases also yielded Manichaean texts, which include nine illuminated book fragments that are relevant for this study. These items are housed in the London, Kyoto, and St. Petersburg collections. In addition to the early expeditions, modern Chinese excavations brought to light one illuminated Manichaean scroll at Bezeklik, which is exhibited in the local museum in Turfan (Xinjiang, PRC) and occasionaly featured in international Silk Road exhibitions.[24]

Understandably, the discoveries in the Turfan region and Dunhuang had a great impact on studies of the Manichaean religion. Not only were these the first primary Manichaean sources ever to come to light, but also they came from a location that clearly confirmed the wide extent of the mediaeval Manichaean world—a notion that previously could be anticipated only in the light of Islamic sources. Prior to these finds the scholarly rediscovery of this religion had to rely on Christian and Islamic polemical accounts, which treated the Manichaeans as enemies and thus documented contact with Manichaean activities in a variety of genres. Secular studies began in the early eighteenth century when Isaac de Beausobre published the first non-polemic history of the Manichaean religion in Amsterdam.[25] The best account of the history of scholarship on Manichaeism is the bibliographical essay of Julien Ries (1988), which summarizes the major themes of scholarly interest. There are currently about fifteen hundred scholarly writings covering a variety of Manichaean historical, religious, and artistic questions.[26]

The birth of Manichaean art studies is directly linked to the discoveries of the Prussian expeditions in the Turfan region. The relatively well preserved and rich works of art found in Kocho ignited an interest that yielded a series of art publications between the 1910s and the 1930s. This era of interest however was followed by a long silence. With the exception of the Manichaean entry by Hambis (1964) in the *Encyclopedia of World Art*, publications on the art of this religion began to reemerge only in the 1980s.

Publications on Manichaean art began with the Prussian expedition reports. The very first mention of Manichaean works of art came in Albert Grünwedel's report (1906) on the 1902–1904 exploration of the

---

[22] Müller 1904a, 1904b.

[23] The first expedition was reported by Grünwedel (1906). The organization and the activities of all four Prussian expeditions have been treated in numerous publications (Le Coq 1913, 1–18; Le Coq 1923, 21–33; Gabain 1960, IX–XXI; Klimkeit 1982a, 23–27; Härtel 1982, 24–46; Yaldiz 1987, 7–13).

[24] Tokyo National Museum 2002, 160–161.

[25] Isaac de Beausobre's book *Histoire (critique) de Manichée et du Manichéisme*, vols 1-2, (1734–1738) is discussed in Ries 1988, 36–42.

[26] Mikkelsen 1997.

ruins at Kocho, followed by discussion of other Manichaean items in Grünwedel's second report (1912) on the 1906–1907 expeditions to the same site. Both publications contain descriptions and line drawings of a few Manichaean objects discussed in the context of the site of their discovery. Soon after Grünwedel, Albert von Le Coq published the first color photographs, accompanied by a detailed description and interpretation of Manichaean artifacts in his monograph on Kocho (1913, Pls. 1–6).

The history of the Prussian expeditions to East Central Asia has been told in detail in the above-mentioned publications (Grünwedel 1906, 1912; Le Coq 1913), and retold in several modern accounts. The most detailed of these include Boyce's introduction to her catalogue of Manichaean script texts (1960) and Härtel's introduction (1982) to an exhibition catalogue of the East Central Asian objects of the Museum of Indian Art in Berlin. Samuel N. C. Lieu's article on Manichaean art and text (1997) also summarized the discovery of the Turfan remains, as well as the exploration of other sites relevant to Manichaean art.

The reports on the archaeological sites and on the activities of the Prussian expeditions were followed by a monograph devoted specifically to Manichaean art by Le Coq (1923). Apart from his editions of Turkic Manichaean texts,[27] Le Coq was the first to systematically discuss many of the currently known art pieces. He worked with meticulous care in describing the artistic features and interpreting religious content. Albert von Le Coq certainly was the founder of Manichaean art studies. Modern monographic treatments of Manichaean art includes the work of Hans-Joachim Klimkeit (1982a) published in Brill's *Iconography and Religion Series,* and two catalogues that have been prepared recently on the Berlin Manichaean remains. The one that was designed and written by this author for the *Art Series* of the *Corpus Fontium Manichaeorum* (Gulácsi 2001) is a comprehensive catalogue of positively identified Manichaean works of art in Berlin illustrated in full with enlarged color plates.[28]

The artistic connections between the Turfan Manichaean remains and the art of late antique and early mediaeval West Asia and North Africa were soon recognized. Le Coq began the integration of Manichaean works of art into a wider art historical context in his 1923 monograph. He also prepared an atlas that systematically linked the style and the iconography of the newly discovered samples of central Asian art to the better known traditions of Persian, Byzantine, Chinese, and Indian art (1925). In her short 1972 article, Emel Esin discussed a few Manichaean examples that exhibit signs of cultural connections. Her survey included not only Berlin examples but also two Manichaean remains (Kao. 0107 and Ch. 0015) that are housed in the British Library in London. In addition to Le Coq's studies (1913, 1923), articles by J. Loubier (1910) and P. Kerstein (1914) connected the Manichaean book covers to Coptic ones. The Persian connections of Manichaean art were first explored by Sir Thomas W. Arnold (1924), who argued that trends developed by Sassanian and Manichaean painting traditions survived in mediaeval Persian art. This work was followed by several sections devoted to Manichaean art in the fifth volume of the *Survey of Persian Art.*[29] These articles discuss the relationship of Manichaean book art to later Persian book painting traditions. Among them are the writings of Arnold (1938) and Ugo Monneret de Villard (1938) on Manichaean paintings as sources of later Persian paintings, an article by Taherzade Behzad on the material used by miniature painters (1938), and a study by Emil Gratzl (1938) on book covers. At the same time, little attention was paid to the local artistic tradition that produced the surviving fragments of Manichaean art. The reflection of the regional material culture in Turfan Manichaean book paintings was pointed out by the present author (1996), and used as an argument for the local production of the paintings.

---

[27] Le Coq's editions of Turkic Manichaean texts were surveyed by Clark (1997, 114–115).
[28] Another catalog, devoted to the "small finds" of the Prussian expeditions, was prepared by Jorinde Ebert and awaits publication.
[29] Arnold 1938.

Although no museum exhibition has been devoted exclusively to Manichaean art, the best examples at the Museum of Indian Art (State Museums of Berlin, Prussian Heritage Foundation) are part of the museum's permanent exhibition, and therefore are described in the exhibition catalogue (Museum für Indische Kunst 1986). Occasionally, these and other Manichaean items are included in traveling exhibitions on Silk Road art and thus also are discussed in the Manichaean section of illustrated exhibition catalogues. These include an English language catalogue by Herbert Härtel and Marianne Yaldiz (1982), a Korean language catalogue edited by the National Museum of Korea (1991), and a Japanese language exhibition catalogue edited by the Tokyo and Kyoto National Museums (Tokyu Kokuritsu Hakubutsukan et al. 1991). Most recently a large Silk Road Exhibition was held in the British Library and accompanied by an extensive exhibition catalogue (Whitfield 2004).

Manichaean pictorial art frequently is discussed in connection with religious studies due to the fact that numerous Manichaean paintings depict well-known religious figures and ritual practices. In her PhD dissertation, Victoria Arnold-Döben (1978) surveyed Manichaean literature to identify the recurrent pictorial symbols used in religious language (e.g., trees, boats, pearls, sun and moon). Arnold-Döben succeeded in identifying themes in Manichaean literature that were prominently featured in Klimkeit's interpretation of Manichaean works of art (1982a). As a response to the interpretation of the largest book painting (MIK III 4979 verso) published in Le Coq's monograph (1923, 53–56), which explains the scene depicting a high-ranking elect in the setting of the Bema festival, W. Bang published a brief article (1924) that drew attention to certain important details of the representation. Charles R. C. Allberry (1938b) used the same book painting (MIK III 4979 verso) portraying the Bema festival as primary evidence for his own treatment of this theme. Allberry surveyed all the textual sources on the Bema and found that none of them contained a clear-cut reference to the sacred meal of the elect. To prove that the meal was indeed part of the Bema celebration, Allberry turned to the book painting, which showed the elects seated next to neatly arranged piles of breads, fruits, and an ornate jar placed in front of a Bema. More recently, Jorinde Ebert also has discussed a number of Manichaean works of art in relation to the Bema scene and the portrayal of Mani (1994). In addition, the iconographic similarity between the appearance of figures in a Manichaean painting (MIK III 4979 recto and MIK III 4959 recto) and Hindu Gods was elaborated on by Banerjee in 1970. This work was followed up by Klimkeit (1980), who viewed the "Hindu Gods" as indicators of religious syncretism in Manichaean doctrine. The subject of the four guardians was explored by Ebert as well (1992).

Since most remains of Manichaean art are found in illuminated books, it is not surprising to find objects of art interest discussed in philological studies. Fragments of illuminated manuscripts were listed and briefly described in a catalogue of Manichaean script texts prepared by Boyce (1960), and numerous such art objects were illustrated in the recent facsimile edition of Sundermann (1996b).[30] The list of individual text editions includes the study of MIK III 6368 by Le Coq (1909b) and the edition of Kao. 0107 by Moriyasu (1997). Sundermann has published the text of a pictorial seal (1985) and two fragmentary pages of a silk codex (1992 b),[31] and a variety of art objects have been cited by Moriyasu (1991) in his discussion of the sources of Uygur Manichaeism.

Since the area where Manichaeism survived the longest falls within the borders of the Peoples' Republic

---

[30] These fragments are seen in Sundermann 1996b Pls. 199b–120b (M 730); Pls. 152–153 (MIK III 4974); Pls. 154–155 (MIK III 4979); Pl. 156a (MIK III 4981a); Pl. 156b (MIK III4981f); Pls. 158a–158b (MIK III 7251); Pls. 159a–159b (MIK III 8259); Pls. 177g–177h (S 30); Pl. 183c (S 42); Pls. 186c–186d (S 49); and Pls. 187a–187b (S 50).
[31] MIK III 4981b, e.

of China, it is hardly surprising that not only the best-known sites of origin, but also the sites of new discoveries are being recognized in China. New discoveries from Turfan include an illuminated scroll found at Bezeklik, which was discussed in a Chinese language article by the Turfan Research Group of the Turfan Museum (Tulufan diqu wenwu guanlisuo 1985). In addition, the question of Manichaean cave sites has been detailed in a Chinese language article by Chao Huashan (1993), which was translated into English (1996), and in the German booklet somewhat similar in subject and argument to that of Chao, written by Klimkeit (1996).

Besides Turfan and Dunhuang in Xinjiang and Gansu Province (northwest China), the other Manichaean site in China is in Fukien Province (southeast China). The two-part study of Chavannes and Pelliot (1911 and 1913) documenting the survival of Manichaeism well after the end of the Tang period catalyzed the interest of Chinese scholars. Ch'en Yüan, who was a leading authority on Chinese history, published a monograph-length article (1923) that included inserts translated from Chavannes and Pelliot's work together with further evidence on the presence of Manichaean activities from Chinese sources.[32] One of his Chinese sources described a Manichaean shrine that later was successfully located on Huan-piao Hill by Wu Wenliang (1957).[33] The site currently is a functioning Buddhist shrine whose famous main image is featured in *Yüang Ming Ch'ing tai su* (1988, 47). It is described in a detailed field study by Bryder (1988 and 1991).

THE CODICOLOGICAL APPROACH

Most remains of Manichaean art are vestiges of illuminated books in extremely fragmentary condition. This means that if we want to learn about Manichaean book art, we need to use a method that enables us to overcome the condition of the corpus. The research principle most suitable for such study is relatively new to art history, but it has been applied frequently in studies of illuminated books during the past twenty years. Most often it is referred to as a codicological approach.

Codicology (lit. "the study of the codex"), as coined by A. Dain in 1949, was considered equivalent to the German *Handschriftenkunde* ("the study of manuscripts"), and it initially referred to a discipline dealing with the history of the book after its completion. Later, codicology acquired slightly different meanings. On the one hand, it became identical with the German *Buchwesen* (often translated as "the structure of the book"), one of the two divisions of paleography. On the other hand, codicology became the study of characteristics specific to various production centers that are observable in the properties of manuscripts.[34] As a neologism, codicology means the study of the book as a cultural product, unlike traditional paleography which tends to study the book in a cultural vacuum.[35] In this broader and more recently acquired meaning, a codicological approach to the study of illuminated books enables art historians to consider the elements of the page together as a whole, and thus examine the miniatures in their immediate context—as book art.

This approach was emphasized first in a methodological treatise by Delaissé in 1976. He pointed out the need for an alternative to the traditional tendency of art historians to study parts of the books in isolation (e.g., miniatures as paintings, or ornate book covers as metalwork) without considering the context of the books and the texts that they illustrate and/or decorate:

---

[32] Bryder 1988, 201 note 1; Lieu 1997, 296.
[33] The history of research is described in further detail by Bryder (1988, 203) and by Lieu (1997, 296–297), who also provides a translation of the relevant section from Ch'en Yüan's study.
[34] In its narrow connotation, codicology pays attention to the details of workmanship, as seen for example in Wright's recent study of the *Vergilius Romanus* (1992).
[35] *Oxford Dictionary of Byzantium* I:476.

We can undoubtedly be deprived of essential elements in our research if, when using manuscripts, we limit ourselves to an exclusive interest and neglect any of the technical aspects of these books. We must, on the contrary, go first to the book as a whole, see how it is made, examine all aspects of its content and only then can we appreciate the consequence of this complete analysis on our own personal interest.... Presented this way, the examination of the different techniques or aspects of our medieval books does not differ from the archaeological method as it is commonly known. As in any other branch of this discipline it consists first in observing and analyzing all the material data concerning objects of the past and in interpreting them afterwards in order to determine the time and place of their execution. Why not therefore use for the medieval book the word archaeology, which not only indicates a method but also suggests a purpose because of its historical significance (Delaissé 1976, 79).

For its focus on the object, Delaissé called his approach an "archaeological approach," noting that other terms could be found to refer to it, such as the German *Handschriftenkunde* or the English *codicology*.[36] Following the example of John Lowden and David Wright, I refer to this holistic, codicological/archaeological approach as codicology. The French word *codicologie* was used for the first time in A. Dain's *Les manuscrits* (Paris, 1949). In his theoretical article Delaissé explained the trends in the use of the word:

Although the word might imply that the codex has become in itself an object of research, the author (A. Dain) sees codicology as an auxiliary discipline, ancillary even to philology. Thus, in spite of the fact that this word is definitely progressive (as is suggested by the title of the book: *Les manuscrits*) it neither puts the manuscript in its proper place nor gives it real importance. Many scholars in different branches of mediaeval studies are unconsciously of the same opinion. Even if they are convinced that the expert knowledge of paleography is no longer a sufficient qualification for research in mediaeval texts, they still consider a wider knowledge of mediaeval book (to call this 'codicology' is quite fashionable nowadays) solely as an instrument to facilitate their own work (Delaissé 1976, 76–77).

Applications of the codicological method to the study of illuminated books recently have become frequent. In his 1984 study centering on the program of Carolingian and Ottonian illuminated manuscripts, Calkins underlined the importance of considering the decorative elements in association with the immediate physical context of the pages that they decorate:

Art historians tend to examine miniatures as paintings—as isolated images to be arranged like photographs or excised folios in a row in order to demonstrate stylistic affinities and development, or like canvases hung on a museum wall, to be contemplated in isolation in their own right. Only passing attention is placed to their context in the book or their relation to the text they illustrate; and almost none to their placement on the page and their relation to such secondary decoration as may accompany them, such as decorative borders, and to the sequence in which they reveal themselves as one turns the page. In its proper environment—as part of a book—an illuminated page is rarely seen one at a time for it usually is seen in conjugation with its facing folio (Calkins 1984, 16).

More recently, the approach outlined by Delaissé was observed in studies by David Wright and John Lowden. In Wright's view, a full codicological description of the illuminated manuscript must precede more specialized studies. Accordingly, he devoted a separate volume to his codicological descriptions of the *Vergilius Romanus* and saved his interpretations for later works.[37] Lowden specifically discussed this methodological framework, referring to it as a "broadly codicological approach," and applied it in his study of the Byzantine Octateuchs, pointing out its relevance as follows:

The importance of codicological method lies in the emphasis that it places on the totality of the book. And its threat, if it has any, should only be to those who feel that any single topic, be it text, illustration, parchment, layout, ruling, or whatever, can be properly understood without reference to other elements that make up a book.[38]

---

[36] Delaissé 1976, 83.
[37] Wright 1992, 5.
[38] Lowden 1992, 10.

The codicological research program presented here was conducted in accordance with the theoretical guidance of Delaissé and the practical examples of Lowden and Wright. The material subjected to a codicological analysis is the corpus of Manichaean illuminated book fragments. The results of this analysis allow us to focus on five issues: the book format and assemblage, the work of the scribes, the work of the illuminators, the physical integration of text and illumination with special attention to the sideways-oriented images, and the various degrees of contextual cohesion between text and picture. Despite the fragmentary condition of the Manichaean corpus, this approach allows us to view illumination in the context of the lost pages of the books they once decorated, thus establishing the basics of Turfan Manichaean codicology.

Practical Steps of Research

The idea of this research was formulated in 1995. The project gradually took shape as the material dictated, with the basic findings and framework presented here crystallizing by 1998. This approximately 3-year period was occupied by intensive fieldwork with the primary sources—their examination and analysis leading to factually based interpretive findings. During the process of figuring out *what to study* and *how to study it*, I had to consider not only the ultimate goal (to reach an understanding of Manichaean book art), but also the severely fragmented nature of the sources. Therefore, the guidance provided by the codicological literature had to be adapted to the needs of this particular research project.

The preparatory steps began with surveying the available literature, which led to the recognition of the need for a securely defined Manichaean corpus, and continued with an intensive preliminary survey of the two Berlin collections, the results of which are discussed in Chapter 1. To facilitate the study of the ca. 200 Manichaean and non-Manichaean fragments (including a large number of non-illuminated manuscript fragments, as well as fragments of textiles and wall-paintings), I started by assembling a photographic record of all the potential primary sources. Such a personal study archive was essential for designing a first-hand codicological study of the fragments.

The on-site research was devoted to the examination and the analysis of the fragments. Most of them not only are small themselves, but contain textual and artistic elements executed on the smallest possible scale within the world of illuminated manuscripts. Therefore, their scrutiny involved the constant use of a magnifying glass (7x enlargement) and occasionally a microscope (16x enlargement), as well as taking measurements with the aid of a precision caliper (which measured as thin of a line as 0.1 mm) and a basic ruler. To record my observations and measurements I created an outline drawing replica for each fragment. This involved tracing by hand the glassed fragments and their basic page elements on onionskin paper and making photocopies of these tracings. The photocopies allowed me to note the measurements (heights and widths of the fragment, margins, headers, columns, line distances, line heights, and even line thicknesses; see Figure 3/8). In order to aid the interpretation of the data gathered in this way, I used sheets of millimeter paper. The positioning of the cutout tracings of the fragments on the millimeter sheets allowed contemplation of the original folio from which they derived in light of the clues provided by the retained page elements. The reconstructions on the millimeter sheets became the prototypes of the computer outline drawings used as illustrations in Chapters 3 and 5. Finally, the assembled archival data were supplemented with professional slides, which allowed me to continue studying the details of the fragments with only a few additional visits to Berlin.

The subsequent six years were taken up with expanding the corpus with non-Berlin fragments, refining my analysis, developing the presentation of the results, and making new discoveries by repeatedly returning to my sources with fresh ideas of how to recover even more information from these meager remains. This included an assessment of the dates associated with the corpus of Manichaean illuminated book fragments, weighing the traditional stylistic dating of the pictorial components of the fragments against historical and scientific dating, the latter of which was commissioned specifically for this study. As discussed in Chapter 2, the results suggest a new way to think about the chronology of style in Manichaean Turfan. The physical and formal characteristics of Manichaean book art are assessed by investigating what is left from the artistry of the bookmakers, scribes, and illuminators in Chapters 3 and 4. If there was a beneficial side to the damaged nature of this art, it is in how it forces us to look at tiny details that might be neglected in the study of more complete works of art, and how it can at times reveal stages of planning and execution that would be hidden in intact finished pieces. At the same time, understanding the techniques and stages of the artists' work is essential for preventing misinterpretations of the fragments.

Recording the trends of book design is one of the most important components of this study, especially because the images on these fragments are not aligned with their texts. On all illuminated manuscript fragments surviving from the Manichaean world of Turfan, the paintings are oriented sideways in relation to the direction of the writing. Due to the fragmentary nature of the remains and the previous lack of a comprehensive approach to their study, this fact has never been recognized before. Through the analysis of 11 reconstructible fragments, Chapter 5 proves that this design principle is followed systematically in this book art. The final intention of this study rooted in the codicological approach was to consider the texts together with their illuminations. The survey and the interpretation of the contextual cohesion of text and image are presented in Chapter 6.

The organization of data into tables proved to be an important tool of analysis. The use of the table format allowed the grouping of the fragments, and/or their certain data, in order to recognize patterns in their various characteristics. The tables also became essential tools for introducing numerical evidence and statistics for this research. An example of the relevance of such tabular analysis may be the study of codex sizes in Chapter 3, where in light of the 11 reconstructible codex folia, patterns could be shown between the sizes of the page elements and the overall size of the codex folio. This recognition allowed assessment of the original size range of an additional dozen codex fragments in light of measurement of their script heights, line spacing, and just one margin retained on them. As a result, it has become clear that there were five different codex sizes in use among the Manichaeans of Turfan, of which only the middle three were used for illuminated editions (see Fig. 3/9).

Art historical studies must rely on illustrations; this one is no exception. The exquisite quality of artisanship preserved on the remains of this art, however, is hard to capture even through superb photographs. As an external aid, the publication of a catalogue of the Berlin illuminated fragments, illustrated with enlarged color facsimiles, provides a wonderful visual reference—second only to viewing the fragments in person.[39] Illustrating the newly discovered secrets of Turfan Manichaean bookmaking has presented a daunting challenge throughout the years of smaller research publications associated with this project. I gradually developed three ways of meeting these challenges. One of them was the use of close-up photographs, which allow for zooming in on the point of discussion, while avoiding the distraction of additional pieces of information preserved on the fragment. These images had to be taken through long hours of collaboration with an expert photographer. Another technique I have found effective for illustrating seriously damaged material is the use of explanatory diagrams that "translate" pages of explanations to a readily understandable image, and that provide the viewer with an impression, deduced from what survives, of the now-lost complete original. My initial sketches have been rendered into publishable form by graphic design experts, who could work masterfully with modern computer technology and who were committed to the extensive collaborative work needed for perfecting these diagrams. All in all, this project together with its inseparable illustrations highlights the benefits of collaborative work with technical experts for art history.

---

[39] Gulácsi 2001a.

TERMINOLOGY

The key terms employed in this study are summarized in an explanatory illustration that features the facing pages of a hypothetical Manichaean codex (Figure 2). For the most part, I have kept the traditional terminology of codicology including the recto and verso designations. Opposite to codices written in Latin and Greek script, Manichaean codices were bound along the right. In Manichaean codices (just like in Aramaic script books, such as used for Arabic or Hebrew) the page to be read first (i.e., the recto) falls on the left side of the open book, and the subsequent page (the verso) is seen on the right side after turning the folio. In cases where the succession of the pages or the folia cannot be established, the uncertainty is marked by a question mark in parentheses (?) placed directly after the questionable element.

Within the text, the horizontal lines of writing in any of the three scripts (Manichaean, Sogdian/Uygur, or Runic) used for writing Manichaean illuminated books in East Central Asia proceed from right to left, that is on the recto from the inner to the outer margin, and on the verso from the outer to the inner margin.[40] Also, the column(s) tend to be tall and narrow compared to the page, on which they are placed closer to the binding of the book. Accordingly, the four margins are not of equal size. Although the relative sizes of the margins can vary from document to document, the following generalizations can be made: the upper margin is the widest, and can be twice the extent of the outer margin; the inner margin is the narrowest, often half the width of the lower margin.

In most Manichaean books, headers were placed in the middle of the upper margin to indicate the content of the text. Although the headers are only as wide as the width of the column(s) beneath them, on facing pages of the open book they are often meant to be read together.[41] Usually the headers were written using a thicker pen and in a larger sized script, and the scribes decorated them by employing colored ink or gilding, artfully elongated letters, and floral punctuation marks.

The traditional terminology of European book illumination that distinguishes miniatures, initial-letters, and borders[42] does not precisely fit the study of Manichaean book art. The problem is that the above categories are not mutually exclusive, and thus are difficult to use as definitions. Regarding their content, Manichaean book illuminations can be divided into two categories. We can distinguish *decorative designs*, that is, decorative ornaments composed of stylized motifs of plants, scarves, and vessels; and *figural scenes*, which are communicative painted scenes that contain human figures. The decorative designs and the figural compositions have distinct locations on the page.

In most cases, the decorative designs contour the main body of the texts along the upper, outer, and bottom margins (marginal), growing out from the headers. In rare cases, decorative designs are found within the column (intracolumnar), beautifying captions within the columns. Manichaean decorative designs are not identical to European borders. Although both are placed along the margins as ornate borders, they differ in content, because small miniature scenes are not contained within the decorative designs. Furthermore, decorative designs do not compare to European initials, because instead of decorating the starting letter, they embellish an entire line and never contain miniatures, as the initials in European books often do.

The figural scenes of Manichaean illuminated codices are placed along the side margins (marginal) or within the texts (intratextual), or they occupy an entire page on their own (full-page). When within texts, the figural scenes split the columns into upper and lower sections, and often claim the full width of the codex

---

[40] For a reproduction of the Sogdian script bifolio MIK III 200, see Sundermann 1996, Pls. 147 and 148 (where the item is referred to under its old accession number So 14411). For a reproduction of the Runic script codex Ch. 0033, see Stein 1921, Pl. CLX.
[41] BeDuhn 2001 (Nos. 7, 11, and 15).
[42] *Oxford Companion to Art*, 557.

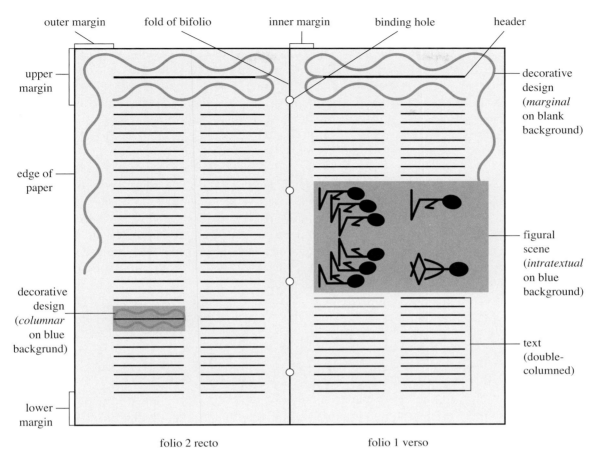

Figure 0/2. Terminology of Manichaean Book Design: Facing Pages from a Hypothetical Illuminated Codex

folio by extending horizontally to the outer margins. Along the margins, figural scenes of smaller scale can stand on their own as the only painted scene on a page. As we shall see Manichaean figural scenes, in any location, are always turned sideways with respect to the text. While the text occupies the page vertically, the miniature utilizes the oblong surface horizontally. These paintings in the context of Manichaean illuminated books correspond to European miniatures.

CHAPTER ONE

IDENTIFYING THE CORPUS OF MANICHAEAN BOOK ART

Among the surviving Manichaean primary sources, the illuminated book fragments enjoy a special place because they allow us to see the art left behind by a religion famous for its book culture. Most of the surviving pieces of Manichaean book art are from an archaeological site at a ruined mediaeval city near the modern oasis town of Turfan, often referred to by its historical Uygur name of Kocho (Chin. Gao-chang). The Manichaean fragments were however recovered together with Buddhist ones, which presents an obstacle to their identification, especially because in many cases shared features of painting style and iconography hamper the differentiation of their distinct origins. In addition, the problem of identification is complicated by the fact that Christian artistic remains also were found in Kocho. These share similarities of format, and possibly iconography, with Manichaean articles. As a result, it is difficult to discern Manichaean artifacts without the confirmation of literary context and specific iconography; no criteria for either have ever been systematically set out.

The lack of a securely identified body of illuminated book fragments hinders research on Manichaean book art, as well as its comparative art historical study. For example, the styles of book painting transmitted into East Central Asia and the ones developed in that region through the activities of the Manichaean church cannot be distinguished without confirmed sources of evidence. In turn, an important group of primary visual sources remains excluded from the study of Manichaean religious life. Therefore, a clearly defined corpus is essential for further research, and a strategy for assembling this corpus is necessary so that Manichaean artifacts can be securely distilled from among the large number of Turfan manuscript remains.

No concerted attempts have been made by previous scholars to address the problem of forming a Manichaean corpus of art. Most specialists have relied on an undefined sense of the "Manichaeanness" of a given piece of art, and due to the subjectiveness of this standard they have included non-corresponding lists of items in their respective corpuses. A comparative listing of items in the two Berlin collections allows us to survey what has been attributed to the corpus of Manichaean book art during the twentieth century (Table 1/1). While the varying contents of the columns in Table 1/1 in part reflect that, understandably, the authors did not aim for comprehensiveness, the differences also indicate that a variety of criteria were used in their selection depending on their respective research purposes.

Albert von Le Coq, the pioneer in identifying Manichaean works of art, had first-hand knowledge about the archaeological sites where the artifacts were found.[1] The logic behind his canon formation was that, along with the unquestionably Manichaean pieces, the same sites were likely to yield less obviously Manichaean objects. The abundant Manichaean texts and wall painting remains found in Kocho Ruin K led Le Coq to reasonably identify it as a Manichaean site, even though it yielded an admixture of Buddhist remains as well. On the basis of this site identification, any artifact of Ruin K that contained motifs unprecedented in Buddhist art had a chance to be Manichaean. On the other hand, this approach is complicated

---

[1] Le Coq 1913 and 1923.

Table 1/1. Illuminated Book Fragments Attributed to the Manichaean Corpus from the two Berlin Collections between 1913 and 2001 (84 examples)

Authors:	_Le Coq_	_Klimkeit_	_Ebert_	_Boyce_	_Gulácsi_
Items:					
Berlin-Brandenburg Academy (27)					
M 23	—	—	—	1960, p. 3	2001, No. 2
M 171	—	—	—	—	2001, No. 6
M 168	—	—	—	—	newly noted
M 233	—	—	—	1960, p. 17	2001, No. 4
M 380 a–b	—	—	—	—	newly noted
M 501 e	—	—	—	1960, p. 34	2001, No. 41
M 501 f	—	—	—	1960, p. 34	2001, App. IV unconfirmed
M 508	—	—	—	—	newly noted
M 556	—	—	—	1960, p. 39	2001, No. 54
M 559	—	—	1994, Fig.10	1960, p. 40	2001, No. 37
M 576	—	—	—	1960, p. 40	2001, No. 1
M 596 a – f	—	—	—	1960, p. 41	2001, No. 47
M 660 a, b	—	—	—	1960, p. 45	2001, App. IV unconfirmed
M 694	—	—	—	1960, p. 47	2001, No. 21
M 730	—	—	—	—	2001, No. 8
M 797	—	—	—	1960, p. 54	2001, No. 13
M 857	—	—	—	—	newly noted Plate 4c
M 871 a	—	—	—	1960, p. 59	2001, No. 10
M 1156	—	—	—	1960, p. 67	2001, No. 25
M 1886	—	—	—	1960, p. 83	2001, App. IV unconfirmed
M 1887	—	—	—	1960, p. 83	2001, No. 12
M 4831	—	—	—	1960, p. 103	2001, No. 20
M 6290	—	—	—	1960, p. 122	2001, No. 38
M 8200	—	—	—	1960, p. 134	2001, No. 56
So 18700	—	—	—	—	2001, No. 41
T.M. 332[1]	—	—	—	—	2001, No. 7
U 246	—	—	—	—	newly noted[17]
Berlin, State Museums (57)					
MIK III 5 d	—	—	—	1960, p. 144	2001, No. 66
MIK III 36	—	—	—	1960, p. 144[3]	2001, No. 42
MIK III 104	—	—	—	1960, p. 144[4]	2001, No. 60
MIK III 134	—	—	1992, Fig. 4	—	2001, No. 43
MIK III 151	—	—	—	—	2001, No. 76
MIK III 4614	1924, No. 3[5]	1982, No. 48[6]	1992, Fig.11	—	2001, No. 65
MIK III 4937	1924, No. 6/c	1982, No. 32	—	—	2001, App. IV unconfirmed
MIK III 4943	—	—	—	—	2001, No. 58
MIK III 4947	1924, No. 6/e	1982, No. 30[7]	—	—	2001, No. 66
MIK III 4956 a–d	—	—	—	—	2001, No. 24, 31, 64
MIK III 4957	1924, No. 5/a	—	—	—	2001, App. IV unconfirmed
MIK III 4958	—	—	—	1960, p. 141	2001, No. 59
MIK III 4959	1924, No. 8ab/d	—	—	1960, p. 142	2001, No. 34
MIK III 4960	—	—	1994, Fig.3	1960, p. 142	2001, No. 57
MIK III 4962 a–c	1924, No. 7/d	—	—	1960, p. 142	2001, No. 23, 55
MIK III 4964	1924, No. 5/e	1982, No. 35	—	1960, p. 142	2001, No. 51
MIK III 4965	1924, No. 8ab/c	1982, No. 33 a,b	—	—	2001, No. 45
MIK III 4966 a–c	—	—	1994, Fig.7	1960, p. 142	2001, No. 18[8]
MIK III 4967 a–c	—	—	—	1960, p. 142	2001, No. 3, 53
MIK III 4968	—	—	—	1960, p. 142	2001, App. IV unconfirmed
MIK III 4969	—	—	—	1960, p. 142	2001, No. 11
MIK III 4970 b, c	1924, No. 5/c, d	1982, No. 36[9]	—	1960, p. 142[10]	2001, No. 50
MIK III 4971 a–c	1924, No. 5/b	—	—	1960, p. 142	2001, No. 49
MIK III 4972	—	—	—	1960, p. 141[11]	2001, No. 30
MIK III 4973	1924, No. 5/f	1982, No. 37	—	—	2001, App. IV unconfirmed
MIK III 4974	1924, No. 7/a	1982, No. 28	—	1960, p. 143	2001, No. 36
MIK III 4975	1924, No. 6/b	1982, No. 34	—	—	2001, No. 67
MIK III 4976	—	—	—	1960, p. 143	2001, No. 19
MIK III 4979	1924, No. 8ab/a	1982, No. 21, 22	1992, Fig. 1	1960, p. 143	2001, No. 32
MIK III 4981 a–f	1924, No. 4b/c	1982, No. 51, 52	—	1960, p. 143	2001, No. 73, 74, 75

Table 1/1. Cont.

MIK III 4983	1924, No. 6/a	1982, No. 49	—	1960, p. 143	2001, No. 15
MIK III 4984	1924, Pl. 6/a	1982, No. 31[12]	—	—	2001, App. IV unconfirmed
MIK III 6252 a–c	1913, Pl. 6/a	—	—	—	2001, App. IV unconfirmed
MIK III 6254	1913, Pl. 6/f	—	—	—	2001, App. IV unconfirmed
MIK III 6255	1924, Pl. 6/d	—	—	—	2001, App. IV unconfirmed
MIK III 6257	—	—	1994, Fig.11	—	2001, No. 33
MIK III 6258 a, b	—	—	—	—	2001, No. 16, 35
MIK III 6261	—	—	—	—	2001, No. 9
MIK III 6265	—	—	—	—	2001, No. 29
MIK III 6267	1924, p. 17	—	—	—	2001, No. 71
MIK III 6268	1924, Pl. 4/e	1982, No. 56	—	—	2001, No. 70
MIK III 6284	—	—	1994, Fig.8	—	2001, No. 44
MIK III 6368	1913, Pl. 5[14]	1982, No. 25, 26	—	—	2001, No. 40
MIK III 6374	—	—	—	—	2001, No. 27
MIK III 6376	—	—	—	—	2001, No. 39
MIK III 6377 a–g	—	—	—	1960, p. 144	2001, No. 14, 17
MIK III 6378 d	—	—	—	—	2001, No. 61
MIK III 6379 a–h	—	—	—	—	2001, No. 22, 46, 63
MIK III 6626	—	—	—	—	2001, No. 46
MIK III 6989 a	—	—	—	—	2001, No. 68
MIK III 7048	—	—	—	—	2001, No. 72
MIK III 7251	1924, Pl. 4/a	1982, No. 50	—	1960, p. 144	2001, No. 5
MIK III 7266	—	—	—	—	2001, No. 26
MIK III 7283	—	—	—	1960, p. 144	2001, No. 48
MIK III 7285	—	—	—	1960, p. 144	2001, No. 52
MIK III 8259	1924, Pl. 7/b	1982, No. 27	1994, Fig.4	1960, p. 144	2001, No. 28
MIK III 8260	1924, Pl. 7/c[15]	1982, No. 29[16]	—	—	2001, No. 69

[1] Lost item; see Gulácsi 2001a, Appendix II.

[2] MIK III 36 is identical to the fragment previously known as IB 6371. The change of catalogue number was due to the introduction of new numbers for fragments that had lost their identification during World War II. This information was kindly provided by Dr. Lore Sander, who was curator and research fellow at the MIK during my research.

[3] MIK III 36 is found in Boyce 1960 under its old number IB 6371.

[4] MIK III 104 is described without accession number as the last entry in Boyce 1960, 144.

[5] In Le Coq's 1923 publication all fragments belonging to the museum are referred to by the old IB prefix.

[6] In Klimkeit's 1982 publication an inconsistent mixture of the new MIK III and the old IB prefixes is used, and in numerous instances the accession numbers are not indicated.

[7] No accession number is given in Klimkeit 1982a, 40.

[8] The separation of the three fragments is discussed in Gulácsi 2001a, Appendix IV.

[9] The item MIK III 4970 b was published as IB 4970 in Klimkeit 1982a, 42.

[10] MIK III 4970 b and c were entered as fragments 4970 a and b respectively in Boyce 1960.

[11] MIK III 4972 a–d was recorded mistakenly under IB 4912 a–d in Boyce 1960.

[12] No accession number is given in Klimkeit 1982a, 40.

[13] No accession number is given in Klimkeit 1982a, 50.

[14] Also published in Le Coq 1924, Pl. 8ab/b.

[15] Instead of the accession number the signature T III 260 was used to identify the fragment in Le Coq 1923, 48.

[16] This piece has no accession number, but the signature T III 260 is given in Klimkeit 1982a, 40.

[17] This illuminated Turkic fragment was first identified as Manichaean by Jens Wilkens (2000, 193–194). Since this is the only fragment in this table identified by Dr. Wilkens, I did not create a separate column for it.

by Le Coq's application of it to the identification of supposedly Manichaean pieces from a partially Buddhist site, Ruin Alpha.[2] Although never aiming to form a corpus, Le Coq made a definitive contribution
by publishing for the first time the best-preserved examples of Turfan Manichaean book art. Ever since,
Le Coq's writings have been consulted by art historians and specialists of religious studies working on ency-
clopedic presentations[3] or comparative studies[4] of Manichaean art.

In publications by Hans-Joachim Klimkeit,[5] most of the book art corresponds to Le Coq's, with new
objects introduced on the basis of a search for possible Manichaean influence on the art of the region. Klimkeit's work on Manichaean art reflects methods of comparative religious studies, and thus his contribution
lies in offering interpretations of works of art that are presented as, and remain, hypothetical. Sometimes
Klimkeit's Manichaean identifications mistakenly include remnants of Buddhist works of art.

While studying various iconographic aspects of Central Asian and Manichaean pictorial art, Jorinde
Ebert has added numerous items with pictorial content to the list of Manichaean illuminated book fragments. Her identifications are based on stylistic features, which frequently enjoy the support of additional
textual evidence. Especially Ebert's discussions of previously ignored, smaller and more damaged fragments
have contributed significantly to the process of canon formation.[6]

The most relevant work for the goal of assembling an illuminated corpus is a publication by Mary Boyce.[7]
While compiling a catalogue of Manichaean manuscripts, Boyce created also a list of Manichaean works
of art that—like all items in her catalogue—are accompanied by Middle Iranian texts written in Manichaean script. Theoretically, every item on her list is accompanied by a Manichaean text. In most cases,
but unfortunately not always, Boyce mentions if a fragment is illuminated, and thus provides a list of items
for the artistic corpus. Since the selection is built on confirmed Manichaean script texts, her identification strategy is the most secure. For creating a comprehensive list of Berlin Manichaean illuminated book
fragments, Boyce's literary catalogue is thus essential. This same strategy also limits its comprehensiveness,
however, because illuminated items with other than Manichaean script texts (e.g., Sogdian and Runic) are
not included in her work, though by content they can be identified as Manichaean according to their content. Due to its literary nature, Boyce's catalogue has escaped the attention of art historians.

The last column of Table 1/1 lists the items identified as Manichaean by the present author, as a preliminary part of this research project,[8] based on the criteria of identification detailed below. The process of
assembling this list incorporated two practical steps. First, by studying the publications of the above-mentioned scholars, a basic group of well-preserved Manichaean items started to emerge. This group however
contained items that were not Manichaean, while also ignoring the smaller, less informative Manichaean
book fragments. Therefore, as a second step, an on-sight survey had to be conducted. In the Turfan collection of the Museum of Indian Art (Musum für Indische Kunst) of the Berlin State Museum, this involved
the personal survey of all Turfan manuscript fragments in the collection. In the Turfan Research Center

---

[2] E.g., MIK III 4975a (Gulácsi 2001a, p. 258).

[3] Hambis 1964.

[4] Grabar 1968, 27–30; Arnold 1924; Monneret de Villard 1938.

[5] Klimkeit 1982. Several items that were published in Klimkeit's work did not make it into my Table 1/1. These were samples of
Manichaean calligraphy (1982, Fig. 53–55), a Manichaean wall painting that remained in Turfan (1982, Fig. 15), all Manichaean
objects that originated in other places than Turfan (1982, Fig. 57–61), and sections of Buddhist wall paintings from Alchi (Jamu-
Kashmir, India; 1982, Fig. 17–20) and Kizil (Xinjiang, PRC; 1982, Fig. 16).

[6] Ebert 1992, 1994, 2003.

[7] Boyce 1960.

[8] Gulácsi 1997 and 2001a, where besides illuminated book fragments, textiles & wallpaintings were also considered to form the
corpus of Manichaean art from among the Berlin Turfan remains.

(Turfan Akademien Vorhaben) of the Berlin-Brandenburg Academy (Berlin-Brandenburgische Akademie der Wissenschaften), the survey had to be accomplished by viewing microfilm[9] and then selecting items for direct examination, with the generous help of the research staff.

A cautious strategy for identification is used for the survey below, with clear justification as to why some items must be added to the corpus of Manichaean book illumination whereas others are moved to the periphery of, or even excluded from, that set.[10] Six worldwide Turfan collections were consulted in order to assemble a corpus of Manichaean book illumination from among all the currently known book fragments recovered from Turfan. These include, in addition to the above-mentioned two institutions in Berlin, the Oriental Institute in St. Petersburg, the British Library in London, the local archaeological museum in the modern city of Turfan in northwest China, and the Otani collection of Ryukoku University near Kyoto, Japan; each of these institutions houses only a few relevant items. The survey resulted in a corpus of 89 fragments. Although in varying sizes and states of preservation, they are all positively identified as remnants of Manichaean illuminated manuscripts.[11]

CRITERIA OF IDENTIFICATION

In the vocabulary of this study, the word *Manichaean* refers to a world religion and not to an artistic style. Accordingly, the term *Manichaean art* is used to connote any and every work of art that was employed in the context of this religion. Art produced in any artistic tradition (whether by artists trained in art schools of Abbasid Persia, or Song China) that was used in association with Manichaean activities (taking place in the Mediterranean region or in West, Central, or East Asia) is Manichaean art.

The secure identification of Manichaean illuminated fragments requires consideration of their literary context. This involves not only the contents of their texts, but also their scripts. Either the content or the use of a script characteristic of this religion can signal the Manichaean association, and often the specific subject of the folio to which the fragments belonged signals it as well. In addition, certain artistic traits that occur frequently within the illumination of items securely identified through their literary context provide aid in the identification of further items. Finally, documentary evidence anchors a few additional Manichaean items to the corpus of Turfan Manichaean book art.

Shortcomings of the Archaeological Context

The Turfan archaeological context cannot be used to decide whether or not a fragment of an illuminated manuscript is Manichaean. Even if one were so inclined, numerous problems would interfere with relying solely on provenance data for identification. Most objects relevant to this study derive from historically mixed sites. Turfan Manichaean artistic materials, similar to solely literary remains, often derive from a

---

[9] In 1996 the microfilm record consisted of rolls of black-and-white negative film.

[10] The overall concept of identification applied here for illuminated book fragments is in accordance with my previous work on identification of Manichaean artistic media from among the holdings of the two Berlin Turfan collections (Gulácsi 1997). The items thus identified include Manichaean illuminated book fragments as well as fragments of textiles and wall paintings (Gulácsi 2001a).

[11] This project involved numerous research trips to Berlin, London, Turfan, and Kyoto. Based on the sound research collaboration between the former East German Turfan research group and the Oriental Institute in the former Leningrad, for the study of the St. Petersburg holdings, I relied on Sundermann's 2001 publication.

Buddhist provenance, such as the stupas of Bezeklik. Vice versa, buildings suspected of being Manichaean, such as Ruin K and especially Ruin Alpha at Kocho, also contained many Buddhist objects. The fact that both of these sites yielded many Buddhist artifacts draws attention to the problem of the Buddhist provenance of Manichaean objects in Turfan.[12] The reasons behind this fact, which also hold true for the more numerous non-artistic manuscript fragments, still await explanation.

In general, when dealing with manuscripts, provenance is a last resort in identification, when the script, language, vocabulary, and subject matter are not sufficiently specific or preserved to allow confirmation of the manuscript's association. Specifically in Turfan, provenance in and of itself contributes relatively little to our understanding of the individual manuscript fragments. Rather, the relevant information is the provenance of the Turfan artifacts *as sets*. The entirety of recovered objects from a specific site characterizes the group to which the individual fragments belong, which in their association may reveal the functional history of the buildings where they were discovered. Why were these objects found together? Why were they found in particular buildings? If Ruin K indeed included a "Manichaean library room," why did that room contain not a single complete manuscript? Answers to questions like these are yet to be proposed.[13]

It is still possible, however, that the provenance data could narrow the possibilities of identification in certain cases. For instance, since only Buddhist and Manichaean texts were found at Ruin Alpha and Ruin K of Kocho, it would be reasonable to assume that the artistic remains from these sites also are going to be either Buddhist or Manichaean. In other words, the archaeological records may be considered as secondary evidence for identification.

Table 1/2 summarizes the available information on provenance; all items attributed to the Manichaean corpus are grouped according to their records of discovery.[14] The 15 objects listed in the first row of the table lack a record of provenance.[15] The second and third rows are devoted to the first expedition, which yielded 35 Manichaean illuminated book fragments from Kocho. Among these, 25 have no records of provenance because they were purchased from the local population. Some well-preserved important fragments are found in this group (e.g., MIK III 4979, see Figures 2/5, 5/9, and Plate 5; and MIK III 4974, see Figure 5/8). Ten artifacts are from the site referred to as Ruin Alpha, which was meticulously described in the published report of the first expedition.[16] These include numerous important pieces, such as the silk codex fragment (MIK 4981 a–f, see Figure 3/7 and Plate 3) and the carbon-dated reconstructible bifolio illuminated with figural scenes (MIK III 8259, Figures 2/2 and 5/7). No objects were recovered from Ruin K during the first expedition because it was regarded as too disturbed and was thus left alone.[17] Twenty-

---

[12] Based upon the inventory book of the MIK, I have gathered all the objects that were designated as deriving from Ruin Alpha and Ruin K of Kocho, and found that many items appear to be, and have been traditionally identified as, Buddhist on the basis of their iconography. For an illustration of such items see Härtel and Yaldiz 1982, Nos. 146 and 148.

[13] A further obstacle results from the condition of the buildings disturbed by "excavations" of the local population, resulting in the acquisition of many objects that subsequently lack a noted archaeological context. Such missing records on the provenance also eliminate the body of evidence necessary to formulate even hypothetical thoughts about the functions of buildings. Disturbed site conditions are frequently referred to in the filed reports of the Prussian expeditions (e.g., Grünwedel 1909, 13; Le Coq 1923, 22).

[14] The source of information for the items housed in the Berlin-Brandenburg Academy was Boyce's catalogue, and for the MIK objects it was the museum's internal inventory book, in which the items are listed according to identification number and provided with brief descriptions and the known records of provenance.

[15] In the case of the items housed in the Berlin-Brandenburg Academy, the loss of records resulted from the introduction of a cataloguing system that organized the objects according to their script and/or language. The abandoning of old package numbers in 1904 affected only the finds of the first expedition (see Boyce 1960, xxi). The MIK objects lost their four-digit identification number and with it their record of origin during World War II. New (one, two, and three digit) numbers were subsequently introduced to keep track of these items. If the objects with new numbers are successfully matched with the descriptions attached to their old numbers, records of provenance can be recovered.

[16] Grünwedel 1906, 55–73.

[17] Grünwedel 1906, 26–27.

Table 1/2. Provenance of Berlin Artifacts Attributed to the Corpus of Manichaean Illuminated Book Fragments (78 examples)

Lost Record (15)

M 23	M 233	M 556	M 576	M 660 a, b	M 797	So 18700
M 171	M 501 e, f	M 559	M 596 a–f	M 694	M 817 a	T.M. 332
						MIK III 5 d

First Expedition: Kocho, Unspecified Site (25)

M 1886	MIK III 4947	MIK III 4967	MIK III 4972 a–c	MIK III 4979
M 1887	MIK III 4962 a–c	MIK III 4968	MIK III 4973 a–c	MIK III 4984
MIK III 134	MIK III 4964	MIK III 4969	MIK III 4974	MIK III 6989 a
MIK III 4614	MIK III 4965	MIK III 4970 b, c	MIK III 4975	MIK III 7048
MIK III 4937	MIK III 4966 c	MIK III 4971 a–d	MIK III 4976 a, b	MIK III 7060

First Expedition: Kocho, Ruin Alpha (10)

MIK III 4956 a–d	MIK III 4958 a, b	MIK III 4960	MIK III 4983	MIK III 7285
MIK III 4957	MIK III 4959	MIK III 4981 a–f	MIK III 7283	MIK III 8259

Second Exp.: Kocho, Unspecified (2)   Second Exp.: Sengim, East Stupa (1)

M 1156	M 4831	MIK III 6274

Second Expedition: Kocho, Ruin K (21)

M 6290	MIK III 6252 a–c	MIK III 6258 a, b	MIK III 6284	MIK III 6376
MIK III 36	MIK III 6254	MIK III 6261	MIK III 6286	MIK III 6377 a–g
MIK III 104	MIK III 6255	MIK III 6265	MIK III 6368	MIK III 6378 d
MIK III 151	MIK III 6257	MIK III 6267	MIK III 6374	MIK III 6379 a–h
				MIK III 6626

Third Exp.: Kocho, Unspecified (1)   Third Exp.: Kocho, Ruin K (2)   Third Exp.: Sengim, Stupa (1)

M 8200	MIK III 7251	MIK III 7266	MIK III 8260

Table 1/3. Provenance of Non-Berlin Artifacts Attributed to the Corpus of Manichaean Illuminated Book Fragments (9 examples)

(St. Petersburg)	(London)	(London)
Kocho, Unspecific Site (4)	Kocho, Unspecific Site (2)	Dunhuang, Cave 17 (1)
S 30 S 42 S 49 a, b S 50	Or. 12452/3 Or. 8218-1699	Ch. 0015
(Turfan)	(Kyoto)	
Bezeklik, Stupa (1)	Kocho, Unspecific Site (1)	
80 TB 65:01	No. 11074	

three items were found at Kocho during the second expedition, all but two from Ruin K. Although these illuminated fragments are more damaged, they do include important pieces (e.g., MIK III 36, Figure 5/ 11 and Plate 8; and MIK III 6368, Figure 5/13 and Plate 3). The last row lists the four artistic illuminated book fragments found during the third expedition, including the remnants of the illuminated *pustaka* (palm-leaf format) from a stupa at Sengim (MIK III 8260, Figure 5/28 and Plate 6).

In the table of provenance for the non-Berlin fragments (Table 1/3), the items are grouped according to their museum collections. Since seven of the nine fragments were purchased from locals at Kocho, their location of discovery is unknown. In one such case, however, a fragment in St. Petersburg (S 49 a–b, Figure 5/20) matches a fragment in Berlin (MIK III 4976 a–b, Figure 5/20), which also was purchased during the first expedition. The two well-preserved Manichaean scrolls (Ch. 0015, Figure 5/22; and 81 TB 65: 01, Figure 5/23) were discovered from Buddhist provenances at Dunhuang and Bezeklik, respectively.[18]

Art in Literary Context: Forming the Reference Group

The secure identification of Manichaean illuminated book fragments begins with the verification of their literary context. By surveying the remains of Manichaean literature, the core of an artistic corpus can be built and a preliminary picture of how Manichaean art looks can be formed. But due to the fragmentary nature of the Turfan literary remains, the contents of the surviving texts confirm their Manichaeanness in only a limited number of cases. Where content is not sufficient, it is the script that can verify connection with this religion, since the Manichaeans were the exclusive users of the "Manichaean script." This script was not applied extensively in any secular contexts, nor was it used in texts of other religions. It was introduced to the Turfan region through the activities of the church, and was known only by those who were trained in a Manichaean environment.[19]

Prior to 1904, the Manichaean script was unknown to the scholarly world. As part of the philological study of the German expeditions' finds, Friedrich Wilhelm Karl Müller identified the unknown script as a special variant of Estrangelo, the script known to be used by the Syriac Christian church.[20] On the basis of religious content, Müller recognized that the texts and their script were Manichaean, and announced the discovery of the first (and to this day the largest) set of primary sources in existence from this religion. By decoding the writing, the texts written on thousands of manuscript fragments in the Middle Persian, Parthian, Sogdian, and Uygur languages could be read.[21]

Gathering artifacts with Manichaean script is the first step in defining the Manichaean artistic corpus among the Turfan remains. At this point, a practical limit is needed that suits the scope of this study, and that separates the illuminated corpus from the non-illuminated book fragments, which are otherwise important as sources elucidating the formation of an artistic book culture as well as the primary literary milieu of the Turfan Manichaean painting tradition. Figure 1/1 indicates the kinds of evidence that carry data relevant to Turfan Manichaean book art. The thousands of Manichaean manuscript fragments that contain only plain texts (the base of the pyramid) preserve data on book-making techniques as well as the rules of page arrangement, which are necessary to understand the codicological aspects of Manichaean books. Means of scribal decoration (the middle of the pyramid), found on far fewer fragments, can be recognized in punctuation decorations and calligraphic writing. Manuscript illumination (the pinnacle of the pyramid), preserved on a significantly smaller amount of fragments, can be studied through the decorative designs of stylized motifs, as well as through communicative figural scenes. Since the ultimate challenge here is to confirm the Manichaean character of those Manichaean works of art that are not accompanied by Manichaean texts, manuscripts with plain texts and those that are decorated by means of scribal decoration are at the periphery of our interest. The illuminated fragments are the most relevant. These con-

---

[18] Stein 1921 Vol. 2, Chapter XXIV, Sec. v–vi; and Yoshida et al. 2000,1.

[19] There are some indications, however, that the activities of Manichaean scribes might have reached farther than that of the church. One such case has been recognized in inscribed magic bowls from Mesopotamia. The bowls place the script in association with items and practices that are understood as belonging to a regional folk religion rather than to the Manichaean church (BeDuhn 1995b, 432).

[20] Müller 1904.

[21] While the Manichaean script was retained in Turfan and used for writing Manichaean texts in the Middle-Persian, Parthian, Sogdian, and Uygur languages, in other areas of the Manichaean world local scripts enjoyed preference. In East Asia, Chinese language texts (the *Hymn* scroll, the *Compendium*, and the *Tractate*) were written exclusively with Chinese characters (Takakasu-Watanabe 1928, 54:1270–1286). In West Asia and North Africa, Greek and Latin scripts were used in most of the Manichaean documents; only a few examples of Manichaean script texts have been found in these areas (Crum 1919, 206–208; Margoliouth 1915, 214–216; Gardner 1995).

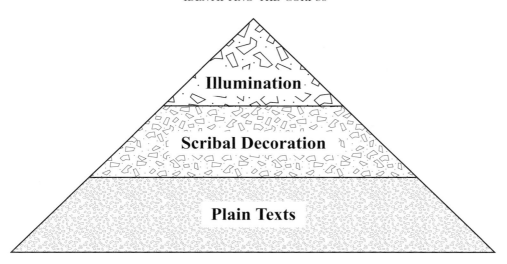

Figure 1/1. Scope of Primary Sources Narrowed for this Study

tain floral and geometric decorations in the forms of decorative designs and more complex communica-tive figural scenes.

Book fragments with decorative designs (e.g., MIK III 4981 a, d, see Plate 2) and/or figural composi-tions (MIK III 4979, see Plate 5) that are accompanied by Manichaean texts form the core of the securely identified Manichaean illuminated corpus (Table 1/4). This core functions as a reference group, consisting of 63 book fragments. Among them, 57 contain writing with Manichaean script. The remaining six can be identified through their Manichaean contents. Four of the six were written in Sogdian script (So 18700 & M 501 e, Figure 5/14 and Plate 6a; MIK III 4614, Figures 5/24 and 6/5b and Plate 8a; and 81 TB 85:01, Figures 5/23 and 6/5; and U 246), and two were in Runic script (T.M. 332; and Or. 1812–1692).[22]

Exclusive Characteristics of the Reference Group

Correlation with features of this reference group permits the identification of further Manichaean illuminated fragments that do not display sufficient textual evidence for their religious affiliation to be determined on that basis. To make such correlations, exclusive characteristics must be identified and used as Manichaean tokens in the survey of the Turfan remains. Among the features that characterize the objects in the reference group, several recurring aspects of format, iconography, style, and technique can be recognized. Some of these attributes are marks of Manichaeanness among the Turfan remains. Before additional Manichaean artifacts can be identified through the aid of these attributes, it is essential to discuss their unique links to Manichaean art production in Turfan.

The Iconography of the Elects
Outer appearance made the Manichaean sacerdotal class distinct from Buddhist monks and Nestorian priests. A connection between garment and religion is clearly documented in both visual and literary

---

[22] For an illustration, see Gulácsi 2001a, No. 7.

Table 1/4. The Reference Group: Manichaean Illuminated Book Fragments Identified by Script and Textual Content (63 examples)

Manichaean Script Text with Decorative Design (29)

Berlin (25):	M 576	MIK III 4966 a	MIK III 4983	*Kyoto (1):*
M 23	M 694	MIK III 4967 b, c	MIK III 6258 b	No. 11074
M 168	M 730	MIK III 4969	MIK III 6377 a, b, d, f	
M 171	M 797	MIK III 4970 c	& III 6379 a	*St. Petersburg (3):*
M 233	M 857	MIK III 4976 a, b	& III 6990 a	S 30
M 380 a, b	M 1881	MIK III 4981 a, d	MIK III 6377 c	S 42
M 508	M 4831	MIK III 4981 c, f	MIK III 7251	S 49

Manichaean Script Texts with Figural Scene (28)

Berlin (26):	MIK III 151 3rd layer	MIK III 4971 a–c	MIK III 7285
M 556	MIK III 4956 b	MIK III 4972 a–d	MIK III 8259
M 559	MIK III 4958	MIK III 4974	MIK III 8260
M 596 a	MIK III 4959	MIK III 4979	
M 6290 b	MIK III 4960	MIK III 6258 a	London (2):
M 8200	MIK III 4962 a, c	MIK III 6265 & III 4966b	Ch. 0015
MIK III 36	MIK III 4964	MIK III 6279 a–i	Or. 12452/3
MIK III 104	MIK III 4970 b	MIK III 6378 d	

Manichaean Content of Text w/ Decorative Design (1)	*Manichaean Content of Text with Figural Scene (5)*			
Berlin (1): U 246	Berlin (3):		London (1):	Turfan (1):
	T.M. 332 So 18700 and M 501 e MIK III 6414		Or. 1812-1692	81 TB 65:01

sources in East Central Asia. Buddhist monks are portrayed, for example, on the walls of Bezeklik's Cave 9, where two groups of them are distinguished by the distinct styles and colors of their garments.[23] The only data concerning the appearance of the Nestorian priesthood in the region consists of a wall painting from Kocho, where a figure interpreted as a Nestorian priest wears two layers of garments—a red and white short coat over a long green alb.[24] A datum specifically on the issue of identity as it is expressed through garment is preserved in the travelogue of Ennin, the Japanese Buddhist monk who visited China in the mid ninth century during the era of persecutions of foreign religions. In 843 CE, he witnessed the martyrdom of Manichaean elects that included their humiliation by depriving them of their white robe and long hair and changing their appearance to that of Buddhists monks.

> Their [the elects'] heads are to be shaven, and they are to be dressed in Buddhist robes and are to be killed looking like Buddhist *sramana*. (*Nittō guhō junrei gyōki*, referring to the year 843 CE)[25]

The elects' appearance is remarked upon in Manichaean textual sources. Although Turfan Manichaean hymns occasionally contain references to the "white-robed elect,"[26] a more authoritative discussion is found in a Manichaean document discovered at Dunhuang known as the *Compendium*, a Chinese language translation of a text prepared in 732 by a high-ranking elect at the request of the Chinese government to provide a description of the religion and its institutions.[27] One of its sections states that the elect wear white garments and white headgear, and states that Mani also is portrayed as dressed in a white robe:

[23] Le Coq 1913, Taf. 16a, b.
[24] Le Coq 1913, Taf. 7a.
[25] Reischauer 1955, 232.
[26] "Let us pray *ara nwydma* to the white-robed elect" (TII D178 II. v. line 12; in Le Coq 1922, 29–30).
[27] According to its colophon, the *Compendium* was composed by a leading member of the church and translated into Chinese (Lieu 1992, 231).

The *a-lo-huan* [here "the elect"] and the higher grades all wear white caps and garments and only the grade of *nu-sha-an* [here "the auditors"] are allowed to retain their ordinary dress…. His [Mani's] being clad in a white robe symbolizes the four pure *dharmākayas*. His occupying his white throne depicts the five *vajra*-lands. (*Compendium of the Doctrines and Styles of the Teaching of Mani, the Buddha of the Light*, 732 CE)[28]

In contrast to the Buddhist and Christian art of East Central Asia, the most common subject matter of extant Manichaean paintings are scenes of religious life, such as alms services, sermons, conversions, and festivals (Plate 7c, f). These paintings show both the elect and lay members of the community. On the basis of evidence on Manichaean garments gained from literary sources, the white robes worn by figures depicted in securely identified Manichaean book paintings can only be interpreted as the garments of the elects. Consequently, these Manichaean paintings constitute primary visual sources of evidence regarding the appearance of the Manichaean priesthood, many details of which were not reported by written sources. A full survey of the representations of ecclesial garments in these paintings would lead to an understanding of the range of outfits known in Manichaean Turfan. Garments distinguish rank, gender, and most likely even regional affiliation of the elects by supplementing the basic white robe with a variety of accessories, such as headgear and robes adorned with golden hems and square patches.[29]

A standard element of the elects' depiction in the paintings of the reference group is their white, robe-like garments (Figure 2/6 and Plate 3). This plain robe covers the body entirely—its tall neckline hides the collarbone, and its length conceals the feet. Unless in an active posture, even the hands are out of view, tucked into the sleeves as the arms are folded in front of the upper body. Fine black lines drawn on the white surface indicate its fullness. The folds are especially heavy around the arms, where the material of the robe gathers as the lower arms of the elects are intertwined beneath the sleeves. The same is true of the folds around the knees of the figures seated cross-legged or on their heels. Among the marks that characterize the elects' appearance, the white robe is the minimum criterion for identification, since the headgear and all other accessories are worn with this uniform robe.

Because the specific white garment depicted in figural compositions is an exclusive token of Manichaeanness, the inclusion into the Manichaean corpus of any Turfan fragment wherein these specific white robes are found is justified through correlation. Among the illuminated book fragments positively identified as Manichaean through their script and textual content, the white-robed elect of both genders can be seen in 12 miniatures of 11 fragments.[30] Similar portrayals are found on an additional 19 fragments discovered in the Turfan region that are not accompanied by Manichaean texts. These include manuscripts, textiles (banners and silk books),[31] and wall paintings.[32]

Remnants of four illuminated book fragments can be identified as Manichaean through the iconography of the elects depicted on them (Table 1/5). Three of these show male elects (MIK III 151 3rd layer, MIK III 6274, and MIK III 6368, Figure 5/13 and Plate 3). One retains only the lower garments of a group of elects standing on lotus flowers (MIK III 6275, Figure 5/25).

---

[28] Haloun and Henning 1952–53, 195 and 194 respectively.

[29] Jorinde Ebert has discussed the accessories associated with the robes of high-ranking elects (2004, 72–83).

[30] The miniatures that portray elects from among the fragments of the reference group are M 555, M 6290, and MIK III 4614, MIK III 4964, MIK III 4971, MIK III 4974, MIK III 4979 recto, MIK III 4979 verso, MIK III 6264 & MIK III 4966 c, MIK III 7285, MIK III 8259, and MIK III 8260.

[31] Textile painting identified through the portal of the elects include MIK III 141 a, MIK III 164, MIK III 4815 & 141 c, MIK III 6189 a & b, MIK III 6251, MIK III 6257, MIK III 6270, MIK III 6283, MIK III 6286, MIK III 6387, MIK III 6388, MIK III 6953, and MIK III 7060. A few additional textile fragments with garments of elects have been identified in the MIK; see Bhattacharya-Haesner 2003 and Ebert 2004.

[32] Wall paintings identified through the portal of the elects include MIK III 4626, MIK III 6915 a–b, and MIK III 6918.

Fully Painted Decorative Designs on Codex Folia

Another distinct characteristic feature of the reference group is the illumination preserved on codex folia. On these pages, decorative designs and figural compositions are painted in a style that is generally best described as a West Asian fully painted style of Turfan Manichaean book art. It is apparent that, among the Turfan remains, codex pages with decorative designs and figural compositions derive solely from Manichaean books, and when codex format and book illumination are recognized together in Turfan, they indicate Manichaeanness. The support of this claim is somewhat problematic since, although several scholarly works touch upon the variety of book formats in East Central Asia,[33] a codicological study of the undecorated Turfan manuscript remains has not been conducted. The above claim is based on my analysis of Turfan collections and published facsimiles of East Central Asian manuscripts. Two preliminary rules have crystallized regarding the utilization of codex format and the presence of fully painted illuminations in such a format.

Concerning the codex shape of East Central Asian books, the following picture emerges. Buddhist texts written in the Middle Iranian and Turkic languages generally follow pustaka (palm-leaf) or scroll formats. Only rarely do they occur as codices, several examples of which are seen among the Dunhuang remains.[34] In Turfan, the Buddhist use of the codex format is documented as a rare exception,[35] whereas it is thought to be the preferred shape for Manichaean and Nestorian Christian manuscripts.[36]

Regarding the use of illumination in codex-formatted books of East Central Asia the following can be noted. Among the Dunhuang remains, illustrated Chinese Buddhist texts are seen in codex format, or codex-like folded forms.[37] The painted scenes on these, however, are composed in manners similar to painted Chinese hand-scrolls where sections of texts are placed between sections of paintings. In such scrolls, either the artwork illustrates the text, or in cases when the painting dominates the scroll, inscriptions interrupt to identify or comment upon the pictures.[38] In any case, since the writing itself is not the subject of decoration, decorative designs are unknown and thus the text is not "illuminated." These observations about painted hand-scrolls apply to the painted Chinese codices. In format and painting style, painted codices exhibit the features of Chinese Buddhist art at Dunhuang from the Tang period. Painted Buddhist codices have not been identified among the Turfan remains. In Turfan, the characteristic distinction between the codices of Manichaean and of Nestorian origin is that while the Manichaean codex remains are lavishly illuminated and heavily gilded, the Nestorian ones are undecorated.[39] Illuminated Nestorian books have not been found in Turfan or in Central and East Asia.[40] In addition, no circumstantial evidence supports the assumption that Nestorian illuminated books existed in Turfan.[41] The remains of wall paintings in the

---

[33] Gabain 1964, 173–176; Gabain 1973, 167–171; and Tekin 1993, 51–70.

[34] Kara and Zieme 1979; Tekin 1980.

[35] Several unpublished fragments of a Buddhist text, U 2972 (T II S 53), were recovered at Sengim. This Uygur manuscript is a hymn or praise, probably to a Bodhisattva (personal communication with Dr. Peter Zieme).

[36] Examples of Christian manuscripts in codex format have been edited by Müller (1908, 1–15), Le Coq (1909, 1202–1211), and Sims-Williams (1985). A sample of Manichaean book fragments in codex format is seen in Le Coq's text editions of 1909 (1047–1061), 1911 (3–61), 1919 (3–15), and 1922 (3–49).

[37] Drége 1979, 17–28.

[38] For illustrations, see Whitfield and Farrer 1990, Nos. 76–79.

[39] An example of a Nestorian codex-formatted book from Turfan is the hymn book (MIK III 45) exhibited in the Museum für Indische Kunst (1986, No. 405).

[40] Personal communication with Prof. Sims-Williams and Dr. Sundermann.

[41] It has been noted that by the sixteenth century the repudiation of images and the hereditary succession of the bishops made the Nestorian movement distinct from the rest of Christianity (see Coakley 1992, 14). Evidence on Nestorian visual art from mediaeval Central and East Asia was surveyed by Jean Dauvillier, in Pelliot 1973 (157–160). In addition Dauvillier also pointed out that the lack of images, which resulted rather from the poverty of the church and the absence of artists than from theological reasons,

Table 1/5. Book Fragments Identified through Elects in Figural Scenes (4 examples)

Scene w/ Male Elects (3)			Scene w/ Garment of Elect (1)
MIK III 151 3rd layer	MIK III 6257	MIK III 6368	MIK III 4975

Table 1/6. Codex Fragments Identified through Decorative Designs (10 examples)

Plain Background (7)			Blue Background (3)	
		MIK III 6379 b, e–h		
M 810 a	MIK III 4962 b	MIK III 6379 d	M 1156	
MIK III 4956 c, d	MIK III 6261	MIK III 6374	MIK III 4956 a	MIK III 7266

Nestorian temple of Kocho do not exhibit an iconography and composition similar to that seen in illuminated Christian books.[42] Although examples of illuminated codices of Eastern Christianity are seen as early as the sixth century,[43] we still cannot presume that the Turfan Nestorian community also engaged in their production. Illuminated books are luxury items that in any context constitute only a tiny fraction of the literary output of a religious community. Painted decoration is an accessory to religious texts, behind the creation of which social reasons are likely to hide.[44] Their production is preconditioned by cultural values that direct the investment of sponsorship into books. In accordance with this reasoning, the existence of decorated manuscripts in Turfan demands to be explained rather than assumed.

Decorative designs executed along the margins on the remains of codex folia in a West Asian fully painted style of illumination are frequently seen on the larger fragments of the reference group (e.g., MIK III 4976 a, d & S 49 a–b, Figure 5/20; M 857 recto[?], see Plate 4c; and MIK III 4983 recto, see Plate 4/b). Similar marginal decorations are preserved on 10 smaller paper fragments (Table 1/6). Among them seven are painted on blank margins of codex folia (M 810 a; MIK III 4956 c, d; MIK III 4962 b; MIK III 6261; MIK III 6374; MIK III 6379 b, e–h; and MIK III 6379 d), and three are found on an unframed blue background (M 1156; MIK III 4956 a; and MIK III 7266).[45] Due to their double-sided codex formats and fully painted illuminations, these 10 fragments are most likely from Manichaean illuminated codices.

Fully Painted Figural Scenes with Token Motifs on Codex Folia
A Manichaean origin for 9 illuminated fragments can be confirmed in light of frequent motifs within the book paintings of the reference group (Table 1/7). Here too, in addition to the motifs (often numerous identifying motifs within one painting), the West Asian fully painted Turfan Manichaean painting style, together with the dominant codex format of the book fragments, aids their identification. The systematic sideways orientation of figural scenes in Turfan Manichaean illuminated manuscripts provides a further criterion to confirm Manichaean origin.

was publicized through Anglican sources in the West. Nevertheless, in Dauvillier's survey no data were found concerning illuminated books. The only examples of decorated texts are seen on funerary inscriptions (Lo Hsiang-Lin 1966; Hamilton and Nui Ru-Ji 1994). The ornamentation of these inscribed stones and decorated paper sheets seems to reflect structural resemblance to illuminated books of the region.

[42] Le Coq 1913, Taf. 7 a–b.
[43] The second earliest datable Christian illuminated book is the Syriac Gospels made by the monk Rabbula in 589, in Zagba, Syria (see Rodley 1994, 104–111).
[44] Lowden 1986, 263–279.
[45] For color illustrations, see Gulácsi 2001a, Nos. 10, 22–27, 63, and 64.

Table 1/7. Book Fragments Identified by Motifs Common in Reference Group (9 examples)

Decorative Disk Motif (2):	Elect w/ Gold-hemmed Cloak (1):	Layman from MIK III 8259 (1):
MIK III 4947 & III 5 d	MIK III 6626 & III 6379c	MIK III 6284
MIK III 4965 verso (?)		
Pomegranate Plant Motif (0):	Figure w/ Crescent Halo (0):	Elements of Alms Service (1):
(also) MIK III 4965 recto (?)	(also) MIK III 6626 & III 6379c	MIK III 6376
	(also) MIK III 4965 recto (?)	
Pool Motif (1):	Military Figure w/ Halo (1)	Felt Carpet and Blue Background (2):
MIK III 6989 a recto	MIK III 134	(also) MIK III 6376
		MIK III 4943 recto (?)
		MIK III 6378 d verso (?)

Within the reference group decorative disks are seen on 15 fragments.[46] They are affixed to the edges of stylized scarves that surround heading-lines (e.g., M 857, see Plate 4c; and MIK III 4981 a, see Plate 2a). In figural paintings, similar disks occur as an attachment to an architectural element and to an ornate border that frames a composition (e.g., MIK III 4971 a–c recto, Figure 5/17a). The disks are often gilded, and on the surface of their gilding two concentric circles are drawn. Two illuminated manuscript fragments are identified on the basis of this motif. One constitutes a small portion of a painted scroll (MIK III 4947 & III 5d, Figure 5/26 and Plate 7c). The fragmentary section of the original composition retains an image of the historical Buddha (one of the four primary Manichaean prophets), identified with the Sogdian form of the name of the Buddha (*bwt*) written on the chest of the figure.[47] Such identification would not be necessary in a Buddhist context, where the subordination of the Buddha figure to the now-lost main figure of the original scene would be unprecedented. By art historical criteria, while the iconography is in full accordance with local Buddhist iconography of the time, the painting style is identical to the Western Asian fully painted style of Turfan Manichaean art (Figures 4/1c, d and 4/4d).

The second item identified on the basis of the decorative disk motif is a solely pictorial fragment from a codex folio (MIK III 4965 verso, Plate 7b). In addition, on its recto(?), the surviving scene contains a pomegranate plant motif growing out from the remaining right shoulder of a side figure that is only partially preserved along the right edge of the image (Plate 7a).[48] Pomegranate plants are often seen on positively identified fragments, mainly within the decorative designs (e.g., MIK III 4981 b, Figure 3/7; and T.M. 332). A Turfan Manichaean textile painting (MIK III 6278) also features numerous pomegranate plants, and preserves a figure with pomegranate branches growing from its shoulders, just like the side figure on the recto(?).[49]

---

[46] In most of the examples decorative disks appear attached to scarves, as seen on numerous positively identified examples, including decorative designs around the headers such as on M 23, M 596 f, M 817 a, So 18700 & M 501 e, T.M. 332, MIK III 4969, MIK III 4974, MIK III 6258 b, MIK III 6377, MIK III 6377 c, MIK III 6626 & 6379 c, and MIK III 7251. In Manichaean figural compositions, disks are attached to scarves as on MIK III 6414 and 80 BT: 65:01, and to vaulted ceilings as on MIK III 4971.

[47] For a reading by Larry Clark, see BeDuhn 2001, 240. An identical reading of the three letters was also given by Kogi Kudara based on an enlarged, slide-projected image (personal communication).

[48] In figural compositions the same plants are seen as greenery, and possibly as an iconographic motif that surrounds the shoulders and heads of certain figures. The produce of the plant is distinct because of the hardened petals that are found at the tip of the fruit, opposite from its stem.

[49] For a color illustration of MIK III 6278, see Gulácsi 2001a, No. 79.

A motif of a pool of water from where the stems of lotus plants grow is frequent within the figural scenes of the reference group (Figure 4/2g and Plate 7e). Well-preserved examples are seen on four fragments (e.g., MIK III 6265 & III 4966 c recto, Figure 2/3b; and 81 TB 65:01, Figures 5/23 and 6/5a).[50] The pond is depicted systematically in a fixed sequence of concentric semi-circles. The internal part is blue, and is surrounded by a thin red line that separates the interior from the green exterior. It is not the *idea* of a motif (pool with lotus plants) in itself that is relevant here, but rather its precise rendering within its Manichaean context. The fragment identified through its pool motif is from a pictorial scroll (MIK III 6989 a, Figure 5/27).

High-ranking elects may be depicted with elaborate halos and dressed in a cloak with a golden hem; an example from the paintings of the reference group can be seen on the image of the Bema festival (MIK III 4979 verso, Figure 2/5b).[51] The fragment identified through the presence of such a ceremonial white cloak is very damaged but retains the gold hem of the originally white garment (MIK III 6626 & III 6379 c).[52] Crescent-shaped halos are part of the representations of these high-ranking elects. Besides these two fragments, the item—already identified through a decorative disk and a pomegranate motif (MIK III 4965 recto[?], see Plate 7a)—also features a crescent-shaped halo around the head of a Manichaean deity, tentatively identified as the Third Messenger.[53] Another unique element of Manichaean book paintings is the depiction of high-ranking military officials, dressed in full, gilded armor, with halos around their helmeted heads, as seen for example in the Conversion Scene (MIK III 4979 recto, Figure 2/5a and Plate 7f) and the King Scene (MIK III 36, Figure 5/11 and Plate 8c). A military figure with halo around his head is a Manichaean identifying mark in a small codex fragment (MIK III 134).[54]

Four smaller pictorial fragments can be identified as remnants of Manichaean codex folia based on motifs similar to the ones seen on the fully painted book paintings of the reference group. One of them (MIK III 6284, Figure 2/3 c) portrays a figure also seen on MIK III 8259, a securely identified Manichaean book fragment (MIK III 8259 folio 1[?] recto, Figure 2/3a), as suggested by Jorinde Ebert due to its headgear, facial hair, and garment, and its grouping with the rest of Uygur nobility.[55] In addition, to the right of the figure is what appears to be a flower bud motif, similar to those frequently seen on lotus plants pictured in figural compositions (Figures 2/7e and 4/2e). Elements of an alms service scene identify another smaller fragment (MIK III 6376). The figures are shown in Uygur male garments, indicated by the traditional side slit.[56] Furthermore, this image features figures seated on felt carpets painted against a blue background. Felt carpets are incorporated in several of the major book paintings within the reference group (MIK III 4979 verso, Figure 2/5; and MIK III 6368 verso, Figure 5/3b);[57] on this latter basis two smaller fragments can also be identified as Manichaean (MIK III 4943 and MIK III 6378 d).[58]

---

[50] The four examples are MIK III 4972 a, MIK III 4974 recto, MIK III 6265 & 4966 c, and 81 TB 65:01.

[51] For a discussion of the golden hem in the Bema Scene (MIK III 4979 verso), see Gulácsi 2001a, 74–75; for a recent article-length study on the subject, see Ebert 2004.

[52] For an illustration of the matched fragments MIK III 6626 & III 6379 c, see Gulácsi 2001a, No. 46.

[53] Manichaean textual sources related to the image of the Third Messenger are briefly discussed in Gulácsi 2001a, 103–104.

[54] For a color illustration, see Gulácsi 2001a, No. 43.

[55] Ebert 1994, 14.

[56] For a color illustration, see Gulácsi 2001a, No. 39.

[57] For an article-length study on the subject of felt carpets depicted on Manichaean book paintings, see Gulácsi 1997.

[58] For a color illustration, see Gulácsi 2001a, Nos. 58 and 61.

Visual Documentary Evidence on Manichaean Artifacts

Since Manichaeanism is an extinct world religion, its art remains have vanished naturally, owing to the passage of time. However, persecutions of the religion also significantly contributed to their disappearance. Persecutions were a constant presence for most of Manichaean history. They devastated the communities, and culminated in martyrdom and public destruction of works of art—mostly book burnings, as noted in the historical record from the territories of the Roman Empire during the fourth and fifth centuries,[59] as well as from Abbasid Persia during the tenth century.

> In 923 CE / 311 AH, at the public gate of Baghdad, the portrait of Mani, together with four sacks of heretical books were burnt. Gold and silver fell out of them (Ibn al-Jawzi, *al Muntazam fi tarikh al muluk wa-al-umam*, before 1201 CE /592 AH).[60]

Manichaean books together with their decorated leather bindings were noted from both territories. In the heat of a polemic composition dated to 400 CE, Augustine of Hippo cried out: "burn all your parchments with their finely-ornamented bindings,"[61]—implying that, together with the parchment folia, the covers were made of a combustible material, most likely leather. Ornate book covers specifically made of leather also were known from Abbasid Persia where the historian, Miskawayh Ahmed Ibn Muhammad, active during the early eleventh century, mentioned the following:

> The supporters of the schismatic al-Hallaj (executed in 921 CE / 310 AH) also imitated the Manichaeans in this respect. Their books were written in gold on Chinese paper, were enhanced in silk and brocade, and were bound in costly leather (*Tajarib al-uman*, before 1030 CE/ 421 AH).[62]

Of all the things such passages tell us about Manichaean books, the comments on the exterior covers of the book have the greatest value for the present purpose because they can be correlated to visual documentary evidence for this part of the book in surviving Manichaean depictions.

Visual documentary evidence supplied by Manichaean paintings provides further data on decorated Manichaean book covers specific to Turfan. A number of Turfan Manichaean paintings portray the use of codices in ritual settings. Elects hold codex-formatted books in Sermon Scenes (MIK III 8259 folio 1[?] recto, Figure 2/3a) and during the celebration of the Bema Festival (MIK III 4979 verso, Figure 2/5 and Plate 6b), just as the portraits of elects and deities on Manichaean textile paintings contain books held in the figures' hands (e.g., MIK III 6286 side 1[?] details 1 and 2, Figure 1/2).[63] As in early Christian book illuminations (see Figures 4/3a and 4/5a), the books shown with the Manichaean figures are in codex format and have decorated covers. The Turfan Manichaean paintings, especially the book paintings, often are detailed enough to make out the types of decorations on the codex covers. Some of them seem to represent a gilded pictorial scene (Plate 6b), whereas others have geometric decorations such as centrally positioned scalloped circles (Figure 1/2b).

Although no intact books with decorated covers have survived from Turfan, three fragments can be recognized as remnants of book covers on the basis of their material, size, and decoration, as well as their

---

[59] For the description of Diocletian's orders (297 CE or 302 CE) to burn the Manichaean leader and their books, see Lieu 1992, 122.

[60] Ibn al-Jawzi, *al Muntazam fi tarikh al muluk wa-al-umam* (Bayrut 1992, Vol. 13, 200); Mez, *Die Renaissance des Islams* (Heidelberg, 1922, 167). The English translation is after Mez 1937, 175.

[61] *Contra Faustum Manichaeum* XIII/18. The translation is from Schaff 1956, 206.

[62] Miskawayh Ahmed Ibn Muhammad, *Tajarub al-uman wa ta'aqib al himam* (edited by H. F. Amedroz and B. Atlow, Baghdad, n. d., Vol. I, 79); the English translation is from Mez 1937, 175.

[63] All together, seven scenes on painted manuscript and textile surfaces portray codices, see Gulácsi 1997, 199.

a: MIK III 6286 side 1(?) detail, main section with   b: MIK III 6286 side 1(?) detail, upper section with
female elect   unidentified figure

Figure 1/2. Books in Turfan Manichaean Paintings
(SMPK, Museum für Indische Kunst, Berlin)

provenance. Regarding material, they are leather. In terms of size, their proportions and measurements are comparable to other Manichaean books from Turfan.[64] The best preserved item can be reconstructed (MIK III 6268, Figures 3/12 and 3/14a). Its technique of decoration is comparable to the early Coptic bindings of Egypt, which also apply filigree cuts in the leather against a gold background.[65] On the basis of such filigree cuts, the second leather fragment also has been interpreted as a book cover by previous scholarship (MIK III 6267, Figure 3/14b).[66] Further, they are both from a locale known to yield such manuscripts. The third leather fragment is considered to be a remnant of a binding on the basis of its material, as well as its gilding and the heavy layers of pigments that are indicative of a figural decoration, most of which has vanished from the leather surface (MIK III 7068, Figure 3/14 c).

Thus, on the basis of visual documentary evidence provided by Turfan Manichaean paintings, it is reasonable to think that actual remains of ornate codex covers, which not only are made of leather and adorned with precise gilded decorations but also derive from a site known to yield Manichaean codex fragments, most likely are to be considered Manichaean (Table 1/8). In this case, the provenance of these covers does play an important role in their identification. The fact that only Buddhist and Manichaean text fragments were found at the same locale as the book covers excludes the possibility of them being inter-

---

[64] Le Coq 1923, 39–40 and Taf. 4/d–e; Henning 1937.
[65] Le Coq 1923, 40; Aslanapa 1980, 60.
[66] These pieces, MIK III 6268 and MIK III 6270, were first published as book covers in Le Coq 1913, 8.

Table 1/8. Berlin Fragments Identified through Documentary Evidence (3 examples)

Leather Book Covers with Decorative Designs (2)		Leather Book Covers with Figural Scenes (1)
MIK III 6267	MIK III 6268	MIK III 7068

preted as Nestorian.[67] In short, visual documentary evidence supported by the provenance of the finds justifies the Manichaean identification of these three items.

Reorganization of Items

The process of assembling the Manichaean corpus required several alterations in the previous arrangement of the material, resulting in a regrouping of fragments involving the items in the two Berlin collections and the one in St. Petersburg.[68] In these institutions, the Manichaean manuscript fragments are stored between two thin layers of glass (in a few cases between glass and cardboard) that have been taped securely together.[69] Many frames contain more than one item, some of which do not necessarily belong together. No record remains concerning the rationale for why certain pieces have been displayed together. In some cases, fragments may have been found together and thus grouped according to their provenance. In other cases, they appear to have been organized according to similarities in their appearance. Nevertheless, the mere fact that they are framed together does not constitute a claim for the Manichaean origin of all the fragments so grouped. Although the logic of framing is unrecorded, one should not assume a lack of it. Since the framing itself could hold information, a documentation of conditions before the alterations is essential.

The new grouping of the fragments involves separation, matching, and omission (Table 1/9). Most of the objects regrouped have been separated from one another; that is, the contents of certain frames have been determined to be unrelated. Separation is crucial in the case of book fragments, because keeping pieces together when no evidence suggests their connection would have created a misleading impression of a page arrangement unconfirmed by other remains. Several fragments have been matched; that is, they are grouped together to form combined entries in cases where evidence suggests that they are from the same manuscript and/or they physically fit together.[70] Yet others have been omitted; that is, they have been excluded from the survey of the Manichaean corpus because they do not fit the criteria of Manichaean origin, and any prior treatment as Manichaean has been by association rather than by independent argument for the item's affiliation with the tradition.[71]

Fragments of Unconfirmed Manichaean Origin

After the above process we are left with 11 illuminated fragments previously treated as Manichaean whose Manichaean identity cannot be confirmed (see Table 1/1; items marked "unconfirmed"). The category of items with unconfirmed Manichaean origin includes illuminations that have been proposed to be Manichaean

---

[67] This is only true for MIK III 6267 and MIK III 6268, since the provenance of MIK III 7048 remains unconfirmed (see Table 1/2).

[68] For a visual documentation of the alterations, see Gulácsi 2001a, Appendix III.

[69] This arrangement had been true for the textile fragments of the MIK as well until the spring of 1996, when the latter were moved into textile-trays and began to be stored horizontally. Nevertheless, for the sake of convenience I refer to the items that are kept in one group (in most cases literally in one glass-frame) as *frames*.

[70] All matches are those of the author except when otherwise noted.

[71] For detailed discussion and illustration of the alterations, see Gulácsi 2001a, Appendix III.

a: Or. 12452/3 recto

b: Or. 12452/3 verso

Figure 1/3. Fragment of Parchment Folio with Intratextual Figural Scene
(British Library, London)

Table 1/9. Regrouping of Fragments Attributed to the Manichaean Corpus (20 examples)

Fragments	*New Grouping*	*Fragments*	*New Grouping*
M 501 e, f	So 18700 & M 501e (Manichaean) M 501 f (omitted)	MIK III 4976 a, b	MIK III 4976 a, b & S 49 a, b (Manichaean)
M 660 a, b	M 660 a (unconfirmed) M 660 b (unconfirmed)	MIK III 4981 a–f	MIK III 4981 b, e (Manichaean) MIK III 4981 f, c (Manichaean)
M 1886/7	M 1886 (unconfirmed) M 1887 (Manichaean)	MIK III 6258 a, b	MIK III 6258 a (Manichaean) MIK III 6258 b (Manichaean)
So 18700	So 18700 & M 501e (Manichaean)	MIK III 6265	MIK III 6265 & III 4966 c (Manichaean)
MIK III 5 a–d	MIK III 5 a–c, e (omitted) MIK 4947 & III 5 e (Manichaean)	MIK III 6377 a–g	MIK III 6377 a, b, d, g & III 6379 a (Manichaean) MIK III 6377 c (Manichaean) MIK III 6377 e, f (unconfirmed)
MIK III 4947	MIK 4947 & III 5 e (Manichaean)	MIK III 6378 a–d	MIK III 6378 a–c (omitted) MIK III 6378 d (Manichaean)
MIK III 4956 a–d	MIK III 4956 a (Manichaean) MIK III 4956 b (Manichaean) MIK III 4956 c–d (Manichaean)	MIK III 6379 a–h	MIK III 6377 a, b, d, g & III 6379 a (Manichaean) MIK III 6379 b, d, f–h (Manichaean) MIK III 6679 & III 6379 c (Manichaean) MIK III 6379 e (Manichaean)
MIK III 4958 a, b	MIK III 4958 (Manichaean)		
MIK III 4962 a–c	MIK III 4962 a, c (Manichaean) MIK III 4962 b (Manichaean MIK III 4966 a (Manichaean)	MIK III 6626	MIK III 6626 & III 6379 c (Manichaean)
		MIK III 6989 a–d	MIK III 6989 a (Manichaean) MIK III 6989 b–d (Manichaean)
MIK III 4966 a–c	MIK III 4966 b (unconfirmed) MIK III 6265 & III 4966 c (Manichaean) MIK III 4981 a, d (Manichaean)	S 49 a, b	MIK III 4976 a, b & S 49 a, b (Manichaean)

by previous scholars but whose characteristics did not meet my own criteria for confirmation. These 11 manuscript fragments are not accompanied by a Manichaean literary context and cannot be correlated with the most striking Manichaean characteristics of art; neither can documentary evidence confirm their Manichaeanness. Despite the fact that their Manichaean origin is unconfirmed by current secure criteria, the possibility still remains that any number of these items may be linked in the future to Turfan Manichaean art production on the basis of criteria different from the ones employed in this study.

CONCLUSION

The process of identifying the corpus of Manichaean illuminated book fragments among the Turfan remains started with a definition that centers on the importance of religious context. In light of this, a core group (reference group) was selected from the remains of Turfan Manichaean manuscripts (identified by their Manichaean script and Manichaean textual content) that contain decorative designs and/or figural com-

a: No 11074 recto(?)

b: No 11074 verso(?)

Figure 1/4. Fragment of Codex Folio with Illuminated Header
(Ryukoku University, Kyoto)

positions (63 examples). In the next step, specific characteristics of these items were verified that together function as a set of exclusively Manichaean markers of Turfan art, including the distinctive white garment of the elects (4 examples) and codex folia (10 examples) that contain fully painted decorative designs and figural compositions with specific motifs (9 examples). Finally, visual documentary evidence was considered together with archaeological context (3 examples).

For the first time in the history of Manichaean studies, therefore, a securely identified artistic manuscript corpus can be verified from among the Turfan remains. It contains 89 items housed in six collections in five countries, with the vast majority of them in Berlin. The group of remains identified through this process form the primary source of evidence for this study of Manichaean book art and also for any further research on book-related pictorial art and book art of Mediaeval East Central Asia.

The Two Berlin Collections (80 Illustrated Book Fragments)

The Museum of Indian Art (State Museums of Berlin) houses 57 Manichaean illuminated book fragments (Table 1/10) of paper, leather, and silk. The paper fragments include three book formats: codex, scroll, and pustaka. Fifty-two items are in a codex format. There are four single-sided scroll fragments accompanied by figural paintings, and there is one illuminated pustaka fragment accompanied by a Manichaean text. The six leather fragments are all book covers and there are four fragments of silk codices.

The Turfan Collection of the Berlin-Brandenburg Academy has 23 Manichaean illuminated book fragments (Table 1/11). They are all paper fragments of codex-formatted books. Twenty-one are remnants of folia and two are bifolia. Detailed descriptions of these items, together with their color facsimiles, are found in the art catalogue (*Manichaean Art in Berlin Collections*) prepared for the Art Series of the Corpus Fontium Manichaeorum.[72]

Other Collections (9 Illuminated Book Fragments)

Four additional Turfan collections in London, St. Petersburg, Turfan, and Kyoto contain a total of nine Manichaean illuminated book fragments (Table 1/12). These were acquired by Silk Road expeditions and local purchases at Turfan during the early part of the twentieth century. Only one item is from the more recent Chinese archaeology conducted during the 1980s.

The Oriental Collection of the British Library in London contains three Manichaean illuminated book fragments (Table 1/12). One is a reconstructible codex folio fragment (Or. 8218-1692, old number Kao. 0107, Figure 5/10) whose paper surface displays remnants of a Manichaean content text (recto) in Runic script and a full-page book painting (verso). The second fragment is from a parchment codex folio (Or. 12452/3, Figures 2/3 and 5/15) containing remnants of an intratextual book painting (recto) and a Manichaean script text (verso). The third Manichaean manuscript relevant for this study in London is a well-preserved paper scroll that contains a Manichaean script confession text written in Uygur Turkic, supplemented with a graffito (Ch. 0015, Figure 5/22). All three items were obtained by the expeditions led by Sir Aurel Stein. The two illuminated codex folio fragments were purchased at Kocho,[73] but the graffito-decorated scroll was discovered among the manuscripts of the sealed vault of Cave 17 at Dunhuang.[74]

Four additional fragments of illuminated codex folia (S 30, S 42, S 49 a–b, and S 50) belong to the collection of the Institute of Oriental Studies of the Russian Academy in St. Petersburg (Table 1/12). About 90 percent of the manuscripts housed in this collection were obtained by the Russian consuls to East Turkistan, who purchased and shipped these finds home during the last two decades of the nineteenth century. Addi-

---

[72] Gulácsi 2001a.
[73] Stein 1924, 590.
[74] Stein 1912, 171–181; 1921, II, 922, 925.

ichaean art production in the region in light of circumstantial evidence supplied by the historical records. The Karabalgasun Inscription, an Uygur stone monument with a trilingual commemorative text in Uygur, Sogdian, and Chinese on the deeds of the Uygur kings erected in the capital city of Karabalgasun (Mong. Ordubalik), mentions that Bügü Khagan rescued four elects from the turmoil of Louyang, taking them back with him to the Uygur realm, and that soon after more elects were sent: "brothers and sisters to enter the kingdom in order to spread and exalt [the religion] there."[11] The Persian historian Gardīzī, who was best informed about the mid eighth century,[12] wrote that "it was customary in the Uygur kingdom for three or four hundred Manichaean priests to gather in the house of the prince to recite the Books of Mani and at the end of the day they would evoke blessing on the ruler before they departed."[13] The Arabic traveler Tamim ibn Bahr, who visited Karabalgasun in the 820s, noted that the Manichaeans (elects) were living outside the capital although their religion was dominant within.[14] By this time, the Uygurs were close to establishing complete military control over the Tarim Basin, some of which was still under and Tibetan Chinese rule.

The Middle Persian hymnbook, the *Mahrnamag* (MIK III 203 [old number M 1], see Figure 3/6a), completed between 808 and 821 CE, documents the ties of the Manichaean church in the Tarim region with the Uygurs of the steppe. The surviving bifolio that preserves four pages of text from this book contains a benediction on the male and female members of the Uygur court, including the ruler Ay Tegrite Kut Bolmish Alp Bilge Uygur Khan; and a colophon states that the writing of this book had already begun in 762 at the Manichaean monastery in Karashashr (Tokharian Agni; Chinese Yanqi):

> [It was] in the year 546 after the birth of the Apostle of Light, [that is] now in the year ... when He [Mani] was raised up in might, and in the year 162 after the raising [i.e., death] of Shad Ohrmizd that this hymnbook, full of living words and beautiful hymns, was begun. The scribe, who had started to write it at the command of the spiritual leaders, was unable to finish it. As he could not devote himself to it, and because he had no time, he wrote [only] a little, [just] a few hymns, and did not complete it. It remained in its incomplete form at this place for many years. It lay around and was deposited in the monastery of Agni [i.e., Karashahr].[15]

The superb artisanship displayed on this fragment, including the black and red blocks of text forming a checkered pattern with the listing of the members of the Uygur court, documents high-quality book production directly associated with the Uygur context.[16]

After the mid ninth century Manichaean art production must have increased in the Turfan area following the foundation of the Tien-shan Uygur kingdom. By 808, the Tien-shan region became controlled and after 841 became inhabited by the Uygurs.[17] With the breakup of the Uygur Steppe Empire, the core imperial Arslan clan with 15 tribes settled in the central Tien-shan, eventually occupying Kocho and Beshbalik by 866.[18] Kocho became established as their winter capital and Beshbalik as the summer one. Although the mid ninth century marked a new demographic and political situation, which transformed the Turfan area, without specific historical records we can only hypothesize about how this era would be reflected in the artistic remains. Such new political conditions most certainly contributed to an increased local produc-

---

[11] Clark 2000, 88.

[12] Czeglédy 1973, 267.

[13] Martinez 1982, 136 (also quoted in Lieu 1992, 240).

[14] Minorsky 1948, 283, 296, 302–303.

[15] This translation of the colophon of the *Mahrnamag* is from Klimkeit (1993, 274).

[16] In light of codicological similarities to illuminated book fragments with similar content (such as MIK III 36 and MIK III 4979) it is possible that the page next to the surviving lists of courtly names and titles might have been illuminated. This idea has been raised already by Müller (1912, 6) and also by Klimkeit (1993, 274 and note 31).

[17] Klyashtorny 1988, 280. For a recent and most thorough discussion of this episode of Uygur history, see Moriyasu 2000.

[18] Czeglédy 1984, 163; Beckwith 1987, 170.

tion of Manichaean art and architecture. From the mid ninth until the late tenth to early eleventh centuries this city was the most important Manichaean center in the world, a cosmopolitan city that offered
much more than safe haven from Abbasid and Tang persecutions.[19]

From the late tenth century, signs of decline begin to surface in the historical records. A variety of primary and secondary data indicates that a strengthening interest in Buddhism started to weaken the Manichaean ties of the Uygur elite around this time.[20] The Uygur-language memoir of a Manichaean priest
named Käd Ogul, referring to events that, according to Takao Moriyasu took place in 983 CE,[21] laments
the tearing down and looting of at least two *manistans* (Manichaean monasteries) in order to build a *vihara*
(Buddhist monastery). Nevertheless, Käd Ogul's memoir itself confirms that a Manichaean community was
still active in Kocho.

> In the time of the Teacher, Astud Farzint, he [Tärkän Tegin] tore down the manistan and built a vihara.
> He also pulled down and took the structural pieces of the *qwndwv kyrw c'ky* manistan which were between and
> within(?). He brought them to erect the vihara. He took the top [?ceiling] *lwqtw*-image(?) decorations and mold-
> ings within the great chamber of this sacred great manistan, and used them to build the vihara. My Lord, (I)
> ... Käd Ogul, unable to suffer any longer, and thinking I should write about the moldings of the manistan, and
> so that later juniors (of the Elect) shall understand (what happened), I have ventured to write briefly (about it)
> in this memorial.[22]

Wang Yen-tö, the Chinese envoy who visited the Uygur court in 981 and 984 CE, also supplied data on
the contemporaneous existence of Manichaean temples in Kocho.[23] Käd Ogul's account, however, is
corroborated through an event of Buddhist appropriation surmised in light of textual and archaeological
evidence. An inscribed foundation stake recovered from the Buddhist temple referred to as Ruin Alpha
in Kocho is dated to 1008 CE, confirming that the site began to be used for Buddhist purposes from that
date. The wooden stake is 83 cm long, carved in the shape of an octagonal cone and inscribed in Uygur
to commemorate the foundation of a Buddhist temple.[24] Understandably, the stake's inscription does not
mention previous Manichaean use of the site, but before housing a Buddhist temple, Ruin Alpha was most
certainly a Manichaean building, as indicated especially by the fragment of a Manichaean wall painting
(MIK III 4624) recovered from there, along with numerous Manichaean text fragments.[25] Further examples
of Buddhist use of previously Manichaean sites are documented by some of the unfortunately undated caves
at Bezeklik. As documented by a recent field study by Takao Moriyasu, Cave 25 contains a Manichaean
wall painting and inscriptions that are now visible from behind a layer of mud-brick wall that was built to
conceal and reshape the earlier Manichaean layer of the cave in order to introduce a subsequent Buddhist

---

[19] The Abbasid persecution already had started in the late eighth century under the rule of al-Mahdi (775–785 CE). See Morony
1984, 408; Lieu 1992, 113–115. The Tang persecution of the Manichaean communities in China started in 843, after the collapse
of the Uygur Steppe Empire in 840 CE. See Lieu 1992, 237–238.

[20] Moriyasu devoted an article-length study to the subject as part of a four-lecture series at the *Collage de France* (2003). Clark
also addressed the political reasons behind the Uygurs' strengthening interest in Buddhism in two unpublished conference papers
in 1994 and 1995.

[21] Moriyasu dated the text on the basis of correlation between references in the text to a Chinese calendar year (ranging between
863, 923, 983, and 1043) and a dated Uygur ruler that he correlated with dates in other sources, considering both 983 and 1043
as possibilities (2004, 178–181).

[22] The translation of the text is from Clark (2005, lines 14–21).

[23] Chavannes-Pelliot 1913, 308.

[24] Moriyasu dated the text on the basis of correlation between references in the text (2001, 154).

[25] Le Coq 1923, 28–31, 36. The text was first translated by W. Radloff (published in Grünwedel 1906), later by Müller in 1915,
and most recently by Moriyasu in 2001 (149–153 and 154–183). 1008 CE as the date of dedication was argued by Hamilton (1992,
xvii), and also Moriyasu (2001, 152), on the basis of correspondence with the Chinese calendar. For a color reproduction of the
wall painting MIK III 4624, see Yaldiz 1987, Fig. 78; or Gulácsi 2001, No. 92.

interior. Moriyasu's study produces accurate dates that the later Buddhist interior was made significantly smaller by the introduction of a mud-brick layer of ceiling vaults and freestanding walls that refashioned and sealed off the previous architectural design, pictorial decoration, and inscriptions associated with the Manichaean use of Cave 25.[26] The Manichaean church, however, still maintained an affiliation with members of the Uygur ruling elite during the early eleventh century, as confirmed by dated primary sources, namely, benedictions and paintings in dated Manichaean books that still refer to and depict members of the Uygur court at this time.[27]

After the early eleventh century, Manichaean datable historical records cease to exist in East Central Asia, and few are the signs that allude to what must have happened to the church and its people. One circumstantial piece of evidence is seen in the scribal artisanship of the Uygur-sponsored Buddhist texts that began to be produced in the early eleventh century. Calligraphy, punctuation decoration, page layout, and even some pictorial qualities indicate that Manichaean scribes and book painters were involved in copying and perhaps occasionally illustrating Buddhist texts.[28] Archaeological data seem to indicate some form of integration. The fact that Manichaean texts were recovered together with Buddhist ones in Kocho, just as in the surrounding sites such as the Stupa at Bezeklik, may suggest that some elects with their holy texts could have been hosted in the Buddhist community and lived their lives affiliated with Buddhist centers. Since there is no evidence for persecution at that time in that area, the demise of Manichaean activities in the Turfan region most likely took place due to a gradual disintegration. Some elects from this region might have resettled in southern China, where a vital Manichaean community was developing in and around Fukien Province by the tenth century.[29]

Since the post early eleventh century phase of gradual disappearance remains undocumented, the circa approximately 270-year epoch of recorded royal patronage, stretching between the mid eighth and early eleventh centuries, is seen today as the historical context of Uygur Manichaeism in the Turfan region. Although it is not impossible that remains of Manichaean art discovered in Turfan may date from before or after this 270-year period, in light of the current state of research it is most likely that the luxurious remains of Turfan Manichaean art were made during this era due to the sponsorship of the Uygur elite. Manichaean activities of the Uygur elite from this time are documented in textual and pictorial primary sources: colophons of religious texts record their involvement in the copying of books,[30] paintings in books and on walls depict their participations in rituals,[31] and benedictory hymns in liturgical texts bless them for their support.[32]

Dating Based on Artistic Evidence

Initial attempts to put forward more precise dates for the remains of Uygur Manichaean art have been based on stylistic and iconographic characteristics, and a hypothetical chronology. It has been noted since

---

[26] Moriyasu 2005, 6–7.

[27] Zieme 1992b, 324; Moriyasu 1980, 334–338; Hamilton 1986, xvii–xviii, note 30.

[28] Moriyasu 1990, 156–158. A Manichaean-style book illumination depicts a Buddhist theme within a Middle Persian language Sogdian script Buddhist text on MIK III 10, an illuminated paper fragment from Kocho. For an illustration and discussion, see Hartel-Yaldiz 1982, 181–182.

[29] Manichaeism became extinct in North China by the tenth century CE. It flourished in southern China, however, expanding from its base in Fukien Province. See Lieu 1992, 267.

[30] For example the colophon of the pustaka book, where a khatun is named as the commissioner (Clark 1982, 159–160).

[31] The carbon-dated book painting on the recto of folio 1(?) of MIK III 8259 depicts high-ranking lay people in Uygur garments wearing court headgear; see Gulácsi 2001, 61. For more details see Gabain 1973, 116, 124, 136. For the wall painting with a damaged section showing Uygur laity, see Gulácsi 2001, 201 or Le Coq 1913, Taf. 1.

[32] Such a reference is found in the benediction of the carbon-dated bifolio MIK III 8259 (Text 2 on folio 1[?] recto), see BeDuhn 2001, 222.

early in Manichaean studies that two distinct stylistic trends are preserved in Turfan Manichaean art: a West Asian (previously "Persian") style, characterized by its similarity to Persian book paintings seen in Islamic illuminated books; and a Chinese style recognizable through similarities to Chinese textile and wall paintings. In addition, certain iconographic motifs had been thought to indicate the age of some Manichaean paintings. Some fragments retain West Asian motifs such as the "flying victories," holding a golden crown above the head of a figure (e.g., MIK 4965, Plate 7a and b), that are frequent in late antique Roman and Parthian art, and are found in mediaeval Persian royal imagery; and female heads, which are used as iconographic symbols in a decorative arrangement within the halo of the figure (e.g. MIK III 6268, Fig. 1/2), also well documented as decorative motifs in Parthian and early Islamic royal architecture. In addition, some Manichaean fragments are distinguished through their use of Buddhist-like motifs, namely open lotus flowers as sitting areas of figures (e.g. MIK III 4959, Fig. 5/1), and a hand gesture that resembles the *vitarka mudra* (e.g. MIK III 4947 & III 5d, Plate 7c) often seen in Buddhist art. According to the stylistic principle of dating, among the "Persian"-looking Manichaean paintings, the ones with Buddhist-like motifs were thought to date from a later period than the ones with West Asian motifs.

The West Asian-looking examples were thought to derive from a prior episode within the history of Manichaean Turfan than the Chinese-looking ones. The idea that an earlier "Persian" and a later Chinese style dominated this art was introduced by Albert von Le Coq in 1923.[33] He modeled his theory on Central Asian Buddhist analogies, according to which an Indo-Persian stylistic era gave way to a Chinese stylistic episode in the Buddhist art of East Central Asia. Without a detailed argument, but in full accordance with the chronology of styles for the Buddhist remains in East Central Asia, Le Coq dated the West Asian-looking Manichaean pieces to the eighth–ninth centuries and the Chinese-looking works to the tenth–eleventh centuries. Although Louis Hambis, in his 1964 entry on Manichaean art in *The Encyclopedia of World Art*, pointed out the lack of proper criteria in dating the Manichaean remains, these hypothetical principles of chronology remained unscrutinized and were employed for dating throughout the twentieth century.[34]

Following up on Hambis's point, I examined the available artistic data relevant for the problem of dating Turfan Manichaean art and published the results in 2003. First, it became clear that West Asian and Chinese artistic trends are indeed readily distinguishable in this art in terms of their basic character and application. The two schools differ sharply from one another in materials and techniques, motif repertoire, composition, and context of use.[35] The artists belonging to the West Asian tradition concerned themselves mainly with book illumination (98 fragmentary paintings document their work), and the Chinese-trained artists worked mostly with textiles and wall surfaces (16 such pictorial fragments are known).[36] In light of this fact, Le Coq's chronology would mean that an era of book illumination was replaced by an era of textile and wall paintings. Currently, no evidence is known that would indicate such a shift in media preference. Instead, the correspondence between media and styles suggests simultaneous employment of artists with divergent training. The artists who worked with the traditional medium of Manichaean art (book illumination) had a different artistic background than those who painted the wall and textile decorations of the manistans. Second, the analysis of iconography also weakened the assumed chronology by demonstrating that the use of West Asian and Buddhist symbols does not correlate with the two painting styles. Buddhist-looking elements are seen frequently in West Asian style images, and Chinese style paintings often con-

---

[33] Le Coq 1923, 18–20.
[34] Hambis 1964, 442–443. For a more detailed discussion, see Gulácsi 2003, 6–7.
[35] See Chapter 4.
[36] Basic trends in the West Asian style of Uygur Manichaean art are well documented, starting from around the thirteenth century, in Eastern Christian (Syriac) as well as Islamic (Persian and Mesopotamian Arabic) book paintings. The style used by the Chinese-trained painter was present in China during the Tang and Northern Song dynasties, that is during the seventh–twelfth centuries (Gulácsi 2003, 18–19, 22–24, 26–29).

tain West Asian symbols.[37] If a break had occurred in the artistic orientation of Manichaean Turfan, one would expect to find a greater correlation of style and iconography between the arts of the old and new eras. Third, inclusion of contextual data presents additional doubt. It is important to note that the Uygurs' great interest in Chinese art and architecture was already documented in Chinese historical sources during the era of their Steppe Empire (744–841 CE).[38] Since the Uygurs' cultural ties with China were earlier and stronger than those with West Asia–Mesopotamia, it is plausible though not necessarily true that the beginning of Uygur sponsorship saw the employment of Chinese-trained artists for Manichaean commissions. Finally, the idea of stylistic dating is further upset by the scientific date on an illuminated codex folio (see below)—this book fragment and others by the same illuminator were painted in the West Asian style during what was supposed to be the Chinese era.

The idea behind the assumed chronology of Manichaean styles in Turfan was based on true trends within Manichaean macro history. The religion, after all, did originate in Mesopotamia, from where it later spread to China. Therefore, it was logical to expect corresponding layers in the art production within the microclimate of Manichaean Turfan. Theories, however, must be tested against analytical data, which in this case must take into consideration the issue of Uygur-Chinese ties. Undoubtedly, West Asian painting style and iconography have older presences in the (lost) overall history of Manichaean art than Buddhist-looking motifs and Chinese painting styles. But the issue of an *older history of a tradition* ought to be kept separate from the *actual dates of production*. Dates in art history connote the time when works of art were made and not the roots of artistic language employed by the artists. Although observations on Manichaean style and iconography may be informative regarding artistic affiliation, without well-matched and securely dated comparative examples, such data cannot be used to mechanically date actual works of art. It is quite likely that through Uygur connections, Chinese-trained artists were employed in Manichaean Turfan, while at the same time the West Asian trends, especially in book art, remained the preference of another group of artists. The above considerations therefore confirm that in the current state of research we are in no position to be able to narrow the dates of Turfan Manichaean art in light of solely art historical data.[39]

MEDIUM HORIZON (126 YEARS)

Scientific evidence permits a more secure approach for dating specific examples of Turfan Manichaean art. Radiocarbon dating, also known as C-14, is widely used to establish the age of archaeological specimens that are between 500 and 50,000 years old. The process is based on the fact that C-14 molecules are absorbed from air by plants and are passed on to animals through the food chain, and therefore into all living organisms. When an organism dies it ceases to absorb C-14, and the amount in its tissue then decreases at a constant rate, which allows scientists to estimate the date when the tissue died.[40] The radiocarbon dating of a Manichaean illuminated codex fragment, whose results were first published in 2003, confirms with 95.4 percent probability that the organic component of its paper was harvested sometime between 889 and 1015 CE (Figure 2/1). Assuming that the writing and painting took place relatively soon after the paper's production, the book was most likely made sometime within (or shortly after) this 126-year period.

---

[37] Such West Asian symbols include a dignitary seating on a throne with his knees spread (MIK III 6286 side 1[?], Fig. 1/2b), portraits of elects with books held at their chest (e.g., MIK III 6283 side 1[?], Fig. 1/2a), and an Iranian incense-burner flanked by kneeling elects (MIK III 8260 recto, Fig. 5/28).

[38] Mackerras 1968, especially pages 12, 18, 25, 29, 37, and 47–50.

[39] For more discussion of styles and dates, see Chapter 4.

[40] *Encyclopedia Britannica* 1987; Bowman 1990.

Radiocarbon Age BP 1090 ± 60
Calibrated age(s) cal AD 978
    one σ   cal AD 897 - 908 959 - 998
    two σ   cal AD 889 - 1015

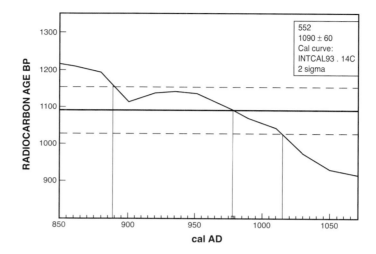

Figure 2/1. Radiocarbon Analysis of MIK III 8259
(Leibniz Labor für Alterbestimmung und Isotopenforschung,
Christian-Albrechts-Universität, Kiel, Germany)

The carbon-dated piece (MIK III 8259, Figures 2/2 and 5/7) is the largest Manichaean illuminated codex fragment currently known, containing both art and text comparable to other pieces of the Manichaean artistic corpus. This torn paper piece is the lower half of a bifolio that once was part of an anthology of religious literature, retaining sections of four Manichaean script texts in the Parthian and Middle Persian languages. The texts include a Parthian parable and a Middle Persian benediction on the religious and secular leaders of the Turfan region on folio 1(?), and a Middle Persian hymn to God (the "Father of Greatness") and a Middle Persian treatise on the origin of the world on folio 2(?).[41] Only folio 1(?) is illuminated. The recto contains a marginal floral decoration and also an intracolumnar painting that depicts a Sermon Scene (Figure 2/3a) on a blue background, oriented sideways. In the lower half of this scene, members of the Uygur royal family (identified by their headgear) are depicted listening to a sermon. In the upper half, two elects seated on lotus supports perform the sermon. Between them is an altar-like cloth-covered table. Bits from a figural scene are preserved along the outer margin. The verso incorporates floral and scarf motifs around one of the names within the benediction. This bifolio's illuminations, especially the well-preserved Sermon Scene (Figure 2/3a), document that the work was by a specific painter, trained in the West Asian tradition, and at the same time link the use of this painter's style to the 126-year era of the carbon date. Since the work of this painter can be recognized on two additional remains, this fragment allows us to consider a significantly narrower period than the years of the historical context for the production of four remains of Turfan Manichaean book art.

The characteristic hand marks of the carbon-dated book painter can be seen in the illuminations of two additional Manichaean book fragments. One is found on two small, recently matched fragments (MIK

---

[41] For the transliteration and translation see BeDuhn 2001, 221–224.

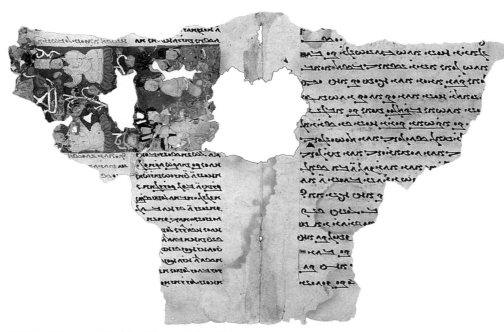

a: MIK III 8259 outer side: folio 1(?) recto, folio 2(?) verso

b: MIK III 8259 inner side: folio 2(?) recto , folio 1(?) verso

Figure 2/2. Carbon-dated Codex Fragment
(SMPK, Museum für Indische Kunst, Berlin)

III 6265 & III 4966 c, Figure 2/3b) that constitute the middle area of the outer margin of a codex folio, retaining on both sides a part from the marginal illumination and bits from the adjacent lines of the text area.[42] The second paper piece with work by the carbon-dated painter is an even smaller fragment (MIK III 6284, Figure 2/3c) that once belonged to the central area of a codex folio.[43]

The close resemblance between these three paintings becomes more obvious when their corresponding sections are viewed side by side (Figure 2/4). The identical facial features (Figure 2/4a) include a gently curving thin black line used for the eyebrows, a more bent and thicker red line for the eyelids, an almost direct angle at the tip of the nose, and an individual short line for the nostril bending backwards in a low angle. The gesture of the sermon-giving elect's left hand (Figure 2/4b) is captured through a teardrop-shaped opening enclosed between the tip of the thumb and the index finger. The second and the third fingers are curled in an even succession, whereas the little finger remains somewhat isolated as it bends and protrudes to the side. Regarding the tablecloth (Figure 2/4c), the diamond shape that resembles the opening of a "box pleat" is drawn with rounded corners on its left and right, and pointed corners at its top and bottom. Another set of connections is seen in the details of the lotus buds (Figure 2/4d). Inside each swollen bud, petals are indicated by an S-shaped oval of a darker color. Finally, the bearded man (Figure 2/4e), who seems to be a particular layman depicted in both scenes, is shown with identical facial characteristics, neckline, and garment.

One other illuminated fragment (MIK III 4979, Figures 2/5 and 5/9, Plate 5), while clearly the work of a different painter, displays a close stylistic connection with the works of the carbon-dated painter. This paper piece constitutes a large section from a codex folio. The recto holds parts of an illuminated header, sections from a text in two columns, and an intracolumnar book painting with the Conversion Scene (Figure 2/5a and Plate 7f). The verso is occupied by a full-page book painting of the Bema Festival (Figure 2/5b). One point of connection regards the naming of a historical figure within the painting of the two fragments. In both cases, a Manichaean script inscription written vertically along the body identifies a high-ranking churchman as Ram-Frazend (Figure 2/6). He is shown as an important elect along the right side of the Bema Scene (MIK III 4979 verso, Figure 2/6a) and as the main figure in the Sermon Scene (MIK III 6265 & III 4966 c recto, Figure 2/6b).[44] Since Manichaean book paintings often depict contemporaneous members of the local community, just as their texts often mention them, the identified figure of these two paintings most likely indicates the temporal closeness of these works of art.

The close stylistic ties that connect the two painters can be easily surveyed through digitally cropped sections of the paintings, placed side by side (Figure 2/7). The similarly depicted motifs include the human face (Figure 2/7a), where red is always used for the outer contour of the faces, the eyelids, the noses, the mouths, and the chins; and black is employed for the eyebrows, the eye contours with the pupils, and the mustaches. A hand gesture resembling the *vitarka mudra* is assumed with both right and left hands in these paintings (Figure 2/7b). In both versions, the index finger and the thumb are touching and the divisions of the palm are captured. While gesturing, the elect's bent arm is held to the side or in front of the body (Figure 2/7c). The folds of the robe over the bent elbows include a characteristic teardrop shape defined by double contours. A further common motif is seen in the depiction of tablecloths and other hanging textiles, such as the diamond-shaped folds of box pleats (Figure 2/7d). Although clearly different hands executed these motifs, their shared technical characteristics indicate painters in close temporal proximity.

In short, four illuminated book fragments can be dated in light of a radiocarbon analysis together when

---

[42] See Gulácsi 2001a, 62–65 and 253.
[43] The artistic ties were pointed out by Jorinde Ebert (1994, 14).
[44] BeDuhn 2001, 227 note 181.

b: MIK III 6265 & III 4966 c recto,
marginal painting with Sermon Scene

c: MIK III 6284 recto(?), intratextual or full-page
painting with unidentified content

a: MIK III 8259 folio 1(?) recto, detail with
intratextual painting of Sermon Scene

Figure 2/3. Three Book Paintings by the Same Carbon-dated Illuminator
(SMPK, Museum für Indische Kunst, Berlin)

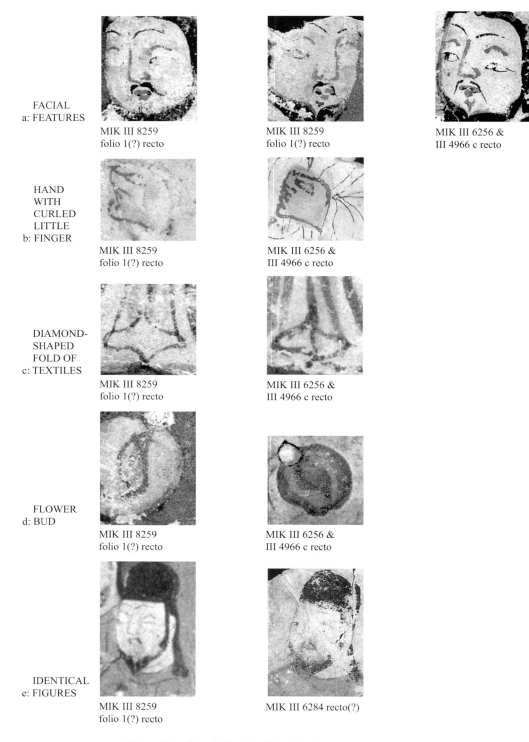

FACIAL
a: FEATURES

MIK III 8259
folio 1(?) recto

MIK III 8259
folio 1(?) recto

MIK III 6256 &
III 4966 c recto

HAND
WITH
CURLED
LITTLE
b: FINGER

MIK III 8259
folio 1(?) recto

MIK III 6256 &
III 4966 c recto

DIAMOND-
SHAPED
FOLD OF
c: TEXTILES

MIK III 8259
folio 1(?) recto

MIK III 6256 &
III 4966 c recto

FLOWER
d: BUD

MIK III 8259
folio 1(?) recto

MIK III 6256 &
III 4966 c recto

IDENTICAL
e: FIGURES

MIK III 8259
folio 1(?) recto

MIK III 6284 recto(?)

Figure 2/4. Correlating Details of the Three Book Paintings

a: MIK III 4979 recto,
detail with intratextual image of Conversion Scene

b: MIK III 4979 verso,
full-page image of Bema Festival

Figure 2/5. Book Paintings in a Style Similar to that of the Carbon-dated Painter
(SMPK, Museum für Indische Kunst, Berlin)

a: MIK III 6265 & MIK III 4966 c recto, detail with   b: MIK III 4979 verso, detail with
Ram Frazend   Ram Frazend on right

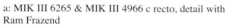

Figure 2/6. The Elect Named *Ram-Frazend* Identified in Two Book Paintings
(SMPK, Museum für Indische Kunst, Berlin)

additional stylistic and textual data are considered. The radiocarbon result gives a 95.4 percent chance that
the largest Manichaean illuminated codex fragment (MIK III 8259) was made sometime during a 126-year
period (between 889 and 1015 CE). The stylistic similarities and the repeated use of a name of an elect indicate a strong connection between the carbon-dated piece and three other Manichaean illuminated book
fragments (MIK III 6265 & III 4966c, MIK III 6284, and MIK III 4979). In light of their pictorial and
textual ties to the carbon-dated example, the dates of production for these four fragments can be narrowed
from the ca. 270-year period to the ca. 126 years defined by the radiocarbon analysis.

NARROW HORIZONS (19, 17, AND CA. 40 YEARS)

Three high-ranking individuals of the Uygur court, a *khatun* (principal wife of the khagan or queen), a khagan,
and a court official, whose existence is recorded in a variety of historical sources, are mentioned on eight
Manichaean illuminated book fragments. The names of dated historical figures allow us to contemplate
the possibility that the books to which these illuminated fragments belonged were made during the times

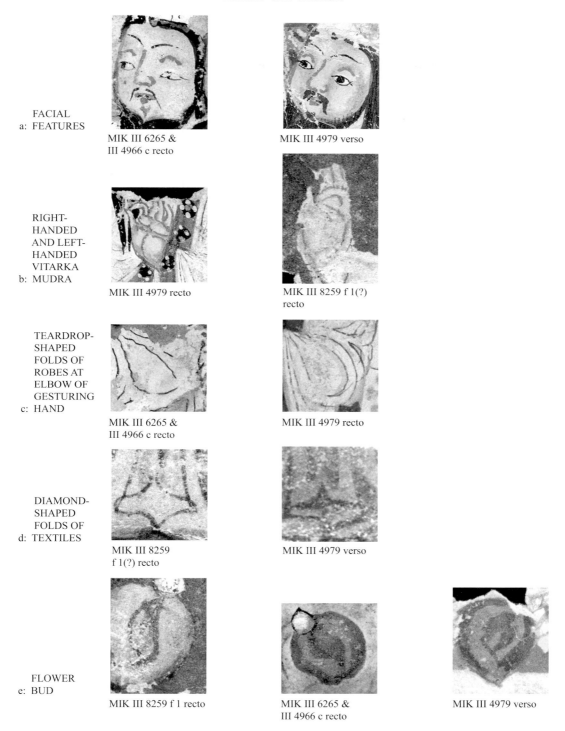

Figure 2/7. Correlating Details of Paintings by the Carbon-dated Illuminator and MIK III 4979

when the people lived. Such textual data result in the possible dating of seven illuminated book fragments. Divided among three groups, all seven are connected to relatively narrow time parameters.

A Historical Date and One Illuminated Book Fragment (MIK III 8260)

The first attempt to date a Manichaean illuminated book fragment, incidentally based on a textual reference to a dated historical figure, was put forward by Annemarie von Gabain in 1958. Gabain worked with the only *pustaka* (Sanskrit for palm-leaf formatted book, also known through the Hindi term *pothi*). The manuscript contains a religious anthology in the Uygur language (MIK III 8260, Figure 5/28 and Plate 6d). Its first folio holds a full-page painting with an *Elect in Paradise Scene* on the recto. This painting consists of two registers. The lower and smaller scene, occupying a third of the page, shows two kneeling elects flanking an incense-burner. Their chins are raised, as if looking up toward the direction of their prayers. The scene within the upper two-thirds, executed on a larger scale, shows an elect with slightly bent upper body, as if looking down onto the realm below his. This elect is seated on his heels next to a low table underneath a flowering tree, from where his headgear is hanging.[45] On the verso, a Manichaean script text in the Uygur language, known as *The Great Hymn to Mani*, begins the anthology with originally as many as a dozen texts on 50 leaves.[46] In accordance to the rule of orientation of book paintings in Manichaean codices, this image is sideways (vertical) to the direction of writing on the verso (horizontal).

In her attempt to date the book, Gabain argued that the Uygur name Kuimsa Xatun Tengrim (Lady Kuimsa, the Queen), mentioned in the pustaka book, referred to the Liao emperor's consort, whose Chinese regal title was T'ai-tsu and who, between 907 and 926, also bore the Chinese title A-pao-chi. Gabain suggested that the name in the Manichaean text is identical to that of the person Taixan Xan Kuimsa Xatun Tngrim (Queen Lady Kuimsa, the Queen) recorded in the colophon of an Uygur language Buddhist manuscript found in Turfan. The Uygur *Taixan*, she reasoned, corresponds with the Chinese *T'ai-tsu*, and thus the Uygur and the Chinese titles must designate the woman also mentioned in the Manichaean pustaka book.[47] In his critical edition of this Uygur Manichaean book, Larry Clark accepted Gabain's argument to date the book to the early tenth century.[48]

The weakness of Gabain's theory, which reduces this dating to only a possibility, is found in the connection between the Chinese and Uygur references. As pointed out by Peter Zieme in 1992, the general nature of these titles renders their tie to the khatun dated in Chinese sources questionable, since in addition to the khatun of the pustaka book, others were also referred to by the same title.[49] Consequently, at the current state of research, it is possible that this Manichaean illuminated book dates from the first quarter of the tenth century, but this dating cannot be confirmed without more solid historical evidence.

Other Historical Dates and Six Illuminated Book Fragments

Further historical data aid us in better understanding the dates of Turfan Manichaean art production. Chinese imperial annals occasionally preserve the titles and the reigns of certain Uygur rulers, but due to the nature of Chinese record-keeping and the way Manichaean religious texts refer to members of Turfan's elite, it is a challenging scholarly task to recognize correspondences between the Chinese and Uygur sources. Two identifications of specific Uygur rulers are accepted today, and therefore have a con-

---

[45] On the subject of the "New Paradise" as the place for the righteous elect after death, see Boyce 1954, 15–23.
[46] The book was reconstructed in a study by Larry Clark (1982).
[47] See Gabain and Winter 1958, 7.
[48] Clark 1982, 159–160.
[49] Zieme 1991, 21–23.

nection with dating artistic remains. Although they both contain hypothetical components, they conform to likely scenarios that keep the current scholarly understanding. The first one relates to the epithet of an Uygur khan who ruled between 1007 and 1024 CE, and is relevant the dating of five illuminated codex fragments. The second one is built around the title of a high-ranking Uygur official who was active around 1008 CE, and is used to date one illuminated scroll. These historical references allow us to connect possibly six illuminated book fragments to the early eleventh century.

A Dated Uygur Khan and Five Illuminated Codex Fragments (MIK III 6368, MIK III 8259, MIK III 6265 & III 4966c, MIK III 6284, and MIK III 4979)

In 1992, Peter Zieme carefully considered the possible dates of an Uygur ruler mentioned in the benediction of an illuminated codex fragment (MIK III 6368, Figure 5/12 and Plate 3) on the basis of research by James Hamilton and Takao Moriyasu. Hamilton, building on Moriyasu, worked with the Chinese sources and proposed that a part of the epithet *Arslan Kutlug Köl Bilgä* (Lion, Blessed Ocean of Wisdom) occurs in Chinese sources, where "Lion" is qualified by *zhi hai* (Whose Wisdom is [like] the Ocean), and designates a khan who ruled the Uygurs between at least 1007 and 1024 CE.[50] The khan's complete epithet, which consists of 19 words—*Kün Ay Tängritä Kut Bolmish Ulug Kut Ornanmish Alpin Ärdämin El Tutmish Alp Arslan Kutlug Köl Bilgä Tängri Xan*—means "Who has Obtained Charisma from the Sun and the Moon God, Who is Imbued with Great Charisma, Who has Maintained the Realm with Toughness and Manly Virtue, Courageous Lion, Blessed Ocean of Wisdom, Divine Khan." Zieme pointed out that 12 words from a very similar epithet (*Kutlug Elig Ay Tängritä Kut Bolmish Kut Ornanmish Alp[in Ärdämin El T]utmish*) also are seen on MIK III 6368. By equating the dated khan's title with that of the khan in the Uygur language benediction of this illuminated manuscript, Zieme proposed to date the fragment to ca. 1007–1024 CE.[51] This torn piece of paper constitutes the upper third of an illuminated codex folio. Both sides are illuminated. Its recto contains parts of a Scribal Scene depicted as a full-page image with sections of a text integrated within the composition. On the verso, an illuminated header surrounds the text in two columns and a Hymnody Scene is painted along the outer margin.

Also in 1992, Werner Sundermann drew attention to the fact that parts of the very same epithet are preserved within a Middle Persian language benediction of another Manichaean illuminated codex fragment (MIK III 8259, Figure 2/2). In this case, only six words can be reconstructed from the original 19-word title—*[Ay] Tängritä Kut [Bolmish Kut O]rnan[mish]*—but it includes the otherwise rare element *Ornanmish* (imbued). Thus, Sundermann raised the possibility that this illuminated fragment, too, may be connected with the dated khan.[52] In addition, this very same fragment (MIK III 8259) happens to be the carbon-dated fragment. If a name of a dated ruler is indeed preserved in its text, then the approximately 126-year potential era of production could be narrowed further to a 17-year period corresponding with the approximate reign of the khan mentioned in the text. Consequently, all four works of art linked to the carbon-dated painter are likely to have been made during (or close to) this 17-year period. In short, in addition to the two illuminated fragments with the name of the dated ruler (MIK III 6368 and MIK III 8259), the three other related book fragments (MIK III 6265 & III 4966c, MIK III 6284, and MIK III 4979, see Figures 2/3 and 2/4) also may date to this era.

We can accept Zieme's and Sundermann's argument to connect Moriyasu's date with two illuminated fragments only under two conditions: first, if the Chinese title indeed refers to the ruler with the better-

---

[50] James Hamilton notes that the Western Uygurs were called the "Arslan Uygurs" in the Lao Chinese records (A-sa-lan-Huei-hu), and that the Song records also refer to the Uygur rulers as "Arslan khans" (1986, xvi).
[51] Zieme 1992b, 324.
[52] Sundermann 1992, 67–68.

Table 2/1. Compared Epithets

MIK III 6368:

(1)	(2)	(3)	(4)	(5)	(6)	(7)	(8)	(9)	(10)	(11)	(12)	(13)	(14)	(15)	(16)	(17)	(18)	(19)
Kün	**Ay**	**Tängritä**	**Kut**	**Bolmish**	*Ulug*	**Kut Ornanmish**	*Alpin Ärdämin*	*El*	*Tutmish*	*Alp*		*Arslan*	*Kutlug*	*Köl*		*Bilgä*	*Tängri*	*Xan*

MIK III 8259:

(1)	(2)	(3)	(4)	(5)	(6)
[Ay]	**Tängritä**	**Kut**	**[Bolmish**	**Kut**	**O]rnan[mish]** ...

MIK III 203:

(1)	(2)	(3)	(4)	(5)	(6)	(7)	(8)
Ay	**Tängritä**	**Kut**	**Bolmish**	*Alp*	*Bilgä*	*Uygur*	*Xan*

preserved Uygur title; and second, if the fragmentary titles actually designate the same ruler who is mentioned in Chinese sources. It is possible that the king with the 19-word title is the one mentioned on the two illuminated manuscripts, but the two epithets are not identical (Table 2/1). The intact section of the epithet that is missing its second half (MIK III 8259) differs in two words from the complete epithet (MIK III 6368). It does not start with *Kün* (sun) and it does not contain *Ulug* (great). It is unclear today how significant such differences might have been at the time for identifying an individual ruler. In addition, the Middle Persian hymnbook, the *Mahrnamag* (MIK III 203, Figure 3/6a), that was completed between 825 and 832 CE, mentions a ruler with a very similar epithet—*Ay Tängritä Kut Bolmish Alp Bilgä Uygur Khan*— thus suggesting the possibility that minor variations might have signaled different rulers.

For greater certainty, further linguistic and historical research must verify how these titles functioned. Until their consistent reference to a specific individual is recognized, we must use the dates only provisionally. The likelihood of this hypothesis, however, is strengthened by the carbon date, since the dates of the khan recorded in historical sources fall within the era defined by the scientific method.

A Dated Uygur Court Official and One Illuminated Scroll (81 TB 65:01)

The most recently dated Manichaean illuminated manuscript is a relatively well preserved letter in a scroll format (81 TB 65:01, Figure 5/23). It contains 135 lines written in the Sogdian language using the Sogdian script. It is a letter written by a bishop (*aftadan*) named Shahryar Zadag to the teacher (*mozhak*) Aryaman Puhr on the occasion of the lunar New Year. Between lines 25 and 26, a pictorial insert decorates the text. This image is organized around a gilded inscription formed by vertically written letters contoured in a thin red line. At the top, the decorated headgear of a male elect is displayed on a golden fluted plate held on top of a red scarf arrangement. At the bottom, beneath the inscription, there is a pool of water from where two lotus stems emerge, producing two lotus supports for figures of musicians.

In 2002, Yutaka Yoshida dated this letter to ca. 1008 CE based on studies by Takao Moriyasu. In 2003, Moriyasu put forward a date for a high-ranking Uygur court official *Alp Totok Öge* (lit. "Tough Military Counselor") mentioned in line 123 of the Sogdian letter. Moriyasu noticed that Alp Totok Öge as "the Head of Kocho" is mentioned in the first stake inscription of Ruin Alpha, which has been dated by him to 1008 CE. Therefore, he argued that the illuminated Sogdian letter must also have been made during the time when *Alp Totok Öge* held his office in Kocho, in or around the year 1008.[53] The conditional element of this dating comes from the fact that *Alp Totok Öge* could have held the position of counselor (*öge*) for two to three decades, which could mean plus or minus about 20 years for the date of the Sogdian letter in relation to the First Stake inscription. Such a variable is tolerable, however, when it concerns relative dates.

---

[53] The reference to the court official in the First Stake inscription is found in line 18. In Moriyasu's translation it reads: "the head of Kocho city, Alp Totoq Öge" (Moriyasu 2003, 2). For the edition and dating of the stake inscriptions, see Moriyasu 2001.

a: MIK III 4981 a, with illuminated header and
first 6 lines of column (H: 7.4 cm, W: 6.0 cm)

b: MIK III 4981 a, detail of header with gold dot
in second to last letter (Manichaean "a")

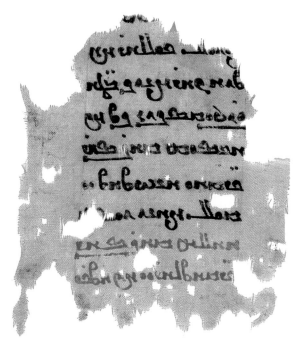

c: MIK III 4981 d, with last 9 lines of column (H: 7.2 cm, W: 6.0 cm)

Plate 2. Fragments of Silk Codex Folia
(SMPK, Museum für Indische Kunst, Berlin)

a: MIK III 6368, recto shown from picture-viewing direction
(H: 11.2 cm, W: 17.2 cm)

b: MIK III 6368 recto, detail (to left
of text area) with elect holding ink pen

Plate 3. Elects in Scribal Duty
(SMPK, Museum für Indische Kunst, Berlin)

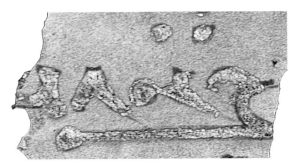

b: MIK III 4983 recto, detail with header in gold ink

a: MIK III 4969 inner side, detail with two lines of text
in gold ink

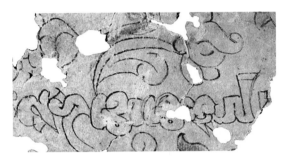

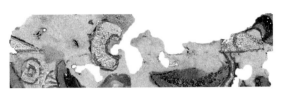

c: MIK III 6258b recto(?), detail with header in gold leaf

d: MIK III 4970b recto(?), detail with
header in black in outline writing

f: M 857 recto(?), detail with header in
orange & green outline writing

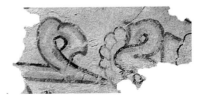

g: MIK III 6377 a recto(?), detail with
header in red & blue outline writing

e: MIK III 4969 outer side (?), detail with header in
orange & green outline writing

Plate 4. Writing in Gold and Multicolored Outline Writing
(SMPK, Museum für Indische Kunst, Berlin; and SBPK, Berlin-Brandenburgische
Akademie der Wissenschaften, Turfanforschung, Berlin)

a: MIK III 4979 recto

Plate 5. Illuminated Folio with Sideways Image
(SMPK, Museum für Indische Kunst, Berlin)

a: Example of West Asian outline drawing style
(So 18700 & M 501 e verso, detail)

b: Example of West Asian fully painted style
(MIK III 4979 verso, detail)

c: Example of Chinese outline drawing style
(MIK III 4614, detail)

d: Example of Chinese fully painted style
(MIK III 8260 recto, detail)

Plate 6. The Four Book Painting Styles of Turfan Manichaean Art
(SMPK, Museum für Indische Kunst, Berlin; and SBPK, Berlin-Brandenburgische
Akademie der Wissenschaften, Turfanforschung, Berlin)

THEOLOGY

 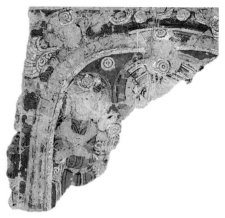

a: *Deity*, Probably the Third Messenger
(MIK III 4965 recto[?], detail)

b: *Unidentified Deity*
(MIK III 4965 verso[?], detail)

DOCTRINE

c: *The Four Prophets* (MIK III 4947 & III 5 d, detail)

d: *Judgement* (MIK III 4959 verso, detail)

RITUAL

e: *Sermon* (MIK III 6256 & III 4966 c recto, detail)

f: *Conversion* (MIK III 4979 recto, detail)

Plate 7. Identifiable Pictorial Subjects (I)
(SMPK, Museum für Indische Kunst, Berlin)

CHURCH
INSTITUTION

a: *Headgear as Emblem of Church Official*
(MIK III 4614, detail)

b: *Elects in Scribal Duty*
(MIK III 6268 recto, deatil)

PATRONS

c: *Ruler and Military Elite,* detail with generals
(MIK III 36 verso, detail)

d: *Ruler and Military Elite*
(MIK III 36 verso)

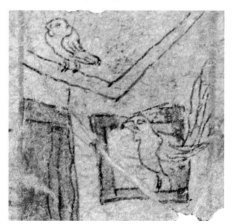

OTHER

e: *Omen* with birds
(M 556 verso[?], detail)

f: Omen with lantern
(M 556 verso[?], detail)

Plate 8. Identifiable Pictorial Subjects (II)
(SMPK, Museum für Indische Kunst, Berlin)

CODICOLOGICAL CHARACTERISTICS: ARTISANSHIP
OF BOOKMAKERS AND SCRIBES IN MANICHAEAN TURFAN

It is well documented in the secondary literature that the Manichaean church placed a special emphasis on its religious books and invested precious materials and extraordinary craftsmanship in their production. Writing in late fourth century Roman North Africa, Augustine of Hippo remarked about the books used by his opponents in a debate with the Manichaean elect named Faustus, mentioning their delicately decorated bindings, white parchment, and black inks.[1] Similarly, al-Jahiz, a Muslim historian who worked in the first half of the ninth century in Abbasid Baghdad, found it relevant to cite a conversation in his discussion of the Manichaeans in which he recorded the impressive quality of their books:

> I am pleased to see the eagerness of the Zindiqs [Manichaeans] in spending money on fine white paper and brilliant ink with a sheen on it, and their desire to get the best possible handwritten and most competent calligraphists, for I have never seen finer paper or better handwriting than what they have in their books.... We may compare the lavish expenditure of the Zindiqs on the production of their books with that of the Christians on their churches. (*Kitab al-hayawan*, prior to 847 CE / 233 AH)[2]

In light of such accounts, it is reasonable to assume that a sophisticated book workmanship was dominant even more in tenth century Turfan, where the Manichaeans enjoyed Uygur royal support. Indeed, luxurious manuscripts are found among the Manichaean remains recovered from Turfan—all in hopelessly fragmentary conditions. Not only is there no complete book among them, but there is not even a single complete illuminated folio. All the adorned remains are torn pieces of varying sizes and varying states of preservation. While the fragmentary paintings on them have been studied in terms of style and iconography from the very beginning of Manichaean scholarship, the torn condition of the pages has eliminated any ambition to reach even a basic understanding of artisanship associated with the production of Turfan Manichaean book art.

This chapter is therefore dedicated to gathering codicological data about the work of bookmakers and scribes in Manichaean Turfan. Like isolated bits of a gigantic jigsaw puzzle, the 89 illuminated fragments retain a useful sample of what was lost. Despite their poor condition, these fragments as a group are informative enough to indicate numerous important characteristics about the illuminated manuscripts made and used in Manichaean Turfan during the mid eighth to early eleventh centuries.

Through a codicological survey presented in this chapter, previously unknown, unique details are revealed about a lost book culture that was well adapted to its mediaeval, East Central Asian milieu. Regarding the

---

[1] In 400 CE, Augustine wrote in his *Contra Faustum*:
Burn all your parchments with their finely-ornamented bindings; so you will be rid of a useless burden, and your God who suffers confinement in the volume will be set free. What a mercy it would be to the members of your God, if you would boil your books and eat them! There might be a difficulty, however, from the prohibition of animal food. Then the writing must share in the impurity of the sheepskin. Indeed you are to blame for this, like what you say was done in the first war between light and darkness, you brought what was clean on the pen, in contact with the uncleanness of the parchment. Or perhaps for the sake of colors, we might put it the other way; and so the darkness would be yours in the ink, which you brought against the light of the white pages. (Schaff 1956, 206)
[2] Translation is from Arnold 1938, 1817.

work of the bookmaker, we learn that illuminated texts were written not only on paper and parchment, but also on silk. Being thin and unsuitably flexible for use as codex folia, silk was cleverly reinforced with paper in order to create silk sheets, thus adapted for the codex format. Alongside the dominant codex shapes, illuminated texts written on paper were also produced in scroll and pustaka formats. The sizes of these formats, just as their proportions, varied greatly. Among the non-illuminated manuscripts the greatest size difference is ten-fold; the illuminated books show a five-fold difference. Intact sets of binding holes along the fold of the bifolia allow us to learn about sewing stations used for bookbinding. In addition, a few examples of delicately decorated leather covers indicate the use of two types of book covers and their techniques of adornment. Regarding scribal workmanship, we learn that the trade of the scribes in Turfan reached beyond the mastery of lettering and the perfect alignment of horizontal lines within columns. The scribes also knew how to elaborate a calligraphic header written across the two upper margins of the facing pages by elongating select letters, or by writing the entire header in multi-colored outline-writing. To mark and decorate certain lines, the scribes also mastered the drawing of delicate floral motifs. The bits and pieces of codicological data retained on the fragments thus constitute primary visual evidence of the Uygur-sponsored epoch of Manichaean book culture.

Similar to books of other religions, the majority of Manichaean books in East Central Asia were not illuminated. They contained only texts, as suggested by the relatively small number of illuminated book fragments within a vast amount, ca. 5,000 fragments, of non-illuminated Manichaean manuscripts discovered in Turfan.[3] Besides being less numerous, the illuminated remains happen to be in an overall poorer state of preservation. Most of them are deprived of features that reflect their physical assemblage. Thus, to be able to understand the basic codicological characteristics associated with the making of Manichaean illuminated manuscripts, especially in terms of assemblage, we must rely partially on data supplied by non-illuminated Manichaean manuscripts, which constitute indispensable sources of supplementary information for the study of the illuminated corpus.

The Making of Illuminated Codices

The codex format dominates among the remains of Turfan Manichaean manuscripts just as among the illuminated corpus, where out of 89 fragments, 78 are from codices. Through a codicological survey, important basic characteristics can be learned about the formal features of these lost mediaeval books, including their physical build, the construction of experimental material such as silk folia, the range of their sizes and proportions, and the types and decorations of their leather covers.

The Structure of Codices

The available evidence on assemblage suggests that Turfan Manichaean codices were composed of only a few, but thick quires. They could contain at least 15 bifolia that were laid on top of, folded, and attached to one another through a small number of binding holes—two, four, or six depending on the height of the codex. The building of such quires necessitated the strengthening of the top and the bottom binding holes by gluing a small piece of paper over the area of the sewing station. This practice is seen only on certain bifolia, probably the ones that were the outermost bifolia of the quires. Occasionally, even the

---

[3] Boyce's catalogue (1960) lists around 5,000 Manichaean script manuscripts in the two Berlin collections. With the addition of Manichaean texts written in Sogdian and Runic script, my survey includes 69 illuminated book fragments from Berlin. In addition there are hundreds of smaller fragments in the Otani collection, many of which are Manichaean. The facsimiles and the edition of these texts are found in a publication by Kudara, Sundermann, and Yoshida (1997).

most lavishly illuminated codices included skillfully spliced sheets of paper. These were created by gluing together smaller pieces of paper in order to reach the desired size of the bifolio, using either a vertical or a horizontal join. Both types of join were cleverly disguised among the page elements. The codicological data surveyed below document the frequent application of these practices in Turfan Manichaean book art.

Quires

A significantly large portion of a Bema hymnbook known as the BBB (Germ. *Bet- und Beichtbuch*) is preserved among the non-illuminated Manichaean remains (MIK III 53 [M 801], Figures 3/1 and 3/2). This extra-small paper codex fragment (9.5 cm in height and 3.8 cm wide) preserves remnants of 48 pages of text on 12 bifolia. Most pages retain large headers written across the facing pages in colored inks (orange-red, red-violet, blue, and green), adorned with calligraphic letters and floral punctuation marks. In 1936, W. Henning examined the BBB's randomly stacked bifolia which were found secured to one another with a non-original, but pre-modern cord. While providing the critical edition of the texts, he identified the correct order of the pages and thus revealed important data on the quire structure of a Turfan Manichaean codex. Originally, this codex consisted of at least three (possibly four) quires with a minimum of 15 bifolia (i.e., 30 folia with 60 pages) in each.[4] The complete book of three quires held a minimum of 45 bifolia (i.e., 90 folia with 180 pages), while four quires would have meant 60 bifolia (i.e., 120 folia with 240 pages).

Among the 12 surviving bifolia, Henning discovered the remnants of two quires (Figure 3/2b). The first (quire 1), which was the first or second quire within the codex, retains three bifolia. On these, the surviving texts start with the *Letter of the Seal* (i.e., the letter written by Mani in prison that was customarily read out during the Bema Festival), followed directly by a set of Parthian and Middle Persian Bema hymns and a collection of Parthian and Middle Persian miscellaneous hymns for the same occasion. The other quire (quire 2), which formed the second or third quire of the codex, begins with Parthian and Middle Persian miscellaneous hymns and continues in Sogdian with a numbered list of Rules of Conduct. Besides reflecting the content of these texts, the headers also show the correct configuration of the 15 bifolia in this quire, since they not only read continuously across the two facing pages, but also are written with the same color of ink (Figure 3/1).

Quire 2 represents a relatively large gathering, since it contains two to three times the number of bifolia seen in the gatherings of East Mediterranean Manichaean codices (Table 3/1). Six well-preserved Greek and Coptic language manuscripts have survived from that westernmost part of the Manichaean world. They include a Greek parchment codex, known as the *Cologne Mani Codex*, and five Coptic papyrus codices. The *Cologne Mani Codex* has 192 pages arranged in eight quires with six bifolia (24 pages) in each quire.[5] The five Coptic papyri, the two *Kephalaia*, the *Homilies*, the *Psalm-Book*, and the *Synaxeis*, employ either four or six bifolia in their quires.[6] The Turfan example shows a comparable page number, either 168 or 224, but

---

[4] Henning emphasized that numerous pages, possibly even more than two bifolia, were missing at the middle of the quire, labeled here as the second quire (Figs. 3/1 and 3/2b). His calculation is based on the fact that the surviving portion retains hymns (folia 11–13) and the Elect's Confession (folio 17). The missing pages contained (1) the end of the hymns and the transition from the hymns to the confession theme; (2) the entire text of the first conduct (i.e., truth telling), which could have been at least as long as the text of the second conduct; and (3) a few lines that begin the confession on the second conduct (i.e., non-injury), the rest of which survives intact on four and a half pages (Henning 1936, 5–7).

[5] Cameron and Dewey 1979, 1. It is a Greek language manuscript about the life of Mani that was discovered in Egypt and now housed in Cologne, but thought to have originated in Byzantium. It is dated by paleography to the late fourth to early fifth centuries. See discussion of Mani's life in the Introduction.

[6] A codicological survey of these manuscripts has not been completed. The partial data published so far suggests that the Dublin

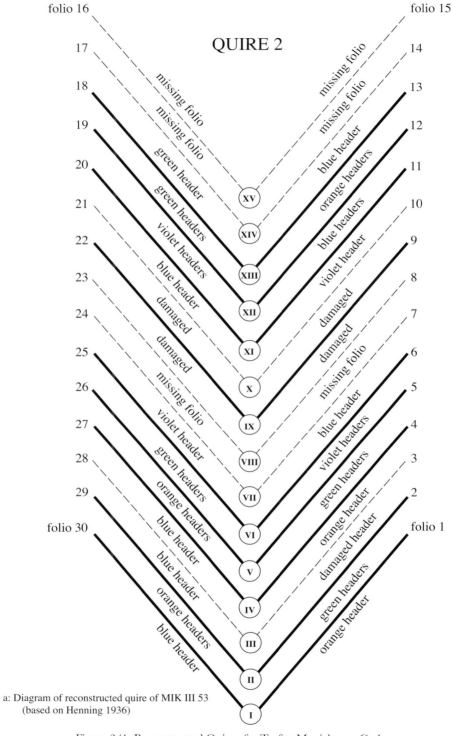

QUIRE 2

folio 16   folio 15

17   missing folio   14

18   missing folio   missing folio   13

19   missing folio   missing folio   12

20   green header   blue header   11

21   green header   orange headers   10

22   green headers   blue headers   9

23   violet headers   violet header   8

24   blue header   damaged   7

25   damaged   damaged   6

26   damaged   missing folio   5

27   missing folio   blue header   4

28   violet header   violet headers   3

29   green headers   green headers   2

folio 30   orange headers   orange header   folio 1

blue header   damaged header

blue header   green headers

orange headers   orange header

blue header

XV XIV XIII XII XI X IX VIII VII VI V IV III II I

a: Diagram of reconstructed quire of MIK III 53
(based on Henning 1936)

Figure 3/1. Reconstructed Quire of a Turfan Manichaean Codex

a: MIK III 53 (H: 9.5 cm W: 2x 3.8 cm)
(SMPK, Museum für Indische Kunst, Berlin)

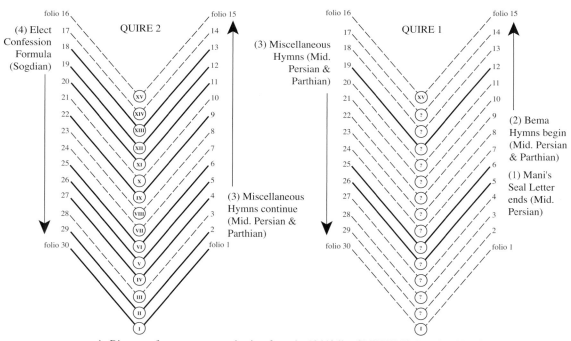

b: Diagram of two reconstructed quires from the 12 bifolia of MIK III 53 (based on Henning 1936)

Figure 3/2. Remnants of a Bema Hymnbook

Table 3/1. Comparison of Manichaean Quire Numbers and Thicknesses

Location (Date)	East Mediterranean Region (4th–8th centuries)		Central Asia (8th–11th centuries)
Language	Coptic Texts	Greek Texts	Iranian Texts
Material	*PAPYRUS*	*PARCHMENT*	*PAPER*
Number of Bifolia in Quire	4 & 6	6	min.15
Number of Quires in Codex	up to 33	8	3 (or 4)
Number of Bifolia in Codex	up to 123	48	45 (or 60)
Number of Folia in Codex	up to 246	96	90 (or 120)
Number of Pages in Codex	up to 492	192	180 (or 240)

a unique quire organization with 15 bifolia in three or four quires.

A possible explanation for the variety in quire thickness may lie in the different materials used for making the folia of the codex. The page number of a substantial codex (ca. 192 pages) seems to have been standard throughout the Manichaean world, whereas the number of bifolia in each quire is drastically different—just as the material of the codex. The fourth to eighth century East Mediterranean Manichaean codices used thinner quires of papyrus and later parchment. The eighth to eleventh century Central Asian Manichaean codices document a preference for only a few, but thicker quires for paper folia. The relative thickness of a papyrus and a parchment sheet compared to the thinness of high-quality paper is the most likely reason behind this phenomenon.

Binding

Tiny holes retained along the folds of fragmentary bifolia are remnants of the sewing stations that were used for securing the individual sheets of bifolia to one another within the quire, and for attaching quires to one another within the codex (Figure 3/3). Either strong thin threads or delicate cords were used for sewing purposes, no examples of which survive. The thread holding together the 12 surviving bifolia of the BBB (MIK III 53, Figure 3/2) is not the thread used in the original codex. Although it is a historical thread discovered together with the manuscript, the bifolia that it held together were found stacked in a false sequence. Also, it appears too crude compared to the delicacy of the book. The correct succession of the bifolia within this gathering, reflected in the current arrangement, was established in light of the content of the text.[7] On these remains, just as on most other Turfan Manichaean codex fragments that retain parts of the bifolio's fold, the binding holes are worn or otherwise damaged, and thus no longer resemble their original delicate sizes and shapes. Examples of worn but intact binding holes can be seen on the extra small non-illuminated bifolio MIK III 103 (Figure 3/3a).[8] Along the fold of this 5.8 cm high parchment sheet, there are two intact binding holes 2.3 cm apart.

Examples of binding holes close to their original condition are preserved on the non-illuminated parchment bifolio MIK III 4990 (Plate 1).[9] The superbly inscribed snow-white bifolio is decorated with headers

---

Kephalaia consisted of four bifolia per quire (Giversen 1986, Vol. I, pp. xxi–xxvi), and the first half of the Psalm-Book had 252 or 256 pages arranged in six bifolia per quire (Giversen 1988, Vol. III, pp. vii–xiv). Psalm-Book part 2 had 234 pages (Giversen 1988, Vol. IV, p. ix). The complete book totaled 486–490 pages.

[7] The manuscript, also known by its old number M 801, was found with its bifolia in incorrect sequence, tied together with a rough cord. Henning, who took upon himself the critical edition of the text, noted the incorrect sequence of the pages and established the correct order, and then reassembled the quire (1937, 3–4).

[8] The bifolio MIK III 103, also known by its old number as M 8110, contains *Hymns to the Living Self* (Boyce 1960, 133). It awaits publication by Desmond Durkin-Meisterernst.

[9] MIK III 4990 is also known under the old number M 178.

a: MIK III 103, parchment bifolio with intact binding holes (H: 5.7 cm, W: 2 x 3.4 cm)

b: MIK III 4983 recto, detail with part
of upper binding hole

c: MIK III 4981 b, detail with
binding hole and binding cord

Figure 3/3. Bindings Holes of Manichaean Codices
(SMPK, Museum für Indische Kunst, Berlin)

Table 3/2. Sample Distribution of Binding Holes on Non-illuminated Codices (5 examples)

Data ⟍ Fragment	Height of Codex	Number of Binding Holes	Distance between Binding Holes	Distance from Upper & Lower Edge
MIK III 53	9.2 cm	2	4.8 cm	2.2 cm
MIK III 101	11.5 cm	2	6.1 cm	3.1 cm & 2.3 cm
MIK III 103	5.8 cm	2	2.3 cm	1.9 cm & 1.4 cm
MIK III 203	21.1 cm	4	4.8 cm	3.0 cm
MIK III 4990	24.6 cm	4	5.7 cm	6.6 cm

written in blue and an unusual green color of ink, with calligraphic letters and floral punctuation marks. The codex to which it once belonged was a tall, medium-sized book, measuring 23.8 cm in height and 10.0 cm in width. Similar sizes and proportions (approximately 2.4:1) are documented among the illuminated codex fragments, making this bifolio a good comparative example for understanding the binding holes of illuminated manuscripts in close to their original condition. The smallest of these holes are less than 0.1 cm in diameter, confirming that a delicate cord or a strong thread was used for the sewing. The four holes are approximately equidistant from one another; measured from top to bottom, their distances are 7.1 cm, 7.6 cm, and 7.4 cm. In contrast, the top and bottom holes are very close to the edges of the parchment: 0.8 cm from the top and 0.7 cm from the bottom.

The small original sizes of the binding holes are also documented on a paper bifolio (**MIK III 203**, Figure 3/6a).[10] This non-illuminated fragment, which is adorned with a variety of scribal decorations, once belonged to a tall codex that was about 21.1 cm high and 12.2 cm wide, and approximately 1.9:1 in its height to width ratio. Three of the four binding holes on this fragment are close to original condition. Their small sizes make them hard to see on regular photographs, but placed against a light source, the bifolio reveals three delicate holes and a torn area around the uppermost binding hole. The latter was either 3.6 or 4.2 cm below the edge of the paper. The bottom hole, visible next to the third line from the bottom, is ca. 3.5 cm from the bottom edge. In this case, the distances between the holes are ca. 4.5 cm (or 5.1 cm), 4.9 cm, and 4.0 cm, counting from the top. The smallest diameter of these holes—0.06 cm—reflects the size of a metal point used for piercing and the thinness of the needle used for threading the binding cords. Besides documenting the delicacy of the binding, this example also shows that in paper codices the binding holes were placed at a greater distance from the edges of the sheet than on parchment codices, most certainly in order to better guard against tearing.

On all well-preserved fragments, the number of binding holes varies between two and four according to the size of the bifolio (Table 3/2). Codices that are under 18 cm in height have only two binding holes. For example, on the twelve 9.2 cm high bifolia remaining from the non-illuminated quire (**MIK III 53**, Figure 3/2a), the two holes are ca. 2.2 cm from the edges of the paper and 4.8 cm from each other. Codices that are between 20 and 35 cm in height have four binding holes, as seen on the remains of the 24.6 cm high parchment codex (**MIK III 4990**, Plate 1) and the 21.1 cm high paper codex (**MIK III 203**, Figure 3/6a). No binding holes are preserved on the fragments of larger size codices.

Due to their damaged condition, there are only six examples with binding holes among the illuminated fragments (Table 3/3). Parts of the uppermost hole are visible on three fragments (**MIK III 4983**, Figure 3/3b; **M 797**, Figure 5/5; and **MIK III 6368**, Figure 5/13). One of the middle holes can be seen on a silk codex fragment (**MIK III 4981 b**, Figure 3/3c). The bottom and one of the middle binding holes are retained on a reconstructible bifolio with a figural scene—the only illuminated fragment with enough data to

---

[10] MIK III 203 is also known as M 1.

Table 3/3. Distribution of Binding Holes on Illuminated Codex Fragments (6 examples)

Fragment	Data	Height of Codex	Number of Binding Holes	Distance between Binding Holes	Distance from Upper & Lower Edge
M 36		22.0 cm	4	5.5 cm	4.5 cm
M 171		18.0 cm	—	—	—
M 797		25.2 cm	4	cm	cm
MIK III 4983		—	—	—	4.5 cm
MIK III 8386		27.8 cm	—	—	6.6 cm
MIK III 8259		29.2 cm	4	6.2 cm	5.3 cm

confirm four binding holes on the originally 29.2 cm high bifolio (MIK III 8259, Figures 3/4c and 5/7).

The small number of binding holes in relation to the height of the book is characteristic of Turfan Manichaean codices, suggesting the possibility that they were bound with a technique similar to that known as Coptic sewing. In this technique, named after its numerous early examples documented from Coptic Christian codices, raised chain stitches not only secure the bifolia within the quires and link all the quires together, but also hold the cover of the codex. The top and the bottom cover, as if they were just additional quires, are stitched to the stack of quires sandwiching the first and the last leaves of the codex, while the spine of the book and the raised sewing stitches remain exposed. Since other binding methods involve more holes, it is possible that this method, or another akin to this technique, was employed in Manichaean Turfan.

Some information about the history of these books is also revealed through the study of the binding holes, suggesting that at one point many of the books to which these fragments belonged were taken apart. The worn quality of the intact binding holes, seen on numerous fragments, indicates natural widening and tearing, and thus prolonged use. The occasional unimpaired paper along the fold of the bifolia, just as the intact holes themselves, indicates that the pages were not torn out from many of these codices, as one might assume based on the poor condition of most remains. Rather, it seems that many of these books were taken apart systematically. Their binding stitches having been cut, the bifolia became loose and eventually separated from their quires; further damage occurred to the already loose sheets. Unfortunately, such data represent traces of the deed only and not its circumstances. It does not help to ask questions such as by whom and for what purpose these books were disassembled. Besides the torn condition of the pages, the fact that there are no intact books among the remains is significant. It seems that what the Turfan expeditions found was not a remnant of a decaying Manichaean library, but rather a decaying repository of book-parts, probably set aside for some kind of non-Manichaean reuse.

Strengthened Binding Holes

The upper and lower binding holes were occasionally strengthened (Figure 3/4) by gluing independent narrow strips of paper along the fold of the bifolio, in order to add an additional layer of paper to parts of the inner margins through which the top and bottom holes were pierced. Although more complete examples of this practice are preserved among the non-illuminated fragments, three damaged cases (MIK III 4966 a, MIK III 4983, and MIK III 8259) are also found within the illuminated corpus.

A well-preserved set of strengthened binding holes can be observed on the verso of a non-illuminated folio whose red ink headers contain calligraphic letters and floral punctuation marks (M 10, Figure 3/4a). The folio measures 21.8 cm in height and 10.5 cm in width, making it a small and slender codex with a height-to-width ratio of ca. 2.1:1. To the left of the text along the inner margin, the halves of two binding holes are preserved on what is left from the strengthened area of the bifolio. The upper hole is 4.0 cm below the edge. The extra piece of paper glued here was originally about 4.5 cm high and 1.0 cm wide.

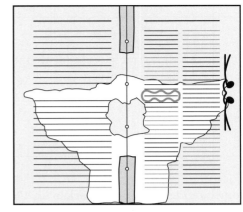

b: Diagram of MIK III 8259, inner side

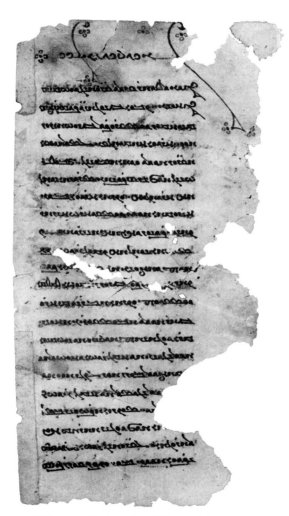

a: M 10 verso with strengthened binding holes

c: MIK III 8259 inner side, detail with strengthened
bindinghole

Figure 3/4. Strengthened Binding Holes
(SMPK, Museum für Indische Kunst, Berlin; and SBPK, Berlin-
Brandenburgische Akademie der Wissenschaften, Turfanforschung, Berlin)

The lower binding hole is 3.8 cm from the bottom edge, but in this case the paper strip was 7.7 cm high.[11] In contrast to the care taken in the handwriting and decoration, the strengthened area gives the impression of a less calculated component of this page.

A telltale sign left from a once strengthened binding hole is seen also on a fragment with a gilded header and an extensive floral decoration (MIK III 4983 recto, Figure 3/3b). On the recto of this folio, to the right of the header, a 3.9 cm long glue strip extends beneath the upper edge of the paper, gradually vanishing toward the binding hole. An additional small drop of glue is seen just beneath the remaining half of the binding hole at 4.9 cm. At this location, these marks can only be interpreted as remnants of a strengthened binding hole. Originally, the extra piece of paper must have reached beyond the binding hole. The length of the strengthening is comparable to that seen on the medium-sized non-illuminated example (M 10, Figure 3/4a). A similar case of a glue-strip along the upper part of the inner margin is preserved next to the illuminated header of another codex fragment that once belonged to a much larger book (MIK III 4966 a). This codex was more than 40 cm in height, as suggested by the ca. 7.0 cm reconstructed height of the upper margin.[12]

An intact strengthened binding hole is evident on a reconstructible illuminated bifolio with figural scenes (MIK III 8259, Figures 3/4 b & c). On the inner side of this bifolio, a 6.9 cm high and 2.4 cm wide paper strip has been glued over the bottom section along the fold, covering symmetrically parts of the two inner margins and the area of the last of the original four binding holes. The paper strip was attached here to provide extra support for the binding hole, and not to mend a previously weakened or torn area of the paper. This interpretation is confirmed by examination of the back side of the patched area (see Figure 2/2b), which is unimpaired and thus was in no need of repair.

The above observations bear important implications for Manichaean bookmaking techniques. The existence of strengthened binding holes in illuminated codices suggests a practice employed routinely in Turfan Manichaean bookbinding, without being considered unsuited for the luxurious, illuminated versions of religious manuscripts. The fact that only certain bifolia received such extra support raises the possibility that the structural stability of the codex required their use only at certain locations within the book. If so, the question naturally arises: On which bifolia were the binding holes in a more vulnerable position than the others? One may hypothesize that the binding holes on the inner- and outermost bifolia of the quire are most likely to have needed extra strengthening.

In light of data preserved within the illuminated corpus, it is possible that only the outermost bifolio of the quire was supplied with extra strong binding holes in Turfan Manichaean book art. This claim is supported by two sets of evidence. On the one hand, examples of bifolia that formed the innermost bifolio of the quires are not strengthened, as documented by one of the reconstructible illuminated bifolia (M 171, Figure 5/4). The four pages of this bifolio contain a well-preserved continuous text, which could have been written only if their two folia were located next to one another at the core of the quire. Numerous other examples of innermost bifolia also do not have strengthened binding holes, attesting to the selective application of this practice. On the other hand, bifolia with strengthened binding holes do not have continuous texts, and are thus likely to have been at the outermost part of the quire. For example, on the only reconstructible bifolio illuminated with figural scenes (MIK III 8259, Figure 4/7), the contents and the layouts of the texts on the two leaves are unrelated, confirming that they were far from one another in the com-

---

[11] An identical strengthening job is seen covering the upper binding hole on MIK III 35, a Runic script codex fragment that contains a bilingual Middle Persian and Uygur hymn of unidentifiable content (Clark 1997, 126, row 74), published by Le Coq 1909b, 1052–1054.

[12] For a color illustration of this fragment, see Gulácsi 2001a, No. 18, p. 45.

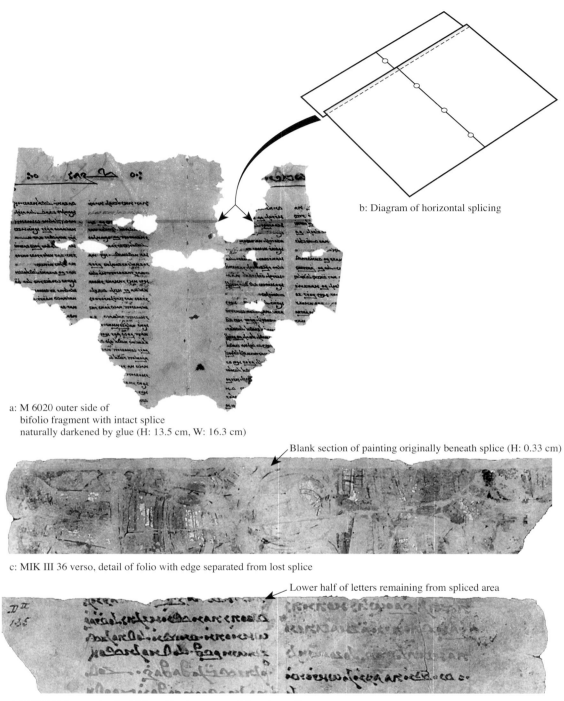

b: Diagram of horizontal splicing

a: M 6020 outer side of
   bifolio fragment with intact splice
   naturally darkened by glue (H: 13.5 cm, W: 16.3 cm)

Blank section of painting originally beneath splice (H: 0.33 cm)

c: MIK III 36 verso, detail of folio with edge separated from lost splice

Lower half of letters remaining from spliced area

d: MIK III 36 recto, detail of folio with edge separated from lost splice

Figure 3/5. Horizontally Spliced Bifolia
(SMPK, Museum für Indische Kunst, Berlin; and SBPK, Berlin-
Brandenburgische Akademie der Wissenschaften, Turfanforschung, Berlin)

pleted quire—a characteristic of bifolia closer to the outside than to the inside of a quire. The strengthened binding hole raises the possibility that this bifolio was in fact the outermost bifolio of its quire. If so, we also know that the quire to which this bifolio belonged was a middle quire in its book, since the texts on the first and last pages are incomplete at their beginning and end, respectively, and thus must have been preceded and followed by other quires in the complete book.

Spliced Bifolia

Among fragments with plain texts and also among the illuminated remains, there are numerous examples of a curious phenomenon—spliced bifolia. These are adjoined sheets created by gluing two pieces of paper next to one another in order to reach the same size as the other bifolia within the quire. Both horizontal and vertical applications of this practice are documented. Either way, a thin overlapping seam runs across the created bifolia, often cleverly disguised between vertical or horizontal elements of the page design.

The practice of horizontal splicing involves uniting a smaller (upper) and a larger, lower oblong piece of paper to make up the complete bifolio (Figure 3/5). An intact example of horizontal joining is found on a non-illuminated fragmentary bifolio that measures 13.5 cm in height and 16.3 cm in width (M 6020, Figures 3/5 a, b). Each folio retains most of the upper margin with decorative headers, the inner margin, and up to 25 lines from the text in two columns. On the inner side of the bifolio, on the recto of folio 2, the header is gilded. Since only the outer margin is missing from the original width of the folio (as indicated by the intact headers), it can be estimated that each folio was around 10.0 cm wide.[13] The original height was most likely between 18.0 and 24.0 cm. The delicate seam, seen across the text area at 3.8 cm below the upper edge of the bifolio, is formed by the 0.13 cm high overlap of two horizontally joined pieces of paper. The upper of the two joined sections is significantly smaller than the lower section, measuring 3.8 cm in height and ca. 20 cm in width. The lower section forms the rest of the bifolio. Within the text area, the horizontal lines of miniscule script (script height 0.12 cm and line spacing 0.4 cm) help to disguise the overlap. On folio 1, the overlap is where the third line of the text was written. On folio 2, it is between lines 2 and 3. Across the blank inner margins the seam is exposed, just as it was on the now-vanished outer margins.

A damaged version of an originally horizontally spliced bifolio is also preserved among the illuminated codex remains (MIK III 36, Figure 3/5 c, d). In this case, the fragment constitutes a portion of the lower section from the two joined pieces of paper, containing some of the lines from a two-columned text area on its recto, and a section from a full-page book painting on its verso. On the recto, the lower section covered the edge of the upper section. One line of the text was written on top of the seam and thus, when the upper section vanished, it took with it the upper half of the writing in this line. Consequently, on the verso we can observe a narrow, 0.33 cm high, blank strip that originally held the glue and was stuck beneath the adjoined upper section of paper. When the upper section became loose, it took away a side section of the full-page figural scene and exposed the blank area of the overlap. The reconstruction of the folio (MIK III 36, Figure 5/11) confirms that the now missing upper section was ca. 3.5 cm high and, based on the preserved original width of the folio (11.0 cm), 22.0 cm wide.[14]

Examples of vertical splicing unite two approximately folio-size pieces of paper into a bifolio (Figure 3/ 6). This is achieved through a thin overlap that runs vertically along an inner margin, as seen on the non-

---

[13] Each folio retains most of the upper margin with decorative headers, up to 25 lines from the text arranged in two columns, and parts of the blank inner margin. The text is written in miniscule script, 0.12 cm high. The lines are spaced every 0.4 cm within the column.

[14] See discussion in Chapter 5.

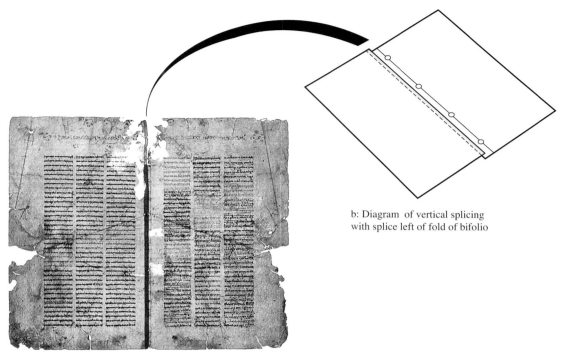

b: Diagram of vertical splicing
with splice left of fold of bifolio

a: MIK III 203, inner side of bifolio on light table to reveal a ca. 0.37 cm
wide double layer of paper in intact splice (H: 21.1 cm, W: 2 x 12.2 cm)

fold of bifolio   edge of splice   edge of splice   fold of bifolio

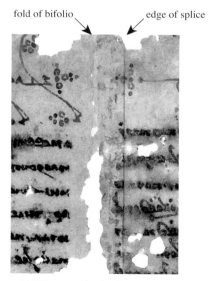

c: M 171 outer side, detail with splice   d: M 171 inner side, detail with splice

Figure 3/6. Vertically Spliced Bifolia
(SMPK, Museum für Indische Kunst, Berlin; and SBPK, Berlin-
Brandenburgische Akademie der Wissenschaften, Turfanforschung, Berlin)

illuminated bifolio already mentioned in connection with its small binding holes (MIK III 203, Figures 3/6 a, b). The photograph taken with a light source behind the bifolio reveals a narrow, ca. 0.37 cm, strip of overlapping paper along the vertical axis. Here, the inner side of the bifolio shows the overlap to the left of the bifolio's fold, allowing us to see that the paper piece used for folio 2 is larger than the one used for folio 1. It contains not only the vertical strip where the two sides are adhered, but also the fold in the middle of the bifolio with the four binding holes. Folio 1 (seen on the right of the bifolio) ends just before the fold, where the doubled area stops.

Among the illuminated remains, another vertical splicing is seen on a reconstructible bifolio with decorative designs (M 171, Figure 3/6 c, d). Here the inner side of the bifolio allows us to see that the inner margin of folio 2 includes the edge of a once independent sheet of paper, which is just a few millimeters less in width than the size of one folio. The vertical, cut edge of the paper is located directly to the left of the fold and the binding holes. Thus, on the inner side of the bifolio, the straight line of the central fold provides a camouflage to the vertical edge of the joined paper with its ca. 0.52 cm wide overlap. On the outer side of the bifolio, we can observe that the larger of the two folia (folio 1) reaches beyond the inner margin into the text area. The vertical edge of the paper is visible along the upper margin, across the floral punctuation mark of the header, continuing downward within the text area, where it contains the first letters of every line. On this side, the joining is more noticeable, which still makes only one of the four pages of the bifolio somewhat cruder than the rest.

The technical details observed on the above examples also indicate the purpose of the practice. In both versions, the result is a full-sized bifolio. In horizontal splicing, a smaller piece of paper (ca. 1/5 of the complete size) is attached to a significantly larger piece of paper (ca. 4/5 of the complete size). The narrow overlapping seam runs across the central part of the pages within the area of the text and the painting. The technique of vertical splicing follows the very same basic principles, except in this case the joined pieces of paper are closer in size and are glued to one another near the fold of the bifolio.[15] The smaller of the two paper pieces is only a few millimeters less wide than the one folio, while the larger of the two is about half a centimeter wider than a folio. The difference between the two widths gives the width of the overlap. By attaching them, the intent is not to strengthen the area of the binding holes, since the binding holes are contained on the larger piece, where a single layer of paper in the middle of the spliced bifolio accommodates them. This area is never doubled among the surviving examples. The goal here, just as in horizontal splicing, is to unite securely and in the least noticeable manner the two pieces of paper, and thus create a regular-sized bifolio.

The observed details also allow us to grasp the culture surrounding this practice. Based on the undoubted fact that small pieces of paper were united to create the needed size, we may hypothesize that this practice was necessitated by a paper shortage resulting from a lack of sufficient sponsorship, and thus write it off as a codicological indicator of a decline. Yet by taking into account additional facts observed on the spliced bifolia, we cannot help but entertain other likely explanations. First, these bifolia are found in superbly executed and often lavishly illuminated luxury codices characterized by the employment of high-quality inks and paints, gilding, and fine scribal and pictorial craftsmanship. Second, the overlapping edges of the adjoined sheets are delicately thin and securely attached at the same time. Third, the visual impact of the seams is minimized by being creatively disguised in between the written and painted contents of the page

---

[15] For three additional examples of vertically spliced illuminated bifolia, see Gulácsi 2001a, No. 59 (MIK III 4958), where remnants of the overlapping area of the two independent pieces of paper are retained along the inner margin; No. 15 (MIK III 4983), where adjacent to the illumination on the recto, a glue-stained strip indicates that the original bifolio to which the fragment belonged was patched; and No. 18 (MIK III 4966 a), where a soiled glue mark along the inner margin of the verso indicates that the bifolio was originally created by joining two independent pieces of paper.

design. There might have been a paper shortage, but that is beyond the point. All these facts clearly document a tradition of craftsmanship that was accustomed to using high-quality materials economically with great attention to details.

Silk Codices

Precious little survives from Manichaean silk codices among the Turfan remains, so it is not surprising that their existence has escaped attention. The evidence about them comes from silk and paper-reinforced silk fragments that are inscribed and illuminated as codex pages found in three groups of objects. The first group consists of six pieces of inscribed and illuminated silk (MIK III 4981 a–f, Figure 3/7 and Plate 2). The second is formed by two Manichaean layers of silk that were reused as reinforcement for a page in a Buddhist booklet (MIK III 151 layers 3 and 5).[16] The third group consists of five inscribed, double-sided, non-illuminated silk folia reinforced with paper (M 6230-4). A close examination of the codicological characteristics of these sources allows us to gain an understanding, undoubtedly incomplete, of what Manichaean silk codices looked like in Turfan.

The silks used for making these codex pages were all high quality and tightly woven with a plain-weave, also known as tabby weave, binding structure (Figure 3/7b). In cloths that have a plain-weave binding structure, single horizontal threads (weft) are woven across in an even pattern above and below the single vertical threads of the loom (warp). The tightness of the weave is measured by counting the number of warps and wefts in a 1 sq cm area. In the six inscribed and illuminated fragments with codex folio–like page layout (MIK III 4981 a–f), the silks contain 60 warps and 50 wefts per sq cm. In the Manichaean layers of the Buddhist booklet (MIK III 151 layers 3 and 5), the silks contain 56 warps and 48 wefts. The non-illuminated, double-sided remains (M 6230-4) contain even finer weave on one side of the paper, with 85–95 warps and 75–85 wefts per sq cm, with a rougher weave with 32–36 warps and 60–70 wefts per sq cm on the other side.[17] Due to the porous nature of the silk fibers, all silk cloths must be sized before the writing or painting could commence in order to prevent the silk from soaking up the liquid ink and paint. We currently have no data on the chemical or biological components of the material used for sizing. It is possible that an alum solution was employed, as documented on Chinese silk manuscripts and paintings.[18]

A unique picture emerges from the available sources regarding the structure of silk codex folia. The one-sidedness of the inscribed and illuminated silk fragments with codex folio-like page layout (e.g., MIK III 4981 b, Figure 3/7a) already suggests that the recto and verso sides of a complete textile folio were composed of two independent pieces of silk. Due to the natural softness of the silk, the two layers required some reinforcement. The five non-illuminated fragments (M 6230–4) still have a paper sheet between their silk layers, suggesting that a paper bifolio was glued in between two layers of silk.[19] A similar supporting paper layer is also preserved between the two Manichaean silk sheets reused in a Buddhist booklet (MIK III 151, layer 5, back side, Figure 3/16c).

It is unclear from the remains how the edges of the paper-reinforced silk sheets were secured, which must have been the case because the process of cutting the silk into the desired shape and size of the bifolio would destroy the structure of the woven fabric along the cut edges. It is possible that an already sized silk would hold its woven structure, especially if prior to cutting it had already been glued to a paper stiff-

---

[16] For the binding structure of the textile, the description, and the color photographs of the items, see Gulácsi 2001a, Nos. 73–75.

[17] Personal communication with Barbara Schröter, the textile specialist of the MIK, who generously devoted her time to the examination of these silk fragments for this study.

[18] Silbergeld 1992, 8.

[19] The fragments are unpublished, but their photographs can be viewed on the Web site of the BBAW.

b: Diagram of
plain-weave binding structure

Weft

Warp

a: MIK III 4981b

Figure 3/7. Remnants of a Paper-reinforced Silk Codex Folio
(SMPK, Museum für Indische Kunst, Berlin)

ener. Straight, cut edges of a silk folio that curiously holds its shape are preserved along the top of the vertically ruled silk folio glued to a paper support (MIK III 151, layer 5, back side, Figure 3/16c). If first the silk sheets were glued to the inner and outer sides of a paper stiffener that was just a bit larger than the needed size of the bifolio, and then all three layers together were cropped into the exact size, the result could have been a bifolio not stiffer, and certainly not thicker, than a parchment bifolio—and thus suited for creating the quires of a codex.

A silk fragment that preserves a binding hole lends support to the idea that the bifolia of silk codices were attached to one another through binding holes, as when the sheets are paper or parchment. An intact small hole is found along the inner margin of an inscribed silk fragment (MIK III 4981 e, Figure 3/3c); in addition to the hole, a small section of a cord is retained. The round shape of the hole was most likely achieved, and preserved, by using a paper stiffener originally attached to the back of this silk. The hole and the cord together seen along the edge of the inner margin not only identify the fragment as part of a recto page, but uniquely in this corpus, document a fashion of binding identical to the one used in paper and parchment codices.

The characteristic trends of page arrangement, documented on Manichaean paper and parchment codex folia, were observed also in silk codices, as suggested by the layouts of the silk folio fragments. On both plain and illuminated silk pages, the headers are written in large script with colored inks that often include calligraphic letters and floral punctuation marks (MIK III 4981 b, Figure 3/7a; and MIK IIII 4981 a, f, Plate 2). The header is placed across the upper margin, directly above the text area. The text is organized into columns and is surrounded by the wider outer and a narrower inner margin between its two sides. The decorative designs originate from the letters of the header and occupy the upper part of the outer margins, and the fragment displays the most frequently used vertical ruling within the columns. One folio from the initial stage of the bookmaking process exhibits thin red-violet ink lines of vertical ruling (MIK III 151, layer 5, back side, Figure 3/16c).

The sideways orientation of directional motifs and figural scenes was also used for silk codices, so that when a footed plate filled with symbolic food is integrated into the floral motifs of the decorative design, it is oriented sideways with the top of the vessel closer to the outer margin. When a figural scene is painted next to a text on a silk page, the figure is oriented at 90 degrees to the horizontal lines of writing. In the only surviving silk example of this practice the writing runs from head to toe in relation to the figure (MIK III 151 layer 3, Figure 3/16c). Although very little survives from the only silk codex page with a figural scene, the relation of the text direction and the figure suggests a page layout analogous to a verso page in a codex.

The small number of silk codex remains (13 fragments), compared to the overwhelming number of fragments surviving from paper codices, suggests a limited use of this medium for books of codex format. Most certainly silk codices, i.e., paper-reinforced silk codices, were a local innovation, in which the originally West Asian book format—codex—and an East Asian material customarily used for writing and painting—tightly woven silk—were united. Since the combination of this format with this material is undocumented from any other context, it is most likely that silk codices were unique to the book art of Manichaean Turfan.

Sizes and Shapes of Codices

The formal variety of Turfan Manichaean illuminated codices has not been studied before. To record the surviving sizes and shapes of Turfan Manichaean book art, the survey below considers measurements taken from the 24 illuminated codex fragments that retain at least three from among ten features of the folio: (1) the height and (2) width of the folia, (3) the ratio of the height and width, (4) the line spacing within the columns of the text, (5) the script height measured by the standard height of the small letters

Table 3/4. Summary of Size Data on Manichaean Codices

Page Elements	Codex Sizes EXTRA SMALL Non-illuminated Codices	SMALL Illuminated Codices	MEDIUM Illuminated Codices	LARGE Illuminated Codices	EXTRA LARGE Non-illuminated Codices
Height	5.0 – 14.0 cm	15.0 – 22.0 cm	23.0 – 30.0 cm	31.0 – 50.0 cm	Over 50.0 cm
Width	3.0 – 14.0 cm	7.0 – 12.0 cm	13.0 – 18.0 cm	19.0 – 30.0 cm	Over 30.0 cm
Proportions	0.7:1 – 3:1	1.7:1 – 2.4:1	1.6:1 – 1.8:1	—	
Line Spacing	0.30 – 0.35 cm	0.30 - 0.67 cm	0.40 – 1.00 cm	0.82 – 1.00 cm	1.2 - 2.5 cm
Script Height	0.10 – 0.20 cm	0.10 - 0.22 cm	0.15 – 0.40 cm	0.35 – 0.50 cm	0.80 – 1.70 cm
Column Width	1.8 – 8.1 cm	4.0 – 8.0 cm	8.0 – 12.0 cm	around 20 cm	over 25 cm
Upper Margin	1.4 – 3.2 cm	2.9 – 3.2 cm	3.4 – 5.9 cm	around 7.5 cm	—
Outer Margin	1.0 – 3.2 cm	1.2 – 3.2 cm	3.1 – 4.6 cm	around 5.5 cm	2.4 cm
Lower Margin	0.8 – 2.3 cm	around 2.4 cm	2.6 – 2.8 cm	around 6.0 cm	2.6 cm
Inner Margin	0.3 – 1.4 cm	0.5 – 1.5 cm	0.6 – 2.4 cm	around 4.4 cm	2.0 cm

(a, e, m, r, and not b, l, p, or g), (6) the column width and numbers on the page, (7) the height of the upper margin, (8) the width of the outer margin, (9) the height of the lower margin, and (10) the width of the inner margin (Figure 3/8). This information is supplemented with measurements taken from seven examples of well-preserved non-illuminated codex remains, in order to provide an overall view on the range of Turfan Manichaean codex shapes and sizes.

Turfan Manichaean codices varied greatly in sizes and shapes (Figure 3/9). Their variety is most striking among the non-illuminated books, where the largest recorded size difference is ten-fold. Although the vertical codex shape does dominate among the remains, there are also examples of square and horizontal non-illuminated codices. Illuminated codices are more limited in variety, occurring in sizes between the extreme dimensions of non-illuminated books. The greatest variation among their measurements is three-fold, although certain aspects of the illuminated page may display a five-fold difference. All known illuminated examples are from vertical codices that display a wide range of proportions. Although the extremes in sizes and shapes are rare, and thus most likely represent exceptions within Turfan Manichaean book art, the existence of codices produced in vastly varied forms does indicate a highly evolved and complex book culture that likely fulfilled a variety of religious needs.

By numerically documenting the trends of sizes and shapes, this survey reveals an interesting set of new information (Table 3/4). For example, the Manichaeans in Turfan apparently preferred the vertical format for their codices (Figure 3/10). Their proportions range between 0.7:1 and 3:1. The 11 cases of reconstructible illuminated folia for which the height and width ratio can be calculated exhibit proportions ranging between 1.6:1 and 2.4:1. The range of shapes happens to be greater among the surviving small-sized illuminated codices (1.7:1 to 2.4:1) than among medium and large illuminated codices (1.6:1 to 1.8:1). The small illuminated codices were often relatively slender, and their heights could reach ca. twice (1.9: 1, 2:1, and 2.1:1) and in one case almost two and a half times (2.4:1) their widths. Regarding the overall sizes of the page elements, we learn that while the actual individual measurements may show an overlap across the size categories, the average sizes of the page elements do increase across the five size categories. The line spacing and script size vary more between the small and medium size groups, whereas they seem to be often the same between the medium and large sized illuminated codices; the same holds true for the margins. This survey also documents the size difference among the four margins. In almost every case, the upper margin is larger than the outer margin, the latter is larger than the lower margin, and the inner margin is always the thinnest. Exceptions to this rule occur when the upper and outer margins, or the outer and lower margins, are the same size.

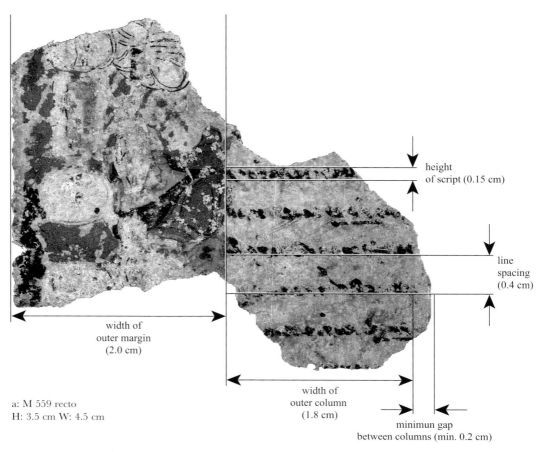

height
of script (0.15 cm)

line
spacing
(0.4 cm)

width of
outer margin
(2.0 cm)

a: M 559 recto
H: 3.5 cm W: 4.5 cm

width of
outer column
(1.8 cm)

minimun gap
between columns (min. 0.2 cm)

Figure 3/8. Measurements of Page Elements on a Codex Folio Fragment
(SBPK, Berlin-Brandenburgische Akademie der Wissenschaften, Turfanforschung, Berlin)

Non-illuminated Codices

Extra-small non-illuminated Manichaean codices from Turfan are well represented through two examples with perfectly preserved bifolia. The smallest bifolio known today from Turfan is a truly miniature book fragment from a parchment codex that measured 5.8 cm in height and 3.4 cm in width (**MIK III 103**, Figures 3/3a and 3/11a). In accordance with the overall dimensions of the folio, the page elements are also miniscule (Table 3/5). The text on the four pages of this bifolio is written in 2.1 cm wide columns in lines that are spaced 0.3 cm apart; the script is only 0.10 cm high. The upper margin is 1.4 cm, and the outer and lower margins are 1.0 cm and 0.8 cm. This bifolio from Turfan resembles the *Cologne Mani Codex*, a parchment codex with a Greek language text from Egypt that measures 4.5 cm in height and 3.5 cm in width. It is comparable in size to the non-illuminated quire with its 12 bifolia discovered in Turfan (MIK III 53, Figure 3/1). Although a third taller at 9.2 cm, the average 3.75 cm width of the folia is similar to that of the smallest bifolia. On the 48 pages surviving from this quire, the text is written in columns 1.9–2.1 cm wide, with lines spaced ca. 0.35 cm apart. The height of the script reaches 0.12 cm. The margins measure 1.5 cm, 1.1 cm, and 1.1 cm.

At the other extreme are extra large non-illuminated codices, with pages that reached over an estimated 60.0 cm in height and 30.0 cm in width (Table 3/6). Among these, one fragment constitutes the lower

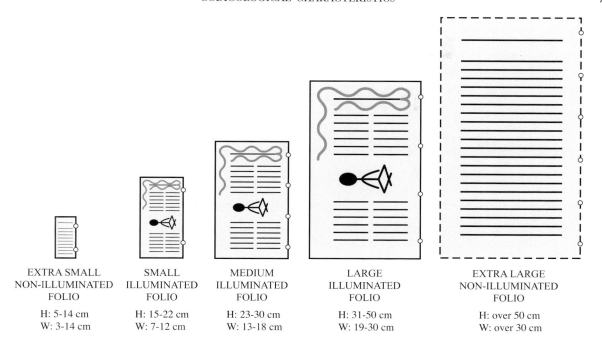

Figure 3/9. Documented Size Range of Turfan Manichaean Codices

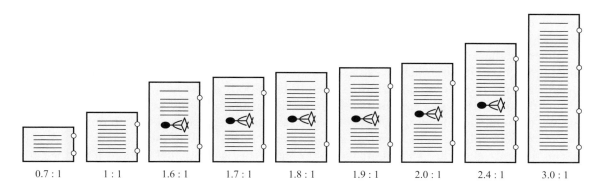

Figure 3/10. Documented Proportion Range of Turfan Manichaean Codices

Table 3/5. Examples of Extra Small Non-Illuminated Codices (5 examples)

Fragment	Measure-ments	Folio Height	Folio Width	H:W Ratio	Line Spacing	Script Height	Column Widths	Upper Margin	Outer Margin	Lower Margin	Inner Margin
MIK III 103		5.80 cm	3.40 cm	1.7 : 1	0.30 cm	0.10 cm	2.1 cm	1.4 cm	1.0 cm	0.8 cm	0.3 cm
MIK III 53		9.20 cm	3.75 cm	2.4 : 1	0.35 cm	0.12 cm	1.8 & 2.1 cm	1.5 cm	1.1 cm	1.1 cm	0.4 cm
M 322		7.5 cm	10.5 cm	0.7 : 1	0.65 cm	0.20 cm	8.1 cm	1.0 cm	1.9 cm	0.9 cm	0.6 cm
M 37		12.7 cm	4.1 cm	3.0 : 1	0.45 cm	0.20 cm	2.4 cm	1.6 cm	1.1 cm	0.9 cm	0.5 cm
M 267 a		14.0 cm	14.0 cm	1 : 1	0.45 cm	0.20 cm	2 x 4.2 cm	3.2 cm	3.2 cm	2.3 cm	1.4 cm

Table 3/6. Examples of Extra Large Non-illuminated Codices (2 examples)

Fragment	Measure-ments	Folio Height	Folio Width	H:W Ratio	Line Spacing	Script Height	Column Widths	Upper Margin	Outer Margin	Lower Margin	Inner Margin
M IK III 38		> 50.0 cm	—	—	0.60 cm	1.70 cm	< 17.0 cm	—	—	2.6 cm	2.0 cm
M 1002, 1006, 1017, 10023, 10028 & 9000		—	35.0 cm	—	0.40 cm	0.13 cm	3 x 8.0 cm	—	2.4 cm	—	—

quarter of a folio whose Manichaean script is 1.7 cm in height (MIK III 38, Figure 3/11e).[20] The current dimensions of the torn paper (height ca. 33.0 cm, width ca. 20.0 cm) suggest that the original height must have been over 50.0 cm and the width was at least 30.0 cm. Another giant, non-illuminated Manichaean manuscript is preserved in six matched fragments (M 1002, M 1006, M 1017, M 1023, M 1028, & M 9000).[21] These fragments retain three columns of text, each 8.0 cm wide. Assuming that the folio had only three columns (3 x 8.0 cm) placed 1.5 cm apart, the original width of just the text area reached 27.0 cm; adding to this the estimated widths of the inner (3.0 cm) and outer margins (5.0 cm), the width of the original folio comes to 35.0 cm.

Illuminated Codices

Remnants of illuminated codices fall between the above-mentioned extremes. They can be divided into three sizes, which for the sake of convenience may be labeled small, medium, and large. These size categories are defined by the 11 reconstructed illuminated folia discussed in Chapter 4, which supplies complete sets of measurements. The size data reveal a simple trend in Manichaean book art—the sizes of the individual page elements roughly accord with the overall dimensions of the folia. This recognition allows us to determine the most likely size category of the more damaged fragments' original folia. As long as they retain at least three measurements (e.g., data on script size and line placement and on one of the margins), they can be grouped with the more complete sets of measurements. Within the currently known corpus of Manichaean book art, there are 13 illuminated codex fragments with original sections from their text and at least one of their four margins. The measurements taken from these fragments correlate with those of the complete folia, and therefore reflect their approximate original sizes. Since these 13 illuminated folia

---

[20] The fragment MIK III 38, also known as M 795, is part of the permanent exhibition of the Museum of Indian Art in Berlin. Accordingly, it is listed in the catalogue of the exhibition (*Museum für Indische Kunst* 1986, 110, No. 398), but it remains unpublished. It is listed as a fragment without records by Boyce (1960, 53 and 141).

[21] The fragments were matched by Werner Sundermann (1973, 29).

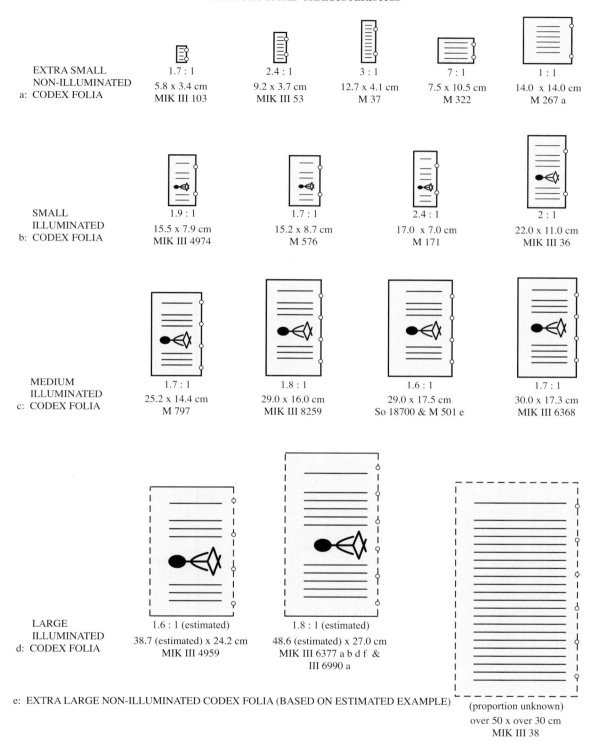

EXTRA SMALL
NON-ILLUMINATED
a: CODEX FOLIA

1.7 : 1
5.8 x 3.4 cm
MIK III 103

2.4 : 1
9.2 x 3.7 cm
MIK III 53

3 : 1
12.7 x 4.1 cm
M 37

7 : 1
7.5 x 10.5 cm
M 322

1 : 1
14.0 x 14.0 cm
M 267 a

SMALL
ILLUMINATED
b: CODEX FOLIA

1.9 : 1
15.5 x 7.9 cm
MIK III 4974

1.7 : 1
15.2 x 8.7 cm
M 576

2.4 : 1
17.0 x 7.0 cm
M 171

2 : 1
22.0 x 11.0 cm
MIK III 36

MEDIUM
ILLUMINATED
c: CODEX FOLIA

1.7 : 1
25.2 x 14.4 cm
M 797

1.8 : 1
29.0 x 16.0 cm
MIK III 8259

1.6 : 1
29.0 x 17.5 cm
So 18700 & M 501 e

1.7 : 1
30.0 x 17.3 cm
MIK III 6368

LARGE
ILLUMINATED
d: CODEX FOLIA

1.6 : 1 (estimated)
38.7 (estimated) x 24.2 cm
MIK III 4959

1.8 : 1 (estimated)
48.6 (estimated) x 27.0 cm
MIK III 6377 a b d f &
III 6990 a

e: EXTRA LARGE NON-ILLUMINATED CODEX FOLIA (BASED ON ESTIMATED EXAMPLE)

(proportion unknown)
over 50 x over 30 cm
MIK III 38

Figure 3/11. Sizes and Proportions of Turfan Manichaean Codices

Table 3/7. Remnants of Small-size Illuminated Codices (8 examples)

Fragment	Measure-ments	Folio Height	Folio Width	H:W Ratio	Line Spacing	Script Height	Column Widths	Upper Margin	Outer Margin	Lower Margin	Inner Margin
MIK III 4974		15.5 cm	7.90 cm	1.9 : 1	0.38 cm	0.12 cm	2 x 2.0 cm	3.0 cm	2.9 cm	2.4 cm	0.5 cm
M 576		15.2 cm	8.70 cm	1.7 : 1	0.30 cm	0.10 cm	3 x 1.8 cm	2.9 cm	2.2 cm	—	—
M 559		—	—	—	0.40 cm	0.10 cm	3 x 1.8 cm	—	2.0 cm	—	—
M 171		17.0 cm	7.00 cm	2.4 : 1	0.60 cm	0.20 cm	1 x 5.0 cm	3.2 cm	1.2 cm	—	0.7 cm
M 23		—	8.70 cm	—	0.67 cm	0.22 cm	1 x 5.0 cm	—	3.0 cm	—	0.8 cm
MIK III 4970 b		—	—	—	0.67 cm	0.17 cm	—	3.2 cm	—	—	—
MIK III 36		22.0 cm	11.0 cm	2.0 : 1	0.40 cm	0.13 cm	2 x 3.4 cm	—	2.4 cm	—	1.5 cm
MIK III 4971 a – c		—	11.6 cm	—	0.50 cm	0.22 cm	1 x 8.0 cm	—	3.2 cm	—	—

cannot be reconstructed, when their incomplete measurements are interpreted in light of the rest of the size data, we are able to determine which of the three size categories their original books belonged to. Thus, this survey allows us to know the size category of 24 Manichaean illuminated codices from Turfan.

Eight fragments document the existence of small illuminated codices that were between ca. 15.0 and 22.0 cm in height and 7.0 and 11.0 cm in width (Figure 3/10 and Table 3/7). The proportion of these codices thus varied between ca. 1.7:1 and 2.4:1. The spacing of the lines in the columns ranged from 0.30 to 0.67 cm, script height was between 0.10 and 0.22 cm, and column width was 4.0 to 8.0 cm. The data on the margins are complete on only two illuminated fragments (MIK III 4974, Figure 4/9; and M 171, Figure 4/5). In this small size category the sums of the margin measurements are upper margins between 3.2 and 2.9 cm, outer margins between 3.2 and 1.2 cm, lower margins around 2.3 cm, and inner margins between 0.5 and 1.5 cm.

The medium-sized illuminated codices were ca. 23.0–30.0 cm in height and 12.0–17.0 cm wide (Figure 3/11 and Table 3/8). There are 11 fragments in this size group. Among them six are reconstructible, thus providing data on the proportions of their folia, such as 1.6:1 and 1.8:1. The line spacing in this group is between 0.4 and 1.0 cm, the script size ranges from 0.15 to 0.40 cm, and the column widths are between 8.0 and 12.0 cm. The four margins gradually decrease in size. The upper margins are 3.4–5.9 cm, the outer margins are 3.1–4.6 cm, the lower margins are 2.6–2.8 cm, and the inner margins are 0.6–2.4 cm. It is important to note the significant variation in size of the texts that could occur even on the four pages of a single bifolio (MIK III 8259, Figure 4/6). A similar size variety within one book is also documented through the two pages of the largest folio in this group (MIK III 6368, Figure 4/13).

Four fragments indicate the existence of large-sized illuminated codices (Figure 3/12 and Table 3/9). Although none of the folia within this group can be reconstructed, it seems that their original measurements reached at least 31.0–50.0 cm in height, and their width varied between ca. 19.0 and 30.0 cm.[22] The two best preserved fragments in this group (MIK III 4959, Figure 4/16; and MIKIII 4976 a, b & S 49, Figure 4/18) allow us to estimate the width of their folia. In both cases the fragments retain data on the number and width of columns, and thus indicate the minimum original width of the page. The writing in this size category is distributed in lines that are 0.82 and 1.00 cm apart, written in scripts that are between 0.35

---

[22] An example is MIK III 4966 a, which constitutes the innermost section of an upper margin, and retains bits from the original edge along the top. The distance of the header from the top edge is 4.5 cm. In accordance with the large size of the folio, the height of the script is 0.7 cm. Four additional illuminated folio fragments indicate large originals. For their color facsimiles, see Gulácsi 2001, No. 17 (MIK III 6377 c); No. 19 (MIK III 4976 a, b, reproduced here as Fig. 5/20); No. 27 (MIK III 6374); and No. 51 (MIK III 4964).

Table 3/8. Remnants of Medium-size Illuminated Codices (11 examples)

Fragment \ Measurements	Folio Height	Folio Width	H:W Ratio	Line Spacing	Script Height	Column Widths	Upper Margin	Outer Margin	Lower Margin	Inner Margin
M 233	—	14.2 cm	—	1.00 cm	0.33 cm	9.4 cm	4.4 cm	3.1 cm	—	0.6 cm
M 797	25.2 cm	14.4 cm	1.7:1	0.90 cm	0.25 cm	1 x 8.7 cm	4.3 cm	4.1 cm	2.8 cm	1.4 cm
M 730	—	14.3 cm	—	0.57 cm	0.22 cm	4.6 & 4.9 cm	2.9 cm	3.1 cm	—	—
MIK III 4979	26.7 cm	15.7 cm	1.7:1	0.55 cm	0.18 cm	2 x 5.8 cm	3.7 cm	—	—	—
Or. 8212-1692	27.0 cm	15.7 cm	1.7:1	0.40 cm	0.15 cm	2 x 3.7 cm	3.5 cm	3.2 cm	—	—
MIK III 4969	—	—	—	0.65 cm	0.18 cm	—	3.5 cm	—	—	0.8 cm
MIK III 4983	—	—	—	0.60 cm	0.20 cm	—	3.4 cm	—	—	1.0 cm
MIK III 8259 fl(?) recto	29.0 cm	16.0 cm	1.8:1	0.60 cm	0.22 cm	5.0 & 5.4 cm	—	2.6 cm	2.5 cm	2.4 cm
fl(?) verso	29.0 cm	16.0 cm	1.8:1	0.65 cm	0.22 cm	5.4 & 5.2 cm	—	2.8 cm	2.6 cm	2.0 cm
f 2(?) recto	29.0 cm	16.0 cm	1.8:1	0.90 cm	0.40 cm	1 x 11.1 cm	—	2.5 cm	2.5 cm	2.4 cm
f 2(?) verso	29.0 cm	16.0 cm	1.8:1	0.82 cm	0.40 cm	1 x 10.9 cm	—	2.8 cm	2.7 cm	2.2 cm
So 18.700 & M 501 e	29.0 cm	17.5 cm	1.6:1	0.85 cm	0.30 cm	1 x 12.0 cm	—	4.0 cm	—	—
MIK III 6265 & 4966 c	—	—	—	0.70 cm	0.30 cm	—	—	4.0 cm	—	—
MIK III 6368 recto	30.0 cm	17.3 cm	1.7:1	1.00 cm	0.36 cm	5.0 & 6.0 cm	5.9 cm	4.1 cm	—	0.9 cm
verso	30.0 cm	17.3 cm	1.7:1	0.75 cm	0.30 cm	1 x 11.5 cm	5.5 cm	4.6 cm	—	1.0 cm

Table 3/9. Remnants of Large-size Illuminated Codices (4 examples)

Fragment \ Measurements	Folio Height	Folio Width	H:W Ratio	Line Spacing	Script Height	Column Widths	Upper Margin	Outer Margin	Lower Margin	Inner Margin
MIK III 4959	—	24.2 cm	—	0.82 cm	0.35 cm	3 x 6.3 cm	—	—	6.0 cm	—
MIK III 4976 a, b & S 49	—	27.2 cm	—	0.95 cm	0.50 cm	2 x 9.3 cm	—	5.5 cm	—	—
MIK III 6377 a, b, d, f & III 6900 a recto[?]	—	27.0 cm	—	—	0.43 cm	—	7.5 cm	—	—	—
MIK III 4958	ca.50 cm	—	—	1.00 cm	0.50 cm	—	—	—	—	4.4 cm

and 0.50 cm high. In accordance with the wider page, the text area may spread to ca. 20.0 cm, including the gap between the columns. In accordance with the larger overall size of the folia, the fragmentary data on margin size indicate a range between 7.5 and 4.4 cm.

Codex Covers

Codex covers were an important, but little documented part of the Turfan Manichaean book culture. The limited available data derive from two groups of sources—the remnants of actual leather covers, including three ornate leather pieces (MIK III 6268, MIK III 6267, and MIK III 7048); and five Manichaean paintings that depict codices with lavishly decorated covers held by male and female elects or deities (MIK III 4979 verso, MIK III 6268 side 1[?] upper scene and main scene, MIK III 6283 side 1[?] and side 2[?], MIK III 8259 folio 1[?] recto, and MIK III 8260 recto). These paintings function as primary documentary evidence on the subject. All in all, these sources allow us to learn about two formats of leather codex covers and eight techniques of leather cover decoration.

Although our sources are limited, and only preliminary comparative studies with contemporaneous West

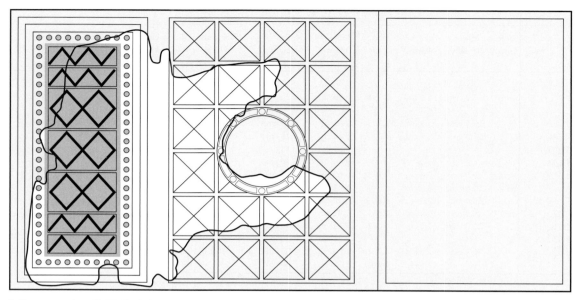

b: Reconstruction of MIK III 6268 (H: ca. 10.0 cm, W: ca. 22.0 cm)

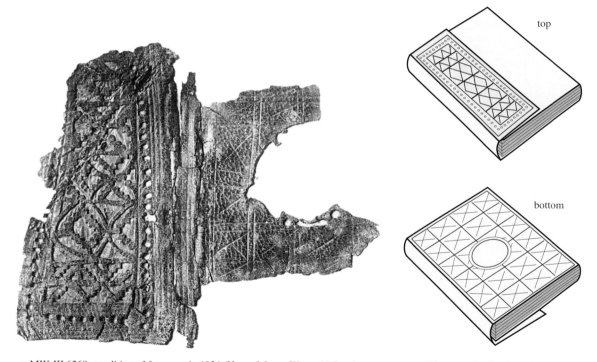

a: MIK III 6268, condition of fragment in 1924 (H: ca. 9.0 cm, W: ca. 11.0 cm)
(SMPK, Museum für Indische Kunst, Berlin)

c: Diagram of codex bound in
cover with flap closure

Figure 3/12. Codex Cover with Flap Closure

Asian book covers have been conducted,[23] the analysis of the available sources permit a few interpretive remarks. Regarding the types of Manichaean codex covers, their design seems to be similar to early mediaeval Eastern Christian and Islamic codices. On the majority of the surviving covers, the decoration was based on leather craftsmanship; their motifs, in both design and execution, are rooted in leather craft. Frames are embossed, holes are punched, concentric ovals are stamped in an even line, and filigree is cut in a complex pattern. The overall design of decoration is built on repetition and geometric order, in sharp contrast to the inside decoration of the book, where the illumination of the folia was dominated by representational themes, including stylized floral motifs arranged in an imaginary creative design in order to fill out the available area, just as in figural scenes. On a few of the covers, however, the decoration seems to be influenced by this pictorial art. The images on these covers appear to have been less complex versions of book paintings, but analogous to them in terms of iconography, color repertoire, and composition.

Documented Formats of Leather Codex Covers

A well-preserved fragment of a reconstructible leather cover indicates that the Manichaeans in Turfan did use a version of codex covers with envelope flaps. This leather fragment preserves filigree-like openwork with underlain gold leaf on a paper backing (MIK III 6268, Figure 3/12). This gilded part of the cover measured ca. 3.0 cm in width and ca. 10.0 cm in height in its original condition, before the shrinking of its one end possibly due to heat damage.[24] The small size in relation to the rest of the cover, together with the elaborate decoration, suggests that this section was the most prestigious area of the cover. Next to it, a larger and less decorative unit measured ca. 6.0 cm in width. This original width can be estimated in light of a remnant of a circular cut that most likely was located not only at mid height, but also along the vertical axis of this section. Similar centrally located circular decorations of book covers are depicted in two Manichaean paintings (MIK III 6286 upper and central images), and also are well documented on early Islamic covers. These observations lead us to view the gilded area as a rectangular version of an envelope flap, and the area with the circle in its center as the lower cover of the book.

No parts survive of the rest of this cover so it is unclear how it was attached to the spine of its book. The upper cover and the spine are missing, along with more than half of the lower cover. To gain an understanding of the possible binding techniques, three early mediaeval cover designs must be considered. First, it seems unlikely that the binding cord of the quires was sewn directly to the spine as in the wrapping covers of the Nag-Hammadi codices that consist of one quire, where the wrapper is handled as the last bifolio. Second, it is possible that the quires were Coptic, sewn to one another with the rear edge of the quire stack exposed, as suggested by the Turfan Manichaean application of a low and even number of binding holes characteristic of this type of early mediaeval bindings in West Asia. If so, this cover must have consisted of two independent parts: the lower cover with the envelope flap and the now lost upper cover, each attached to the quires as if they were the first and the last quire of the stack. Third, if the cover was more similar to later Islamic covers with envelope flaps, the spine was then part of the cover. This possibility is weakened by the fact that the Manichaean fragments do not preserve traces of how the quires were attached to the cover since, other than the binding holes, no sewing marks seem to be left on the fragments.

The existence of a different kind of book cover, a wrapping cover, is also documented in Manichaean Turfan (Figure 3/13). A Manichaean book painting depicts a rectangular object displayed on a low decorated table next to a sitting male elect (MIK III 8260 recto, Figure 3/13a and Plate 6d). In light of the

---

[23] Loubier 1910, 33; Le Coq 1923, 40; Grohman - Arnold 1929; and Gratzl 1938, p. 1976.

[24] Kocho, where the fragment was waiting its rediscovery for ca. 1000 years, is located in the desert of the Turfan Depression—one of the hottest places on the planet.

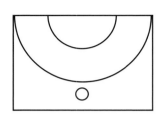

a: MIK III 8260, detail with leather-wrapped book on table (SMPK, Museum für Indische Kunst, Berlin)

b: Interpretation of MIK III 6280, detail of leather wrapper from frontal view

c: Comparative image of a leather wrapper (Arabic MS 321, Beinecke Libr., Yale)

Figure 3/13. Leather Wrappers

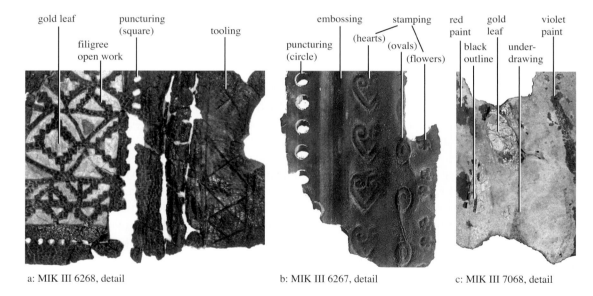

a: MIK III 6268, detail

b: MIK III 6267, detail

c: MIK III 7068, detail

Figure 3/14. Techniques of Leather Decoration Documented on Manichaean Codex Cover Fragments (SMPK, Museum für Indische Kunst, Berlin)

details of its representation, this object is best interpreted as a codex-formatted book in a protective leather wrap. It is shown from the front. It is defined by black contour lines that outline the overall rectangular shape with a height to width ratio of 1:1.4. Two prominent parallel semi-circular lines are drawn on its front. The lower one, reaching two-thirds down the front of the object, seems to be the rounded edge of the overlap, since directly beneath it, there is a small round circle that most likely represents a button used for closing the case. The upper circular line at the upper one-third of the object seems to be a decoration that echoes the shape of the flap (Figure 3/13b). The interpretation of this rectangular object as a book in a wrapping cover is aided by the analogous shapes of wrapping covers known from West Asia, the earliest ones of which are from the Nag-Hammadi finds from Egypt dated to the fourth and fifth centuries.[25] The Nag-Hammadi leather wrapper design is identical to that of a nineteenth-century Archaic manuscript cover illustrated here (Figure 3/13c).[26]

Decoration Techniques on Fragments of Leather Book Covers

Even in their damaged condition and small numbers, Turfan Manichaean book covers document a superb quality of craftsmanship in leather decoration (Figure 3/14). On the first two fragmentary covers (MIK III 6267, Figure 3/14a; and MIK III 8268, Figure 3/14b), eight techniques can be distinguished—dyeing, embossing, stamping, tooling, puncturing, cutting, gilding, and painting. These are used in combination, creating densely decorated surfaces. In addition, a pictorial means of leather decoration is also documented on one fragment (MIK III 7048, Figure 3/14c), which seems to have been decorated with a painting only, without the use of any leather decorating techniques.

Dyeing is the least intrusive decoration on the surface of the leather cover. Since dyeing is done at the end of the tanning process, most likely the bookbinder was not involved with it, but worked with already dyed hides. As documented by the brown and the red-violet ornate cover fragments (MIK III 6267 and MIK III 6268) and the depiction of the orange-red undecorated wrapping cover (MIK III 8260 recto, Figure 3/13a), dyed leather may be used for book covers with or without additional decorations—a large variety of which survive on the three cover fragments.

Embossing involves working the reverse side of the leather in order to create a protruding linear decoration in a low relief on the obverse. This technique is seen in the presence of two parallel protruding lines with a deep round-bottomed groove between them that frames a larger section of the overall design (MIK III 6267 and MIK III 6268).

Tooling of the leather entails the impressing of delicate lines onto the obverse side without cutting into the surface. Metal tools are used for this process, all with dull blades in a variety of shapes. Tooling marks created the parallel and crossing lines of the surviving back cover portion of the reconstructed cover (MIKIII 6268). On this damaged cover, just as on better-preserved Islamic covers, tooled decoration is understated and is used to surround more prominent central motifs.

Stamping requires the use of metal drive punches (also known as single axis stamps) that are impressed with the aid of a mallet onto the obverse side in order to introduce delicate sunken motifs. Motifs stamped beneath one another create three parallel lines on one of the cover fragments (MIK III 6267). The surviving motifs include an open heart, a set of two concentric ovals, and a quatrefoil flower, the latter of which is used in pairs. The tools of the Manichaean bookbinder most certainly included a metal punch set with a large variety of motifs, similar to modern tools.

Puncturing, cutting fully perforated holes, is achieved by driving a metal punch through the leather.

[25] Doresse 1972, Fig. 10; Rudolph 1983, Figs 14–16.
[26] Shailor 1994, 55.

The holes may be of different shapes, depending on the shape of the tool. The two cover fragments (MIK III 6267 and MIK III 6268) document two shapes from the Manichaean repertoire of this tool: one with a rounded square blade and another with a fully circular blade. In both cases, the small cut holes are distributed evenly in a linear pattern and are used to frame units within the overall decoration.

Openwork cutting of the leather results in delicate decorative gaps that form a negative design against a distinct surface used as a background. A complex version of this kind of decoration is preserved on the flap of the reconstructed cover (MIK III 6268). Here, a series of stepped and arched bands are cut out from the leather. Based on the evenness and the complexity of the design, it is most likely that not a knife, but rather delicate drive punches were used to create these filigree cuts.

Gilding on Manichaean book covers is seen in two forms. One involves the use of underlain gold leaf, where a thin sheet of gold is glued to paper that can be seen through the decorative openwork cuts of the leather. The cut leather protects the gold layer by rising higher than the gold surface, and also by exposing only small areas of the gold sheet at a time (MIK III 6268). This technique of gilding is identical to gilding in book illumination, where a gold sheet is glued against a paper. The other technique adheres the gold leaf directly onto the leather surface; it was used in a pictorial decoration (MIK III 7048).

Paint was also applied to leather codex covers, as seen on a likely remnant of a leather cover (MIK III 7048). This fragment of a thick leather piece—and thus unlikely to have belonged to a parchment scroll—retains a gold leaf in the shape of a crescent halo glued to the surface, as seen in Manichaean book paintings. On this leather piece, black outlines, red and red-violet paints, and gilding are integrated into an image in the manner of Manichaean book painters. Undoubtedly, any pictorial decoration would be much more vulnerable and significantly less durable on the surface of a book cover than inside the book. If this painting was indeed on the surface of a book cover, then it must have been supplemented with a protective device, such as a cut layer of leather framing the units of the painting applied on top of the painted surface. Additional cloth wrappings may have been used as well to protect the gilded leather covers.

The Making of Illuminated Hand Scrolls and Pustakas

Both scroll and pustaka were favored in mediaeval East Central Asia, although these two book formats are distinct in appearance, primary context of use, and origin. Their mere existence alongside the dominant codex format for Manichaean illuminated manuscripts is unique to Turfan. A variety of codicological, scribal, and pictorial features connect the scroll and pustaka fragments with the illuminated codex fragments, confirming that all three formats were fully integrated in Turfan Manichaean book art. Despite their formal and technical integration, the small number of the surviving scrolls and pustakas seem to indicate a rather limited use of these types of books for specific, well-defined Manichaean purposes.

Hand Scrolls

Scrolls have a long documented history in the Manichaean tradition. A secondary datum is available already from fourth-century West Asia, in which the Syrian bishop, Ephrem Syrus (who died in 373 CE) records how Mani himself used a scroll:

> According to some of his disciples, Mani also illustrated the figures of his ... doctrine, ... using pigments on a scroll.... He accordingly states: *I have written them* [the teachings] *in books and illustrated them in colors. Let the one who hears about them verbally, also see them in visual forms; and the one who is unable to learn them from* [words] *learn them from pictures.* (Refutations 122.31–127.11)[27]

---

[27] Reeves 1997, 262–263.

By the time of Mani (216–276 CE), the codex format had started to be preferred more and more for texts in West Asia, although scrolls were still dominant for textual and pictorial purposes.[28] Most likely the painted horizontal scroll became traditional within Manichaean circles following its use by Mani, and subsequently remained in fashion until the mediaeval period in Manichaean Turfan.[29]

Although documented in significantly fewer fragments than codices, the hand scroll is the second most frequently employed artistic format, used for illuminated letters and pictorial books in Manichaean Turfan. Six single-sided painted and/or illuminated fragments of varying sizes and states of preservation are interpreted as remnants of scrolls. They include three fragments of pictorial scrolls each with a series of framed scenes, two remains of illuminated letters written as formulaic greetings between high-ranking church officials, and one well-preserved textual scroll with a graffito at its end. No fragments of silk scrolls are found among the remains. The one painted silk fragment (MIK III 6275) that was initially thought to have possibly derived from a silk scroll[30] is now confirmed to have been part of a hanging scroll-like painted textile, based on its warp alignment.[31] Since neither silk nor parchment scrolls are known from Manichaean Turfan, the discussion below is limited to the structures and sizes of paper scrolls.

Structure of Scrolls

Manichaean scrolls from Turfan are long strips of paper that are stored in rolled-up fashion, as scrolls are in other cultures. To access the content, only a relatively small portion of the complete scroll (an approximately shoulder-wide section held in the hands of a person or rolled out on a table) is exposed at a time, while the rest of the manuscript is rolled up. This manner of access is employed for both textual and pictorial scrolls, despite the divergent orientation of the two. In Manichaean Turfan, the pictorial scrolls are horizontal, with their contents arranged from right to left, whereas the textual scrolls are vertical, with their lines distributed from top to bottom. Their length varied greatly, as indicated even by the two more or less intact examples, whose complete lengths are respectively 10 times and 46 times their widths (Ch. 0015, Figure 5/22; and 80 TB 65: 01, Figure 5/23).

Unlike the case of silk, the nature of both paper and parchment production necessitates the joining of pre-manufactured standard units of material in order to reach the desired length. Among the six artistic Manichaean scroll fragments, three preserve the adjoined sections of their paper. They all contain overlaps, measuring between 0.1 and 0.3 cm, in which the subsequent section of the paper is tacked beneath the end of the previous unit. The ca. 260 cm long Sogdian illuminated letter (81 TB 65:01, Figure 5/23) contains six roughly equally cut sections (ca. 42 cm) glued to one another, in addition to the shorter pictorial insert (ca. 17 cm). Across or beneath the joins and a few adjacent lines are red seals[32] that are stamped over the writing. The location of the stamps exclusively on the joins suggests that their role is to certify that the joins are intact, and that nothing has been surreptitiously removed from the letter in transit. Identical techniques of joining can be seen on the textual scroll with the graffito, but without the use of certifying

---

[28] Since no painted scrolls survive from late antique Roman times, their existence has been deduced from a variety of evidence; this continues to be a subject of debate (Shapiro 1979, 48).

[29] This important subject still awaits detailed investigation.

[30] Le Coq 1913, discussion of plate 4b; Klimkeit 1982a 46. The idea that this composition could have been part of (or copied from) a scroll is supported by a variety of characteristics, which make the image analogous to fragments of pictorial hand scrolls in terms of overall composition and size.

[31] As confirmed by the textile analysis of Barbara Schröter, the textile specialist of the MIK, this silk contains 32 paired warps and 29 single wefts. In contrast to our expectation, the warps are oriented vertically with respect to the painting. Vertical warps mean that if this silk indeed belonged to a scroll, then that scroll was oriented vertically, with its scenes painted beneath one another. Since no such layout is documented from Manichaean Turfan, it is most likely that this textile was some version of a hanging scroll (Gulácsi 2001a, 174, note 231).

[32] On the subject of Manichaean seals, see Sundermann 1985b and 1996, 103.

seals (Ch. 0015, Figure 5/22), and on one of the pictorial scroll fragments (MIK III 4975, Figure 5/25).

Pictorial inserts of letter scrolls survive in two instances. They are distinct from the regular adjoined sections in both joining technique and function. In the well-preserved Sogdian letter (81 TB 65:01, Figure 5/23), we can observe how an already inscribed scroll was cut between its lines 25 and 26, and a painted section was glued in between the cut edges. As evidence that no space had originally been left for an insert between the lines of the text, the paper with the painting is adhered by its edges beneath lines of text. An analogous pictorial insert survives on the other illuminated letter fragment (MIK III 4614, Figure 5/24), where only bits of the vanished text can be detected adjacent to the overlapping layers of the paper along what remains from the rest of the scroll. In both cases, the function of the patching is to add an originally independent painting to the letter scroll. The solution of combining a pictorial and a textual area by cutting the text into two and gluing the desired addition between the cut edges combines the works of two craftsmen (a scribe and an illuminator), confirming that the two were indeed distinct, working in separate environments, somewhat isolated from one another. Judging from the content of the pictorial inserts, it is possible that a stack of such paintings were stored ready to be used in the scriptoria of the highest-ranking leaders of the Manichaean church.[33]

The basic accessories of Turfan Manichaean scrolls may have included rollers and protective covers. It seems that at least the longer scrolls were rolled with the aid of a wooden roller, as suggested by one example. At the end of the long textual scroll with the graffito (Ch. 0015, Figure 5/22), the paper was gradually narrowed to a trapezoid-shaped cut. This end was wrapped around and adhered to a rod, which became the core of the roll.[34] In this case, the original rod is preserved as a roughly carved piece of wood that is ca. 11 cm long and less than 1 cm in diameter. No roller was attached to the other relatively well preserved shorter scroll of the illuminated letter (81 TB 65:01, Figure 5/23). It is possible that textile or reed-based woven protective covers were wrapped around the scrolls, as suggested by examples discovered in Dunhuang,[35] although no protective covers have been identified in association with Manichaean scrolls.

Size Variety of Scrolls

Undoubtedly, the six surviving scroll fragments do not constitute a representative sample of the full variety of formal qualities. They nevertheless allow us to form a basic understanding regarding Turfan Manichaean scroll sizes. Since data on their lengths is not available, the size categories discussed below are based on their widths, which, just like their script sizes and line distances, are comparable to the corresponding data of codex formatted books—a feature that fully integrates the scrolls with the rest of the Turfan Manichaean corpus. Based on their intact widths, then, the surviving Manichaean illuminated scrolls can be termed small, medium, or large (Figure 3/15 and Table 3/10).

Small scrolls were around 10.0 cm wide. This size category is represented by the textual scroll with a graffito at its end (Ch. 0015, Figure 5/22) that measures 10.5 cm wide. This scroll is dedicated to one Uygur-language text, a formulaic confession of sins, written in ca. 340 Manichaean script lines.[36] The horizontal lines of writing orient this manuscript vertically. The height of the script is 0.4 cm, distributed in lines 1.1 cm apart throughout the 424.0 cm (over 14 feet) long paper surface. Sixteen pieces of paper are spliced together in order to form the scroll, each measuring between 25 and 34 cm.

---

[33] For more on this subject, see Chapters 4 and 5.

[34] Similar thin wooden rods are seen attached to the ends of other scrolls found in Dunhuang. See Giès-Cohen 1995, 74 (No. 38).

[35] Tenth-century silk and reed scroll covers found by the French expedition at Qianfodong are described in Giès-Cohen 1995, 68 (Nos. 33a and 33b).

[36] From this well-preserved text only the first few lines are missing (Asmussen 1965, 193).

Table 3/10. Summary of Size Data on Manichaean Pictorial and Illuminated Scrolls

Elements	Sizes	Small Illuminated Scrolls	Medium Illuminated Scrolls	Large Illuminated Scrolls
Width		Around 9.5 cm	Around 13.0 cm	Around 27.0 cm
Length		430.0 cm	—	263.0 cm
Proportions		46:1	—	10:1
Line Spacing		1.1 cm	—	ca. 2.0 cm
Script Height		0.2 cm	—	0.8 cm
Line Width		8.0 cm	—	Ca. 24.0 cm
Picture Height		1.2 – 3.2 cm	11.7 cm	Over 24.0 cm
Margins (along length)		0.6 – 0.9 cm	0.6 –0.7 cm	1.0 cm

Medium-size scrolls were around 13.0 cm wide. The one fragment that documents this size category preserves its intact width (MIK III 4975, Figure 5/25), measuring 12.7 cm. On this pictorial scroll, the scenes were distributed horizontally, placed next to one another separated by decorative borders and blank sections. Beneath and above the painting, parts of a narrow black margin (0.6 cm) remain visible. It is possible that another, more fragmentary scroll (MIK III 6989 a, Figure 5/27) had a similar size and design. This small, also pictorial scroll fragment preserves three design elements: parts of the blank bottom margin (min. 0.7 cm), the intact height of a decorative border formed by five layers of a border pattern frequently seen in Manichaean illuminated codices (1.5 cm), and a pool motif (originally ca. 1.5 cm high) from the painting itself. The scale of the figures and other motifs and accessories seen on these scrolls is identical to the sizes of the corresponding motifs on Manichaean illuminated codices.

Large scrolls are documented by three examples, whose original width was around 27.0 cm. The best preserved of them is the Sogdian illuminated letter (81 TB 65:01, Figure 5/23), which measures 26.0 cm in width and 268 cm in length. Comparable to this is the more fragmentary illuminated letter (MIK III 4614, Figure 5/24) whose reconstructed width reached ca. 27.5 cm. The similarly large pictorial scroll with the image of the Buddha (MIK III 4947 & III 5 d, Figure 5/26) is reconstructed to have been 27.6 cm in width.

Pustakas

The structure of books in pustaka format is characterized by oblong folia that are placed between wooden covers without permanent binding. The stacked folia are held horizontally in front of the reader. On the top of the stack is the recto page of the first folio. The reader then turns the folio along its horizontal axis upward to access the verso, and starts creating a new stack with the verso pages facing up. In order to keep the folia together, occasionally one or two binding holes are pierced through the page. These holes are isolated within the text area by blank circles. Loose cords lead through the holes to connect the folia, allowing just enough room to turn the pages.

This book format originated in India. The shape of the palm leaf as the preferred material for writing in South Asia had a long-lasting influence on the way manuscripts were written in the Indian subcontinent and areas under India's cultural influence.[37] The pages of such books can be made from a variety of materials such as palm leaves, bronze plates, and paper.[38] Since palm leaf is the original material associated with this

---

[37] *Dictionary of Art* Vol. 20, 327.
[38] Losty 1982, 8–10.

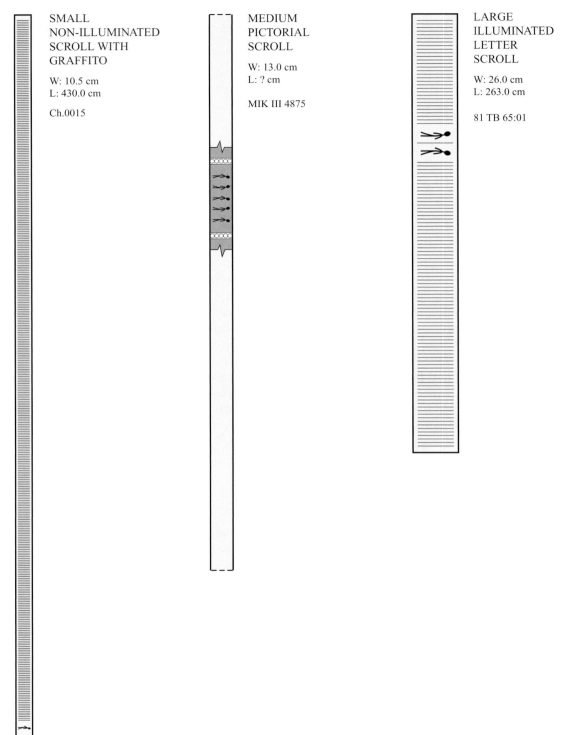

SMALL
NON-ILLUMINATED
SCROLL WITH
GRAFFITO

W: 10.5 cm
L: 430.0 cm

Ch.0015

MEDIUM
PICTORIAL
SCROLL

W: 13.0 cm
L: ? cm

MIK III 4875

LARGE
ILLUMINATED
LETTER
SCROLL

W: 26.0 cm
L: 263.0 cm

81 TB 65:01

Figure 3/15. Documented Sizes of Turfan Manichaean Illuminated Scrolls

book design, it has been referred to by the Sanskrit term *pustaka* (book) or the Hindi *pothi* (book). Although in earlier literature Central Asian books of this format were referred to by the modern Hindi word,[39] the term *pustaka* may be preferred here for its temporal closeness to the object under discussion.[40]

Within the corpus of Manichaean art, there is only one illuminated pustaka book, possibly dated to the early tenth century (see Chapter 2). It retains approximately a third of the original manuscript, which was an anthology of Manichaean literature adorned with a full-page painting as the frontispiece of the book (MIK III 8260, Figure 5/28). This pustaka book measures 6 cm in height and 21.5 cm in width. Five lines of Manichaean script writing are spaciously distributed on each page. The script height reaches 0.4 cm and the line spacing is 1.1 cm. These measurements are comparable to the writing seen on large illuminated codices.

The integration of the unusual pustaka shape with the usual characteristics of Manichaean book art within this manuscript suggests an atmosphere of craftsmanship open to innovations. It is possible that the patron's preference influenced the choice of a characteristically Buddhist book format and the Chinese style painting at the beginning of the book. Both features are unique among the remains of Turfan Manichaean book art.

No protective covers are preserved with this manuscript. Nevertheless, the location of a full-page book painting as the frontispiece on the recto of the first folio suggests that in original condition, this book was enclosed within protective wooden boards or cloth wrappers, as seen in modern Buddhist examples.

THE WORK OF THE SCRIBES

Writing texts and adorning them with basic means of decoration was the work of the scribes in Manichaean Turfan. The overall appearance of the texts is identical in plain and illuminated manuscripts. They are arranged in one, two, or occasionally three columns, the widths of which are defined by vertical ruling. Most often the lines within the columns were written without any aid of horizontal ruling, attesting to the skills of these copyists. With utmost care, the texts were written in three scripts: Manichaean, Sogdian, and Runic. Within the overall corpus of Turfan Manichaean manuscripts, scribal decoration is relatively rare. When encountered, it occurs almost exclusively within Manichaean script texts. The amount and complexity of scribal decoration is the highest on the illuminated fragments. These adornments include the use of colored inks, calligraphic letters, and simple decorative motifs.

Ruling

The layout of the page is defined, at least partially, at the first stage of the scribal work, which is ruling. In Turfan Manichaean book art, ruling is used to set the width and length of the columns and the sizes of the adjacent four margins, but it does not indicate any further plan for the decoration of the page. For example, a ruled page contains no indication whether a header is planned for the upper margin, nor does it designate whether the page will have marginal illumination. Most important, the ruling does not signal to the scribe whether the writing of the text will have to be interrupted by leaving room for intratextual or full-page book paintings. At the ruling stage, the layout of illuminated codex pages is identical to the

---

[39] The term *pothi* is used frequently (e.g., in Le Coq 1923, 16; Gabain 1964, 174; Clark 1982; Klimkeit 1982a, 40; Museum für Indische Kunst 1986, 141).
[40] My use of *pustaka* is based on Lore Sander's work (1968, 34).

layout of non-illuminated ones. On all pages the standard ruling pattern varies only in accordance with the dimensions of the page and the number of columns.

The standard ruling pattern of Turfan Manichaean manuscripts consists of vertical markers and only rarely includes additional horizontal aids (Figure 3/16). Vertical ruling marks the two sides as well as the starting and finishing lines of the columns. For this purpose, a relatively thick line drawn in diluted red-violet ink is used; it is often hardly visible or completely faded away on many remains. Such red-violet vertical ruling lines are the only means of ruling on extra small, small, and medium size books, whose texts are written with small and medium size scripts. The ruling begins where the first line of the column is to be located and it ends at the last line of the column. It runs uninterruptedly across the middle of the page even if intracolumnar book paintings are added later. The vertical lines did come in handy for the painters, who placed the bases of the marginal images onto the ruling of the outermost column, carefully avoiding any letter that accidentally hangs into the margin (MIK III 6265 & III 4966 c recto, Figure 3/16a). In intracolumnar scenes, the painter often aligned the upper and lower sections of the image with the ruling of the outer and inner columns of the page (e.g., the Sermon Scene, MIK III 8259 folio 1 recto, Figure 2/3a). Occasionally, horizontal ruling was added to the vertical ruling to assure the straightness of the writing, but this occurs only for medium to large size scripts. For this purpose a graphite-like grey, or the above mentioned red-violet line is employed. On pages with horizontal ruling, the writing may be beneath (MIK III 4976 a, b & S 49, Figure 5/20), or across the ruling lines (MIK III 7285 verso, Figure 3/16b).

One fragment preserves a rejected page with a ruling mistake (MIK III 151, layer 5, back side, Figure 3/16c). This paper-reinforced silk fragment was intended for a silk codex, but due to the ruling mistake was never used for a Manichaean book. It survives reused, as part of the back support in a now-fragmentary Buddhist paper scroll. This silk surface retains four red-violet lines of vertical ruling, indicating that this page was intended for two columns of text. The distribution and execution of ruling, which is identical to the ruling pattern seen on Manichaean codex pages made of paper, confirms that this piece of silk was intended for Manichaean use at one time.[41]

Writing of the Texts

A variety of scripts, languages, and creative means of masterfully executed writing constitutes an important characteristic feature of the Turfan Manichaean remains, attesting to a complex and highly developed literary culture. The most common script is the Manichaean script, which on the illuminated fragments is used for writing Middle Persian, Parthian, Sogdian, and Uygur. The Sogdian script is seen for writing Sogdian and Uygur languages, whereas the rare Runic script is preserved for Uygur language texts only. Although the vast majority of texts on the illuminated fragments are in Manichaean script, 12 are found in Sogdian and 2 in Runic. Within the texts of Turfan Manichaean manuscripts, the three scripts are all written in horizontal lines from right to left. Occasionally, when a figure is identified on a painting (Figure 2/6 and Plates 6b, 7c, and 7e) his or her name is written vertically from head to toe across the garment, or next to the person. The examples feature Manichaean and in one case Sogdian scripts. The practice is frequent on book paintings, and is also employed on Manichaean textiles and wall paintings.

The letters themselves are carefully defined with an even flow of ink in both the smallest and largest script sizes. Miniscule writing, seen on numerous fragments, is further evidence of the skill of the scribes. An example of a minute-size script can be seen on M 559 (Figure 3/8), where the height of an average letter is 1.5 mm; the thickness of the pen was around 0.5 mm.[42]

---

[41] For more discussion and color reproductions see Gulácsi 2001a, pp. 168–169, No. 76.
[42] See Gulácsi 2001a, No. 37; other manuscripts written with a minuscule script include No. 60 (MIK III 104 verso).

a: MIK III 6265 & 4966 c recto, detail with vertical ruling along edge of marginal figural scene

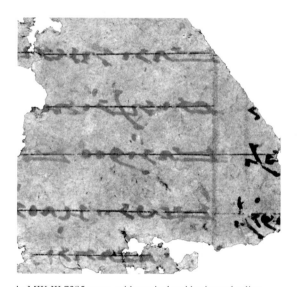

b: MIK III 7285 verso, with vertical and horizontal ruling

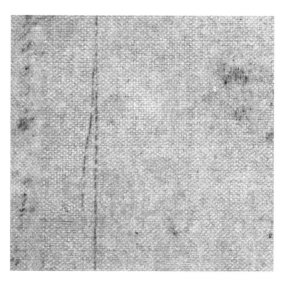

c: MIK III 151 back side, detail of rejected silk sheet with ruling mistake

Figure 3/16. Ruling Documented on Turfan Manichaean Book Fragments
(SMPK, Museum für Indische Kunst, Berlin)

The words may also be written in a stretched manner. Besides the occasional spreading out of the last few words at the end of a column in order to reach the ruling evenly,[43] the entire texts of hymns may be altered by cantillation, which involves rendering a word into phonetic components, separating syllables by horizontal dashes either extending from the bases of the letters or as separate strokes. This way of writing indicates that the text is a hymn, to be sung aloud. This practice proves that some of these illuminated books were used in liturgy. An example of a cantillated text is seen on a reconstructible bifolio (M 797, Figure 5/5a). The spacious and relatively large handwriting (3.8 mm in height, with a space of ca. 1 cm between lines) is in accordance with such practice.[44]

When needed, the scribes must leave larger blank areas within the columns. This occurs either for the later addition of a vernacular translation to a preceding text or to add an intracolumnar book painting. In cases when the manuscript is not finished, the blank area may be found on the surviving fragments of Turfan Manichaean books. Due to their diverse functions, the two gaps are of distinct appearance within the overall page design. A gap left blank for translation begins at the completed end of a passage to be translated, and a new passage begins below it, as seen on a fragment with scribal decoration (M 17). The gaps on this page were left within the Middle Persian language text to be filled in with a vernacular translation, as confirmed by a parallel text.[45] In contrast, the intracolumnar paintings are centered on the page. Above the paintings, the texts in both columns are interrupted in mid-sentence. Beneath them the text continues in each respective column (e.g., MIK III 4974, 6/4). Since no mark on the page indicates the planned illumination, most likely the scribe was orally instructed to leave room for an intracolumnar painting. The same scenario no doubt applies when whole pages are left blank, with the text on the previous page resuming on the page following the one left blank. Signs of such situations seem to be found only at the beginning of the surviving Manichaean books of Turfan.[46]

Supplementing the actual manuscript fragments is a primary visual source that also documents the work of Turfan Manichaean scribes (MIK III 6368 recto, Plate 3). This fragment retains more than a third of the original pictorial content of the image, showing Elects in Scribal Duty. Similar to other Manichaean book paintings, this composition is a stylized rendering of reality. It omits certain elements of the depicted event, while adding imaginary elements appropriate to the subject. The scribes in this scene are male elects, set up to work outside under grape-bearing arbors. Although grape arbors are often seen in the Turfan oasis, the painting most likely shows a stylized setting rather than an actual work area. The neatly arranged trees are analogous to the portrayal of trees in the Manichaean wall painting at Bezeklik.[47] The points of similarity include the straight tree trunks with diverging branches, the round leafy flowers, and the grapes hanging from the crown. Such stylization, however, does not interfere with the presence of descriptively accurate

---

[43] Manichaean script examples of this practice include two illuminated fragments, see Gulácsi 2001a, No. 30 (MIK III 4972 a recto) and No. 19 (MIK III 4976 a recto). The Sogdian script examples can be observed on MIK III 6368 verso (Fig. 5/13b) and on the matched fragments So 18700 & M 501 e verso, (Fig. 5/14b).

[44] The only other example of cantillation within the illuminated corpus is found on MIK III 4967a, above the intracolumnar book painting of the verso of the folio fragment. Although the text is too fragmentary to be identified, its cantillation confirms that it was a hymn, suggesting that the fragment is from an illuminated hymnbook. Here, too, the handwriting is large and spacious (3.8 mm in height, with ca. 1 cm between lines). For color facsimiles and further discussion, see Gulácsi 2001a, 124–125 (No. 53).

[45] MacKenzie 1994, 195. Another example of an uneven gap is found on the recto of MIK III 198, where the Uygur language text of the so-called Argu colophon, similar to the texts on other colophon fragments, continues beneath the gap. Curiously, however, the text here does not need translation because it is already written in the vernacular (personal communication with Larry Clark); also, the area left blank is somewhat larger in the inner column than in the outer column, which is a layout undocumented in any other intracolumnar book painting.

[46] For the discussion of this point, see Chapter 6.

[47] Moriyasu 1991, Pl. 1–2.

visual details.[48] The elects are seated on their heels behind two rows of low desks covered with decorative red, blue, green, and gold cloths. On the desks in front of them are vertically ruled pieces of paper. The inkwells and the lines of writing on the page are omitted. Seated with erect upper bodies, all but two are holding ink-pens. The pointed tip of this writing instrument is accurately portrayed in one pen (seen in the left hand of the fourth figure from the right in the upper row, Plate 3b). Among the seven surviving scribes, three hold two pens. Unlike book paintings in mediaeval Europe that show scribes with a wide-bladed knife used for corrections in their left hand,[49] the Manichaean scribes hold two identical pen-like instruments. A possible explanation for this may be the use of distinct pens for different colors. This practice is confirmed by the measurements of line thickness of letters written in different colors on the same page by the same scribe, which show differences that must be attributed to the use of separate pens. In addition, it is also possible that placing a pen in both hands alludes to an actual copying routine, where the scribes may use a dry pen as a pointer over the original texts in order to eliminate copying mistakes.[50]

Scribal Decoration

A great variety is reached through the creative combination of a few simple methods of scribal decoration in both plain and illuminated Manichaean manuscripts in Turfan. At the core, there are four basic techniques: the use of inks in 6 different colors, the employment of monochrome and multi-colored outline-writing, the inclusion of occasional calligraphic letters, and the drawing of simple motifs to enhance the regular punctuation and diacritical needs of the text. Although these adornments occur mostly in the header, sometimes they are also seen at the starting and ending lines of the page and within the body of the text.

Colored Inks and Gilded Writing

Besides their superb black ink, the scribes of Turfan Manichaean manuscripts used a wide range of colorful inks, including red (i.e., red-orange), violet (i.e., red-violet), blue, green, and gold. At the current stage of research, the material composition of these inks remains unknown.[51] We can only surmise some basic facts, such as the use of some high-quality soot for black ink and powdered gold for gold ink. In addition, letters cut from gold leaves and enhanced with red outlines are also part of the writing repertoire. It is possible, but remains unconfirmed that the pigments within the rest of the inks were most likely identical to the pigments of the paints used in Manichaean book art.[52] It is clear, however, that colorful inks were

---

[48] For a discussion of the documentary value of Turfan Manichaean book painting, see Gulácsi 1997.

[49] Brown 1994, 77 and 114.

[50] Another hypothetical explanation for this Manichaean representation might relate to the workshop practice of the contemporary Irish scribe, Timothy O'Neill. In order to secure the even flow of the ink from his quill-pen, O'Neill does not dip his pen into the ink well directly. Rather, he uses a brush as an intermediary between his ink well and the quill. He dips and squeezes out the extra moisture from the brush, and then he swipes the tip of the quill on the brush. He is thus able to control the evenness of ink. While writing, he holds the brush in his left hand, thereby giving an appearance similar to the one in the Scribal Scene. The consistently even amount of ink observable on Manichaean texts indicates a careful practice, identical or at least very similar to the contemporary one used by O'Neill (Simms 1993).

[51] Personal communication with Prof. Dr. Yaldiz (Museum für Indische Kunst, Berlin). The greatest repertoire of ink colors used in the headers is documented in the quire fragments MIK III 53, discussed by Henning (1937, 4–5). See Fig. 3/1. For a brief discussion of possible paint materials, see Whitfield 2004, 294.

[52] The categories of materials and techniques employed in modern art history, building on primarily European and/or modern data, do not always match up with the actual practice of other cultures. Thus, without actual testing, we can only assume that in Turfan Manichaean book art, the difference between *paints* and *inks* was identical to what is known about them today: paints contain three basic ingredients (pigment, binder, and solvent), whereas inks just two (pigments and solvent). See Mayer 1991, 203–204 and 291.

employed for a variety of practical and decorative purposes in both illuminated and plain manuscripts.

Red ink was chosen most frequently to enhance black ink text in a variety of ways. On a more practical side, it was used to draw circles around the punctuation marks as well as delicate floral motifs within scribal decorations. In addition, red ink was often used for writing. Headers can be red. Within the body of the text, red ink helps to distinguish the captions and highlight the beginning or ending lines.[53] A purely decorative way to introduce color to the page is by writing in alternating sequences of red and black blocks of lines. These occur in great variety. The beginning and ending two or three lines in a column can be red, as can the first lines resuming a text and beneath an intratextual miniature. Another, more complex way to decorate the page is to create a red and black checkered pattern between two or three columns by writing adjacent blocks of 5–8 lines in these two colors.[54]

The other ink colors are used primarily for writing the line of the header across the upper margins of the two facing pages, as seen for example on a well-preserved parchment fragment, where the inner side of the bifolio preserves parts of two headers (MIK III 4990 folio 1[?] verso and folio 2[?] recto, see Plate 1). The two folios originally had other, now-lost pages between them. On the surviving folia, one of the headers is green, on the verso of folio 1(?), and it retains the first half of the original full header that would have read across the full length of the facing pages. A faint impression of some green pigment deposited from the second half of the original header confirms that indeed the now-missing, originally facing page contained the rest of the header in green. The use of five different colors for the headers is documented on the remains of the extra small codex quires remaining of the Bema service-book (MIK III 53, Figure 3/1a), where the content of the pages confirms that headers written continuously across the upper margins of the two facing pages are in a single ink color.[55]

Crysography, writing in gold, is preserved on four illuminated fragments.[56] Examples are seen for both the use of actual gold ink and lines of letters cut from gold foil. Similar to red ink, gold ink may be used in the headers of lavishly illuminated pages, just as in the two first lines of the page. Gold ink is seen on two fragments within the illuminated corpus. One contains a gold ink header (MIK III 4983 recto, Figure3/2b, Plate 4b), in which the body of the letters are outlined in red ink. The only other surviving example contains parts of the first two lines of the page (MIK III 4969 folio 1[?] recto, Plate 4a). Due to the nature of the technique, letters cut from thin gold sheets are used for the larger scripts, mainly in the headers. In such gilded headers, geometric shapes resembling the letters themselves are cut and glued to the paper, as seen on one folio fragment that retains only bits from a once lavishly illuminated header (MIK III 6258b recto[?], Plate 4c). The pointy tip of an 'ain ('), most of the loop from a "y," and the elongated horizontal baseline of a "k" are still preserved from the Manichaean script header.[57] An intact version of the very same technique is employed in the vertical inscription found in the Sogdian letter scroll's pictorial insert (81 TB 65:01, Figure 6/5). Here, too, the letters are outlined in red ink, the practice of which is observed on all surviving examples of gold writing.

---

[53] Red ink to write the beginning or ending lines of the page can be seen, e.g., on MIK III 4974 verso, Fig. 5/8b; and MIK III 8259 folio 1(?), Fig. 5/7a–b; full-stops in red are seen e.g. on MIK III 4974 recto, Fig. 5/8a.

[54] This can be best observed in the texts of three illuminated fragments: on MIK III 36, Fig. 5/11a; MIK III 4979, Fig. 5/9; and MIK III 8259 folio 1(?), Fig. 5/7.

[55] Since the quire remains are stored under glass, I relied on Henning's publication of the fragment in 1936. Henning established the order of the folio based on the textual content, and at the same time conformed the color sequence of headers—an important rule of scribal decoration and Manichaean codicology (1936, 4–8).

[56] An additional, non-illuminated Manichaean codex fragment with gold writing in both of its headers is M 798d.

[57] BeDuhn 2001, No. 16.

Monochrome and Multicolored Outline Writing

Outline writing is an effective way to set the headers apart from the rest of the text on the page. In this decorative writing, the letters are larger, ca. two or two and a half times the size of the regular script. Their shapes remain identical to the usual version except that they are all defined by contour lines. A simple version of this is done in one color, as documented on the two sides of one folio fragment (MIK III 4970b recto, Plate 4d). In this case, the contours of the letters are captured in black ink.[58] A more complex version is present on a larger group of illuminated fragments, almost exclusively within their headers.[59] In that case, the letters are conveyed by two sets of two ink colors, introducing a sense of space as if the letters were not two-, but rather three-dimensional. In the finished calligraphy, each letter is outlined in two parts. The outer half of the letter is written with a red colored line, and the inner half with a green colored line (MIK III 4969 outer side[?], Plate 4e). In the red portion, a thin, intense red line is covered over by a thicker, diluted version of the same ink. In the green portion, a thin black line is covered over by a thicker, diluted green line. The combination of these two colors is present in all letters, occasionally alternating between their inner and outer parts (M 857 recto[?], Plate 4f). On one example of such a header, surviving from the largest known illuminated codex folio, blue ink is used instead of the green (MIK III 6377a recto[?], Plate 4g).

A slight three-dimensionality is captured in this way of writing compared to the rest of the writing on the page. A sense of depth is introduced to the flat page surface in two ways. On the one hand, each of the doubled lines creates an impression of modeling, as if the body of the letters themselves were made of something three-dimensional, such as the rounded surface of rope. This effect is achieved by using a thinner line (black and red) of a more intense color compared to the thicker translucent line drawn on top of the thinner one (green or rarely blue over the black, and orange over the red). On the other hand, the overlapping components of certain letters introduce an additional way to create the impression that some parts of the letters are closer to the viewer than others. When the contour-defined "lines" of such a letter intersect, one is depicted as covering the other, as seen for example in a Manichaean 's' (MIK III 4969 inner side[?], Plate 4e). The first part, the triangular part, of the letter covers the area where the second, hooked portion of the letter begins. A similar sense of space is also alluded to on the monochrome example (MIK III 4970b recto, Plate 4c) where the first fully visible letter, a Manichaean "h," is rendered with a flat top, captured as if the viewer was looking down onto it from a high horizon.

Calligraphic Letters

Calligraphy, or "beautiful writing," is a term used frequently in connection with mediaeval book art. Most often it evokes the basic artistry associated with the handwriting of scribes, who then are referred to as calligraphers. Indeed, the highest quality of handwriting is a standard feature on most remains of both plain and illuminated Turfan Manichaean manuscripts. To distinguish the general execution of letters from extraordinary ways of writing, I restrict the use of calligraphy here for connoting only the writing of artistically enhanced letters. In Turfan Manichaean book art, individual, calligraphic letters are included within the words of the headers written with letters of regular shape. As suggested by the identical handwriting seen on different parts of the page, the very same scribe who wrote the rest of the text on the page

---

[58] One fragment, M 1887, documents that during the initial stage a light grey underdrawing was used, which would not be visible in the completed version. It is possible that this unfinished header was part of a practice folio (Gulácsi 2001a, No. 12).

[59] The only surviving exception to this is a caption written against a blue background within a column (MIK III 4979 recto, Fig. 4/8).

executed the headers together with their few calligraphic letters. This fact, among numerous others, attests to the exceptional skills of these scribes, who were indeed calligraphers.

The presence of calligraphy in Turfan Manichaean art is confined by three conditions: specific script, specific letters, and specific locations. The script elaborated is always the Manichaean script. The two other scripts used in Turfan Manichaean books, Sogdian and Runic, are not modified in this way. This fact seems to attest to the West Asian source of this art. The letters best suited for being decorated this way are often the letters with open and possibly long stems such as "g," "t," and "l" (Figure 3/17), in addition to the letters "a," "v" (= b with 2 dots), "ch," "h," and "sh." Calligraphic letters are employed primarily in the headers, but occasionally we do find them as the first letter of the page.

In terms of execution, Turfan Manichaean calligraphy is dramatic. Calligraphic letters are always enlarged, usually by 3–5 times, but occasionally as much as 10 times the size of the regular version of the same let-ter on the page. While they maintain the recognizable shapes of ordinary letters, they always incorporate elongated stems that reach into the blank area of the upper and side margins, often in a striking manner, sharply contrasting with the regular monotony of the handwriting within the rest of the header and espe-cially on the rest of the page.[60] This can be seen for instance on the parchment bifolio MIK III 4990 (Fig-ure 3/17a and Plate 1), where the first letter of the header, a Manichaean "g," stretches downward in a diagonal line along the outer margin beyond even the third line of the column (Figure 3/17a), and to the second line (Plate 1). A similar calligraphic dynamism is found on another bifolio fragment (M 7981, Fig-ure 3/17b) where the letter "h" gives the scribe the opportunity to reach with a diagonal stroke down-ward to the left, to the outer margin.

Punctuation Decoration and other Scribal Ornaments

Occasionally, simple decorative motifs are added to the writing as textual accessories in both illuminated and plain Turfan Manichaean manuscripts. Conveyed in red, blue, and/or black inks, three basic motifs are encountered most frequently on otherwise non-illuminated pages in both illuminated and non-illumi-nated manuscripts.

The simplest of scribal ornaments are red circles around the marks of punctuation, which may occur as single or double dots (e.g., MIK III 4990, Plate 1; and MIK III 4981a, line 3, Plate 3). These circles are often used in pairs drawn close to one another, each surrounding one of the two black dots placed at mid height of the script at the end of a sentence. The circles are relatively small. Their height stays below the height of the script.

The floral diacritical marks are found around the headers. These consist of a few curving lines arranged in a manner to resemble petals to form the diacritical marks. Since they are used along the upper margin, sometimes around the enlarged calligraphic letters of the header, they stick out through their relative iso-lation compared to the rest of the densely written text of the page, as seen for instance on the parchment folio (e.g., MIK III 4990, Figure 3/17a), and other examples of headers of non-illuminated paper folia (M 7981, Figure 3/17b; M 7984, Figure 3/17c; and M 4a, Figure 3/17d). In addition to floral diacritics, often the corner of the calligraphic letters as well as the beginning and the end of the complete line of the headers are decorated with such simple floral motifs. Being improvised by the scribes, the number of pet-als and their overall arrangements vary.

A somewhat more ornate means of scribal decoration is the use of tapering floral motifs before and after the captions marking the beginning or end of texts in the body of the columns (M 797 detail, Figure 3/18a;

---

[60] The five examples of calligraphic letters found in the headers of illuminated manuscripts are M 576 recto, M 233 recto and verso, M 797 folio 2(?) verso, MIK III 4983, and MIK III 4981 b.

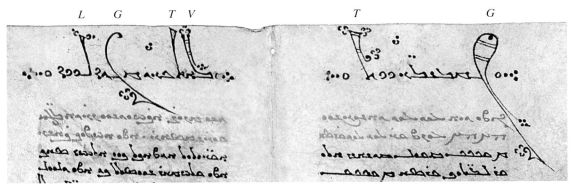

a: MIK III 4990 outer side, detail

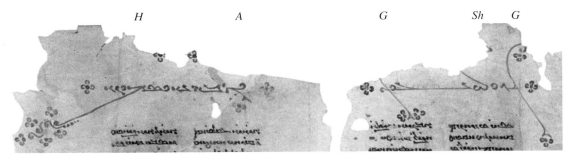

b: M 7981 outer side, folio 1 recto & folio 2 verso, detail

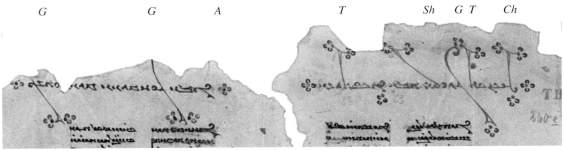

c: M 7984 outer side, folio 1 recto & folio 2 verso, detail

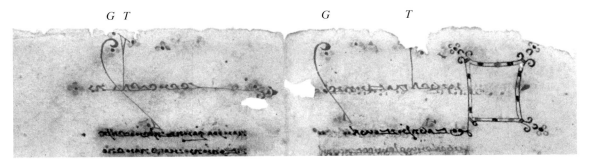

d: M 4a outer side, folio 1 recto & folio 2 verso, detail

Figure 3/17. Examples of Calligraphy and Scribal Decoration
(SMPK, Museum für Indische Kunst, Berlin; and SBPK, Berlin-Brandenburgische
Akademie der Wissenschaften, Turfanforschung, Berlin)

a: M 797 folio 1(?) recto, detail of text area
with floral motif

b: M 279 recto, detail of upper margin
with abstract design

c: M 403 verso, detail of outer margin
with abstract design

d: M 411, M 427, & M 5391 verso, detail
of outer margin with abstract design

e: M 4a folio 1(?) verso, detail of outer
margin with abstract design

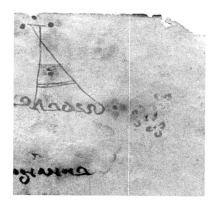

f: M 4b folio 1(?) verso, detail of
upper margin with abstract design

Figure 3/18. Examples of Scribal Decoration
(SBPK, Berlin-Brandenburgische Akademie der Wissenschaften, Turfanforschung, Berlin)

MIK III 4990 detail, Figure 3/17a; and M 171 folio 1(?) recto, Figure 5/4a). The first of these motifs, to the right of the caption (i.e., preceding it), gradually widens to the script height. The second, placed symmetrically at the end of the caption, gradually narrows from the height of the script to a point. One example of this is seen on an illuminated bifolio, where the ornaments are placed at the beginning and at the end of two red lines of a caption that identifies the melody to which the hymn was to be sung.[61]

The one additional type of scribal decoration in this book art may be labeled as abstract designs. These are ink drawings created in association with the very first letter of the page and occasionally around select letters of the headers. Although simple, these decorations are creative compositions, examples of which include variations of curving and swirling motifs closely related to the shapes of their letters (M 297 verso detail, Figure 3/18b;[62] M 403 verso detail, Figure 3/18c; and M 411 & M 427 & M 5391 verso detail, Figure 3/18d) and geometrical motifs, whose shapes are more independent from the letters they are attached to. Such geometrical shapes are seen in a rectangle with slightly concave sides that emerge from the vertical stem of a letter "ch" (M 4a detail, Figure 3/18e) and a triangle that spreads above the first word of its header, which reads "completed" (M 4b, Figure 3/18f).[63]

Conclusion

Despite the torn condition of these sources, the above codicological study has revealed a significant amount of evidence on the technical aspects of Turfan Manichaean book culture, together with the overall sequence of work produced by a variety of artisans. The process of production started with the bookmakers, who measured, cut, and adjoined (if so needed) the writing surfaces, transforming them from the already manufactured paper, silk, or parchment into writing surfaces in sheets and/or rolls. The preliminary nature of this kind of work is documented by numerous codex and scroll fragments that retain the traces of the bookmakers' work beneath the writing. The scribes supplied the ruling and wrote the texts, often adorning them with basic means of textual decoration. Although ruling and writing are both basic scribal tasks, they seem to represent a collaborative effort of scribes with different skills and ranks. Calligraphy and scribal decoration on the same page seem to have been produced by the scribe who also took care of writing the texts. After the scribes' work was accomplished, the illuminators took over. That illumination was added subsequent to text copying is indicated by the illuminators carefully avoiding the occasional bits of letters hanging into the area of their paintings. As we shall see, the illuminator's task was to embellish the calligraphic headers with decorative designs and to paint figural scenes—smaller ones along the outer margins and more complex intracolumnar and full-page images on surfaces left blank for them by the scribes. It seems that, at the very end of the process, the bookmakers took care of binding the manuscripts according to the needs of their specific formats.

The codicological data gathered here is specific to a ca. 300-year-long era of Manichaean book culture, which is tied to the Uygur patronage of the church in the Turfan region. There, too, the activities of the Manichaean church heavily relied on book production as the most important artistic medium, just as documented by al-Jahiz in West Asia. In his writings about the Manichaeans, the Muslim historian (cited at the beginning of this chapter) emphasized how lavishly the Manichaean community he knew in early ninth century Baghdad spent its resources on purchasing the best quality paper and ink, and commissioning the most accomplished scribes.[64] In Turfan, the Manichaeans had a chance to spend even more lavishly on

---

[61] BeDuhn 2001, No. 13.

[62] The recto of M 279 also retains evidence of vertical splicing. To the right of the text, the now departed spliced folio (which also contained the lower tip of the calligraphic letter "G") has revealed a glue strip.

[63] Boyce 1975,161.

[64] For the citation from al-Jahiz's *Kitab al-hayawan* (Arnold 1936, 1817), see the first page of this chapter.

importing good quality raw materials such as ink, paper, and silk from China, and gold and lapis lazuli from neighboring regions of Central Asia. Yet spending on scribes and bookmakers would not have been possible, because prior to the appearance of the Manichaeans, book production was little known in East Central Asia. Therefore, it is reasonable to assume that the Manichaean community established local book production centers that were directly linked to them, perhaps initially drawing skilled personnel from the church's West Asian institutions. It is possible that in addition to lay people, some members of the elect specialized in bookmaking and scribal work, as suggested by a Turfan Manichaean book painting that depicts Elects in Scribal Duty (MIK III 6368 recto, Plate 3).

Furthermore, the above codicological data recovered from the remains of Turfan Manichaean book culture is essential for contextualizing the Turfan evidence in light of the better-known history of West Asian and, to a lesser degree, East Asian book art. This material provides some essential missing links in the history of the development and transmission of traditions of book production and illumination across Asia. The Manichaeans were not only receivers of these arts, but evidently innovators in them as well. The task of future studies will be not only exploring the more than 1000-year history of Manichaean book art, but also gaining an understanding of how the Manichaeans contributed to the formation of the mediaeval book art shared by Jewish, Christian, and Islamic communities in mediaeval West and Central Asia.

CHAPTER FOUR

THE WORK OF THE ILLUMINATOR: THE FOUR BASIC PAINTING STYLES OF TURFAN MANICHAEAN BOOK ILLUMINATION

While any previous understanding of Manichaean codicology has been prevented by the fragmentary condition of the remains, an appreciation of Manichaean book illumination has been present from the earliest stages of scholarship. Bits surviving from Manichaean book paintings had been noted as the remains of a superb mediaeval pictorial tradition. Indeed, the exquisite details associated with the work of the illuminator can be observed on intact portions of larger book paintings, such as the one illustrated here (MIK III 4979 verso, Plate 7b). Being a close-up to the central right part of a full-page painting with a male elect raising a book to his chin, this well-preserved section of a larger image allows us to admire the work of the illuminator—from at least a 1000-year distance. The original size of the enlarged area illustrated is ca. 3.8 cm high and 2.7 cm wide. Within the red contour of the face, violet tint defines the cheeks. The black facial hair along the cheek and the mustache are indicated through the thinnest lines of Manichaean book painting. The miniscule scale of representation seen here is impressive, especially deriving from an age without magnification and artificial light. The gold leaf is glued beneath the surrounding layer of powdered lapis lazuli paint. Although the materials, techniques, and quality displayed here are present on the vast majority of the remains, some other Manichaean book paintings display distinctly different styles of illumination, thus suggesting a complex history worthy of an art historical study.

In order to gain a general understanding about the work of book illuminators preserved among the remains of Turfan Manichaean manuscripts, a necessary step is to identify and describe the basic technical trends ("styles") that have not been recognized before. The pictorial analysis presented here defines four distinctly different Turfan Manichaean style groups. Through the introduction of comparative visual sources, it becomes clear that the roots of two Manichaean styles are West Asian, while the other two are Chinese. A detailed survey will demonstrate that these styles differ in their basic character and application. The painters of the West Asian tradition mainly concerned themselves with manuscript illumination (98 fragmentary paintings document their work). The ones trained in the Chinese tradition mostly worked with textiles and wall surfaces (13 such pictorial fragments are known) and left behind only a few book paintings (2 manuscripts fragments have been found).

The interpretation of this art historical data in light of historical sources results in new views regarding how pictorial art developed in Turfan between the mid eighth and early eleventh centuries. Until now it has been thought that an earlier "Persian" and a later Chinese style dominated Manichaean art, just as the arts of Buddhist East Central Asia. Although only four codex fragments can be dated securely from one of the West Asian style groups (see Chapter 2), I suggest that definite time parameters can be determined for the use of these painting styles in Manichaean Turfan, in light of their stylistic and contextual relation to the dated book fragments and historical evidence. By demonstrating that the West Asian roots ruled the traditional media of Uygur Manichaean art until the early eleventh century, this study eliminates a fossilized assumption within the history of East Central Asian art. But before looking into the details of what survives from the art of the book painters in Manichaean Turfan, the special terminology used here must be clarified.

The term "West Asian" refers to the "Persian" roots of Uygur Manichaean art. "West Asian" is a con-

venient compromise between "Iranian," "Mesopotamian," and "Persian," all of which can be only partially justified. We could use "Iranian," since most Uygur Manichaean pictorial art is found in manuscripts
written in Iranian languages (Middle Persian, Sogdian, and Parthian). We could select "Mesopotamian,"
because Mani (216–276) was active in mid third century Mesopotamia and, as documentary sources confirm, he himself painted the *Picture-Book* for which he must have employed a painting style popular in his
culture. Since the use of Mani's *Picture-Book* (most certainly copies of it) is documented throughout the
Manichaean world, we can rightfully assume that this lost Mesopotamian painted work influenced the
later formation of Manichaean art. A reason for "Persian" may be supported by the fact that Uygur Manichaean illuminations show stylistic connections with later, Islamic Persian book art—as noted in numerous publications. The origin of what I call here the "West Asian" style Uygur Manichaean art, however,
is not Persian. Rather, it derives from the amalgamation of a variety of West Asian artistic traditions that
existed during late antiquity and early mediaeval times but by now are lost or little documented. This varied West Asian cultural environment with its Semitic, Greek, and Iranian components is also the birth-
place of Manichaeism.

The designation "Chinese" for roots of two other groups of Uygur Manichaean art is due to their stylistic relationship with Chinese pictorial art of the Tang and Song dynasties. As we shall see, the use of
Chinese styles by the Manichaeans in the Turfan region, possibly already prior to the mid ninth century,
resulted from the intense cultural ties of the Uygur ruling elite with Tang China. Furthermore, after the
fall of the Uygur Steppe Empire (841 CE) and the resettling of two Manichaean clans of the Uygurs in the
Tian Shan region and east of Dunhuang, local and "imported" Chinese artists contributed to the creation
of these works of art.

The term "style" also requires some clarification due to the wide range of its possible connotations. While
in general style always connotes a variety of artistic elements that together constitute a manner of expression, depending on one's research interest, this manner of expression can be narrowed to that of an individual, widened to include a group of contemporaneous artists, or extended to encompass generations of
artists who worked in a similar fashion during an entire era.[1] To fit the nature of the Uygur Manichaean
material, the working definition of "style" used here is the most inclusive. Restrained by the fragmentary
condition and the limited number of sources, the defining criteria is based on the materials and techniques
employed by generations of painters, in addition to which motifs, compositional characteristics, and a variety of Uygur Manichaean media displaying similar characteristics will be considered.

Although style is one of the foci of this investigation, an understanding of the styles is not the ultimate goal
here. The study of painting styles is used here as a tool for extracting information from the remains regarding
the circumstances of their creation. Since documentary writings on Uygur Manichaean art are not available, we
are left with primary artistic materials as our only sources of evidence. Analyzing this art according to materials
and techniques, motifs, composition, and context of use enables us to assess workshop practices, visual thinking,
and the professional ties of the painters to West and East Asian pictorial traditions. The stylistic and contextual relationship of these paintings to the carbon-dated book painting (MIK III 8259 folio 1(?) recto, Figure
2/3a) helps us to confirm that the use of the two traditions was simultaneous—an art historical piece of
evidence for the multi-cultural character of the Turfan Manichaean community.

THE WEST ASIAN FULLY PAINTED STYLE

In the quest to define the style observed in the paintings of the four dated codex fragments (MIK III 8259,
Figure 2/3a; MIK III 6265 & III 4966c, Figure 2/3b; MIK III 6284, Figure 2/3c; and MIK III 4979,

---

[1] *McGraw-Hill Dictionary of Art* 1969, Vol. 5, 250.

Figure 2/4) and numerous other comparable examples of Uygur Manichaean art, I searched for traits of craftsmanship apparent in the four areas of materials and techniques, motif repertoire, composition, and context of use. Among these, the materials and techniques proved to be the most distinctive, since they are clearly recognizable on 66 Manichaean paintings that are also connected through reoccurring motifs, compositional qualities, and context of use. Their shared visual language documents the painters' common training experience. While some painters were contemporaries working side by side, others no doubt belonged to subsequent generations of the same workshop. In either case, a specific painting style is displayed in their works.

Materials and Techniques

Due to the varying degrees of surface damage that exposes the stratigraphy of the paintings, we can observe that the painting program incorporated five layers that roughly correspond with the stages of the work: underdrawing, gilding, painting, detailing, and supplying the blue background. For the underdrawing an ink-pen and diluted red-violet or grey ink was used. For the gilding the gold leaves were cut with straight edges. In order to reach the desired form of gilded motifs the artist had to paint the blue background over the edges of the gold leaf and draw definition onto its surface. For painting, paints and brushes were needed. The paints were composed of mineral pigments and an organic binder.[2] The illuminators' favored color-set consisted of at least nine hues. These included red, red-violet, and blue, which were frequently employed together with their tints or shades, and were supplemented with black and white. Only occasionally, green, yellow, and brown completed the palette. On the surface of the paint and the gold leaf, essential details were drawn by ink-pens and painted with a brush. At the very last stage, the painter often applied a blue background, filling in the blank areas and framing the composition in a blue rectangle.

To illustrate these characteristics, a section of a decorative design and a figural composition are presented in Figure 4/1. The decorative design derives from the upper margin of a codex folio, MIK III 6258 b (Figure 4/1a), where bits from the header's large gilded letters are retained above the remnants of leaves, scarves, and gilded disks painted against a blank background. Identical painting technique and materials were used in the carbon-dated painting, from which the upper right section is enlarged in Figure 4/1b. Since most of the white coating on the elect's body has flaked off, we can observe how the underdrawing defined the basic contours of the seated form. Originally, no areas were left blank. Even the exposed body parts (hands, neck, and face) received a layer of paint. The surface of the paint was further treated, as seen on the lotus petals and the remaining patches of the figure's face and robe. The varying thicknesses of these lines (e.g., underdrawing of the body, facial features, and folds of robe) indicate that the illuminator employed several pens, each with a distinctly sized tip. The now uneven edges of the blue background around the figure resulted from the flaking off of the white paint that was slightly overlapped by the blue.

Motifs

Looking through the 68 fragmentary paintings that document this style, a large body of motifs and their components become familiar to us. Their digitally cut sections are placed side by side for an easy survey (Figure 4/1). Despite shared characteristics, clearly, different hands executed them. Our concern here is neither their meaning nor their origin, but rather the way they were depicted.

---

[2] A preliminary analysis that aimed to verify the mineral content of the pigments used on MIK III 4983 (Fig. 3/3b and Plate 4b) confirmed the presence of protein in the paint (personal communication with Joseph Riederer, Rathgen-Forschungslabor, Berlin).

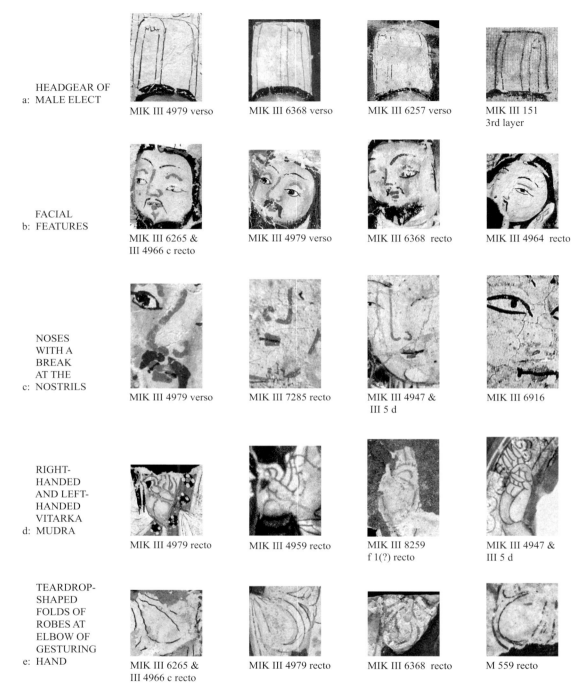

HEADGEAR OF
a: MALE ELECT

MIK III 4979 verso   MIK III 6368 verso   MIK III 6257 verso   MIK III 151 3rd layer

FACIAL
b: FEATURES

MIK III 6265 & III 4966 c recto   MIK III 4979 verso   MIK III 6368 recto   MIK III 4964 recto

NOSES
WITH A
BREAK
AT THE
c: NOSTRILS

MIK III 4979 verso   MIK III 7285 recto   MIK III 4947 & III 5 d   MIK III 6916

RIGHT-
HANDED
AND LEFT-
HANDED
VITARKA
d: MUDRA

MIK III 4979 recto   MIK III 4959 recto   MIK III 8259 f 1(?) recto   MIK III 4947 & III 5 d

TEARDROP-
SHAPED
FOLDS OF
ROBES AT
ELBOW OF
GESTURING
e: HAND

MIK III 6265 & III 4966 c recto   MIK III 4979 recto   MIK III 6368 recto   M 559 recto

Figure 4/1. West Asian Fully Painted Style of Uygur Manichaean Art: Samples of Reoccurring Motifs (I)

The samples related to the depiction of the human figure begin with the headgear (Figure 4/1a) worn by most male elects. This tall, white hat has a wide flat front and narrower sides, at the top of which the cloth is slightly gathered. The depiction of the human face (Figure 4/1b) also follows a routine. The outer contour of the faces, the eyelids, the noses, the mouths, and the chins are always in red; the eyebrows, the eye contours with the pupils, and the mustaches are always in black. The bridge of the nose and the nostrils (Figure 4/1c) are drawn with two separate lines, often with an actual gap between them. A hand gesture, similar to the Buddhist *vitarka mudra* (Figure 4/1d), is assumed with both right and left hands in Manichaean art.[3] In both versions, the index finger and the thumb are touching and the divisions of the palm are captured. While gesturing, the figure's bent arm is held to the side or in front of the body (Figure 4/1e). The folds of the robe over the bent elbows include a characteristic teardrop shape defined by double contours.

Decorative details also incorporate standard elements. Halos (Figure 4/2a) often contain a middle band formed by a sequence of squares, each with a dot or a circle in its center. The very same pattern arranged in straight layers is occasionally used to frame miniatures. The nimbuses of religious dignitaries and heavenly beings may contain a crescent rim (Figure 4/2b). Such crescents are formed by twisted metallic-looking bands and are often gilded. Similar crescents decorate flat breads to be consumed in the daily sacred meals of the elects. A further common motif is seen in the depiction of tablecloths and other hanging textiles (Figure 4/2c). The diamond-shaped fold of a "box pleat" survives on four paintings; other folds are defined in a flower-like shape (Figure 4/2d). When the textile is white or gold, its flower folds are captured in black lines. In some paintings, diamond and flower folds are employed side by side.

Flowering plants are frequently incorporated into both figural compositions and decorative designs. Side stems often conclude in flower buds (Figure 4/2e) with slightly oval bodies and middle openings. The main stems may end in floral sequences (Figure 4/2f) formed by a petal-ring and a five-petaled shoot. Our final example is the pool motif (Figure 4/2g). The characteristic swirl of the water is symbolized by spiraling dark blue lines and even darker blue patches. The water-bank is formed by two red bands, and the surrounding area is indicated by a ring of green grass. Every example of the pool motif in this art incorporates these elements.

Composition

Compositional assessments are burdened, but not prevented, by the fact that no painting is intact in this style. Although the more or less complete examples total less than a dozen, all remains display the recognizable traits of density, balance, and visual hierarchy, which are well represented on the carbon-dated book painting (MIK III 8259, Figure 2/3a).

A balanced density dominates throughout. Compactness is reached not only by the tight placement of the figures, but also through real and imaginary additions such as foliage, textiles, furniture, food, or halos. When blue background is employed, it too contributes to a sense of density. Regarding balance, all the well-preserved scenes are arranged symmetrically, and this effect is often accomplished by a clever distribution of visual weight.

Hierarchy is conveyed via a variety of means, one of which is size difference. This, however, is only rarely archived through the scale of the figures. Most often the associated sitting areas, headgear, and halos

---

[3] In Manichaean art the left-handed gestures are always secondary to a gesture assumed by the right hand, which enjoys a special significance not only in the art but also in the literature of this religion; for other examples and literary references, see Gulácsi 2001a, No. 32, note 3.

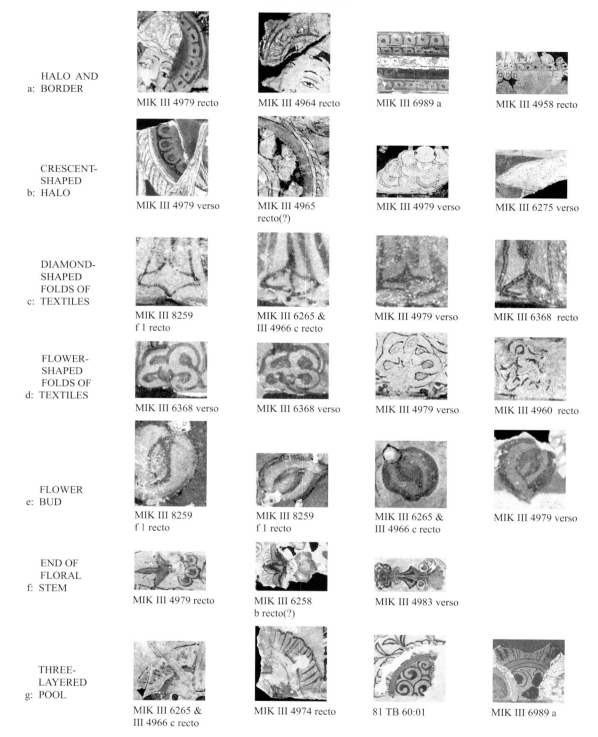

HALO AND
a: BORDER

MIK III 4979 recto   MIK III 4964 recto   MIK III 6989 a   MIK III 4958 recto

CRESCENT-
SHAPED
b: HALO

MIK III 4979 verso   MIK III 4965 recto(?)   MIK III 4979 verso   MIK III 6275 verso

DIAMOND-
SHAPED
FOLDS OF
c: TEXTILES

MIK III 8259 f 1 recto   MIK III 6265 & III 4966 c recto   MIK III 4979 verso   MIK III 6368 recto

FLOWER-
SHAPED
FOLDS OF
d: TEXTILES

MIK III 6368 verso   MIK III 6368 verso   MIK III 4979 verso   MIK III 4960 recto

FLOWER
e: BUD

MIK III 8259 f 1 recto   MIK III 8259 f 1 recto   MIK III 6265 & III 4966 c recto   MIK III 4979 verso

END OF
FLORAL
f: STEM

MIK III 4979 recto   MIK III 6258 b recto(?)   MIK III 4983 verso

THREE-
LAYERED
g: POOL

MIK III 6265 & III 4966 c recto   MIK III 4974 recto   81 TB 60:01   MIK III 6989 a

Figure 4/2. West Asian Fully Painted Style of Uygur Manichaean Art: Samples of Reoccurring Motifs (II)

a: "St. John" on folio 27 verso of the Syriac Gospel Book Dawkins 58 (1238 CE), Bodleian Library, Oxford

b: "Maqama of al-Rahba" on folio 32 verso of the St. Petersburg Maqamat, S 23 (c. 1240 CE), Russian Academy of Sciences

Figure 4/3. West Asian Comparative Examples from the early 13th century

in Oxford, contains four fully painted author portraits inserted as sideways-turned columnar images at the beginning of each *evangelion*. The portrait of John on the verso of folio 27 (Figure 4/3a) is damaged and thus allows us to observe technical details also employed in Uygur Manichaean book paintings. Remnants of the underdrawing are seen along the proper right of the figure, where diluted red lines indicate the contours of an arm and the hip area. In addition, to model the folds of the garment, blue with white stylized highlights are used for the shirt, and green with black stylized shades for the cloak of the figure.

Illuminated books produced in Baghdad during the thirteenth century, like the St. Petersburg copy of the *Maqamat*, also exhibit similar means of modeling (Figure 4/3b). Being one of the best preserved among the 13 copies of the *Maqamat*, this manuscript was discussed by both Richard Ettinghausen in 1962 and Oleg Grabar in 1984 as a prime source of Islamic pictorial art from the reign of the Abbasid dynasty.[18] Just as the Manichaean artist in Turfan during the tenth century, the Baghdad painter in the 1240s employed one color with its shade (blue with dark blue, violet with dark violet, green with dark green.) and white or black to indicate the texture of draperies, grass, and water. At the same time, to capture the folds of white garments, both artists used thin black lines on the white paint.

---

[18] Ettinghausen 1962; Grabar 1984. For recent discussions by Stefano Carboni and Anas B. Khalidov, see Petrosyan et al. 1995, 80–82 and 144–155, respectively.

Such technical similarities in and of themselves cannot be used to prove that tenth-century Uygur Manichaean book art influenced thirteenth-century Syriac Christian and Abbasid Islamic book art. Although the idea of the Abbasid connection has been raised repeatedly (without comparative art historical analyses),[19] this claim remains historically unsubstantiated, since there is no evidence for any Manichaean community in Central Asia after the early eleventh century. The above stylistic correlations, however, can be used to suggest that this style of Uygur Manichaean book art from the late ninth to early eleventh centuries shares a common West Asian origin with Syriac Christian and Abbasid Islamic book art of the early thirteenth century.

Arnold in 1938 already implied the idea of common roots as he hypothesized about how an Abbasid Manichaean tradition could have been transmitted to the Uygurs during the ninth and tenth centuries. In his article on the origins of Persian book art in the *Survey of Persian Art*, he gathered detailed references to the lavish decoration of West Asian Manichaean books from Christian and Islamic documentary writings, in light of which he deduced the following possible sequence of events: In Iran "under Arab rule, up to the early part of the tenth century, there was a group of painters enjoying the patronage of the Manichaean sect," who, after the Manichaean commissions vanished, may have found "employment in the Muhammadan courts, and add[ed] their contribution to the sum total of what is roughly described as Persian painting." In addition, Arnold also hypothesized that those painters who were themselves Manichaeans (elect or laity) might have fled from Abbasid persecution (ninth-tenth centuries) with the rest of the church eastward and thus were responsible for transmitting a "Persian" style of painting to East Asia.[20] Arnold imagined a likely scenario of what might have happened to art and the artist after the religion, with which both were associated, was persecuted to extinction in one locale. In addition, however, we must take into consideration that the Uygurs offered rich commissions and royal support for safe missions starting already from the mid eighth century. At least from then on a well-organized Manichaean church, active in book production, was present in Turfan. Since historical sources on this subject can little help our work, we might be able to turn to art historical evidence if future comparative studies produced reliable art historical data that document the West Asian artistic ties of the Manichaean community in Turfan.

The West Asian Outline Drawing Style

Strikingly different materials and techniques are used on another group of Manichaean remains (Table 4/2). The decoration of 32 fragments lack the complex layered painting program. Instead of heavy gilding and colorful paints, these images are conveyed in distinct black contours of skilled draftsmanship with occasional light coloring. To distinguish this style from the above described one, I refer to it as the "West Asian outline drawing" style of Uygur Manichaean art.[21]

Materials and Techniques

The scenes and decorations conveyed in this style are ink drawings that are occasionally supplemented with gilding and light coloring. Within these tinted drawings, the motifs and their details are defined in black or sometimes red-violet, contours drawn with a thin ink-pen. The even thickness of the lines indicates not only that the draftsman employed a fine ink-pen and not a brush, but also that he worked with one such pen

---

[19] Arnold 1924, 19–23; Bussagli 1963, 111; Hambis 1964, 433, 439, 443; Klimkeit 1982, 19.

[20] Arnold 1938, 1818.

[21] The term "outline drawing" is used mainly in illuminated manuscript studies (Brown 1994, 91). Analogously to "fully painted," its use is appropriate since most of the examples in this style are fragments of illuminated books.

Table 4/2. Examples of the West Asian Outline-drawing Style (32 examples)

Decorative Designs	TM 332 verso	MIK III 4971 a–c recto
On Codex Pages (26)	MIK III 4967 b verso	MIK III 4971 a–c verso
M 23 recto	MIK III 4967 c recto	MIK III 4971 d verso
M 23 verso	MIK III 4967 c verso	
M 171 f 1 verso	MIKIII 4981 a (silk codex)	
M 171 f 2 recto	MIK III 4981 f (silk codex)	*On Scrolls (0)*
M 233 recto	MIK III 4970 b, c verso(?)	No evidence
M 576 recto	MIK III 4970 c recto(?)	
M 730 recto	MIK III 6261 recto	*On Pustakas (0)*
M 730 verso	MIK III 6261 verso	No evidence
M 871 recto	MIK III 7251 verso	
M 871 verso		*On Textile Banners (0)*
M 1887 recto	*Figural Scenes*	No evidence
M 1887 verso	*On Codex Pages (6)*	
M 4831 recto(?)	M 6290 b recto	*On Wall Paintings (0)*
So 18700 & M 501 e verso	M 8200 recto	No evidence
TM 332 recto	MIK III 4970 c verso	

and not with several of distinct thicknesses. For gilding, he adhered cut pieces of gold leaves whose rough shapes were altered by line drawings on their surfaces. For coloring, diluted paint and a brush were needed. While no traces of underdrawing remain detectable, preliminary planning must have been implemented for the efficient utilization of the available space. The lack of costly pigments and the complex painting process makes this style less expensive and quicker to complete than the fully painted illuminations.

The above-described features can be seen for example within the decorative designs from the verso of the fragmentary codex page M 23 (Figure 4/4). Here, the concluding motif of a marginal decoration is formed by a series of scarves with disks conveyed in uninterrupted thin black lines and light traces of coloring. The figural composition belongs to the verso of a fragmentary codex folio (So 18700 & M 501 e verso, Figure 5/14b and Plate 6/c). A young flute player remains from among a series of such figures along the outer margin of the page.

Although the two West Asian styles of Uygur Manichaean art have distinct appearances, they are often employed together within one composition (Figure 4/5). The gold leaves in fully painted book paintings frequently incorporate extensive outline drawings. An example for this is seen in the diadem held by two angels over the open crescent halo of a Manichaean mythical figure, probably the Third Messenger, found on the recto(?) of a fragmentary codex folio (MIK III 4965 recto[?], Figure 4/5a and Plate 7a). The line drawing of this gold diadem is almost identical to the details of a footed plate filled with symbolic food from a solely outlined decorative design (M 23 recto, Figure 4/5b). Points of similarities between the two include the pearled edges conveyed by a series of tiny circles, the side motifs of the three curly stems, and the central motif of a stylized flower formed by concentric circles and a pearl rim. Numerous additional cases are seen for the combined occurrence of the two styles.[22]

Motifs

Although the limited number of West Asian outline drawings precludes an overall survey of recurring motifs, by looking through remnants of this style, we notice that several motifs are defined in manners

---

[22] The list of images in the fully painted style that contain extensive outline drawings includes book paintings such as Nos. 45, 57, 58, and 66 in Gulácsi 2001a.

a: M 23 recto

b: M 23 verso

Figure 4/4. Examples of the West Asian Outline Drawing Style of Turfan Manichaean Art
(SBPK, Berlin-Brandenburgische Akademie der Wissenschaften, Turfanforschung, Berlin)

identical to their fully painted versions. A substantial set of examples is seen among vegetal motifs. These
are numerous, for flowers and vines are frequently incorporated into the decorative designs and the figural
scenes of both styles (Figure 4/6). Arranged side by side, the visual survey of these motifs contains the
fully painted versions on the left (Figure 4/6, columns 1–2) and the outline drawings on the right (Figure
4/6, columns 3–4).

The first example is a flower bud with a twisted central petal (Figure 4/6a). It is illustrated here through
the underdrawing of a damaged painted and gilded motif (MIK III 4969 folio 1[?] recto), an intact fully
painted bud (MIK III 4983 verso), and two torn outline drawings (MIK III 4970 c recto[?] and MIK III
4967 c). The second motif is a lotus bud (Figure 4/6b) conveyed with a few downward bending leaves
at the stem of a funnel-shaped bloom that often concludes in a set of parallel bands. Only the last example in this row (M 4831 recto[?]) is a line drawing, whereas the rest are from fully painted illuminations.
The third motif is a rose-like flower (Figure 4/6c) composed of two curled lateral pedicles and a bloom
with a series of petals along a round core. The fully painted example is an underdrawing from a decorative design (MIK III 4969 folio 1[?] verso) whose components reflect the basic trends seen on three examples executed in outline drawings (MIK III 7251 verso, MIK III 4964 c verso, and M 23 recto). The final

a: MIK III 4965 recto(?), detail with crown from full-painted image

b: M 23 recto, detail with footed plate from line-drawn image

Figure 4/5. Examples of Draftsmanship in the Two West Asian Styles of Turfan Manichaean Art (SMPK, Museum für Indische Kunst, Berlin; and SBPK, Berlin-Brandenburgische Akademie der Wissenschaften, Turfanforschung, Berlin)

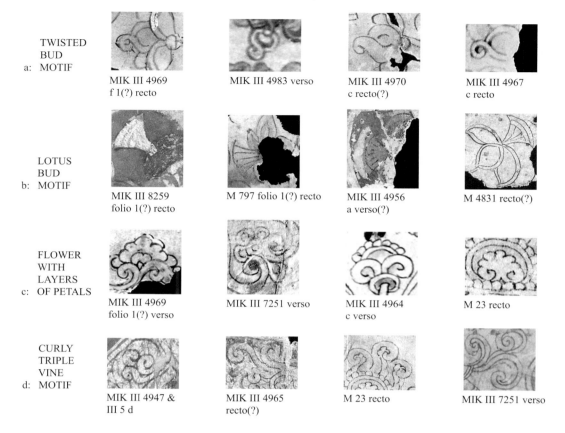

Figure 4/6. West Asian Fully Painted & Line Drawing Styles of Turfan Manichaean Art: Samples of Reoccurring Motifs

motif is a curled trefoil vine (Figure 4/6d). The first two examples are on gold leaves in fully painted figural compositions (**MIK III 4947 & III 5d**; and **MIK III 4965 recto[?]**), and the last two are outline drawing in decorative designs (**M 23 recto** and **MIK III 7251 verso**).

Composition and Context of Use

Just as in the similarities of materials and techniques, the motif correlations also support the idea that line drawings are unpainted, skillfully drawn renditions of the fully painted designs. The close connection of the two styles is also reflected in their composition and context of use.

On the bits and pieces of torn pages remaining from this style, we can recognize certain compositional features familiar to us from fully painted images. In this style too, figural compositions are used as marginal, intracolumnar, and possibly full-page scenes.[23] The reconstruction of the most complete outline drawing, retained on three small paper fragments (**MIK III 4971 a–c recto**, Figure 5/18d), shows that the basic page arrangement and the composition of the intracolumnar image on the recto are identical to those of

---

[23] Regarding full-page illuminations, besides one tiny fragment of a seated figure (**MIK III 4971 d**) that derives from the central part of a page and thereby forms part of an intracolumnar or a full-page scene, we have no evidence for their existence.

the carbon-dated fragment (MIK III 8259, Figure 5/7d). In both scenes, the image is organized into an upper and lower section. The upper section contains a main figure flanked by two side figures. The lower section features lesser-ranking figures seated in two groups, facing toward one another.

The West Asian outline drawing style of Uygur Manichaean art is connected solely to illuminated books (Table 4/2). All remnants belong to codices. Two silk fragments indicate the use of this style in silk codices. The integration of outline drawings with the textual parts of manuscripts is identical to fully painted illuminations. One fragment documents this style in a book that also contained a fully painted scene.[24]

Dating and Origin

We have seen that these two styles are connected through numerous ties, indicating that the outline drawings are less decorative versions of the fully painted illuminations. Regarding the issue of dating, no evidence makes us think that the simpler outline drawings predate the fully painted images in the Turfan region, or vice-versa. Their shared motif repertoire, compositional principles, context of use, and employment within the same composition and within the same book can only be interpreted as signs of simultaneous existence. Although this evidence is not suited for the dating of individual fragments, it suggests nevertheless that the outline drawing style was also in use in Turfan between the late ninth and early eleventh centuries.

It is well documented that outline drawings, just as fully painted images, were used in illuminated manuscripts of the Mediterranean region during late antiquity.[25] An example for the early medieval presence of outline drawings in West Asia is found in a Syriac Bible from 932 CE (Add. 14594) in the collection of the British Library (Figure 4/7a). The first page of this parchment codex is decorated with a simple ink drawing of a clerical figure identified as "the Bishop of Abba." In addition to the medium, the context, and the basic technique of illumination, this early tenth century image is connected to the Uygur Manichaean examples through the sideways positioning of the image within the page.

The technical ties recognized between the outline drawing and fully painted scenes may also impact upon our understanding of the question of origin. An illuminated collection of poems, know as the *Diwan* of Sultan Ahmad Jalayir, made in Baghdad in ca. 1402 (Figure 4/7b) contains the earliest known examples of Islamic outline drawings. In this royal manuscript, wide margins surround the poems of Sultan Ahmad. The margins on the last eight pages are decorated with pastoral scenes conveyed in delicate black contours enhanced with occasional gold and light blue pigments.[26] Since very few Persian line drawings survive even from the fifteenth century, these illuminations were initially considered later additions to the manuscript. In 1965 Basil W. Robinson, however, suggested that the lightly tinted drawings of this *Diwan* must date together with the book. His argument was based on the recognition that the style of these drawings accords with other fully painted scenes of the period.[27] Earlier examples of tinted drawings in Central Asian book art have been known only through an early fourteenth century illuminated copy of Rashid al-Din's *Universal History*. The pages preserved from the ca. 1330 edition from Ilkhanid Tabriz, in the Topkapi Sarayi Müzesi in Istanbul, retain Mongol court scenes.[28] Although a light coloring is prominent in its paintings, the heavy outlines clearly dominate, placing them stylistically in between the line drawings and the opaque painted scenes of later Islamic manuscripts.[29]

---

[24] Gulácsi 2001a, No. 20.
[25] Brown 1994, 91.
[26] Gray 1977, 52; Badiee 1996, 320.
[27] Robinson 1965, 18.
[28] Rogers (ed.) 1986, 69 and Fig. 44.
[29] It has been suggested in numerous publications that the technique of ink drawings in Islamic book art, occasionally highlighted

a: "The Bishop of Abba," folio 1 recto of the Syriac
Gospel Book add. 14594 (932 CE), British Library, London

b: Sultan Jalayir's *Diwan*, 32.29-37, detail with marginal
pastoral scene on unspecified folio recto (1403 CE),
Freer Gallery of Art, Washington DC

Figure 4/7. West Asian Comparative Examples from the mid 10th and the early 15th centuries

Robinson's claim for the fourteenth-fifteenth century existence of line drawings in Baghdad together
with the Syriac and Manichaean examples suggests that an outline drawing technique of book illumination was known among artists active in West Asia most likely during the entire medieval period. Examples
in relatively large quantity and high quality from the ninth to early eleventh centuries are found among
the remains of Uygur Manichaean art. It is possible that in Turfan, the closeness of the Chinese tradition
of monochrome ink paintings increased the popularity or catalyzed the development of an already existing
West Asian style. As we shall see, both monochrome and fully painted Chinese painting techniques were
known to and employed in Uygur Manichaean circles.

---

with light washes, resulted from a Chinese influence (*chinoiserie*) on the Central Asian pictorial tradition; see e.g. Blair and Bloom
1994, 28; Allen 1985, 122; Badiee 1996, 320.

Table 4/4. Examples of the Chinese Outline Drawing Styles (3 examples)

On Codex Pages (0)	On Pustakas (0)	On Textile Banners (2)
No evidence	No evidence	MIK III 164
		MIK III 6270
On Scrolls (1)	On Wall Paintings (0)	
MIK III 4614	No evidence	

dian-language letter written on a paper scroll. Curiously, neither inscriptions nor texts written in Chinese were ever found in the immediate contexts of these works of art.[36]

Dating

No remains from among the two Chinese styles of Uygur Manichaean art have been dated securely. Radiocarbon dates are not available, and the single date put forward based on a historical reference by Annemarie von Gabain in 1958[37] was shown to be unfounded by Peter Zieme in 1992 (see discussion in Chapter 2). Thus, at this point, the safest way to estimate the dates of these styles in Manichaean Turfan is through a consideration of the immediate historical, religious, and artistic contexts of the remains.

Based on the known historical decline of Manichaeism in the Turfan region during the early eleventh century, we can no longer think that the two Chinese-rooted styles of this art succeeded the era of the West Asian styles. In addition, the distinct media preferences of the Chinese and West Asian styles support the idea that the use of Chinese styles in Manichaean Turfan was contemporaneous with and complementary to that of the West Asian styles.

But since when were the two Chinese styles employed in Uygur Manichaean art? The first Manichaean community in Turfan in the seventh century was Parthian and Sogdian based. Its art production (if any) was most likely connected to Mesopotamia and West Central Asia. Regarding Chinese-style art production in Turfan, Sarah E. Fraser's study on artists and workshop practices in 1998 showed that prior to the ninth century a relatively small range and humble quality characterized local Chinese art there.[38] The remains of the Chinese styles of Uygur Manichaean art do not comply with this characterization. In addition, it is unlikely that a significant portion of the local Chinese population had ever converted to Manichaeism, since only two Chinese language Manichaean text fragments have been found there,[39] compared with the several thousand fragments in Parthian, Sogdian, and Turkic languages. Thus, there is reason to doubt that the local Chinese population was responsible for the introduction of high-quality Chinese pictorial art to the Manichaean community, just as it is unlikely that this higher quality art appeared in Turfan prior to the start of Uygur sponsorship in the mid eighth century.

Between the mid eighth and the mid ninth centuries, the political power, and the growing wealth, of the Uygurs was unparalleled in Inner and East Asia. Throughout the second half of the eighth century, they benefited from the weakness of the Tang government, which, in exchange for military support during and after the An Lushan rebellion (755–762), allowed the Uygurs to plunder Loyang and kept on buying their endless supply of horses. In addition, by the early ninth century the Uygurs acquired control of

---

[36] For the transcription and translation of Middle Persian, Sogdian, and Uygur language texts associated with the remains of both Chinese styles of Uygur Manichaean art, see BeDuhn 2001, Nos. 65, 69, 80, 81, and 91.
[37] Gabain and Winter 1958, 7.
[38] Fraser 1999a.
[39] Thilo 1991, 161–170; Sundermann 1991, 171–174; and Mikkelsen 2003.

a: *Vaiśravana Riding Across the Waters* (before 1035 CE), detail with main figure, British Museum, London

b: *Banner with Bodhisattva* (before 1035 CE), detail, British Museum, London

Figure 4/10. Comparative Examples of Chinese Paintings from Dunhuang from the early 11th century

the northern Silk Road, gaining regular income from protecting long-distance trade and any other traffic. The artistic output of the Turfan region was undoubtedly boosted by the arrival of Uygur control in the early ninth century. Simultaneously, the once solely nomadic Uygur society and culture went through dramatic changes. Already in their steppe homeland there was evidence of agriculture, industry, commerce, towns, literacy, world religions, and also an increased appetite for luxuries.[40] It is certainly possible that major Uygur-sponsored Manichaean art projects involving Chinese-trained artists started in the Turfan region with the conversion (mid eighth century). The likelihood of such sponsorship increases at the time when the Uygur control of Turfan began (early ninth century), and is most probable after the Uygur relocation to the Turfan region (mid ninth century; Figure 4/11b).

The middle of the ninth century represents a turning point in both Uygur and Manichaean history. Following a series of events that led to the disintegration of the Uygur Steppe Empire in 841, the era of Uygur influence on Tang politics ended. The Tang government, being confident in the loss of Uygur mil-

---

[40] Mackerras 1968, especially pages 12, 18, 25, 29, 37, 47–50.

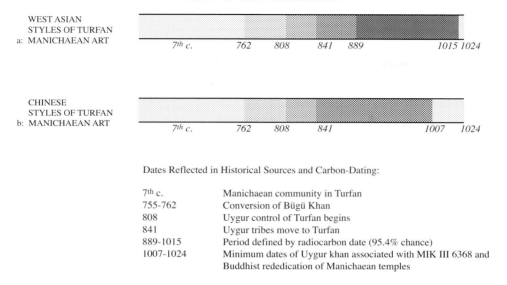

Dates Reflected in Historical Sources and Carbon-Dating:

7th c.	Manichaean community in Turfan
755-762	Conversion of Bügü Khan
808	Uygur control of Turfan begins
841	Uygur tribes move to Turfan
889-1015	Period defined by radiocarbon date (95.4% chance)
1007-1024	Minimum dates of Uygur khan associated with MIK III 6368 and
	Buddhist rededication of Manichaean temples

Figure 4/11. Likelihood of Manichaean Art Production in the Turfan Region

itary might, targeted especially severely the Manichaean communities of Chang'an and Luoyang during the persecutions of 843. Those not killed were sent to join the newly resettled Uygur tribes in the Tian Shan region and Gansu. Others fled to the south where the Tang control was minimal.[41] Analogous to Arnold's assessment of the effect of the Abbasid persecution on the formation of Uygur Manichaean art, it seems reasonable to assume that the partially Chinese Manichaean communities of Chang'an and Luoyang also included Manichaean artists (elects or laity) trained in Chinese schools, who were amongst those who fled.

Origin

The complex Sino-Uygur relations included a little-documented, but significant cultural component. Already between the mid eighth and mid ninth centuries a Chinese cultural influence among the Uygurs was relatively strong. They acquired goods through trade and princesses through diplomatic ties, and with these also came admired aspects of art and architecture. Chinese historical annals show that Chinese builders worked already on the steppe among the Uygurs, and the Chinese text of the Karabalgasun inscription from the early ninth century may signal the presence of a significant Chinese populace among them.[42] In addition, the Chinese style remains of Uygur Manichaean art from Turfan form a group of visual evidence, indicating not only that such cultural connections continued after the Uygurs settled in the Tian Shan region, but also that they had access to high-quality art.

The roots of these two Uygur styles are well demonstrated through comparative examples of Chinese paintings produced during late Tang and early Song times in imperial circles and Dunhuang. The basic technical and stylistic ties between the Uygur Manichaean and other Chinese styles are illustrated here by four Chinese paintings that were selected as comparative examples on the basis of their similar sub-

---

[41] Lieu 1992, 238.
[42] Mackerras 1968, 50.

ject, stylistic likeness, and temporal closeness to the Manichaean examples. Despite differences in media, scale, and condition, the similarity of these examples in technique, iconography, and expressiveness confirms that Uygur Manichaean art formed a part of Chinese pictorial art during ca. the ninth to early eleventh centuries.

The Chinese-trained painters who worked for the Manichaeans in Turfan employed techniques similar to those used by the most famous imperial painters. The first comparative example shows emperor Wudi (r. 561–578 CE) depicted in the "Emperors Scroll" in the collection of the Museum of Fine Arts in Boston (Figure 4/9a). The first part of the scroll is thought to be a later, probably Northern Song dynasty copy of the Tang original, while the second half is attributed to Yan Liben (d. 673 CE).[43] Emperor Wudi belongs to the first part of the scroll. Although executed on different scales, the details defining the face of the emperor in the scroll and of the Manichaean dignitary in the wall painting (MIK III 6918) are strikingly similar to one another in the eye, the ear, and the nose area. In both depictions the artists placed three upward curling lines at the corner of the eye. They captured the ear by using an outer fleshy loop from within which the antihelix protrudes in a manner resembling a mug-handle. They defined the area of the nose by combining a hook-shape for the nostril with a line leading toward the corner of the mouth. Similar traits are present on the rest of the imperial faces throughout the Boston scroll. Although the actual reasons behind the close correlation between the Manichaean leader's and emperor Wudi's face may be lost forever, it is clear that both artists relied on common techniques of portraiture, and thus the two depictions are connected through a shared visual language. The Manichaean wall painting was painted by an accomplished artist who was familiar with a technique of expressiveness well known to Chinese court painters, and used it to convey dignity and power in Manichaean Turfan. To capture the actual physical likeness of the individual was not the goal in the portraits of the time. None were painted from life, but from a vision of the moral qualities involved.[44] The image of a dignitary, secular or religious, included a specific group of lines in the formation of the face that were standard within the Chinese tradition.

Besides fully painted works, linear ink paintings were also popular in Chinese imperial circles at the time. A monochrome ink image of a bodhisattva from the collection of the Shoso-in Nara (Figure 4/9b) has been traditionally considered to be closely related to Tang court paintings, especially to the style of Wu Daozi (ca. 710–760).[45] Through its sole figure, this large banner displays a fine carbon ink painting of its era comparable to the work of Chinese court painters. The banner is dated to the eighth century partially on the basis of an assumed connection to the style of Wu Daozi,[46] but also through the presence of a crescent shape and the side bows of a Sasanian-looking headgear popular in Tang Buddhist art (as seen e.g. on Figure 4/9b).[47] Without the crescent addition in the front, this type of headgear is encountered in the West Asian style of Uygur Manichaean art (e.g. 81 TB 65:01, Figure 6/5a). Although the scale difference makes a comparison of the brushwork unjustified, a similarity in the basic appearance of the Shoso-in bodhisattva and Uygur Manichaean ink paintings can be recognized, as in the case of the image of a young male elect retained on the surviving side panel of a Manichaean hemp banner (MIK III 4624).[48] Both figures

---

[43] This dating is based on Cahill 1980, 24; it is held by the Asian Collection of the Museum of Fine Arts in Boston (personal communication with Ann Bennett, the curator of the collection). In 1994 Dietrich Seckel (1993, 22) referred to the scroll as an early copy of the original attributed to Yan Liben. Recently Su Bai considered it to be an early Song copy (1998, 149 & note 30).

[44] Farrer 1993, 107.

[45] See Sickman and Soper 1988, 172–174.

[46] For a discussion of his style, see Stanley-Baker 1996.

[47] The approximately square surface of the vertically joined two sheets of hemp support measures 138.5 cm in height and 133 cm in width (Shôsô-in Office, 1989, xliv, No. 143).

[48] Gulácsi 2003, 25; for a color illustration, see Gulácsi 2001a, No. 78.

are defined in bold lines that capture creatively the desired human form, the characteristics of the garment, and the necessary iconographic clues. They display virtuosity through bold brushwork that freely discloses the starting and finishing points of the strokes. In the Manichaean case, the simplicity of the monochrome lines is enhanced with a layer of gold paint that once coated the entire surface of the banner.

The roughly contemporaneous East Central Asian existence of these Chinese painting techniques has been well documented through Buddhist pictorial art from Dunhuang, where a variety of silk paintings survived in Cave 17. Before it was sealed, this small side chamber functioned as a depository of no-longer-used books and banners. Most of its contents date from before the early eleventh century.[49] One of the best preserved high-quality silk paintings from this site, dated by Roderick Whitfield on stylistic grounds to the middle of the tenth century, portrays Vaiśravana (Figure 4/10a).[50] Only a few temple banners decorated with monochrome line drawings demonstrate the existence of this painting style in Dunhuang. The selected portrait of a bodhisattva (Figure 4/10b) was also dated to the middle of the tenth century by Whitfield on stylistic grounds.[51] Until now the fragmentary condition of the Manichaean remains prevented us from recognizing that not only the Buddhists in Dunhuang, but also the Manichaeans in Turfan utilized high-quality Chinese pictorial art.

Conclusions

The above study of painting styles preserved on the remains of Turfan Manichaean manuscripts has revealed a variety of important information that sheds new light on not only previous understandings of Turfan Manichaean painting styles and their origins, but also the local development of this book culture. A simple numerical survey of styles together with the consideration of data provided by scientific dating and historical sources results in the elimination of a fossilized assumption associated with this book art.

We have learned that four basic technical trends (styles) are documented from among the remains. While further research will undoubtedly be able to refine this initial view of Manichaean painting styles, this survey has shown that the paintings of the manuscript illuminators working for Manichaean purposes in Turfan fall into two styles that are Western Asian in origin (a fully painted and an outline drawing style) and two that are of Chinese origin (again a fully painted and an outline drawing style). These four styles differ from one another in terms of their material and technique, motif repertoire, composition, and context of use.

The understanding of their context of use especially provides fresh insight regarding the formation of the Turfan epoch of Manichaean book art. This book art was dominated by Western Asiatic traditions of manuscript illumination. All but two examples from among the 89 fragments of Manichaean illuminated books are decorated by artists working in these traditions. The remaining two examples display Chinese pictorial trends in their paintings, which are documented in greater numbers on the fragments of Manichaean textile and wall paintings recovered from Turfan.

After considering evidence provided by scientific dating together with a stylistic analysis, it has become clear that we can no longer think in accordance with the currently accepted stylistic stratigraphy of Buddhist art in East Central Asia, based on apparent regional trends in wall painting, when it comes to establishing the dates of Uygur Manichaean manuscript fragments. The material surveyed here does not follow

---

[49] For the latest theory regarding the reasons of closing the cave in the early eleventh century, see Rong (1996, 23) and its assessment by Sarah E. Fraser (1999b, 57). For another interpretation that pays attention to the function and the physical context of the cave, and thus argues for a mid thirteenth century closing, see Huntington 1986.

[50] Whitfield and Farrer 1990, 20–23, 34.

[51] Whitfield and Farrer 1990, 20–23, 70.

the Buddhist analogy according to which an earlier "Persian" presence gave way to a later Chinese primacy in the local styles employed in the medium of mural art. Even though West Asian art has a more ancient history in Manichaeism than East Asian, the evidence presented here indicates that Manichaean usage of the two artistic traditions was complementary and roughly contemporaneous in Turfan (Figure 4/11). The traditional West Asian roots of the art used in the book medium were maintained until the end of Manichaeism in the region. The art of book illumination flourished in this period and impacted upon the creation of Manichaean wall and textile paintings. At the same time, the Turfan Manichaean community also employed Chinese-trained painters, whose paintings on silk banners and wall surfaces introduced East Asian renditions of Manichaean themes that complemented, but did not replace, the still dominant West Asian character of Uygur Manichaean book art.

CHAPTER FIVE

PATTERNS OF PAGE ARRANGEMENT: INTEGRATION OF TEXT AND IMAGE

The orientation of Manichaean manuscript fragments illuminated with figural scenes has presented an unexpected puzzle for scholars and book publishers alike. In most reproductions, these torn painted pieces of paper are featured with their texts in illegible directions that are never encountered in publications of non-illuminated Manichaean manuscripts. The phenomenon is well demonstrated through an orientation experiment conducted with a small remnant of a codex folio illuminated with a figural scene (MIK III 4959, see Figure 5/1). On one of its sides, this torn paper piece contains parts of six lines from a Middle Persian language text written in Manichaean script and four figures out of which two, seated on lotus flowers, are fully preserved. Instinctively, one would orient this fragment in accordance with the direction of its painting (Figure 5/1a). But by doing so, we make the text illegible: the lines become vertical with the letters running from the feet to the heads of the figures. By rotating the paper piece 90 degrees clockwise, the painting turns sideways and the lines of the text become horizontal, but now the letters are upside-down (Figure 5/1b). As we continue turning another 90 degrees, the painting becomes upside-down and the lines of the text vertical (Figure 5/1c). Finally, by placing the fragment into its last possible position, we reach a direction from which the text can be read but now the painting is on its side (Figure 5/1d). This experiment proves that the solution to the problem does not depend on how one holds the fragment. No matter how it is oriented and re-oriented, the relationship of the page components does not change. On this piece, just as on all other currently known examples of Manichaean illuminated fragments, as we shall see, the figural scenes and the texts are not aligned.

With one exception, the issue of how to position correctly the fragments of Manichaean illuminated books has escaped scholarly attention. In all major art publications during the twentieth century (including Albert von Le Coq's two books related to Manichaean art in 1913 and 1923, Louis Hambis's entry on Manichaean art in the *Encyclopedia on World Art* in 1964, Herbert Härtel's and Marianne Yaldiz's Manichaean chapter in their exhibition catalogue of Silk Road art in 1982, and even Hans-Joachim Klimkeit's study on Manichaean art and calligraphy in 1982) the focus was on the paintings of the Manichaeans and not their book art. Accordingly, the illuminated pages were featured from what may be called the picture-viewing direction. Showing both sides of a folio in this way, however, results in irreconcilable differences in the direction of the texts, as seen for example on the fragment with the Elects in Scribal Duty and Hymnody Scenes (MIK III 6368, Figure 5/2a and b). From the picture-viewing direction, the text runs in vertical lines, from toe to head next to the elects; on the side with the musicians, the vertical lines of writing run from "head-to-toe" in relation to the direction of the figures.

Only Le Coq has considered in some of his art historical studies how these fragments were bound.[1] Being familiar with the religious and cultural context of Turfan remains and having published numerous Turkic Manichaean texts, Le Coq occasionally referred to the fact that the fragments were bound originally

---

[1] The facsimiles of Manichaean text editions that occasionally contained fragments with figural scenes did feature the fragments correctly, from the text-reading direction; see e.g. Sundermann 1996, Plates 152–153, 154–155, and 159.

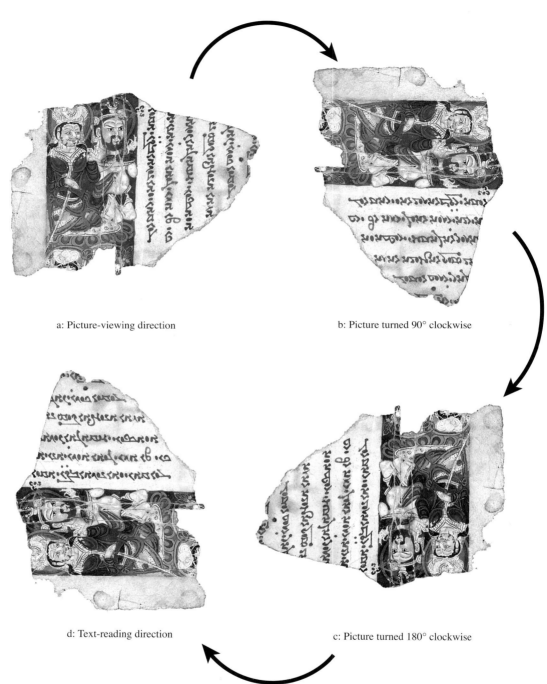

a: Picture-viewing direction

b: Picture turned 90° clockwise

d: Text-reading direction

c: Picture turned 180° clockwise

Figure 5/1. Orientation Experiment with a Fragmentary Illuminated Folio (MIK III 4959, recto)
(SMPK, Museum für Indische Kunst, Berlin)

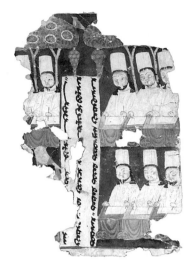

a: Recto: *Elects in Scribal Duty* & Text with
vertical lines of letters written from bottom to top

b: Verso: *Hymnody Scene* & Text with
vertical lines of letters written from top to bottom

Figure 5/2. The Picture-viewing Direction of a Fragmentary Illuminated Folio (MIK III 6368)
(SMPK, Museum für Indische Kunst, Berlin)

according to what we may call the text-reading direction.[2] When the very same fragment is shown this way (Figure 5/3a and b), the Manichaean script lines of writing are horizontal, running from right to left on both sides. The figures are on their sides, with their heads closer to the outer margin of their pages, that is in opposite direction from one another on the two pages. Besides brief remarks in connection with certain fragments in his 1923 book, Le Coq never illustrated, nor further explored the phenomenon of non-aligned illustrations. His concerns lay elsewhere. Although later scholarship on Manichaean art relied heavily on Le Coq's pioneering publications, his comments on correct orientation had no impact: the reproductions have remained misaligned, and an important aspect of Manichaean book art has stayed unexplored.

To follow up on Albert von Le Coq's findings, this chapter is dedicated to mapping out the consistency of the sideways picture orientation within the corpus of Manichaean illuminated manuscripts. It is not the goal here to find an explanation to the ultimate question of *why*. The reason for the practice can be contemplated only when the basic facts about Manichaean book art are understood. Therefore, our current task is to document a unique system of page arrangement, well disguised by the fragmentary nature of this corpus.

Not a single undamaged Manichaean illuminated manuscript has ever been recovered. Although the scroll in the Turfan Museum in Xinjiang (81 TB 65:01, Figure 5/13) is in a relatively good state of preservation, just as the first leaf from the pustaka (palm-leaf) book in Berlin (MIK III 8260, Figure 5/28), the vast majority of the illuminated remains—the ones in codex format—are extremely fragmentary. This damaged condition naturally hinders the study of their page arrangement, but it also makes it essential to conduct a survey. In order to document the basic rules of book design, we must gather clues from all surviving sources and then use their synthesis to recover the patterns of page arrangement. By integrating data

---

[2] Le Coq 1923, 49–50.

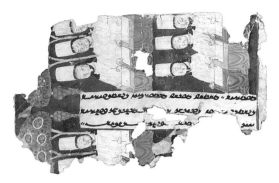

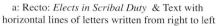

a: Recto: *Elects in Scribal Duty* & Text with
horizontal lines of letters written from right to left

b: Verso: *Hymnody Scene* & Text with
horizontal lines of letters written from right to left

Figure 5/3. The Text-reading Direction of a Fragmentary Illuminated Folio (MIK III 6368)
(SMPK, Museum für Indische Kunst, Berlin)

gained from physically disjointed sources into a coherent system, we will be able to reconstruct at least some of the basic trends observed in Turfan Manichaean book design.

This study of layout is based on the 89 Manichaean illuminated book fragments currently known. Here we examine these sources according to their book formats (codex, scroll, and pustaka) and types of illumination (decorative designs and figural scenes). First, the best-preserved illuminated folia will be reconstructed. Among them are two bifolia with decorative designs and eight additional mostly folio fragments with figural scenes. All 11 examples retain enough information to study their original layouts and sizes. As we shall see, the page design of these rebuilt folia documents a consistent pattern in the physical integration of text and illumination, and thus conveys a system. Similar to modern books, when an illustration is wider than can be accommodated by the width of the page, the pictures in mediaeval Manichaean books are featured at right angles to the text. The figural scenes, and some motifs in the decorative designs, are oriented sideways with the heads of figures (or the tops of the plates in the decorative designs) always closer to the outer margin. Since this pattern of orientation is maintained on both sides of the codex folio, the relationship between the text and the picture is different on the two sides, and the direction of the figures in relation to the text always identifies which page is the recto and which is the verso.[3] Second, the rules that defined this system are tested against the smaller and more damaged remains in order to prove that the layout of all currently known Manichaean illuminated codex fragments conforms to this pattern of alignment. Third, in order to consider the locations of all illuminations on the remains of this book art, codex pages with both decorative designs and figural scenes are surveyed. On the one hand, such an overview allows us to confirm the rules of page arrangement. On the other hand, it helps us to record the surviving patterns of placement of illuminations, and thus gain an understanding about the designs of Manichaean illuminated codices. Finally, our attention shifts to Manichaean illuminated manuscripts in hand scroll and pustaka formats. A survey of them confirms a pattern of page arrangement identical to the one seen in codex format in Manichaean Turfan, that is, the use of horizontal lines of writing and the sideways-oriented pictures.

---

[3] Just as in all books with Semitic scripts, the writing proceeds from right to left on both sides of the folio, and the page to be read first (i.e., the recto) falls on the left side of the open book, while the subsequent page (i.e., the verso) is seen on the right side after turning the folio.

Diagrams are provided to illustrate the reconstructed folia. In these, white areas defined by black contours indicate the actual shape and the relative size of the fragment surviving from the original folio. The grey areas defined by continuous black contour lines mark the reconstructed sections, and broken black contour lines indicate the hypothetical sizes in cases where the original measurements cannot be verified with certainty. Circles symbolize the binding holes along the folds of the bifolia. Regarding the content of the page, black lines mark the lines of writing in the header along the upper margin and within the columns of the texts. Since most of the texts are written in black ink, grey lines are used to signal the occasional presence of writing in red ink. The presence of decorative designs is indicated through the use of a meandering thick grey line.

Stick figures are used to capture the positions and locations of human or anthropomorphic divine beings within the figural scenes of the reconstructed pages (Figure 5/4). The five positions in which the figures are featured in this Manichaean art include standing, sitting on heels, sitting cross-legged, sitting on a throne, and flying. As integral components within the diagrams of page layout, these stick figures also capture the orientation of the figural scenes on the pages.

Figure 5/4. Symbols of Figures Painted on Blue Background

Reconstructible Codex Fragments with Decorative Designs

Within the corpus of Manichaean illuminated manuscripts two fragments with decorative designs are preserved well enough to accurately reconstruct their original sizes. They both represent large sections of bifolia, and their page layouts fully accord with those of non-illuminated Manichaean manuscripts from Turfan: the text area has horizontal lines of writing, there is a header above the text, margins have systematic widths around the text, and along the fold of both bifolia remnants are binding holes.

These two bifolia provide data on the layout of eight pages from two now-lost Manichaean illuminated codices in different sizes. One of them derived from a medium-size book of 18.0 × 7 cm (M 171), and the other from a large book of ca. 25.2 × 14.4 cm (M 797). Regarding the elements of the pages, the text areas are arranged in columns of horizontal Manichaean script lines, and the upper margins contain a header on each page (Table 5/1). On three from among the eight pages, the headers are written in large outlined

Table 5/1. Page Elements of two Reconstructable Codex Fragments with Decorative Designs (8 examples)

Number of Codex Pages	Texts	Illumination
M 171 folio 1 recto	Manichaean script	none
M 171 folio 1 verso	Manichaean script	decorative design with sideways footed plate
M 171 folio 2 recto	Manichaean script	decorative design
M 171 folio 2 verso	Manichaean script	none
M 797 folio 1(?) recto	Manichaean script	decorative design
M 797 folio 1(?) verso	Manichaean script	none
M 797 folio 2(?) recto	Manichaean script	none
M 797 folio 2(?) verso	Manichaean script	none

letters and illuminated with decorative designs. The painted floral and scarf motifs emerge from among the letters along the upper margin and continue down the outer margins. In one case, a footed plate filled with symbolic food is placed next to the header at the outer margin. This plate is oriented sideways, at a 90-degree angle to the direction of the writing, with the rim of the plate toward the edge of the page. On five pages, the headers are not illuminated but are written in larger script in red ink and incorporate elongated letters with floral punctuation marks.

The two books to which these pages belonged were unevenly decorated, as suggested by the variety of layouts on their subsequent pages. The four subsequent pages surviving from the smaller book (M 171) show decorative designs distributed symmetrically along the outer margin of the two facing pages (folio 1 verso and folio 2 recto), and the previous page (folio 1 recto), just like the following page (folio 2 verso), are both non-illuminated. The four pages remaining from two different parts of a quire from the larger book (M 797) also document an uneven distribution of the decorative designs, since among the four only one page is illuminated.

Bifolio with Decorative Designs on Two Facing Pages (M 171)

The most intact codex fragment illuminated with a decorative design is a bifolio that preserves four subsequent pages from the middle of a quire (M 171, Figure 5/5). The Manichaean script text, which reads continuously from folio 1 recto to the verso of folio 2, is arranged in a single narrow column on each page. On the two facing pages, that is at the inner side of the bifolio, the calligraphic headers are decorated with floral and scarf motifs and a sideways-turned footed plate of symbolic food. On both pages the illumination culminates within the upper half of the outer margin (Figure 5/5a and c). On the outer non-illuminated side of the bifolio, the headers that were written with enlarged script in red ink incorporate a few elongated letters and several elaborate floral punctuation marks (Figure 5/5b and d).

Only the lower margin is missing from the original height of these folia. With the 23 lines of text (24 lines of text on folio 1 verso), the current height is 17.0 cm. Assuming that the lower margin was not wider than the outer margin (ca. 1.0 cm), the estimated original height comes to ca. 18.0 cm. The current widest extent of the fragment accurately captures the original width of the folia. The width was ca. 7 cm, including a narrow inner margin (0.5 cm), a single column (ca. 5.5 cm), and a narrow outer margin (ca. 1.0 cm).

Bifolio with Decorative Design on One Page (M 797)

The second-largest codex fragment with a decorative design is a more damaged bifolio (M 797, Figure 5/6). It is unclear from the one-columned Manichaean script text how the two folia succeeded one another. One of them, folio 1(?) contains cantillated writing. Its recto is illuminated with fully painted floral motifs that

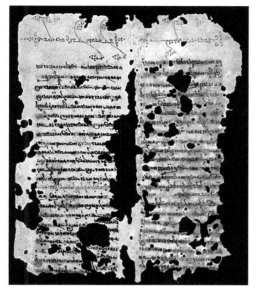

a: M 171 outer side, folio 1 recto & folio 2 verso

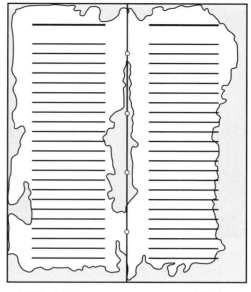

c: M 171, folio 1 recto folio 2 verso

b: M 171 inner side, folio 2 recto & folio 1 verso

d: M 171, folio 2 recto folio 1 verso

Figure 5/5. Reconstruction of an Illuminated Bifolio (M 171)
(SBPK, Berlin-Brandenburgische Akademie der Wissenschaften, Turfanforschung, Berlin)

a: M 797, folio 1(?) recto & folio 2(?) verso

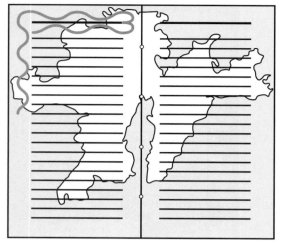

c: M 797, folio 1(?) recto   folio 2(?) verso

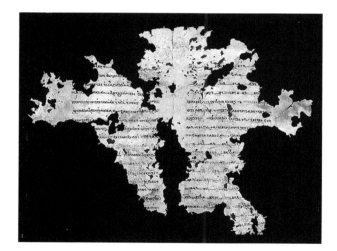

b: M 797, folio 2(?) recto & folio 1(?) verso

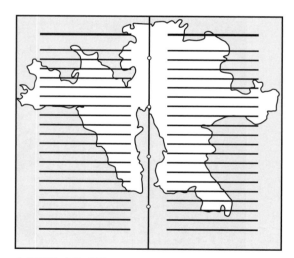

d: M 797, folio 2(?) recto   folio 1(?) verso

Figure 5/6. Reconstruction of an Illuminated Bifolio (M 797)
(SBPK, Berlin-Brandenburgische Akademie der Wissenschaften, Turfanforschung, Berlin)

reached down to at least the middle of the outer margin. The non-illuminated verso retains bits from the header's elongated two letters and the floral punctuation marks. Both sides of folio 2(?) are non-illuminated. The current measurements of the bifolio are ca. 22 cm for the height and ca. 28.7 cm for the width. The proposed original size of each folio comes to ca. 25.2 cm in height and at least 14.4 cm in width.

The original width is relatively well represented on both folia. The 1.4 cm widths of the inner margins are intact, as are parts of the 8.7 cm wide text areas. The current width of the outer margin on folio 1(?) is 4.1 cm. The torn edges of the floral motifs on the recto suggest that bits are missing from the current widest extent. A 4.3 cm wide blank outer margin preserved on folio 2(?) suggests a conservative estimate for the original widths of the outer margins on all pages. Thus, the approximate original width comes to minimum 14.4 cm.

The original height can only be estimated. The current size of the upper margin is 3.9 cm on folio 1(?) recto, where remnants of the floral illumination just barely fit on the area above the header, raising the possibility that at least a few millimeters are missing along its current extent. The text area on this page retains 21 lines that amount to 18.1 cm in height. Assuming that the text contained only 21 lines, and that the lower margin was just somewhat narrower than the outer margin, it is likely that a minimum of ca. 3.2 cm is missing from the original 25.2 cm height of the folio, including ca. 0.4 cm from the upper margin, and 2.8 cm as the complete height of the lower margin.

RECONSTRUCTIBLE CODEX FRAGMENTS WITH FIGURAL SCENES

Within the corpus of Manichaean illuminated manuscripts are nine codex fragments illuminated with figural scenes that can be reconstructed. One of them is a bifolio with clear binding holes. The others are fragmentary folia with occasional bits from the binding holes. Among the nine, five retain enough evidence to actually calculate their original sizes. Four additional folia can be reconstructed hypothetically since, although they retain clear data on their original layouts, their damaged margins leave a small range of possibilities for their dimensions. Nevertheless, the original page layouts and either the intact height or the intact width are restored in all cases. The components of the pages, including especially the horizontal lines of writing in Manichaean, Sogdian, and Runic scripts, together with the occasional remnants of the binding holes, unquestionably verify that these fragments derive from books in the usual codex format that were decorated with unusual sideways pictures.

These reconstructed fragments allow us to understand the layouts of 20 pages remaining from nine now-lost Manichaean codices illuminated with figural scenes. Although these pages show a considerable variety in terms of their content and layout, their basic page elements remain consistent. They all accommodate texts written in horizontal lines in Manichaean, Sogdian, or Runic scripts; and two types of illuminations—decorative designs and figural scenes (Table 5/2).

The reconstructions confirm that the illuminated books to which these folia belonged were unevenly decorated. On all nine fragments, the layout of the recto and verso sides are only identical when the page is not illuminated (MIK III 8259 folio 2[?]), although even here the text area is situated differently on the page due to the standard differences in width between inner and outer margins. All illuminated folia feature different layouts on their two subsequent sides. On two folia, the recto is non-illuminated but the verso contains a full-page figural scene (Or. 8212-1692 and MIK III 36). On three folia, one side contains a figural scene and the other a decorative design (M 576, So 18700 & M 501 e, and MIK III 4974). On three other folia, both sides contain figural scenes at different locations (MIK III 4979, MIK III 6368, and MIK III 8259 folio[?]1). Unfortunately, this group of fragments provides no information on facing pages. The one bifolio (MIK III 8259) documents a case when one section of the book was heavily illuminated with both decorative designs and figural scenes, while another section was not adorned at all.

Table 5/2. Page Elements of 11 Reconstructable Codex Fragments with Figural Scenes (20 examples)

Number of Codex Pages	Texts	Illumination (Decorative Design & Figural Scene)	
Or. 12452/3 recto	Manichaean script	none	figural scene (intratextual)
Or. 12452/3 verso	Manichaean script	none	none
Or. 8212-1692 recto	Runic script	none	none
Or. 8212-1692 verso	none	none	figural scene (full page)
M 576 recto	Manichaean script	decorative design	none
M 576 verso	Manichaean script	decorative design	figural scene (intratextual)
So 18700 & M 501 e recto	Sogdian script	decorative design	none
So 18700 & M 501 e recto	Sogdian script	decorative design	figural scene (marginal)
MIK III 36 recto	Manichaean script	none	none
MIK III 36 verso	none	none	figural scene (marginal)
MIK III 4974 recto	Manichaean script	decorative design	figural scene (intratextual)
MIK III 4974 verso	Manichaean script	decorative design	none
MIK III 4979 a–d recto	Manichaean script	decorative design	figural scene (intratextual)
MIK III 4979 a–d verso	none	none	figural scene (full page)
MIK III 6368 recto	Sogdian script	none	figural scene (full page)
MIK III 6368 verso	Sogdian script	decorative design	figural scene (marginal)
MIK III 8259 folio 1(?) recto	Manichaean script	decorative design	figural scene (intratextual)
MIK III 8259 folio 1(?) verso	Manichaean script	decorative design	figural scene (marginal)
MIK III 8259 folio 2(?) recto	Manichaean script	none	none
MIK III 8259 folio 2(?) recto	Manichaean script	none	none

A Bifolio with an Intratextual Scene (MIK III 8259)

In terms of actual size, the largest Manichaean codex fragment with a figural scene is a torn bifolio (**MIK III 8259**, Figure 5/7). The fragment can be correctly oriented in light of the horizontal lines of its Manichaean script texts and the vertical fold along the middle of the bifolio. The recto and verso sides of the two folia can be determined based on the location of the outer and inner margins in relation to the text area. The sequence of the two folia, however, cannot be confirmed. We know only that they did not follow one another directly within the quire. The illuminated folio is designated here as folio 1(?). The recto of folio 1(?) retains parts of two columns with an intratextual book painting and a marginal decorative design. The verso holds parts of two columns with an intracolumnar decorative design and a marginal figural scene. Both sides of folio 2(?) are occupied by Manichaean script writing in one column. The current measurements of the bifolio are 18.8 cm in height and 29.2 cm in width. The size of the once-intact double leaf reached approximately 29.2 cm in height and 35.4 cm in width, which made each folio 17.7 cm in width.

Determining the original height of any page will reflect the height of all pages. From the original height of this bifolio, only the bottom margin remains intact, while a large section from the text area, as well as the entire upper margin is missing. The height of the text area and that of the upper margin can be calculated by a combination of two kinds of data retained on the "inner side" of the bifolio, i.e., on the surface of folio 1(?) verso and folio 2(?) recto. These are (1) the rhythmic sequences of alternating ink colors of the text together with (2) the even distribution of binding holes along the fold of the bifolio.

First, let us consider the original size of the text area. On folio 1(?) verso, the text is organized in alternating sections of six lines in red ink and six lines in black ink. The lines are written with a relatively small script height (0.22 cm in black ink and 0.19 in red ink) and, without the aid of horizontal ruling, are spaced uniformly 0.6 cm apart within the columns. The broken upper edge of the fragment allows us to see the

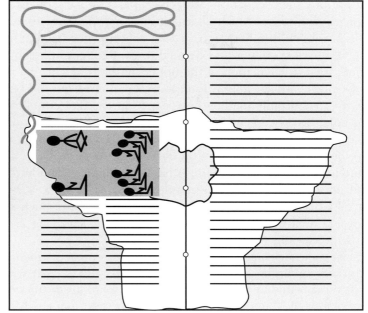

a: MIK III 8259 folio 1(?) recto &
folio 2(?) verso

c: MIK III 8259 folio 1(?) recto   folio 2(?) verso

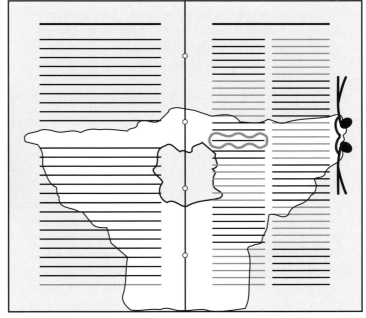

b: MIK III 8259 folio 2(?) recto &
folio 1(?) verso

d: MIK III 8259 folio 2(?) recto   folio 1(?) verso

Figure 5/7. Reconstruction of an Illuminated Bifolio (MIK III 8259)
(SMPK, Museum für Indische Kunst, Berlin)

last lines of one such sequence. Altogether, parts of five sequences are retained. In all known examples of intact pages with texts in such alternating colors, the sequences are used in even numbers. This fact suggests the possibility that here, too, at least six sequences were employed. Six color sequences would mean that the text area on this page extended to ca. 22.2 cm in height.[4]

Second, for the calculation of the upper margin's height, the binding holes provide the needed clue. A relatively intact binding hole is found at ca. 5.3 cm from the bottom edge.[5] The other, much less intact but clearly recognizable binding hole is seen at ca. 12.4 cm above the bottom. This could not be the top binding hole, because even if we calculate only five sequences of text and the upper margin as the missing area, the hole would be too far down from the upper edge to be the top binding hole (i.e., more than 5.3 cm). Based on the location of the surviving two, most likely there was one other binding hole between them and another one above them. A bifolio equipped with four binding holes positioned at approximately 5.3 cm from the top and bottom margins, and spaced at ca. 6.2 cm from one another (2×5.3 cm $= 10.6$ cm, plus 3×6.2 cm $= 18.6$ cm), would reach ca. 29.2 cm. Such a page height would accommodate a 22.2 cm high text area with the six color sequences, the surviving 2.7 cm high bottom margin, and an upper margin with a height of ca. 4.3 cm.

Regarding the original width, among the three page elements that together define the width of each folio (the inner margin, text, and outer margin), the 2.1 cm wide inner margins and the 11.1 cm wide text area remain undamaged, while only some parts from the outer margins are preserved. Observations on margin sizes of Manichaean book fragments (see Chapter 3) suggest that the outer margins are usually the second widest after the upper margin, extending at least as wide as the height of the bottom margin. Thus, it is safe to assume that the now-lost outer margin, in its narrowest possible width, most certainly was between the estimated height of the upper margin (4.3 cm) and the surviving height of the bottom margin (2.7 cm). The mathematical mean of these two measurements (ca. 3.5 cm) gives a reasonable estimate for the approximate original width of the outer margin. Adding up the width of the individual page elements (ca. 3.5 cm for the outer margin, 11.1 cm for the text, and 2.1 cm of the inner margin) yields a minimum of ca. 17.7 cm as the width of one undamaged folio.

A Folio with Intratextual and Marginal Scenes (MIK III 4974)

The most intact Manichaean illuminated codex folio retains an extensive painting program (MIK III 4974, Figure 5/8); the horizontal lines of Manichaean script writing align the fragment. In this case, the sequence of the two sides is determined by the content of the surviving continuous text, which starts on the recto and continues on the verso. Thus, the recto is the side with remnants of an illuminated header and a text area, which is interrupted with an intratextual figural composition. Here the heads of the figures are closer to the outer margin, just as seen on the illuminated recto of the previous reconstruction (MIK III 8259, folio 1[?] recto). The verso holds the continuation of the text and a remnant of a decorative design seen beneath the mostly vanished header. The current measurements of the fragment are 13.4 cm high and 7.9 cm wide. The size of the once-intact folio was ca. 15.5 cm high and 7.9 cm wide.

Approximately the entire original width of the page is retained. On the recto, the 4.5 cm width of the text area suffered no damage, and the ca. 0.5 cm inner margin seems to be complete at several locations, as indicated by strait sections of a rim that formed as the bifolio tore along its fold. Similarly, the current

---

[4] The height of the text area can be calculated by adding the height of the six sequences to the distance that separates them. On folio 1(?) verso, in column 1, the height of one complete sequence is ca. 3.8 cm, and the distance between the sequences is ca. 0.6 cm. In light of this measurement the height of the text comes to 22.2 cm (6×3.2 cm $= 19.2$ cm plus 5×0.6 cm $= 3.0$ cm).

[5] The current edges of the torn hole are between 5.1 and 5.5 cm from the bottom margin.

a: MIK III 4974 recto

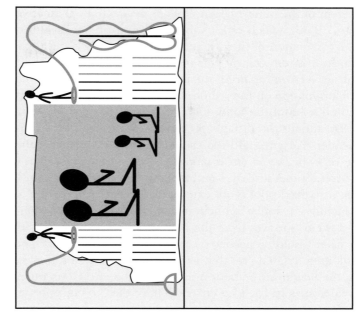

c: MIK III 4974 recto

b: MIK III 4974 verso

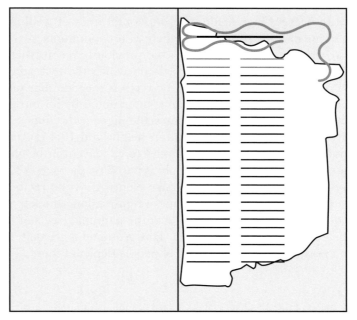

d: MIK III 4974 verso

Figure 5/8. Reconstruction of an Illuminated Folio (MIK III 4974)
(SMPK, Museum für Indische Kunst, Berlin)

widest extent of the outer margin, 2.9 cm, seems to be indicative of its original width. These measurements add up to 7.9 cm, which reflects the minimum original width of the folio.

For the calculation of the original height, the upper and the lower margins need to be considered, since although the 10.2 cm central part of the page (including the full extent of the text with its intratextual book painting) survives unimpaired, the margins above and below the text area are severely damaged. The program of illumination on the recto retains clues for the original size of these marginal areas. The upper margin, on both sides of the folio, includes a faint header that marks approximately the middle of the upper margin. By adding the distance between the first line of the column and the header (1.3 cm), the height of the header (0.4 cm), and the estimated distance between the top of the header and the upper edge of the page (1.3 cm), ca. 3 cm is gained as the minimum height of the upper margin. The bottom margin, which currently measures 1.3 cm, is illuminated on the recto. By turning the page to the picture-viewing direction, a stylized pool motif can be recognized. On several Manichaean codex pages the marginal decoration includes a similar semicircular pool of water from where lotus flowers emerge. In this case, only a half (ca. 1.0 cm) survives from the pool motif. Therefore, the vertical extent of the margin can be assessed through what would be needed to complete the semicircular pool motif (ca. 2.0 cm) and an additional narrow blank area (ca. 0.3 cm) that was most likely present at the edge of the paper. In light of these considerations, the height of the bottom margin is 2.3 cm. Consequently the estimated minimum original height of the folio comes to ca. 15.5 cm, including the 3.0 cm upper margin, the 10.2 cm text area, and the 2.3 cm bottom margin.

A Folio with an Intratextual Scene and a Full-Page Book Painting (MIK III 4979 a–d)

The two best-preserved Manichaean book paintings were initially found on four fragments (MIK III 4979 a–d, Figure 5/9).[6] Once again, the horizontal lines of writing align the fragment. Since the outer and inner margins did not survive, and there is no continuous text on these pages, for determining the recto and verso sequence we must turn to the previously reconstructed examples (**MIK III 8259** and **MIK III 4974**). On these, the recto was the side on which the text proceeded from head to toe in relation to the direction of the figures. Thus, here the recto is the side that retains parts of an illuminated header and a Manichaean script text in two columns interrupted by an intratextual figural scene. The other side is the verso with a full-page painting. If correctly aligned, the dimensions of the remains do not extend beyond that of fragment a, which is 25.5 cm in height and 12.4 cm in width. In light of the calculations below, the original size of the intact folio comes to ca. 27 cm in height and 18.5 cm in width.

The assessment of the original height is based on the verso's full-page pictorial program and is confirmed by the resulting proportions of the page elements of the recto. By turning the verso to the picture-viewing direction, the orderly arrangement of figures along the left and right sides of the composition becomes apparent. On the more intact left side of the painting, elects of varying ranks are seated in four rows, looking to the center of the composition. This grouping is partially mirrored along the right side of the painting in the positioning of elects and lay people depicted there. The symmetry of the two sides suggests that

---

[6] The remnant of this folio has been assembled from numerous torn paper segments, and in its current condition consists of two independent fragments. Although two small fragments (c and d) were lost during the Second World War, an old photograph allows us to consider all four fragment of the page; see Gulácsi 2001a, Appendix II, 245. The large piece (hereafter fragment a) and the surviving smaller independent pieces (hereafter fragment b) do not physically match, but undoubtedly belong together. The approximate dimensions of fragment a are 25.5 cm in height and 12.4 cm wide, while fragment b extends to 3 cm high and 2.9 cm wide (their measurements are approximate, since the piece is in the permanent exhibition under thick plastic layers). In most publications the two fragments are referred to as MIK III 4979, without distinguishing the independent fragments through the use of letters a and b.

a: MIK III 4979 a-d recto

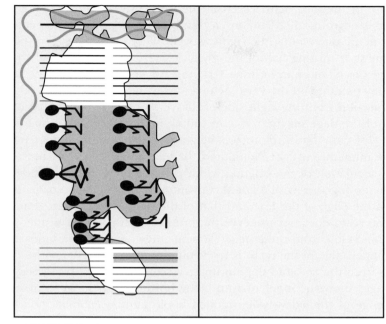

c: MIK III 4979 a-d recto

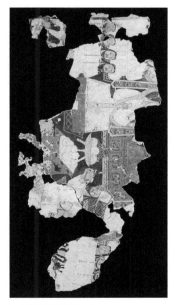

b: MIK III 4979 a-d verso

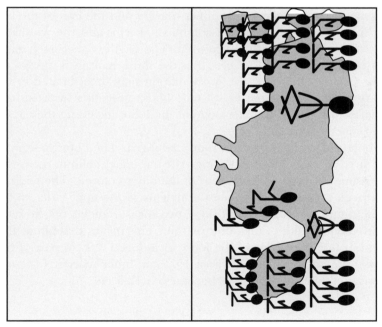

d: MIK III 4979 a-d verso

Figure 5/9. Reconstruction of an Illuminated Folio (MIK III 4979a–d)
(SMPK, Museum für Indische Kunst, Berlin)

the width of the four figures seen in the third row along the left side (5.2 cm) together with the edge of the blue background (0.3 cm) and a thin blank margin along the edge of the paper (0.6 cm) were approximately maintained along the right, as well. If so, the third row of figures along the damaged right side of the painting is missing half of the fourth elect (0.6 cm), the small strip from the blue background (ca. 0.3 cm), and the blank margin (min. 0.6 cm). All in all, ca. 1.5 cm is missing from the right side of the full-page book painting on the verso, which makes the original height of this folio to be ca. 27 cm. The missing 1.5 cm section from the right side of the verso's full-page book painting corresponds with the area of the bottom of the page on the recto, including a bit from the last line (0.1 cm) and the height of the bottom margin (1.4 cm). Thus, the recto's height is defined by the upper margin (3.7 cm), the text area together with the miniature (ca. 21.9 cm), and the bottom margin (1.4 cm), reaching ca. 27 cm.[7]

The calculation of the original width is made possible by considering the codicological data preserved on the recto together with a noted convention of Manichaean page arrangement reflected in the alignment between the edge of the text and that of the pictorial program along the inner margin seen on the recto. Since the recto does not preserve the original widths of the header and the text area, our task is to consider what is lost from these page elements together with the inner and outer margins.

The inner edge of the recto is unevenly torn. Not only the entire inner margin is missing, but also large sections from the text and the intratextual painting. Better-preserved examples of Manichaean illuminated book pages show the inner margin being bordered by the vertical ruling along the inner columns as well as the edge of the sideways-positioned book painting.[8] Since the pictorial program of the recto's painting is largely complete, only a few millimeters (ca. 0.3 cm) seems to be missing from the area where the miniature reached the inner margin. This lower area of the book painting contains flowering bushes and duck-like birds (MIK III 4979 recto, detail, Figure 5/8). Thus, the width of the first column, that is the distance between the edge of the inner margin and the end of the lines, must have been close to 7.3 cm. Adding the distance between the columns (0.6 cm) and the widths of the two columns (14.6 cm) results in 15.2 cm as the width of the text area. The width of the inner margin can only be hypothesized. Manichaean codicological data suggest that the inner margin is always the thinnest of all the margins of the page (see Chapter 3). Here, the inner margin may be estimated to have reached ca. 1 cm, since the bottom margin's estimate came to 1.4 cm. Thus, altogether approximately 1.3 cm is missing from the widest extent of the surviving inner edge of the folio, including the ca. 0.3 cm area of the miniature and the ca. 1 cm inner margin.

The outer edge of the recto is more damaged. The outer margin has entirely vanished and sections of the text area are torn, too. Knowing that the intact column measured 7.2 cm, we can calculate that 1.4 cm is missing from the widest extent of the outer column. The width of the outer margin in Turfan Manichaean book art is often between the heights of the upper (here 3.6 cm) and bottom (here 1.4 cm) margins. The mathematical mean of these two measurements on the recto (2.5 cm) gives a good estimate for the approximate width of the outer margin. This means that altogether ca. 4.0 cm is missing from the widest extent of the outer edge of the folio, including a 1.5 cm part of the text area and a 2.5 cm outer margin. Using the above clues (text area 15.0 cm, inner margin 1.0 cm, and outer margin 2.5 cm), the estimated original width of the page becomes ca 18.5 cm.

---

[7] This section includes an upper text area (5.2 cm) with alternating sequences of four red and four black lines,; the book painting (12.0 cm), and a lower text area arranged similarly to the basic design of the upper text area (currently 4.6 cm). In light of the verso's pictorial clue, the last traceable line must have been the very last line of the main text. If so, the lower margin was ca. 1.5 cm.

[8] The inner margin, defining the edge of both the text and the book painting, is seen on four Manichaean illuminated codex fragments (MIK III 8259 folio 1[?] recto, MIK III 4974 recto, MIK III 6368 verso, and MIK III 4958 recto).

A Folio with an Intratextual Scene (Or. 8212-1692)

In its current condition Or. 8212-1692 (Kao. 0107 in early publications) constitutes approximately two-thirds of an illuminated folio (Figure 5/10). The horizontal lines of the Runic script text align the fragment. The sequence of the two sides can be recognized in light of the relationship between the directions of the text and the outer margin, since we know that on a recto page, the lines of the text proceed from the inner margin and end at the outer margin. Thus, in this case the recto is the side that preserves parts of a header and two columns of a Runic text, and the verso is the side on which the traces of a full-page book painting are found. The dimensions of the fragment are 10 cm in height and 8 cm in width. Based on the reasons presented below, it is most likely that the approximate original size of the folio reached ca. 14.6 cm in height and 11.3 cm in width.

For the reconstruction of the original height, the layout of the recto and the composition of the book painting on the verso are both informative, but only allow us to reach a hypothetical result that nevertheless can be confirmed in light of Manichaean pictorial data gained from a comparative example. From among the page elements on the recto, the calculation of the height of the upper margin is the most secure. The distance between the header and the first line of the text is 1.4 cm. The height of the writing in the header is 0.2 cm. Above the header, currently 1.4 cm is retained. Remnants of floral motifs in this part of the page suggest that only a small section is missing from along the upper edge of the folio. This section must have contained the now-vanished parts of the floral motifs and a blank area along the edge of the folio, all in all an estimated ca. 0.5 cm. Together with it, the original height of the upper margin reached ca. 3.5 cm (including the 2×1.4 cm retained illuminated area, the 0.2 cm line of the header, and the missing 0.5 cm).

The calculation of the text area's height on the recto is more difficult. Below the upper margin, the text is organized into two columns written in sequences of alternating groups of red and black ink lines that form a checkered pattern. The sequences on this page are rather long, containing 10 lines each and extending to 4.6 cm in height. Line spacing, and hence the gap between two subsequent sequences, is ca. 0.5 cm. Remnants of the text confirm two color sequences, making 20 lines in each column. This means that the minimum vertical extent of the text area was 9.7 cm (including the 2×4.6 cm sequence plus the 0.5 cm line distance that separated the two sections).

The verso's pictorial program supports the idea that only two color sequences were part of the columns on the recto. The book painting on the verso depicts a version of a Bema Scene, which is also seen as a full-page book painting on the verso of MIK III 4979 (Figure 5/9). As my recent study concludes, points of comparison between these two paintings include identical details of iconography (figures and components of the scene) and composition (location of main and side figures, and the objects of the setting).[9] In both paintings, the central area consists of two main elects with gesturing hands and elaborate garments, a book-reading elect, and containers of food. In both paintings, the central area is flanked by side areas formed by elects and other figures arranged in rows, looking toward the center of the composition. On the verso of Or. 8212-1692, the central area defined by the two main elects measures 7.4 cm.[10] Along the left side, the painting retains parts of three elects. Since we have seen that only ca. 0.5 cm is missing from the upper margin on the recto, this would leave room on the verso for only the rest of the third seated elect and a narrow margin, resulting in ca. 3.6 cm for this side of the painting. In light of the symmetrical arrangement of the better-preserved Bema Scene, we can assume that this painting, too, was composed accordingly, and thus, along the right side of the central episode, originally there was a ca. 3.6 cm

---

[9] Gulácsi 2005.

[10] The ca. 6.5 cm for the central area was measured between the outer rims of the two main figures' halos.

a: Or. 8212-1692 recto

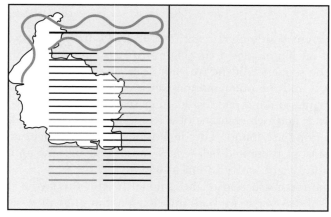

c: Or. 8212-1692 recto

b: Or. 8212-1692 verso

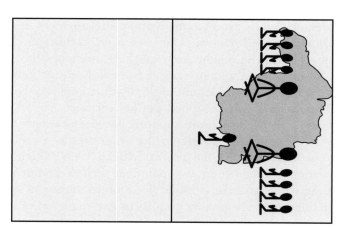

d: Or. 8212-1692 verso

Figure 5/10. Reconstruction of an Illuminated Folio (Or. 8218-1692)
(British Library, London)

area filled with rows of elects. In terms of folio sizes, this logic means that the width of the sideways-oriented full-page scene, that is the height of the codex folio, was 14.6 cm, including the two 3.6 cm side areas and the 7.4 cm central area of the scene. For the layout of the recto, a 14.6 cm height includes a 3.5 cm upper margin, a text area with two color sequences in 9.7 cm, and a bottom margin of 1.4 cm. In light of Manichaean codicological data, 1.4 cm is a reasonable estimate on this page, since the bottom margin is expected to be between the sizes of the inner and outer margins.

The original width of this folio can be calculated based on the retained sizes of the page elements of the recto and Manichaean codicological data. The outer margin is more or less intact at its widest preserved extent (2.8 cm). Assuming that only a few millimeters are missing from it, the original width of the outer margin must have been ca. 3.0 cm. The text area contains remnants of two columns (3.5 cm each) and a gap between them (0.3 cm); thus its original width is calculated to be 7.3 cm. The inner margin's width can only be hypothesized. Since in Manichaean book art the inner margin is often less than half of the outer margin, an estimate of ca. 1.0 cm seems reasonable. This would mean that ca. 2.2 cm is missing from the inner part of the folio, at the widest section of the fragment.[11] These measurements total 11.3 cm as the estimated size for the original width, including the 3.0 cm for the outer margin, the 7.3 cm text area, and the 1.0 cm inner margin.

A Folio with Traces of a Full-Page Book Painting (MIK III 36)

The fragment MIK III 36 preserves a large section from the upper central area of a folio (Figure 5/11). The Manichaean script text aligns the fragment. The text in relation to the outer and inner margins identifies the recto as the side with the text. Here, the lines of writing proceed from the narrower inner margin toward the wider outer margin. The verso is the side with the full-page book painting, showing a seated ruler with rows of soldiers. Although no original edges survive, this paper piece does have two straight edges. The vertical one formed along the middle fold when the original bifolio tore into two sheets. The horizontal straight edge, seen along the top, is a cut that once was overlapped slightly with a now-vanished piece of paper glued here in order to patch the upper section of the folio.[12] In its current condition the dimensions of the fragment are 10.0 cm in height and 10.3 cm in width. The proposed original measurements of the folio are ca. 22.0 cm for the height and 11.0 cm for the width.

The original height of this folio can be proposed in light of a combination of evidence including the pattern of text arrangement on the recto, the symmetrical composition of the full-page book painting on the verso, and Manichaean codicological data. On the recto, the upper and bottom margins have completely vanished. From the text area parts of five sequences are retained from the alternating blocks of red and black lines of writing.[13] On all illuminated fragments with identical red and black line sequences, the

---

[11] On the verso, this 2.2 cm area would correspond with the bottom of the book painting, where piles of food were depicted in the lower center of the composition, for the pictorial reconstruction.

[12] The broken text on the recto and the missing parts of figures on the verso indicate that the straight-looking line at the top of the fragment is not the actual upper edge of the page. On the verso, along the side with the half figures, a delicate blank strip can be observed. Although looking misleadingly similar to a narrow margin that surrounds painted scenes, the thin blank strip is not a margin. Rather, it shows a glued section where an extra piece was added to the paper to complete the needed size of the folio. When this added section was lost, it exposed a narrow glue strip that had held the two joined pieces of paper together. Beneath the overlap, the glue strip remained blank. The missing upper part of the verso was occupied by a minimum of a narrow margin and one more column of figures (i.e. two figures situated above and below one another) whose hands, extended to the left of their bodies, are still visible.

[13] In the first (inner) column, each sequence contains five lines. Within the corresponding sections of the second (outer) column the number of lines squeezed into the available area varies between 5 and 6 lines. Although the line numbers differ, the height of all sequences is standard (1.75 cm).

a: MIK III 36 recto

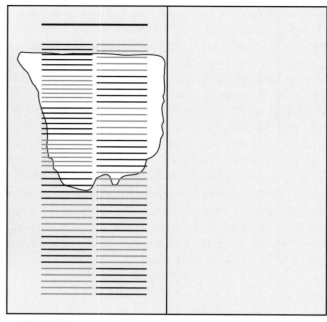

c: MIK III 36 recto

b: MIK III 36 verso

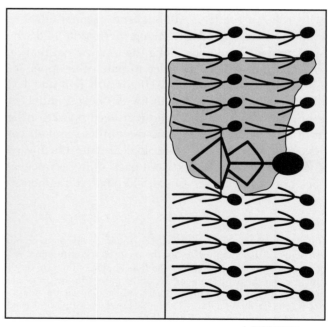

d: MIK III 36 verso

Figure 5/11. Reconstruction of an Illuminated Folio (MIK III 36)
(SMPK, Museum für Indische Kunst, Berlin)

first block of the sequence on a page is red, suggesting that the top surviving sequence of the first column could be the first sequence on this page. The pictorial program on the verso can help us judge how much is missing from the text area. The remnant of the verso's painting suggests that a symmetrical composition occupied this page. The large figure of a seated ruler is likely to be found at the vertical axis of the composition. The location of the ruler on the verso corresponds with the middle of the fourth color sequence on the recto. If we imagine a mirror symmetrical composition for the verso, then the recto must have had at least eight red and black sequences in each column. If indeed eight color sequences were on the recto, then an additional three sequences must be missing, all three beneath the ones that survive and none above the first remaining sequence. What does this mean in centimeters?

In accordance with the above reasoning, only two lines and the upper margin are missing from the top of the page on the recto. This area would accommodate one additional soldier along with the missing half of the soldier at the current edge of the fragment, as well as a thin margin (ca. 3.5 cm) on the verso. On the recto, this approximately 3.5 cm contained the now-missing two lines from the text area (0.5 cm) and an upper margin (ca. 3.0 cm). The suggested vertical axis of the painting is currently at 7.5 cm from the edge of the fragment. Adding the 3.5 cm missing from the top of the page to this measurement means that if the ruler indeed represents the vertical axis, then the complete folio's midpoint was at ca. 11.0 cm (3.5 cm plus 7.5 cm); the original height was thus ca. 22.0 cm. The plausibility of this estimate can be evaluated by checking the results on the recto, where the estimated height of the upper margin comes to ca. 3.0 cm, the text area with 8 red and black sequences in each column amounts to ca. 17.5 cm,[14] and the bottom margin is ca. 1.5 cm.

The original width of this folio is almost fully preserved at the widest extent of the fragment, as indicated by the page elements of the recto, where sections of the inner margin (1.5 cm), as well as the text area (7.0 cm), are undamaged. The idea that only a small part (ca. 0.7 cm) is missing from the complete outer margin (estimated at 1.8 cm), is suggested by the corresponding section of the verso's pictorial program. The verso's full-page book painting shows the seated ruler surrounded by rows of figures in military armor. The area equivalent to the recto's outer margin is occupied by the heads of the standing solders. The missing section contained a tiny part from the helmet and the halo of the most complete figure, together with the edge of the blue background, as well as a narrow blank space along the edges of the paper. In light of the proportion of the figures and the overall scale of the painting, the estimate for the missing width is ca. 0.7 cm. On the recto, this 0.7 cm belonged to the blank outer margin. Taken together, the proposed original widths for the page elements on the recto are inner margin 1.5 cm, text 7.0 cm, and outer margin ca. 2.5 cm (1.8 cm plus the now missing 0.7 cm). They total ca. 11.0 cm.

A Folio with Traces of an Intratextual Scene (M 576)

The fragment in the poorest condition within the reconstructible group preserves the upper three-quarters of a codex folio (M 576, Figure 5/12). The horizontal lines of Manichaean script text in relation to the outer and inner margins allow us to align the fragment and distinguish the two sides. The recto is the side on which an illuminated header and a text are clearly visible. The verso suffered considerable surface damage that left only a vaguely detectable illuminated header, and only traces of the continuation of the Manichaean script text and its intratextual book painting. The current measurements are 11.6 cm for the height and 8.2 cm for the width. The proposed original size comes to a minimum 14.1 cm for the height and ca. 9.2 cm for the width.

---

[14] Each sequence is ca. 1.75 cm high and there are eight of them in each column (8 × 1.75 cm = 14 cm). The spacing between the sequences is ca. 0.5 cm, and there are seven of them (7 × 0.5 cm = 3.5 cm). Thus the height is ca. 17.5 cm.

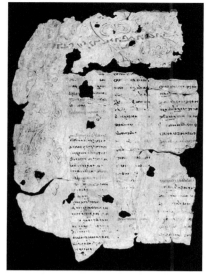

a: M 576 recto

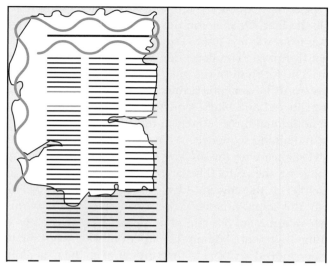

c: M 576 recto

b: M 576 verso

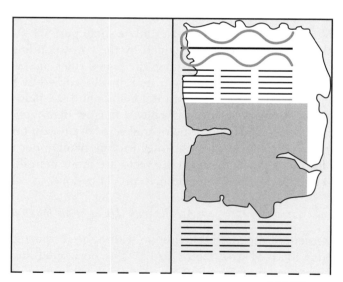

d: M 576 verso

Figure 5/12. Reconstruction of an Illuminated Folio (M 576)
(SBPK, Berlin-Brandenburgische Akademie der Wissenschaften, Turfanforschung, Berlin)

The original width is reflected well on the page elements of the recto. On this page, the header stretches along the entire width of the three columns at approximately the middle of the surviving upper margin. The torn gap seen within the upper margin does not represent a missing piece from the original folio. Rather, it resulted from a gradual separation of once-connected paper parts. By aligning the paper of the upper margin from its currently separated position with the rest of the page, the header becomes parallel with the text. In general, the headers on Manichaean manuscripts are as long as the width of the column(s) of the page. Since the header's phrase "The Beautiful Hymn-Incipits" is complete, most likely its width represents the width of the text area. If so, no additional column, just a narrow inner margin is missing from the original width of the folio.[15] Adding up the outer margin's ca. 2.2 cm, and the text area's ca. 6.0 cm, to the inner margin's estimated ca.1 cm, the original width of the folio comes to ca. 9.2 cm.

To reach a likely estimate for the original height of this damaged folio, we must turn to the data preserved on the verso and compare it to the layout seen on better-preserved Manichaean illuminated fragments. Although most of the content on this side has vanished completely, on the wrinkled paper surface, red color traces the shape of a ribbon in the upper margin, and smeared black and red lines indicate lines of writing in the header as well as in three short columns of text. Beneath the columns, a blurry, multicolored area confirms that at one time a book painting was inserted into the text area, separating it into two halves. In the Berlin corpus of Manichaean art, three reconstructible codex folia (MIK III 4974 recto, MIK III 4979 recto, and MIK III 8259 folio 1 recto) contain intratextual figural compositions. In each case, the painting is placed in the center of the text area, with equal amounts of lines of writing above and below the picture. Since the upper margin usually occupies a greater area than the lower margin, the intratextual scene is rarely found in the middle of the page—the exception being MIK III 4974 recto, where the symmetry of the pictorial program around the intratextual scene required equal heights for the upper and lower margins.

On the verso of M 576, the height of the remaining pictorial area (i.e., the distance between the beginning of the blue background beneath the last line of the upper text area and the bottom edge of the fragment) is 6.6 cm. Above the painting, the intact text area with its eight lines of miniscule writing extends to 1.7 cm. The height of the upper margin measures ca. 2.6 cm. Since in well-preserved Manichaean codex pages with floral illumination the lower margin's height is frequently the same as the section of the upper margin above the header, here a likely minimal estimate for the lower margin is ca. 1.5 cm. Thus, a minimum 3.2 cm area that contained eight lines of text (1.7 cm) and the lower margin (1.5 cm) is missing from this page. All in all the minimum original height of the folio is 14.1 cm, including the upper margin (2.6 cm), the upper text area (1.7 cm), the book painting (min. 6.6 cm), the lower text area (1.7 cm), and the lower margin (1.5 cm). It is possible that the intratextual painting occupied a larger section of the page, and/or the bottom margin was taller, and consequently the folio was a few centimeters greater in height.

A Folio with a Full-Page Book Painting and a Marginal Scene (MIK III 6368)

With its well-preserved sections of marginal and full-page book paintings, MIK III 6368 constitutes the upper third of an illuminated codex folio (Figure 5/13). The horizontal lines of Sogdian script align the fragment. The recto, on which the writing proceeds from the inner to the outer margins, contains part of a full-page book painting that incorporates a textual area into its pictorial program. The verso is the side on which the text proceeds from the wider outer margin on the right, toward the inner margin on the left. This side retains an illuminated header and a text arranged in two columns bordered by a figural

---

[15] Due to the fragmentary condition of the manuscript, Reck considered the possibility that the header was longer (i.e., preceded by an extra word) on the recto (1990, 46).

a: MIK III 6368 recto

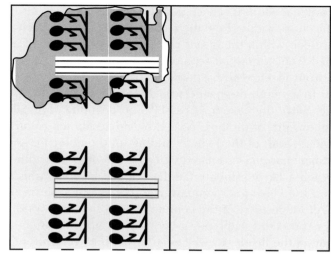

d: MIK III 6368 recto

b: MIK III 6368 verso

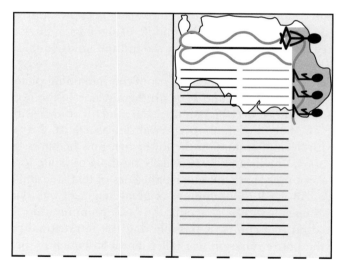

d: MIK III 6368 verso

Figure 5/13. Reconstruction of an Illuminated Folio (MIK III 6368)
(SMPK, Museum für Indische Kunst, Berlin)

composition along the outer margin. The current dimensions are 11.2 cm for the height and 17.2 cm for the width. The original height of the folio reached a minimum of 27.8 cm, and its width was 17.2 cm.

The original width of this folio is more or less intact. On both sides, the current widest extent remaining from the inner margin (0.8 cm) represents the approximate complete width defined on one side by a straight edge that formed along the fold as the sheet separated from its bifolio. Bordering the inner margin on the recto is a full-page book painting (16.3 cm). From the outer margin's blank area just a tiny section is retained (ca. 0.1 cm). Since no full-page Manichaean book painting preserves the area of the outer margin, we can only guess its original width here. It could have been as wide as the inner margin on this page (ca. 0.9 cm). It is more likely however, that the outer margin on the recto was rather narrow (0.1 cm), as suggested by comparison with the upper margin of the recto, which is similarly thin (ca. 0.1 cm). Working with the latter estimate, the widths of the page elements on the recto are ca. 0.9 cm for the inner margin, 16.2 cm for the pictorial area, and ca. 0.1 cm for the outer margin, resulting in 17.2 cm as the minimum original width of the folio. On the verso, this 17.2 cm width is occupied by the inner margin's ca. 0.9 cm, the text area's 12.1 cm, and the outer margin's 4.1 cm marginal figural scene on a blue background and its ca. 0.1 cm blank border.

To judge the original height of the folio, we ought to consider the page elements of the verso and the pictorial program of the recto, as well as Manichaean codicological data. On the verso, the text area just barely preserves an important clue, permitting the reconstruction. The text is divided between two columns. The first (outer) column starts with five lines in red ink. The sixth line is completely missing except for tiny sections of two letters, one in the middle and one at the end of the line. Both are in black ink. The fact that here the sixth line is in black ink, just like the first lines remaining from the second (inner) column, suggests that originally this text area contained alternating sequences of red and black ink lines. More than two sequences can be suspected, since it is unlikely that an intratextual book painting was part of the verso, because the marginal figural composition on this page is not oriented toward the area where an intratextual painting would be. Rather all figures along the margin face toward the header, where a gold-robed preaching elect is depicted. How many color sequences are missing? On the other four examples of illuminated folia with texts arranged in a checkered pattern (MIK III 8259 fl[?] verso, MIK III 36, MIK III 4979 recto, and Or. 8212-1692 recto), the sequences are in even numbers: two, four, six, and eight. Undoubtedly more than two sequences were part of this page. If four sequences were employed, each column would have contained four 5-line sequences, amounting to ca.19.0 cm in height. One sequence measures 4.0 cm and four of these reach 16.0 cm. The gap, that is the line distance, between two sequences is 1.0 cm, so between four sequences there would be three such gaps, totaling 3.0 cm. The upper margin on the verso (ca. 5.8 cm) is defined by a straight edge along its top that can be considered to be representative of the original upper edge of the folio. Since the lower half of the page is completely missing, the height of the bottom margin can only be hypothesized. It is likely that the height of the bottom margin was similar to the ca. 3.0 cm distance seen between the header and the edge of the page. By adding the estimated 3.0 cm height of the bottom margin to the 19.0 cm text area, and the 5.8 cm height of the upper margin, the minimum original height of the page comes to 27.8 cm.

The 27.8 cm height for the recto would mean that the full-page pictorial program incorporated at least two text areas, each with three lines of text written on a ca. 2.5 cm high blank block (5.0 cm). Above the upper and below the lower text areas were the two 5.5 cm side sections from the painting program (11.0 cm). These estimates would leave 11.8 cm between the two text blocks for the central part of the full-page composition. Since only a 3.7 cm portion is retained from this central part of the page, it is possible that the 11.8 cm was not dedicated solely to the pictorial program, but that it incorporated another text area in the very middle of the page. Either way, 27.8 cm seems to be a reasonable estimate for the original height.

Folio with Decorative Designs and a Figural Scene (So 18700 & M 501 e with So 10650 a)

Three fragments retain most of the upper half and a small section from the lower half of a codex folio with a Sogdian script text (So 18700 & M 501 e with So 10650 a, Figure 5/14). The recto is the side that preserves small parts from the illuminated upper margin from the area just below the now-lost header and a large section from the non-illuminated outer margin to the left of the text. The verso also contains sections from the illuminated upper margin from the area beneath the header, which is no longer part of the page. The outer margin, which on the verso is to the right of the text, is illuminated with a figural scene. Scarf motifs, similar to the ones seen along the upper margin, are repeated in between seated figures that are oriented sideways. The current size of the now physically joined two fragments (So 18700 & M 501) is 12.8 cm in height and 15.0 cm in width. The third fragment, which most likely derived from the lower part of the page, measures 8.2 cm in height 3.2 cm in width. The estimated original height of the folio reached ca. 28.5 cm and the width ca. 17.7 cm.

Regarding the original height, currently there are 14 lines of text and parts from the upper margin on each side of the physically joined fragments. It is most likely that at least 10 lines are missing from the text area, as suggested in a recent study in which the fragment, So 10650 a, with parts of 10 lines, has been identified as belonging to this folio. The subject and formal qualities of the text on So 10650 a are identical to that of the joined fragments. The lines are written in identical handwriting, script size, and line spacing, suggesting that this fragment must have belonged to the same codex, possibly to the lower half of this illuminated folio.[16] An additional 10 lines would mean that the text area on these pages consisted of at least 22–24 lines, depending on whether So 10650 a preserves text sections overlapping with lines 13 and 14 of our fragment, or not. The height of the upper margin in its current condition measures 1.6 cm, which represents less than half of its original height of ca. 4.5 cm. The 14 lines of the text area occupy 11.3 cm. The additional 10 lines take up 8.2 cm. The line spacing is 1.0 cm. Thus, a text area with 24 lines would have reached 20.5 cm in height. The lower margin can be estimated to be ca. 2.5 cm. In light of this data, the likely original height of the folio was around 28.5 cm.

Only small sections are missiong from the current 15.0 cm widest extent of the folio. The outer margin measures 4.0 cm. Since on the verso the top of the figure's head is lost, we can assume that ca. 0.5 cm is lacking from its original width. The widest extent of this one-columned text seems to be indicated at two locations. On both sides of the page a vertical line of ruling is seen along the outer margin. On the recto the edge of a scarf motif suggests the possibility that the word beneath the scarf was the first word of the page, continuing the text from the previous folio. Thus, the text area was most likely 11.7 cm wide. No parts of the inner margins are retained. In light of the width of the outer margin, it probably was relatively wide, ca. 1.5 cm. Taken together, the original width of the complete folio can be estimated to have reached ca. 17.7 cm.

A Parchment Folio with an Intratextual Scene (Or. 12452/3)

This torn illuminated parchment (Or. 12452/3) represents a small area from the central inner part of a codex folio (Figure 5/15). The horizontal lines of Manichaean script writing align the fragment, and the direction of the writing in relation to the figures of the book painting allow us to distinguish the recto and verso sides. The side with the book painting is the recto. Here, a section of the inner margin can be seen to the right of the painting. The heads of the figures are toward the left, where originally the outer margin was located. The two lines of text preserved above the painting confirm that the image was an intratextual

---

[16] Reck 2005.

a: So 18700 & M 501 e recto

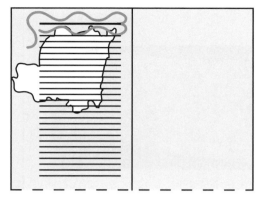

c: So 18700 & M 501 e recto

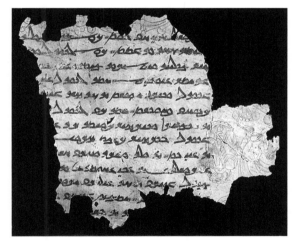

b: So 18700 & M 501 e verso

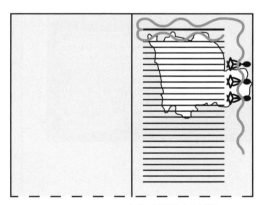

d: So 18700 & M 501 e verso

Figure 5/14. Reconstruction of an Illuminated Folio (So 18700 and M 501 e)
(SBPK, Berlin-Brandenburgische Akademie der Wissenschaften, Turfanforschung, Berlin)

a: Or. 12452/3 recto

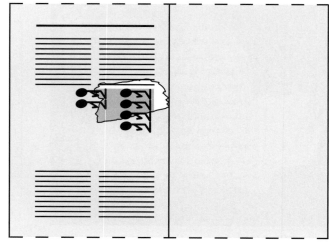

c: Or. 12452/3 recto

b: Or. 12452/3 verso

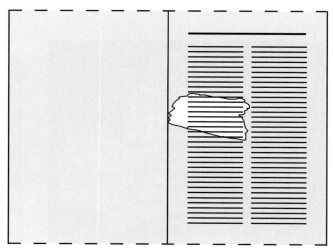

d: Or. 12452/3 verso

Figure 5/15. Reconstruction of an Illuminated Folio Fragment (Or. 12452/3)
(British Library, London)

scene. The non-illuminated side is the verso, and retains 11 lines from the inner column of the text, small areas from the gap between the columns, and a section of the inner margin. In its current condition the fragment measures 4.75 by 8.9 cm. Based on a reconstruction of the original layout, the folio's height was between 24.2 and 32.6 cm, and its width reached a minimum of 18.2 cm.

The calculation of the original width is made possible in light of the page elements of the verso, which leave us to estimate only the width of the outer margin. On this side, a relatively wide inner margin in its current 2.5 cm size indicates the minimum width of the original inner margin. The 5.8 cm width of the inner column is intact. Sections remaining from the blank area that separated the two columns suggest that the columns were placed a minimum of 0.6 cm apart. Thus, the original width of the text area comes to 12.2 cm, including the widths of the two columns (11.6 cm) and the gap (0.6 cm) that separated them. This 12.2 cm approximately corresponds with the original horizontal extent of the book painting on the recto. Knowing that in Manichaean book art the inner margin, which here measures 2.5 cm, is likely to be the thinnest among the four margins, an estimate of 3.5 cm for the outer margin is reasonable. All in all, the widths of the page elements add up to a minimum of 18.2 cm as the most likely measurement for the original width.

Although much less information is preserved concerning the height of this folio, its vertical extent can be estimated with accuracy when the fragmentary page elements of the recto are interpreted in light of analogous contents of better-preserved Manichaean illuminated codex folia. First, let us consider the area of the book painting that originally occupied a minimum of 10.0 cm from the page height. By turning the fragment to the picture-viewing direction, we notice that the retained portion of the painting shows close resemblance to one of the best-preserved intratextual book paintings, the Conversion Scene (MIK III 4979 recto, Figure 5/9), in terms of composition (and iconography). It is most likely that this scene, too, consisted of rows of seated figures balanced symmetrically along the now-lost vertical axis of the composition. At its current widest extent, the remaining right half of the image measures 4.0 cm. The original right half of the image was approximately 5.0 cm. This half of the composition was occupied by four seated figures at the lower right and two seated figures together with parts of the central area at the upper right. If indeed the group of four figures once took up the entire lower right of the painting, just as in the well-preserved Conversion Scene, then the intact image must have contained two ca. 5.0 cm halves. The original 10.0 cm width of the image included a now-missing ca. 2.0 cm central area with most certainly a main figure in the upper center flanked by side figures seated on carpets.

Continuing the investigation of the original page height, we ought to consider the text that sandwiched the book painting on the recto. As all better-preserved examples of pages with intertextual scenes confirm (such as MIK III 8259 folio 1[?] recto, Figure 5/7; MIK III 4979 recto, Figure 5/9; and MIK III 4974 recto, Figure 4/8), the writing started in the upper section of the inner column whose lines continued beneath the painting before leading the reader to the outer column of this page; the columns were evenly divided by the painting. In the case of this parchment folio, the complete text area with equal amount of lines above and beneath the image can be estimated to have taken up between 7.2 cm and 15.6 cm, depending on the number of lines that formed each column. Intercolumnar scenes enclosed by 12 lines of text (six lines above and six lines below the painting) are documented on two examples (MIK III 4979 recto, Figure 5/9; and MIK III 4974 recto, Figure 4/8), whereas 26 lines of text (13 lines above and 13 lines below the painting) are seen on one fragment (MIK III 8259 folio 1[?] recto, Figure 4/7). On this parchment fragment, the intact line height (0.12 cm) and line spacing (0.6 cm) preserved on the verso reflect the arrangement also seen in the partially preserved lines on the recto. Assuming that a minimum of six lines (3.6 cm) and a maximum of 13 lines (7.8 cm) were part of each column both above and below the painting, the vertical extent of the writing comes to either 7.2 cm (2 × 3.6 cm) or 15.6 cm (2 × 7.8 cm). Thus, the text area of the recto, including its intratextual book painting (10.0 cm) occupied a minimum of 17.2 cm and a maximum of 25.6 cm from the page height.

The upper and bottom margins are the final elements of the page relevant for establishing the original height of the folio. Based on the fact that the inner margin on this fragment, which in most examples of Turfan Manichaean book art is the thinnest, measures 2.5 cm, it can be estimated that the bottom margin was somewhat wider than the inner margin, ca. 3.0 cm. Following the same trend in codicological data, it is reasonable to assume that the upper margin was the widest, ca. 4.0 cm. Thus, the upper and lower margins together reached ca. 7.0 cm on this folio.

These calculations and size estimates suggest that the original height of the fragment was a minimum of 24.2 cm and a maximum of 32.6 cm. On both sides of the intact folio, this height was occupied by a ca. 4.0 cm high upper margin, a text area of between 17.2 cm and 25.6 cm that included the book painting on the recto, and a ca. 3.0 cm high lower margin. As on all other currently known examples of Manichaean illuminated codex fragments, here, too, the book painting is oriented sideways, with the heads of the figures toward the outer margin.

INTERPRETATION OF NON-RECONSTRUCTIBLE ILLUMINATED CODEX FRAGMENTS

On the 26 six pages of the 11 codex remains (two with decorative designs and nine with figural scenes) reconstructed above, the textual and pictorial components are systematic in terms of their location and orientation, and thus convey a set of basic rules. These rules can be summed up in the following points:

TEXT: The lines of the texts are horizontal
                             The lines of the texts proceed from right to left on each side

DECORATIVE DESIGN: Decorative designs are placed along the upper and outer margins

FIGURAL SCENE: The figural scenes are painted sideways, at right angles to texts
                             The heads of the figures are closer to the outer margins on each side

Besides exhibiting a consistent application of these principles, the reconstructed folia also show that the direction of the lines within the text in relation to the outer margin (with or without decorative design) and to the direction of figural scenes is different on the recto and the verso. On each page the lines of the text are standard. They proceed from right to left. It is the borders of the page that change between the two sides of the folio, since the margins around the text are symmetrical on the two facing pages of the book. The margins on the verso mirror the margins on the recto. The margins also dictate where to place the decorative designs in relation to the text area, and in which direction to paint the figural scenes. Accordingly, the recto and verso sides are distinct in terms of the relationship of their page elements:

RECTO: The lines of the text run from the inner margin to the outer margin
          Decorative designs are above and to the left of text
          The heads of figures are closer to the outer margin
          The lines of text read from toe to head of the figures

VERSO: The lines of text run from outer margin to inner margin
           Decorative designs are above and to the right of text
           The heads of figures are closer to the outer margin
           The lines of text read from head to toe of the figures

For example, even on the smallest fragment, when a section from a text and a figural scene (with a directional component) are retained, the physical relationship of the two identifies the recto and the verso sides. On the rectos, the lines of the text proceed from toe to head in relation to the adjacent figures, that is, the writing in the lines begins from the inner margins and concludes at the outer margins. On the versos, the lines of the text proceed from head to toe in relation to the figures, starting from the outer margins and ending at the inner margins. The same is true for any folio fragment on which a section from the text is preserved together with either the outer or inner margins.

The majority of Manichaean illuminated codex fragments are so damaged that their original folia cannot be reconstructed. But their correct orientation and the sequence of the two sides can be determined in light of the rules observed on the reconstructed pages. As a result, some information can always be learned about the original layouts and the sizes. Three examples will illustrate the application of these rules. They illustrate that despite their damaged condition and small sizes, the fragments retain a rich body of information about Manichaean book art. They can be aligned correctly and, in most cases, the sequence of their two sides can be established. Much of their original page layout can be established, as well as the original size of their folia. Through this four-step analysis (alignment, sequence, layout, and size), all currently known Manichaean illuminated codex fragments can contribute to this study, which is therefore comprehensive in scope.

Folio Fragment with Two Figural Scenes (MIK III 4959)

The fragment with which the orientation experiment was conducted at the beginning of this chapter can be easily understood in light of the above rules of page arrangement (MIK III 4959, Figure 5/16). The text-reading direction correctly aligns this double-sided paper piece. When placed in this position the lines of writing are horizontal, running from right to left. The side with the two figures and the text is the recto, since the writing here proceeds from the inner to the outer margin, that is from toe to head in relation to the neighboring figures. The verso in this case contains only a part of a figural scene with the heads toward the right—to the now-lost outer margin of the page.

Numerous additional pieces of information are preserved on this fragment about the original page layout. We learn that this torn piece of paper derived from the bottom middle part a codex folio, since on both sides it retains a section from the original edge along the ca. 1.8 cm high blank bottom margin. The recto accommodated both a text and a figural scene. The text was organized into columns of ca. 6.4 cm wide each, as confirmed by the last line visible directly above the figures. The inner edge of this column is indicated by a gap (ca. 0.5 cm), and the outer edge is signaled with a floral scribal decoration just under the last letter of the line. The figures beneath the text area were part of either a wide marginal scene, or more likely a full-page composition that integrated textual areas within a pictorial program, as documented on MIK III 6368 recto (Figure 5/13). Six seated figures can be deciphered from this area of the original composition. They are arranged in pairs, seated beneath one another in three rows. The distribution of the three pairs of figures was roughly analogous to that of the columns in a way that at the end of each column, a pair of figures was painted. The two intact figures are the middle pair. Beneath their lotus seats, the remnants of two halos and headdresses confirm the lower pair. The paper beyond the heads of the two intact figures is torn. But, directly above the halo of the bearded one, the edge of the paper retains bits of violet

a: MIK III 4959 recto

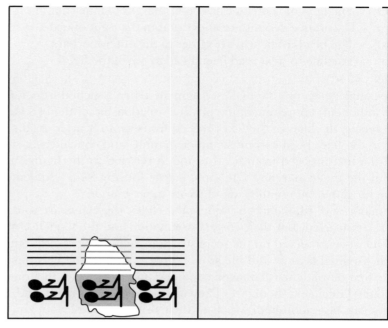

c: MIK III 4959 recto

b: MIK III 4959 verso

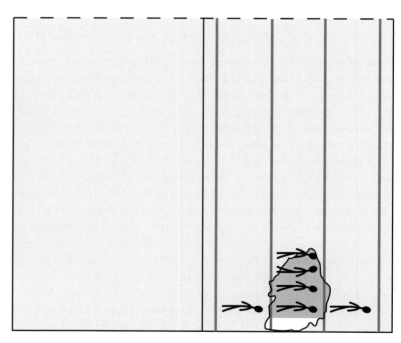

d: MIK III 4959 verso

Figure 5/16. Interpretation of an Illuminated Folio Fragment (MIK III 4959)
(SMPK, Museum für Indische Kunst, Berlin)

pigment, suggesting the possibility that these colors were part of the now-lost lotus seats of the upper pair. The verso was devoted solely to a pictorial program. Here, parts of two golden lines suggest that originally three narrow registers (each 6.5 cm wide) were filled with units of figural scenes; the one preserved is the middle of the three. From the area of the lower register only bits from the blue background are retained. From the upper register, only unidentifiable bits from some motifs are preserved. These three registers in size and distribution accord with the three-columned page layout of the recto.

Regarding the original size, this folio was rather large. The text area in itself, including the three columns (3 × 6.4 cm) and the two gaps between them (2 × 0.8 cm) was 20.8 cm wide on this page. In light of such a size, it is reasonable to assume that the inner and outer margins together might have been around 4.0 cm, making the folio's width at least ca. 24.8 cm. The size of the script (0.4 cm), the line spacing (1.0 cm), the width of the columns on the recto (6.4 cm), and the gap between the two columns (0.8 cm) are approximately one-third larger than seen on the two largest reconstructed fragments (MIK III 8259, Figure 5/7; MIK III 4979, Figure 5/9). Such an overall size of the page elements supports the hypothesis that this fragment derived from a minimum 24.2 cm wide illuminated codex, whose height most likely exceeded 40.0 cm.

Fragments of Two Subsequent Folia with Three Figural Scenes (MIK III 4971 a–d)

The four illuminated fragments discussed here represent parts of two subsequent folia of a book in codex format (MIK III 1971 a–d, Figure 5/17). The horizontal lines of Manichaean script in relation to the wide outer margins and the directions of the sideways figures allow us to correctly orient these fragments, judge the layout of their pages, and identify the recto and verso sides. But the succession of the two folia cannot be confirmed. Folio 1(?) is indicated through the three largest fragments (a–c), and folio 2(?) is preserved through the smallest paper piece, fragment d, seen adhered to fragment a.

From the recto of folio 1(?) bits of the text and sections of a figural scene remain. On fragment a, the figural scene shows the upper left of an intratextual composition with bits from a centrally positioned and haloed elect and the upper body of a male elect along the side. Through an architectural arching frame, this scene extends to the area of the outer margin, where bits from a carpet and the knees are preserved from a seated elect, suggesting that the main scene was flanked by at least two such figures along the outer margin. Fragment b preserves the upper body of a male elect from the marginal section of the main scene, as well as a stroke from the last letter of the last line from the text above the intratextual scene. Fragment c holds the headgear of three male elects beneath a register line that must have belonged to the lower half of the intratextual scene that, similarly to the upper half, was most likely arranged symmetrically. A symmetrical arrangement is often employed for the figural scenes in Manichaean book art, as shown for example on an analogous composition preserved on the reconstructed bifolio MIK III 8259 (Figure 5/3).[17]

From the verso of folio 1(?), fragment a retains parts of the main text and the lower half of the outer margin, which is blank on this side. Fragment b shows three seated male elects and an ink dot, indicating the starting stroke from a letter seen underneath the last elect. The location of the figures along the upper

---

[17] The original layout of folio 1(?) recto is not fully understood, since the surviving data do not retain any information on the contents of the upper and lower margins. Comparative examples of better-preserved and reconstructed pages suggest that two different arrangements could have been accommodated within the original design on this page. On the one hand, it is possible that the page was arranged similarly to the folio with the two *putti* (MIK III 4974 recto, Fig. 4/4). In this case, the lower margin would be blank and the upper margin would contain a header, possibly with a decorative design. On the other hand, it is also possible that the page layout was analogous to the reconstructed page with the scribes (MIK III 6368 recto, Fig. 5/9). In this case, the upper and lower margins would be used for a pictorial program that used the intratextual area as part of a full-page figural scene that hosted a few lines of text, above and below the central scene.

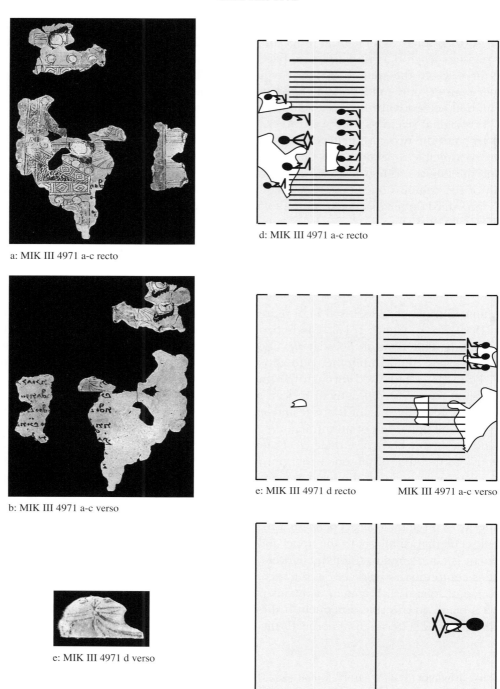

a: MIK III 4971 a-c recto

d: MIK III 4971 a-c recto

b: MIK III 4971 a-c verso

e: MIK III 4971 d recto   MIK III 4971 a-c verso

e: MIK III 4971 d verso

f: MIK III 4971 d verso

Figure 5/17. Interpretation of four Fragments of two Illuminated Folia (MIK III 4971 a–d)
(SMPK, Museum für Indische Kunst, Berlin)

half of the outer margin with the blank lower part of the same margin preserved on fragment a confirms that the figural scene concluded above the middle of the outer margin and that its seated figures faced toward the top of the page. Fragment 'c' holds bits of five lines from close to the inner margin.

Folio 2(?) is represented solely by a tiny piece of paper, fragment d, found adhered to the verso of fragment a, covering up part of the latter's text and also concealing the tiny section remaining from its own recto. It is most likely that fragment d represents a small part of the adjacent folio. The visible side retains the upper body of an elect, which belonged to either a full-page or an intratextual book painting.[18]

Regarding the original size, we learn that these fragments derived from a relatively small codex, on the pages of which the height of the script was ca. 0.2 cm, written with a line spacing of 0.5 cm. In light of the interpretation of the recto's layout on folio 1(?), especially that of the intratextual book painting, it is most likely that the minimum width of the folio was around 11.0 cm. This estimate compares well to the widths of two reconstructed fragments (Or. 8212-1692, Figure 5/10; and MIK III 36, Figure 5/11).

Folio Fragment with a Figural Scene (M 559)

Even small fragments such as M 559, interpreted in light of the rules of page arrangement, contribute important bits of information to our current understanding of Turfan Manichaean book art (Figure 5/18). The horizontal lines of Manichaean script writing retained on both sides align the fragment. The figures to the right of the text indicate the outer margin on a recto page. On the other side, the blank area to the left of the text identifies the verso.

Regarding the original layout of the folio, this fragment derived from an area close to the middle part of the outer margin, as suggested by the composition of the book painting. The section that remains from this marginal scene shows seated figures arranged in a symmetrical manner, facing one another as they flank a small table set up in the near background. A similar example of a symmetrical composition along the outer margin is preserved on the only reconstructed bifolio with figural scenes, MIK III 8259 (Figure 5/7). In that case, flying figures are depicted facing one another approximately at the middle of the outer margin. Thus, it is quite likely that the symmetrical arrangement of figures within the marginal scene on M 559, too, was harmonized within the overall page design by this section of the scene being centered along the outer margin.

The minute size of the page elements suggests that this fragment belonged to a small codex. A small-scale execution characterizes both the writing and the painting. The marginal scene occupies 1.9 cm, defined between the ruling of the outer column and the narrow 0.1 cm blank edge of the page. The width of the outer margin is 2.0 cm. In addition to the marginal figural scene, the recto preserves eight lines from the outer column of a text and a section of the gap that separated two columns on the page. The width of the column is 1.82 cm. Within the column, the writing is miniscule; the height of the script is as tiny as 0.1 cm, and the line spacing is 0.4 cm. From the gap between the two columns, 0.23 cm remains. These measurements compare well to that of the non-illuminated verso, although they are not identical.[19] Regarding the actual size, the presence of at least two columns indicates a ca. 6.7 cm wide folio. Such a page width, as well as the overall sizes of the page elements, compares well to that of the reconstructed codex folio with the two putti (MIK III 4974, Figure 5/8), which was 15.5 cm in height and 7.9 cm in width. A convincing size comparison, however, can be made also with the most damaged fragment among the reconstructed

---

[18] A similar reconstruction of the recto of fragments MIK III 4971 a–c was presented by Dr. Jorinde Ebert at the conference entitled *Annemarie von Gabain und die Turfanforschung*, held in Berlin in 1994.

[19] On the verso, the blank outer margin is 2.1 cm wide. Eight lines of script define a column that reached 1.75 cm in its width. The 0.2 cm blank area to the right of the column confirms that this page, too, was occupied by at least two columns of text.

a: M 559 recto

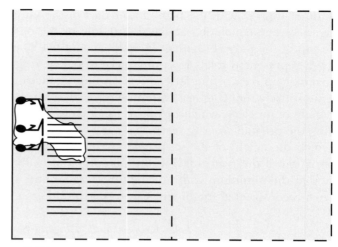

c: M 559 recto

b: M 559 verso

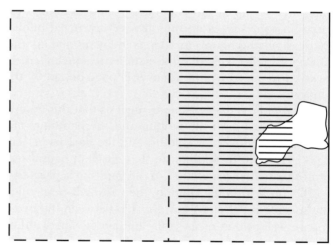

d: M 559 verso

Figure 5/18. Interpretation of an Illuminated Folio Fragment (M559)
(SBPK, Berlin-Brandenburgische Akademie der Wissenschaften, Turfanforschung, Berlin)

folia with figural scenes (M 576, Figure 5/12), which retains three columns written in minute script and was thus somewhat larger at 14.1 cm high and 9.2 cm wide. It is possible that M 559 belonged to a folio with three columns on each page. An additional 2.1 cm width for the third column (1.9 cm) and the additional gap (0.2 cm) would make the folio's estimated original width 8.8 cm.

LAYOUTS OF ILLUMINATED CODEX FRAGMENTS

Like pieces in a picture puzzle, the fragments allow us to accumulate data toward the goal of understanding Manichaean book design. To obtain a full record on the question of page layout, the survey below investigates two types of illuminations (decorative designs and figural scenes) in arbitrary separation from one another. First, the more simple case of decorative designs is discussed, since a clear understanding of their placement aids the consideration of location possibilities for the figural scenes on even the smallest codex remains.

Locations of Decorative Designs

Decorative designs consist of flowery plants that occasionally incorporate scarves, fruits, and plates with symbolic food. They are always associated with the text of the page in one of two possible ways. They are either *marginal*, that is they surround the text area in varying degrees along the upper, outer, and lower margins; or they are *intratextual*, that is they are placed within the columns fully enclosing one line or one word in it (Figure 5/19). Within the currently known corpus of Manichaean book art, 41 fragments preserve 59 codex pages with 61 examples of decorative designs.

The 59 surviving examples of codex pages with decorative designs confirm that in Turfan Manichaean book art such illuminations were used to adorn the page above and alongside the columns (marginal) and, more rarely, also to distinguish the beginning of certain passages within the column (intratextual). Most examples of decorative designs are marginal. Marginal decorative designs always grow out from the header, which is placed along the middle of the upper margin. Via the dominating floral or scarf motifs, the decoration spreads from between the letters in the header and surrounds the text, filling out the upper, outer and lower margins, leaving blank on all examples the area of the inner margin. Not even along the upper margin does the decoration intrude to this innermost, blank part of the codex page. Rarely, there is illumination within the area of a column. The surviving cases of columnar decorative designs suggest that, through this means of illumination, the first line of a new section of the text may be singled out within a column on a highly adorned page. The line is highlighted through pictorial means, through the use of either blue background around a calligraphic script line, or floral motifs painted around the calligraphic script. In either case, the intratextual illumination is executed by taking up two lines from the area of the column.

There are only two examples of decorative designs within the columns of the text, where they incorporate floral decoration and thus draw attention to the beginning of a new text in the column (Table 5/3). The illuminated words are written with outlined letters that are circa twice the size of the regular script on the page. This larger, outlined script together with the illumination occupies an area equivalent to that normally occupied by two lines within the column. In both cases, the pages are richly illuminated, incorporating figural scenes and/or marginal decorative designs.

Marginal decorative designs always start along the upper margin, since the header placed in the middle of the upper margin is the source of all such decorations; there are 33 examples of such decorative designs along the upper margins (Table 5/4). Of these, four pages are intact enough to show that the illumination concludes within the area of the upper margin, directly around the header. The additional 29 pages

a: Decorative design in text on recto

b: Decorative design along the upper margin on verso

c: Decorative design along the upper and outer margin on recto

d: Decorative design along the upper, outer, and lower margin on verso

Figure 5/19. Integration of Text and Decorative Design on the Turfan Manichaean Codex Page

Table 5/3. Decorative Design within Text Area (2 examples)

Word Enclosed in Floral Motifs (1)	*Word Enclosed in Blue Background (1)*
MIK III 4979 recto	MIK III 8259 folio 1(?) recto

Table 5/4. Decorative Design along the upper Margin (33 examples)

Only Upper Margin Decorated (4)	M 1887 recto	MIK III 4972 b verso
M 576 verso	M 1887 verso	MIK III 4979 a-d recto
M 1156 recto(?)	T.M. 332 recto	MIK III 4983 verso
MIK III 4974 verso	T.M. 332 verso	MIK III 6258 b recto_
MIK III 7251 verso	So 18700 & M 510 e recto	MIK III 6258 b verso
	MIK III 4966 a recto	MIK III 6261 recto
Only the Decorated Upper	MIK III 4966 a verso	MIK III 6261 verso
Margin Survives (29)	MIK III 4969 folio 1(?) recto	MIK III 6377 a, b, d, f, &
M 596 b recto(?)	MIK III 4969 folio 1(?) verso	III 6379a & III 6990a recto
M 596 f recto(?)	MIK III 4969 folio 2(?) recto	MIK III 6377a, b d, f, &
M 596 f verso(?)	MIK III 4969 folio 2(?) verso	III 6379a & III 6990a verso
M 730 recto	MIK III 4970 c recto	MIK III 6377 c recto_
M 730 verso	MIK III 4972 b recto	MIK III 6377 c verso

Table 5/5. Decorative Design along the upper and outer Margins (21 examples)

Only the Upper & Outer	*Only the Decorated Upper &*	MIK III 4970 b verso
Margins are Decorated (5)	*Outer Margins Survive (15)*	MIK III 6265 & III 4966 c verso
M 171 folio 1(?) recto	M 23 recto	MIK III 6626 & III 6379 c recto
M 171 folio 1(?) verso	M 23 verso	MIK III 8250 folio 1(?) recto
M 576 recto	M 233 recto	M 797 folio 1(?) verso
MIK III 4981 a (silk)	M 694 verso	MIK III 4967 b verso
MIK III 4981 f (silk)	So 18700 & M 501 e verso	MIK III 4967 c recto
	MIK III 4956 a recto	MIK III 4967 c verso
	MIK III 4956 a verso	MIK III 6368 verso

retain only the illuminated upper margins, so we cannot confirm whether the decoration was actually terminated along the upper margin.

Decorative designs also often conclude along the outer margins as suggested by the remains of 20 pages (Table 5/5). On five of these, the floral and scarf motifs originate from between the letters of the header, spread along the upper margin, continue adjacent to the area of the text along the outer margin, and stop at approximately one-third or one-half, of the page. Beneath the design, the area of the outer margin, and most certainly that of the bottom margin, remains blank. On 15 additional fragmentary pages we cannot confirm whether the illumination concluded along the outer margin. Since these pages contain sections of only the outer margins or parts of the upper and outer margins, it is possible that their illuminations continued along the lower margins, as seen on a few fragments.

Four pages confirm that decoration could surround the text along the upper, outer, and lower margins (Table 5/6). Two pages retain decorations next to and below the area of the text as indicated by both sides of the hypothetically reconstructed pages of matched fragments (MIK III 4958 a, b & S 49, Figure 5/20). Besides the illustrated case, we can observe decoration beneath the last line of the text on two other fragmentary pages.

There are also 18 additional fragments with decorative designs possibly derived from one of the margins

a: MIK III 4976 a, b & S 49 recto

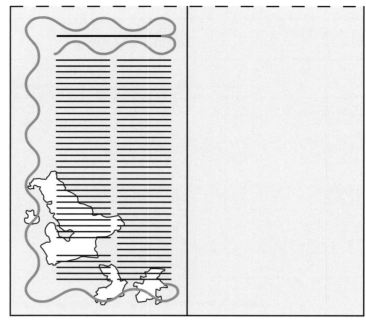

c: MIK III 4976 a, b & S 49 recto

b: MIK III 4976 a, b & S 49 verso

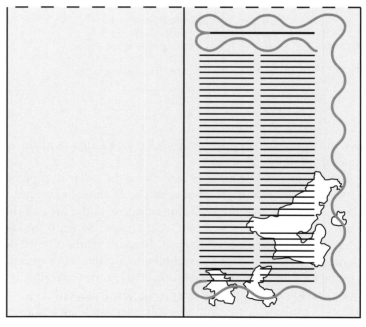

d: MIK III 4976 a, b & S 49 verso

Figure 5/20. Interpretation of Four Illuminated Folio Fragments (MIK III 4976 a, b & S 49)
(SMPK, Museum für Indische Kunst; and Russian Academy, St. Petersburg)

Table 5/6. Decorative Design along upper, outer, and lower Margins (4 examples)

Only Decorated Outer & Lower Margins Survive (2)	*Only Decorated Lower Margin Survives (2)*
S 49 & MIK III 4976 a, b recto	M 4931 recto
S 49 & MIK III 4976 a, b verso	M 4931 verso

Table 5/7. Decorative Designs at Unidentifiable Marginal Location (18 examples)

Decorative Design on Other Side of Page (18)		
M 596 d recto(?)	MIK III 4962 b recto	MIK III 6379 b, e–h recto
M 596 d verso(?)	MIK III 4962 b verso	MIK III 6379 b, e–h verso
M 817 a recto	MIK III 4972 c, d recto	MIK III 6379 d recto
M 817 a verso	MIK III 4972 c, d verso	MIK III 6379 d verso
MIK III 4956 c, d recto(?)	MIK III 6374 recto	MIK III 7266 recto
MIK III 4956 c, d verso(?)	MIK III 6374 verso	MIK III 7266 verso

of the page (Table 5/7). Since they did not preserve any text, or bits from the writing within the header or within the columns, we do not know which margin they adorned. Depending on the size of their original folia, they could derive from the upper margins above or below the header, or they could have been part of either the outer or the lower margins.

Locations of Figural Scenes

Within this corpus, 59 pages of 36 fragmentary codex folia are illuminated with figural scenes. The figural scenes divide among three types based on their locations: *marginal, intratextual,* and versions of *full-page* (Figure 5/21). In every case, when a text accompanies the painting we can confirm that the figural scenes are oriented sideways on the codex page with the heads of the figures closer to the outer margin. Since the location also impacts upon the size and dimensions of the image, each type offers a unique shape for the pictorial program that is integrated into the layout of the specific page as well as the overall book design.

The survey below confirms the use of these three locations for complex, communicative pictorial purposes among the remains of Turfan Manichaean illuminated codices. Marginal figural scenes are found within the strip of the outer margin adjacent to the area of the text, intratextual figural scenes are painted at the middle of the text area splitting the two or three columns of the page into halves, and full-page figural scenes may be executed as one large composition or several smaller scenes arranged next to one another in registers, or in framed cubicles. In every case, the paintings are oriented sideways in relation to the writing, with the heads of the figures closer to the outer margin.

Marginal Figural Scenes

The margins around the texts offer a relatively limited space for painting. The upper margin, being occupied by the header, does not contain figural scenes among the surviving examples of this art. Even when the corner area—where the upper and outer margins overlap—holds a figure, that, too, is part of the outer margin's program. In this corpus, it is only the outer and bottom margins that accommodate marginal figural scenes, always sideways.

Depending on the size of the page, the height of the outer margin may be between ca. 15.0 and 40.0 cm, and its width varies between ca. 2.0 and 5.0 cm. The outer margin takes up roughly a fifth of the page width. Since these long and narrow areas are used for sideways-oriented scenes, rows of figures seated on their heels are used most frequently in these compositions. Several are complete enough to see that their

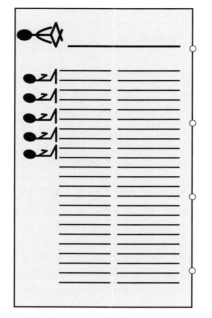

a: Figural scene marginal on recto

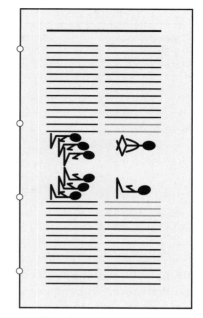

b: Figural scene intertextual on verso

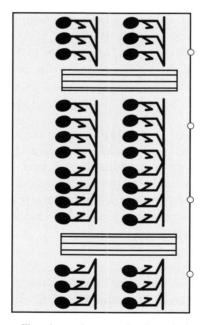

c: Figural scene intertextual and marginal
on recto

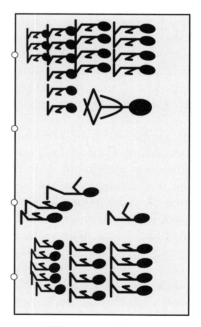

d: Figural scene full page on verso

Figure 5/21. Integration of Text and Figural Scene on the Turfan Manichaean Codex Page

Table 5/8. Figural Scenes along the outer Margins (12 examples)

Marginal Scene Facing Upper Margin (4)	Marginal Scene Facing Center of Outer Margin (5)	Marginal Scenes Flanking Intratextual Scene (2)
So 18700 & M 501 e verso	M 559 recto	MIK III 4974 recto
MIK III 4971 a–c verso	MIK III 4972 a verso	MIK III 4971 a–c recto
MIK III 4972 a recto	MIK III 6265 & III 4966 c recto	
MIK III 6368 verso	MIK III 6265 & III 4966 c verso	Unclear (1)
	MIK III 8259 folio 1(?) verso	MIK III 4956 b recto

marginal compositions were not connected to intratextual scenes; rather, they remain isolated, adorning the page along the side of the text.

Twelve fragmentary pages show figural scenes along the outer margin (Table 5/8). Although none of the marginal areas survive unimpaired, the remains clearly reflect three compositional trends: (1) Marginal scenes facing the upper margin feature the main figure of the composition next to the upper margin, with a row of additional figures facing in his direction. This arrangement is employed on four fragments, including the page with the musicians (MIK III 6368 verso, Figure 5/13), where an elect, seated cross-legged and making communicative gestures with his hands, faces toward lay musicians and singers, who are seated on their heels. (2) Marginal scenes facing the center are symmetrically arranged. Two groups of seated figures evenly distributed along a vertical axis face in each other's direction. The central sections of such marginal scenes are seen on five fragments, such as the scenes with the female elects (M 559 recto, Figure 5/15). (3) Marginal scenes flanking intratextual scenes represent a unique case. These consist of decorative figures that are placed on the two upper corners of the intratextual scenes, partially occupying a small area of the outer margins. Two examples are preserved, including the page with the music-playing putti (MIK III 4974 recto, Figure 5/8) where the composition is retained in relatively good condition. Another, more fragmentary example of this type of marginal figural scene is also preserved (MIK IIII 4971 a–c recto, Figure 5/17).

Fragments with scenes from beneath the text area represent an ambiguous case of marginal illumination. Only four fragmentary pages retain sections of larger figural compositions from along an area of the bottom margin (Table 5/9). These figures may have belonged to full-page compositions that were painted around the text area of the page. Among these, one fragment (MIK III 4959 recto, Figure 5/16) is large enough to show that the middle of the page contained an intratextual scene.

Intratextual Figural Scenes

Intratextual figural scenes are paintings inserted into the center of the text area on the page, claiming a significant portion from it for the pictorial program. The picture always splits the text into an upper and a lower half. The insertion of the pictures into the text area makes the images arbitrarily break each column: the passage contained in a column above the painting continues below the painting within the same column.

Sections of intratextual figural scenes are found on 17 codex pages (Table 5/10). It is interesting that no fully reconstructible remains document the existence of a folio on which both sides were illuminated with intratextual scenes. The program of illumination on the two sides of these folia is never identical. Instead, on the other side of the page with the intratextual scene, we find either only a text, or a text with a marginal figural scene, or a full-page figural scene. On seven fragments, the recto contains an intratextual scene, but the text is not interrupted with such a scene as it continues on the verso. On five fragments, the text on the other side of the page with the intratextual painting is decorated with a marginal figural scene. On another five fragments, the back of the page with the intratextual scene is occupied by a full-page image.

Table 5/9. Figural Scenes along the Bottom Margin (4 examples)

Fragments of Figures Beneath the Text (2)	*Figures beneath the Text Connected to other Scenes (2)*
M 8200 recto	MIK III 4959 recto
MIK III 4958 recto	MIK III 4974 recto

Table 5/10. Intratextual Figural Scenes Preserved from Manichaean Books (17 examples)

Intratextual scene with text on other side of page (7)	*Intratextual scene with marginal scene on other side of page (5)*	*Intratextual scene with full page scene on other side of page (5)*
M 556 recto	MIK III 4964 recto	MIK III 4979 recto
M 569 a–f recto	MIK III 4967 a recto	MIK III 6258 a recto
M 6290 b recto	MIK III 4970 b verso	MIK III 7285 recto
MIK III 4958 recto	MIK III 4971 a–c recto	MIK III 6378 d recto(?)
MIK III 4960 recto	MIK III 8259 folio 1(?) recto	MIK III 6379 d recto(?)
MIK III 4974 recto		
MIK III 6379 d recto[1]		

[1] At the time of writing *Manichaean Art in Berlin Collections*, I did not recognize the correct orientation and the sequence of the two sides of this tiny fragment. (Gulácsi 2001, No. 63, p. 142). The side with the deer-head is the recto, and it must be held with the nose of the dear pointing up, toward the top of the page. The reasons behind this orientation are the following: (1) the deer-head could have only belonged to an intratextual scene, since it is painted to the right of a decorative design, and (2) the page must have a text since decorative designs can only originate from headers in Manichaean book art. The verso retains the section from the outer margin, on which the decorative design concluded. Beneath it, the margin was blank. Therefore the remnants indicate that this page originally contained a text with a header, and a decorative design that concluded along the outer margin.

Table 5/11. Full-page Figural Scenes Preserved from Manichaean Books (8 examples)

Full-Page Figural Scene (5)	*Full-Page Figural Scene with Integrated Text (1)*	*Full-Page Scenes Arranged in Registers or Cubical (2)*
MIK III 36 verso	MIK III 6368 recto	MIK III 4959 verso
MIK III 4956 recto(?)		MIK III 4967 a recto
MIK III 4956 verso(?)		
MIK III 6257 verso		
Or. 8212-1692 verso		

Full-Page Figural Scenes

As their designation suggests, full-page figural scenes are complex paintings that occupy the entire surface of the codex page with a pictorial program. There is, however, a variety of ways to accomplish this. Within the corpus of Turfan Manichaean book art, parts of full-page figural scenes are confirmed in eight cases (Table 5/11). Five examples document full-page scenes that fill out the entire page surrounded by only narrow margins on all four sides. Two examples, however, show pages that are primarily devoted to a figural composition while at the same time also host relatively small, embedded text areas. The painting program on these pages utilizes all areas of the page around the text, including all the spaces that surround the text (i.e., what appear to be the upper, outer, and lower margins around the text) as well as the area between the text-units (i.e., what appears to be the intratextual area of the page) for a continuous scene. Within the texts areas, the lines of writing are continuations from the previous page, as seen on MIK III 6368 recto (Figure 5/14), and possibly MIK III 4959 recto (Figure 5/16). Among these eight remains, there is one fragment (MIK III 4956, Plate 7a–b) with full-page figural scenes on both sides. It is possible

Table 5/12. Full-page or Intratextual Figural Scenes Preserved from Manichaean Books (18 examples)

Figural Scene on other Side of Page (12)	MIK III 4956 d verso(?)	_Text on other Side of Page (5)_
M 501 f recto(?)	MIK III 4962 a verso	MIK III 104 recto
M 501 f verso(?)	MIK III 4962 c recto	MIK III 6376 recto
MIK III 134 recto(?)	MIK III 6284 recto	MIK III 6378 d verso(?)
MIK III 134 verso(?)	MIK III 6284 verso	MIK III 7283 recto
MIK III 4943 recto(?)		MIK III 6226 & III 6379 c recto
MIK III 4943 verso(?)	_Unknown other Side (1)_	
MIK III 4956 d recto(?)	MIK III 4971 d recto	

that this piece of paper derived from a solely pictorial book. On both sides a deity is portrayed in the center of an elaborate composition.[20]

An additional 18 cases show examples on which the figural scenes are at the middle area of the page but the extent of their pictorial program cannot be confirmed (Table 5/12). They could either be part of full-page figural scenes or intratextual compositions. Among these, 12 cases show images on both sides of the folio. Unfortunately, the original extent of their compositions, that is, whether they were full-page or intra-textual scenes, cannot be confirmed. In five cases the other side of the illuminated page contains a text. In one case, we do not know the content of the other side of the fragment since it adheres to another paper piece (MIK III 4971 d, Figure 5/17).

LAYOUTS OF ILLUMINATED HAND SCROLL AND PUSTAKA FRAGMENTS

Besides the numerous codex fragments, a few illuminated manuscripts in other than codex formats are also documented among the Manichaean remains in Turfan. Seven examples are known today: six in hand scroll and one in pustaka formats. The texts in them are written in scripts extensively used in Manichaean codices in Turfan, including Manichaean and Sogdian. In relation to the horizontal lines of the writing, the paintings, which are all figural scenes, are positioned sideways on these fragments.

Illuminated Hand Scrolls

The hand scrolls, or rolls, in the Turfan Manichaean context are one-sided manuscripts made of narrow and long strips of paper that are stored in a rolled-up fashion. Their lengths and widths vary. The scrolls are documented in rather limited numbers compared to the vast amount of remains in codex format. Among the non-illuminated Manichaean manuscripts, there are several letters in scroll format, and also examples of Manichaean texts written on the back of reused Chinese scrolls.[21]

Relevant for this study are six illuminated scroll fragments (Table 5/13), all one-sided. Two survive in excellent condition, preserving the entire text and almost completely the scroll itself. Both of them, as well as an additional more damaged fragment, are primarily textual scrolls with a relatively small section of the complete scroll being devoted to a figural scene. Based on the dominance of the text, we may call them *illu-minated textual scrolls*. Among the six scrolls, three belong to this category. The other three are much more

---

[20] For a detailed discussion on the iconography of the two scenes, see Gulácsi 2001a, 103–107.

[21] Although the circumstances of how these came about falls outside of the scope of the current study, it is important to note that the reasons for their creation are not known today. It is possible that the Manichaeans kept a collection of non-Manichaean texts in some of their monastic libraries, including Buddhist texts and travel-logs in Chinese, in scroll formats. But it is unclear whether indeed the shortage of paper made them write their own text on the back of these Chinese scrolls.

Table 5/13. Fragments of Illuminated Hand Scrolls (6 examples)

Text with Figural Graffiti (1)	*Letter with Figural Scene (2)*	*Fragment with Figural Scene Only (3)*
Ch. 0015	81 TB 65:01	MIK III 4947 & III 5 d
	MIK III 4614	MIK III 4975
		MIK III 6989 a

fragmentary. They are small, one-sided torn pieces of paper with remnants of a figural composition on each. Curiously, none of them retain any textual components. Since the Manichaeans did have a picture-book tradition, it is likely that these fragments derived from scrolls devoted solely to painting. Based on a likely exclusive dominance of the figural scenes in them, we may refer to them as fragments of *pictorial scrolls*.

The six scrolls discussed here represent our only primary sources on Manichaean illuminated scrolls. Thus, our task is to probe the data retained in them regarding the question of physical integration of the two components to one another and to the scrolls. In cases where text and painting appear together on the same scroll, we need to confirm their relative orientation. This investigation is necessarily informed by the other cases in which the illuminated scrolls are primarily textual, or exclusively pictorial, and how in each respective case the paper surface is utilized.

The orientation of these scrolls at first seems ambiguous. Without the evidence of bindings, as in codices, we must rely on the content in order to judge how they were held. It is clear that the right-to-left writing direction of all West Asian scripts defines the use of the writing surface let it be *codex* (that opens from right-to-left) *horizontal scroll* (that rolls from right-to-left), or vertical scroll (the lines of which read from right-to-left). The problem is that on all examples of Manichaean illuminated scrolls, there is a direction conflict between the textual and pictorial components—just as on the codex remains. Being already familiar with a similar case of divergent positioning of texts and figural scenes on the codex remains, it is easier to accept the idea that the illuminated textual scrolls are vertical scrolls with sideways scenes. In them, the texts are written with the usual horizontal Sogdian and Manichaean scripts in lines beneath one another on a vertical scroll. When the textual scrolls contain figural scenes, the pictures are oriented sideways in relation to the writing. The surviving fragments of solely pictorial scrolls suggest that Manichaean scrolls in Turfan were oriented in different ways for textual and for pictorial use. *The text always uses the scroll surface vertically*, as confirmed by the horizontal lines of writing placed beneath one another, forming a continuous, long column on the vertical scroll surface. *The picture always uses the scroll surface horizontally*, as suggested by the orientation of the figures, which are distributed on a horizontally held surface, with the heads of the figures closer to the upper edge of the scroll. In light of this it seems logical to assume that the Manichaean illuminated scrolls were created by copying or inserting scenes from horizontal scrolls into texts in vertical scrolls.

Textual Scroll with a Figural Graffito (Ch. 0015)

The best-preserved Manichaean manuscript in this corpus is the famous *Manichaean Confession of Sins* text, known by its Middle Persian formal title as the *Xuastanift* (Ch. 0015, Figure 5/22). Although it is not illuminated, this Uygur language manuscript is relevant for our study because at the end of the text a graffito-like simple outline drawing of a standing layman is present.[22] This scroll was used during the ritual of confession, when it was rolled out in sections by the reader, and read aloud as a formulaic confession.

Regarding its basic formal qualities, this scroll is small, measuring 10.5 cm in width and 430.0 cm in length. Being uniquely undamaged, it preserves even its own original rolling-rod. At the very end of the scroll, the paper was cropped into a pointed shape, wrapped around and glued to a small, roughly carved

---

[22] A similar graffito-like addition can be observed on another Manichaean fragment (MIK III 38). For a Dunhuang example of a graffito, see Sims-Williams and Hamilton 1990, 77–78.

a: Last 83 from 338 lines of text

Figure 5/22. Textual Scroll with a Graffito (Ch. 0015, detail)
(British Library, London)

wooden stick used as a rolling aid. The text is written in 338 lines. The height of the script is ca. 0.4 cm and the lines are placed every 1.2 cm without horizontal ruling in a long column. Between the vertical ruling, the width of each line is ca. 8.85 cm. Along the two edges of the paper, the narrow margins are ca. 0.65 cm wide on the right and ca. 0.55 cm wide on the left.

Regarding its orientation, this scroll is vertical, that is, the wooden roller was held in front of the reader horizontally, and the scroll was unrolled by pulling in a vertical direction. The horizontal lines of Manichaean script text employ the surface accordingly, running line by line from top to bottom, and thus orient the manuscript vertically. The writing itself, as always, proceeds from right to left. A small figure of a layman (6.9 cm high) is drawn, in ink, at 6.2 cm distance from the last line. In relation to the text, the layman is positioned sideways, with his head closer to the right margin.

Illuminated Textual Scroll (81 TB 65:01)

The most recently discovered, relatively well-preserved, illuminated scroll is a Sogdian language Manichaean letter in the collection of the local archaeological museum in Turfan (81 TB 65:01, Figure 5/23). It was found deposited in a stupa at Bezeklik, near Turfan, and is relevant for our study because it contains a lavishly illuminated pictorial insert. Although tearing impairs the ends of most lines, as well as the lower part of the painting, the surviving large portion of the original scroll is in excellent condition. Being a formulaic letter of New Year greeting sent to a high-ranking church official, the scroll was rolled out in sections by the reader (and most likely read aloud to the receiver).[23]

Regarding its format, this scroll is large, measuring 26.0 cm in width and 268.0 cm in length. It contains 135 lines of text in black ink, 7 round seals stamped in red ink across the writing throughout the scroll, and one colorfully painted and generously gilded figural scene. The text is written in a large script, ca. 1.0 cm (check) high. The lines are placed at every ca. 2.0 cm, filling the 26.0 cm wide paper surface without leaving blank any space as margins (except for a few lines indented according to epistolary rules). Around the figural scene, however, there is a ca. 1.0 cm wide margin in all directions.

This is a vertical scroll. The paper surface is dominated by the horizontal lines of Sogdian script text, which align the scroll vertically. Between lines 25 and 26 the paper was cut and an elaborate figural scene was glued into the scroll. The viewing direction of this scene does not accord with the reading direction of the text. Within the pictorial insert, the heads of the figures are toward the right. Thus, while the text utilizes the scroll surface vertically, the scene used the scroll surface horizontally. It is inserted into the text on an originally independent piece of paper. Therefore, in this illuminated manuscript, too, the painting is sideways in relation to the direction of writing.

A prominent inscription within the pictorial insert makes the orientation of this illuminated textual scroll confusing. The painting is centered around a Sogdian script line, placed along the vertical axis of the composition. Here, the writing is vertical, just as seen in the much less dominating inscriptions of names seen on Manichaean textiles and wall painting, in addition to book paintings. The letters in such vertical inscriptions are written not simply beneath one another, retaining their original orientation, but rather the complete line is turned 90 degrees counter-clockwise compared to the regular horizontal lines of the texts. Hence, they form a vertical line of text that invariably proceeds from top to bottom of the writing surface, and from head to toe of any accompanying figures. The phenomenon of vertical inscription is confined to pictorial contexts in Manichaean book art.

Fragment of an Illuminated Textual Scroll (MIK 4614)

The most damaged example of an illuminated textual scroll is a one-sided torn piece of paper with a large figural scene and bits of letters from the now-lost text (MIK 4614, Figure 5/24). Data preserved on this fragment suggest that it belonged to a letter written on a large scroll that also contained a pictorial insert,

---

[23] For color illustrations, see Yoshida et al 2000 and Tokyo National Museum 2002, 160–161.

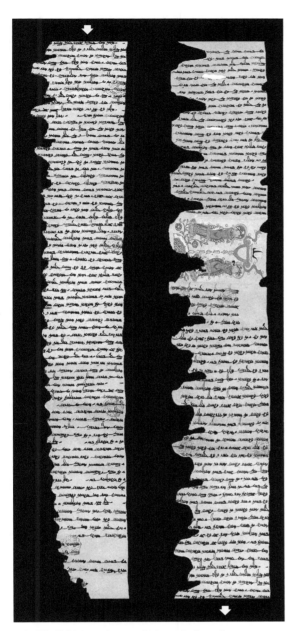

a: 81 TB 65:01 (complete scroll shown in 2 parts)

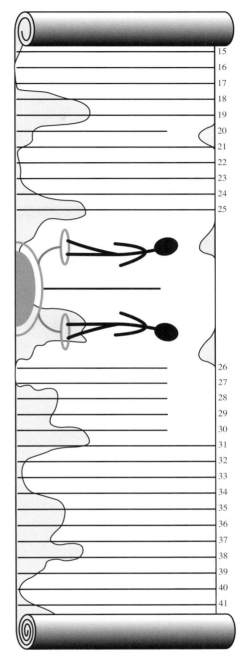

b: 81 TB 65:01

Figure 5/23. Reconstruction of an Illuminated Letter Scroll (81 TB 65:01)
(Turfan Antiquarian Bureau, Turfan, China)

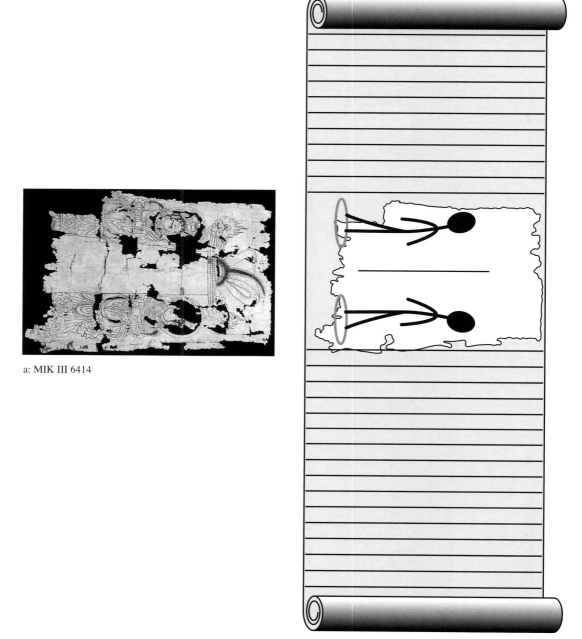

a: MIK III 6414

b: MIK III 6414

Figure 5/24. Interpretation of an Illuminated Letter Scroll Fragment (MIK III 4614)
(SMPK, Museum für Indische Kunst, Berlin)

similar to the Turfan Museum's scroll (81 TB 65:01, Figure 5/23).

This scroll in original condition was ca. 27.5 cm wide. Above the heads of the figures the torn section of the paper retains parts of the original edge. Toward the feet of the figures, the petals remaining from a lotus flower under each suggest that they were standing on lotus supports, much like the figures in the Turfan Museum's scroll. On that scroll the area of the two lotus plants, together with the pool and the blank margin beneath them, takes up approximately one-quarter of the scene, in light of which it seems that here, too, ca. one-quarter (ca. 5.5 cm) is missing from the original image. In accordance with the large size of the scroll, the text was written in a relatively large script. Bits remaining from letters along the right edge of the fragment allow us to estimate a script height of ca. 0.8 cm.

Regarding its orientation, the scroll to which this fragment belonged was a vertical, textual scroll that contained a sideways figural scene. The scene was drawn on an independent piece of paper and physically inserted into the body of the scroll, as documented by the ca. 0.5 cm wide overlapping glued edges preserved on both the left and right sides of the figural scene. Only tiny bits are retained from the text area. Along the right rough edges of the fragment, a few strokes are preserved from a line that resumed the text beneath the figural scene. In addition, a highly faded inscription is found between the two figures. Identical to the Turfan Museum's scroll, the line of the inscription is written vertically with the letters on their sides, 90 degrees counter-clockwise, proceeding from top to bottom in relation to the direction of the figures. Here, too, the vertical writing is confined to the inscription, and is not to be mistaken with the writing direction used systematically in Manichaean manuscripts.

Fragment of a Pictorial Scroll (MIK III 4975)

The largest portion surviving from a pictorial scroll is found on a badly damaged fragment (MIK III 4975, Figure 5/25). Although torn and faded, it preserves important data regarding the physical characteristics and the orientation of its original, suggesting that this fragment belonged to a medium-sized scroll devoted solely to pictorial communication.

We know that this fragment was part of a medium-sized scroll because approximately the complete original height, 13.0 cm, is intact. The area that retains the vertical extent happens to be the section on which two independent pieces of paper were glued to one another in order to lengthen the paper surface. This indicates that the scroll continued to the left of the painting. We also notice that this scene was displayed on a blue background, which terminates along the top and bottom without a frame. At the vertical edge of the scene, most likely on both ends, a border-like decoration was drawn consisting of circles drawn tightly next to one another within two straight lines. Since the blue background already defines a rectangular area for the image, this decorative finish functions as an extra visual unit to conclude the painting.[24] In light of the lengthening of the scroll, most certainly another decorative border started off the next figural scene to the left of where the surviving fragment is torn.

The pictorial content is also informative about the original layout of this scroll. The painting utilized the scroll surface horizontally. The two elects displayed on lotus supports indicate the symmetrical arrangement of the original scene, in which most likely four elects flanked a central area with an object or another figure. This now-lost central area was the most prestigious part of the scene, and most certainly it was also located at the very center along the vertical axis of the composition. This interpretation is suggested by the gradual scale increase of both the elects (2.8 and 3.5 cm between feet and elbows) and their lotus-supports (2.0 and 2.7 cm) as they get closer to the assumed center.

---

[24] Only one other Manichaean painting preserved, on silk, shows identical features of format: blue background, unframed top and bottom edge, and elaborate vertical border (MIK III 6278). For more detailed discussions, see Gulácsi 2001a, 174–175; and 2004, 289.

b: MIK III 4975

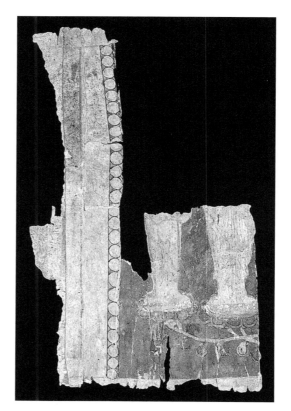

a: MIK III 4975

Figure 5/25. Interpretation of a Pictorial Scroll Fragment (MIK III 4975)
(SMPK, Museum für Indische Kunst, Berlin)

b: MIK III 4947 & III 5 d

a: MIK III 4947 & III 5 d

Figure 5/26. Interpretation of two Matched Fragments from a Pictorial Scroll (MIK III 4947 & III 5d)
(SMPK, Museum für Indische Kunst, Berlin)

The observed size increase and the assumed symmetry as principles for the overall organization allow us to consider the original width of this scene as well as to contemplate that of the complete scroll. The horizontal extent of the remaining left-side section, including the reconstructed missing edge of the larger lotus flower (5.6 cm), together with the now-lost central lotus flower (ca. 3.4 cm) and the repeated two elects on the right side (5.6 cm), suggest that the original scene was a minimum of 14.6 cm wide.[25] The original height of the painting area preserved along the decorative border is 11.7 cm. It is most likely that several such scenes, possibly each separated from one another by decorative vertical edges and blank sections of paper, were part of this painted scroll. The minimum of two such paintings, including the start and the end of the scroll, would make the horizontal extent only ca. 40.0 cm, which is about one-tenth of the *Xuastanift* (Ch. 0015, Figure 5/22; 9.5 cm wide and 430 cm long), and a little more than one-sixth of the Turfan Museum's scroll (81 TB 65:01, Figure 5/23; 26 cm wide and 263 cm long). Although it is impossible to determine the original length of the scroll in question, if it contained 15 scenes of ca. 20.0 cm for each scene and the gap between scenes, it would have reached the not unreasonable length of ca. 300 cm.

Two Matched Fragments of a Painted Scroll (MIK III 4947 & III 5 d)

A relatively well preserved section from an exquisite one-sided painting is found on two matched fragments (MIK 4947 & III 5 d, Figure 5/26). Although these remains are insignificantly small compared to the overall layout of the painted scroll to which the scene belonged, they do preserve some useful pieces of data on issues of the original format.[26] The blue background and a decorative border defined the area of the painting. Along its top, the fragment retains a section of an elaborate border. It is gilded and detailed, with delicate red lines drawn on the surface of the gold. Most likely an identical border ran along the bottom edge, and the scene between them utilized the scroll surface horizontally. Similar gilded top and/or bottom edges are also preserved on three Manichaean codex paintings (MIK III 4959 verso, Figure 5/16b; MIK III 7283 recto, and possibly MIK III 4967 a recto).[27]

The original dimensions of the scene, and thus the vertical extent of the scroll, can be hypothesized in light of a recent study that reconstructs the scene through its most plausible iconography.[28] It is most certain that along the upper right and left, two haloed figures flanked the main figure in the original scene. Such a composition would make the horizontal extent of this visual unit to be ca. 20.6 cm. The fragment in its current width (5.8 cm) retains a large section from the right half of the painting. In its original condition, the width of the image would have been a minimum of ca. 10.3 cm, assuming that ca. 2.5 cm is missing from the right edge, including the missing section of the Buddha figure and the right edge of the scene, and ca. 2.0 cm along the left from the area before the vertical axis of the scene. Regarding the vertical extent, with the most often assumed arrangement of four figures around the central deity, the conservative estimate comes to a minimum of 27.6 cm, approximately twice the current size of the fragment (13.6 cm). This height estimate suggests a large scroll, comparable to the size of the Turfan Museum's scroll (81 TB 65:01).[29] If indeed five figures were depicted in the original image, it is most likely that

---

[25] It is most likely that the central lotus flower was the largest (possibly 0.7 cm larger than the previous flower), although in another scene with lotus-supports (MIKIII 8259 folio 1[?] recto), all the flowers are approximately the same size, and thus it is not impossible that the middle flower in this image was the same size as the neighboring flowers (2.7 cm).

[26] For a discussion of these two fragments, see Gulácsi 2001a, 146–148.

[27] For illustrations see Gulácsi 2001a, Nos. 48 and 53.

[28] Gulácsi 2001a, No. 66. For a reference to Dr. Ebert's research on this subject, see Chapter 6 note 30.

[29] For a detailed discussion on the reconstruction with four figures around the central deity, based on an iconographic argument, see Ebert 2005b. If only two figures had flanked the central being, the height of the original scroll would have been around 21.0 cm. In light of the size repertoire of Manichaean scrolls surviving from Turfan, both the smaller (ca. 21.0 cm) and the larger (ca. 27.6 cm) reconstructed sizes are possible for the height of the original scroll.

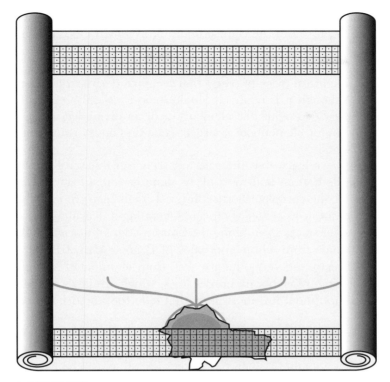

b: MIK III 6989 a

a: MIK III 6989 a

Figure 5/27. Interpretation of a Pictorial Scroll Fragment (MIK III 6989 a)
(SMPK, Museum für Indische Kunst, Berlin)

the four side figures portrayed the four prophets venerated in Manichaeism, including Mani, Jesus, Zara-thustra, & the historical Buddha;[30] and the central figure represented God, the Father of Greatness.

A Small Fragment of a Painted Scroll (MIK III 6989 a)

The last example is a one-sided torn piece of paper that seems to derive from another painted scroll (MIK III 6989 a, Figure 5/27). Although it is relatively small, measuring only 3.2 cm in height and 5.5 cm in width, this fragment retains two recognizable elements: a decorative edge and a pool motif. These well-preserved but undoubtedly minor elements of a larger scene do convey some minimal information about the format of the original scroll.

From the decorative edge, we learn that the relevant scene on this scroll was surrounded by an elab-orate, decorative line along its bottom and most likely along its top. In stacked layers of five bands (red, blue, gold, green, and violet), the complete border line is 1.5 cm high. In each band a motif of a square (ca. 0.3 cm × 0.3 cm) with a dot in its center is repeated, creating a delicately detailed linear pattern. Sim-ilar bands are also preserved in stacks from along the bottom edge of a scene (MIK III 4958 recto)[31] and more frequently in single bands from within the halos of figures (MIK III 134 recto[?], MIK III 4964 recto,[32] and MIK III 4979 recto and verso, Figure 5/9) from illuminated Manichaean codex fragments. In light of versions of other types of elaborate border lines, which are never documented to have enclosed in a full frame the entire composition, it is most likely that here too, the decoration ran only along the top and bottom of the scene.

The pool motif is also informative, especially regarding the scale and the composition of the original image. Above the decorative edge, the area surviving from the painting contains two stylized bush-like motifs, partially overlapping a pool motif. Such pool motifs are often seen on Manichaean codex fragments. In this image, the diameter of this pool motif, including the blue water, the two red bands, and the green grass, measures ca. 1.3 cm. This scale is comparable to the pool motifs seen on codex fragments, suggest-ing that the scale of this scroll painting was in accordance with that of codex illuminations.

In addition, the pool motif suggests that this fragment came from the lower middle section of a larger scene. In all of the more complete scenes with pool motifs (MIK III 8259 folio 1[?] recto, Figure 5/7; MIK III 6265 and III 4966 c recto; and 81 TB 65:01, Figure 5/22), the pool is located in the lower center of a symmetrically arranged composition. Always, it functions as the source from where a lotus plant emerges to support elects, other beings, and altar-like tables. The stems of such lotus plants may be shown inside the water (MIK III 6265 and III 4966 c recto) or just emerging from the green, glass-like area around the water (81 TB 65:01, Figure 4/22; and also MIK III 4972 a recto and verso, Figure 5/9). Here no parts of lotus stem are retained. But, since in Manichaean art there are no examples of pool motifs without lotus plants, it is most likely that this pool, too, was the source of lotus supports at the lower center of a larger, symmetrically arranged composition.

The Illuminated Pustaka Folio (MIK III 8260)

The *pustaka* (Skt. *pustaka*, "book") or *pothi* (Hind. *pothi*, "book") format is well documented in late Antique and Mediaeval East Central Asia, where it is used primarily for Buddhist manuscripts. This format is rooted in the employment of palm leaves as the main writing material in South Asia. Originally, cuts from the leaves of a broad-leaved palm tree (i.e., talipat or palmyra) naturally yielded sheets of rectangular, long

---

[30] As listed in the introduction of the *Kephalaia* (7.18-8.7, see Gardner 1995, 13).
[31] See Gulácsi 2001a, No. 59.
[32] See Gulácsi 2001a, Nos. 43 and 51.

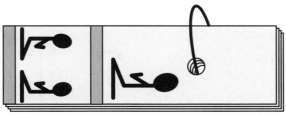

a: MIK III 8260 recto

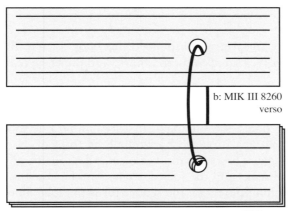

b: MIK III 8260
verso

c: U82 recto

d. MIK III 8260 recto

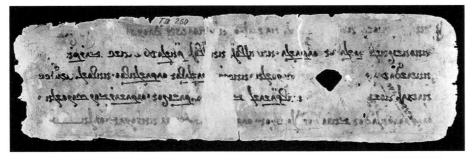

e. MIK III 8260 verso

Figure 5/28. Illuminated Manichaean Pustaka Book
(SMPK, Museum für Indische Kunst, Berlin; SBPK, Berlin-Brandenburgische
Akademie der Wissenschaften, Turfanforschung, Berlin)

Table 5/14. Fragments of the Illuminated Pustaka Book (38 examples)

Illuminated Folio (1)	*Unilluminated Folia (37)*				
MIK III 8260	U 82	U 90	U 97	U 84	U 108
	U 86	U 91	U 98	U 75	U 79
	U 83	U 92	U 99	U 85	U 105
	U 81	U 80	U 100	U 76	U 109
	U 87	U 93	U 101	U 77	U 110
	MIK III 189	U 94	U 102	D 258, 18	
	U 88	U 95	U 103	U 106	
	U 89	U 96	U 104	U 107	

and narrow, double-sided writing surface, which defined this book format. But already in historical times other materials, such as metal, ivory, Himalayan birch bark, and paper were also employed to make books in this format.

When assembled into a book, the pustaka folia are loosely stacked and secured to one another through one or two binding holes cut at one-third distance from the edges along the middle part of each sheet. Cords are threaded through the holes, loose enough to allow lifting one folio from the stack and laying it on its back. For reading, the pustaka is placed horizontally in front of the reader. The lines of the text parallel the longer edge of the page. The recto and verso sides look identical to one another in their page layouts, and thus, if the binding breaks and the folia scatter, only the content can verify which page of the folio is to be read first. After finishing the recto, the reader turns the folio along its horizontal axis to assess the verso. For storage the pustaka book is placed between two wooden boards and wrapped in a cloth.

Within the currently known corpus of Turfan Manichaean book art, there is only one illuminated manuscript fragment in this format (Table 5/14).[33] It was written in the Uygur language with Manichaean script. The complete book originally contained more than 50 loose leaves, out of which 38 double-sided folia have been identified. Among these, only the first folio is illuminated. The other 37 sheets contain only text.[34] In order to learn how the text and the figural scene were integrated in this book, we will focus on the illuminated folio (MIK III 8260), since the layout of its verso is identical to the page arrangement on the rest of the surviving fragments.

The first folio of the "Turkic Manichaean *Pothi*-Book," as it is known in the field, contains a full-page figural scene (MIK III 8260, Figure 5/28). We can rightfully assume that the painting is on the recto, since this image functions as a frontispiece to the texts. On the verso we find the beginning of an anthology of Manichaean religious literature. On this side, just like on all the other pages of the 6.0 cm high and 21.5 cm wide folia, five horizontal lines are written in Manichaean script beneath one another. In relation to the text area, the figural scene on the recto is oriented sideways, with the heads of the figures to the right.

The composition of the painting suggests that the artist fitted the image to the pustaka format. When we turn the recto to the picture-viewing direction, we can access two connected scenes, placed beneath one another to fill out the unique shape of the page. Just above the middle of the upper scene is the binding hole. It is smartly integrated into the painting by being enclosed between the bending flowery branches and the trunk of a tree. Just like on other examples of Manichaean paintings, a vertical inscription is found in the lower scene. Here, the name of the elect on the left is written in front of the figure along the blank area of the page near to the center just above the fire altar.

---

[33] In addition there are only a few examples of non-illuminated Manichaean fragments in pustaka format, see Sundermann 1981, 140.

[34] The surviving folia of this Turkic Manichaean book were reassembled and its text was edited by Larry Clark (1982). For the enumeration of the surviving 38 folia, see pp. 168–180.

This pustaka book is primarily a book of texts adorned with one painting. The way the text utilizes the page is in accordance with the usual use of the pustaka format. Each folio is oriented horizontally with the Manichaean script text being written in horizontal lines that proceed from right to left. Only one page among the 76 pages (38 folia) surviving from the complete manuscript is devoted to a book painting. This painting is oriented sideways in relation to the direction of the writing in the rest of the book. By favoring the picture-viewing direction one would instinctively intend to hold the book vertically. Nevertheless, the consistency of sidewise orientation of figural scenes in relation to the direction of the writing on codex fragments suggests that the unique Manichaean way of integrating text and image into illuminated books was maintained also in pustaka format.

CONCLUSION

It is a complex task to make sense out of the preserved data regarding the original layouts of the 89 remains of Manichaean illuminated manuscripts. A preliminary step in their study is to note the most basic facts about them. First of all, these remains are fragments of illuminated manuscripts, retaining texts and/or illuminations. The illuminations are either simple decorative designs or more complex figural scenes. Most of the remains contain texts together with illuminations, but a dozen fragments have only figural scenes. Second, on all currently known examples, a direction conflict is present between the text and the figural scenes when the two are together. Systematically, the figures are oriented sideways in relation to the horizontal lines of writing. On pages that are either solely textual (and/or decorated with only decorative designs) or contain only figural scenes and no texts, naturally, there is no direction conflict. Finally, even the smallest fragments can retain useful data on the layouts of their originals. Therefore, a survey of all the available sources allows us to reach a basic understanding of how the undamaged versions of Turfan Manichaean illuminated books looked in terms of their layouts. Indeed, using a thorough analysis of their layout features, a variety of discoveries can be made about the originals of these fragments.

Regarding the formats of the original books, the fragments document that the Manichaeans in Turfan used three distinctly different book formats for their illuminated manuscripts: codex, scroll, and pustaka. The vast majority of the remains, 85 fragments, derive from the double-sided folia of illuminated codices. A significantly smaller group, six fragments, is from illuminated scrolls; these are all one-sided. Within the corpus, only one illuminated fragment is from a pustaka book. This folio, just as all pustaka folia, is double sided and reflects a uniquely pustaka shape.

Regarding their general contents, the remains of Manichaean manuscripts in Turfan indicate the existence of three kinds of books: text-books, illuminated text-books, and picture-books. Tens of thousands of Manichaean book fragments are known today. The vast majority of these are from plain, non-illuminated manuscripts that were devoted solely to texts. Therefore, we may refer to them as text-books. Since these are not illuminated, their survey falls outside the scope of this study. Most of the artistic book remains, 88 fragments, derive from illuminated manuscripts that also contain text. Although these, too, were primarily text-books, pictorial decorations adorned their pages. To distinguish them, we may refer to them as illuminated text-books. In these, the pages of texts without illuminations are identical to that of the text-books in layouts and other formal qualities. Only a few examples, 4 from among 12 fragments with solely figural scenes, are intact enough to indicate the existence of books that contained no text, just communicative pictorial scenes. It is most likely that the books to which these fragments belonged were *picture-books*. There is a well-documented tradition of solely pictorial books in the Manichaean tradition, reaching back as far as the time of Mani. Since on these fragments no texts are associated with the paintings, it is quite likely that they are from versions of picture-books.

a: " St. John" on folio 27 verso of the Syriac Gospel Book
Dawkins 58 (1238 CE), Bodleian Library, Oxford

Figure 5/29. Syriac Gospel Book with Sideways Image

Due to the fact that the textual and pictorial components utilize the codex, scroll and pustaka formats in divergent ways, several correlates are seen between the formats and the basic contents in these sources:

FORMATS:	Codex	ORIENTATIONS:	Text-Books	- vertical codex
	Scroll			- horizontal codex (rarely)
	Pustaka			- vertical scroll
				- horizontal pustaka
CONTENTS:	Text-books		Illuminated Text-Books	- vertical codex
	Illuminated Text-Books			- vertical scroll
	Picture-books			- horizontal pustaka
			Picture-Books	- horizontal scroll

(1) In cases when the content is solely textual (text-books), thousands of text fragments document vertical codices with only an insignificant number of exceptions in square and horizontal codex shapes (see discussion in Chapter 4). The textual scrolls are vertical and the pustakas are horizontal. (2) In cases when contents are devoted to texts supplemented with decorative designs and figural scenes (illuminated text-books), the codices are vertical, the scrolls are vertical, and the only pustaka example is horizontal. Their orientation is confirmed by the horizontal lines of writing, binding holes, margins, and other page elements. In all these books, the sideways figural scenes introduce their own use of the paper surface, disregarding the orientation of the texts. All illuminated textual codices are vertical, but in them the figural scenes use the codex pages horizontally. All illuminated textual scrolls are also vertical, but with their figural scenes using the paper horizontally. Also, in the one example of an illuminated pustaka book, which as all traditional pustaka books is horizontal, the figural scene employs the paper surface sideways in relation to the text, making the illuminated page vertical. (3) There are a few codex and scroll fragments on which the contents are solely pictorial, indicating the existence of picture-books in Manichaean Turfan. The remains of the pictorial scrolls derive from unquestionably horizontal scrolls. They, together with the horizontally oriented scenes incorporated into the illuminated text scrolls, suggest the existence of picture-books in a horizontal scroll format. Much less information survives about solely pictorial codices. Only one pictorial folio fragment (MIK III 4965) is likely to derive from a picture-book in codex format. Unfortunately, it does not preserve data on the location of its binding, leaving us without a confirmed orientation. In light of the consistent horizontal use for paining in illuminated textual codices, though, and the analogous example of the pictorial scrolls, it is not impossible that horizontal codices were used for pictorial purposes among the Manichaeans in Turfan. Future comparative studies with the West Asiatic tradition of horizontal codices (Islamic and Eastern Christian) may shed light on this question.

Besides searching for the roots of the *Picture-Book* tradition and the use of horizontal codices in early mediaeval West Asia, future studies will also have to address the reason behind the development of sideways-oriented illustrations. While in Manichaean Turfan sideways-oriented illustrations are the norm, in West Asian Christian & Islamic book illumination sidewaysness is an exception. Nevertheless, in Syriac and Armenian illuminated Gospelbooks and also in a variety of Islamic manuscripts, this unique practice was followed as seen for example on a Syriac Gospelbook (Dawkins 58) from 1238 CE housed in the collection of the Bodleian Library (Fig. 5/29).

CHAPTER SIX

THE WRITTEN AND THE PAINTED MESSAGE:
CONTEXTUAL COHESION OF TEXT AND IMAGE

Paintings in mediaeval illuminated manuscripts often *illustrate*, that is visually comment upon, their associated texts. For instance, images are much-needed components in didactic treatises, and without diagrams and/or images with greater artistic ambition, some scientific texts would surely be less comprehensible.[1] Also, battle scenes may accompany the discussion of military victories in illuminated histories. These book paintings show close contextual cohesion with their texts. Such close association between the textual and visual components of the mediaeval book, however, is not always the case. Recent publications on illuminated Byzantine liturgical manuscripts point out the lack of contextual cohesion between the painting and the writing, and suggest that the illuminations in a certain group of manuscripts may play primarily a decorative role, transforming their books into luxury items.

The remains of Manichaean illuminated manuscripts exhibit a strikingly unique relationship between text and image. Already their physical integration does not fit our expectations; the paintings in Manichaean codices are exclusively oriented sideways, so the heads of the figures are always closer to the outer margins, as confirmed through our examination of the entire corpus of currently known Manichaean illuminated book fragments. So far, however, observations regarding the correlation of their written and painted components have been made only in connection with individual fragments,[2] and no comprehensive survey has been attempted by which generalizations on this subject can be made.

To determine the pattern of contextual cohesion between text and image in mediaeval Manichaean book art, the entire corpus must be subjected to an analytical survey. To that end, our investigation here focuses solely on the subject matter of illuminated book fragments, both written (identifiable texts) and painted (identifiable illumination), and carefully considers all the available sources of evidence. Among the 89 illuminated fragments, 73 are torn sections of codex folia or bifolia. Seven are parts of illuminated hand scrolls, and one constitutes an almost complete folio of a pustaka (palm-leaf formatted) book. 67 fragments preserve information on the two sides of codex folia, and six fragments derive from bifolia and supply data on four pages. All in all, the 73 codex fragments analyzed for this project provide information on 158 pages.[3] The one folio fragment from a pustaka book yields data on two pages. Because of the variety of possible page layouts, some pages may hold texts only, others may contain only illumination and no text, and occasionally a few folio fragments may have blank sides. Thus, depending on their contents, both sides of all double-sided fragments will not necessarily be relevant.

On the basis of numerical data, we can demonstrate the fact that on the surviving pages of Turfan Manichaean illuminated books the vast majority of pictorial subjects do not show close association with the written messages. Instead of visually commenting upon the writing, most book paintings decorate the manuscript by depicting general scenes from the religious life of the Manichaean community and thus exhibit only a rather loose, but nevertheless appropriate, contextual cohesion to the texts.

---

[1] Weitzmann 1959, 5–29.
[2] Klimkeit (1982, 38) considered the connection between a Scribal Scene and its associated text on MIK III 6368 recto.
[3] These include 6 bifolia (6 × 4 = 24) and 67 folia (67 × 2 = 134).

SURVEY OF IDENTIFIABLE TEXTS

On the 89 fragments surviving from Manichaean illuminated books, 45 texts can be identified, based on the fact that they retain large enough sections of literature whose genre and sometimes content can be determined. The translation and identification of these Iranian and Turkic *illuminated Manichaean texts* were achieved through decades of accumulated studies mostly by F. W. K. Müller, Walter Henning, Albert von Le Coq, Ernst Waldschmidt, Wolfgang Lentz, Werner Sundermann, Christiane Reck, Yutaka Yoshida, Jason BeDuhn, Annamarie von Gabain, Hans-Joachim Klimkeit, Takao Moriyasu, and Larry Clark.[4] Regarding the enumeration of identified texts, it is important to remember that texts may continue from one page to the other, unlike figural scenes. When this is recognized, both sides of the fragment are indicated as one entry. If a text is identified only on one side of the folio, the other side with the unclear content is considered separately. If sections of two different texts are retained on the same page of a folio, that page will appear twice in the listings. Table 6/1 presents an overview of these texts, organizing them in columns according to their literary genres: hymn, religious prose, benediction, colophon, omen, and letter; and in rows according to the types of their illumination: decorative design, figural scene, and both.

Hymns

Hymns are verses of praise for mythological or other religious figures that are meant to be performed orally in a ritual setting. Since hymns are frequently written down, they form a standard part of religious literature. In some cases their performative nature is documented, when the melody used for singing them is recorded on the page, as seen on an illuminated folio where the header reads "in the melody of the gods" (M 730 recto).[5] Characteristic phrases of glorification and blessing are seen in Manichaean hymns. The first example cited below celebrates Mani, and the second example exalts and blesses God, the Father of Greatness:

> You, whom one should worship with a reverent mind,
> My respected and famous father, my prophet Mani:
> We prepare ourselves for you, to worship you with humble mind.
> Accept now, O object of desire and trust, all the worship of everyone
> (MIK III 8260 verso, Figure 5/28).[6]

> The greatest of immortals, the king of eternities,
> Who is good, sovereign Zurvan,
> Who is established on the throne amidst his own greatness:
> He gladdens all gods with the five divine gifts,
> And those twelve primeval ones of his,
> Before him they evoke blessing in the four directions.
> And may he be blessed and praised
> (MIK III 8259 folio 1[?] verso column 2, Figures 2/2 and 5/7).[7]

Altogether, 21 illuminated Manichaean texts can be identified as hymns, including an illuminated page of a hymn index (Table 6/2). The subjects of these hymns include the Father of Greatness, the Third Messenger, the Prophets, and Mani, as well as lesser known themes and unidentifiable subjects. These 21

---

[4] For a publication history, see BeDuhn 2001.
[5] BeDuhn 2001, 213.
[6] Translation by Larry Clark, after BeDuhn 2001, 240.
[7] BeDuhn 2001, 223.

Table 6/1. Overview of Literary Genres and Types of Illumination in Identifiable Texts (39 examples)

Type of Illumination	HYMN (15 texts)	RELIGIOUS PROSE (8 texts)	BENEDICTION (8 texts)	OMEN (6 texts)	LETTER (1 text)
DECORATIVE DESIGN ONLY (19 pages)	M 23 recto M 23 verso M 233 recto M 576 recto M 730 recto M 730 verso M 797 folio 1 (?) recto MIK III 4970 b recto MIK III 4970 b verso MIK III 4981 a (silk folio) MIK III 4981 f (silk folio) MIK III 4983 recto	M 171 f 1 verso & f 2 recto M 694 recto MIK III 4976 a, b recto MIK III 4976 a, b verso So 18700 & M 501 e verso	MIK III 4974 verso		
FIGURAL SCENE ONLY (14 pages)	*M 559 recto & verso* *MIK III 8260 verso*	*MIK III 8259 folio 1(?) recto*	*MIK III 36 recto* MIK III 4959 recto *MIK III 6368 verso* *MIK III 8259 folio 1(?) recto* *Or. 8212-1692 recto*	M 556 recto M 556 recto M 556 recto *M 556 recto* *M 556 recto* M 556 recto	
FIGURAL SCENE & DECORATIVE DESIGN (6 pages)	MIK III 8259 folio 1 verso	*MIK III 6368 recto* So 18700 & M 501 e recto	*MIK III 4974 recto* *MIK III 4979 a, b recto*		*81 TB 65:1* (scroll)

Italics indicates associated identifiable figural scene.

Table 6/2. Hymns Preserved from Manichaean Illuminated Books (21 examples)

Hymn to the Father of Greatness (5)	Hymn to Mani (5)	Unidentifiable Hymns (6)
M 559 verso	M 23 recto	M 559 recto
M 730 recto	M 797 folio 1 verso	M 797 folio 2 recto
M 730 verso	MIK III 4981 a	M 797 folio 2 verso
M 797 folio 1 recto	MIK III 4981 f	M 797 folio 2 verso
MIK III 8259 folio 1(?) verso	MIK III 8260 verso	MIK III 4970 b recto
		MIK III 4970 b verso
Hymn to the Third Messenger (1)	Other Hymns (2)	
MIK III 4983 recto & verso	"First of the Righteous"	Hymn Index (1)
	M 233 recto	M 576 recto
Hymn to the Prophets (1)	"Fortunate for Us"(Huyadagman)	
M 23 verso	M 233 verso	

hymns are retained on 12 fragmentary folia that once formed parts of 10 illuminated codices (nine paper and one silk) and one illuminated pustaka book.[8]

Hymns may be collected in hymnbooks or service-books, or in anthologies of religious literature, all of which existed in Manichaean Turfan. From among the decorated fragments surveyed above, three folia contain more than one hymn and thus most likely represent leaves from three illuminated hymnbooks: the folio with a hymn index on its recto with additional damaged text on its verso (M 576, Figure 5/5); the folio with "First of the Righteous" and "Fortunate for Us" on its two sides (M 233);[9] and the bifolia (M 797, Figure 5/5) with a "Hymn to Mani" and three additional unidentified subjects. Service-books, such as the famous BBB (MIK III 53, Figure 3/2), contain hymns together with prose relevant for a specific ritual. Although the eight bifolia surviving from the BBB are exquisitely written and do contain scribal decoration in their headers, they are without paintings. Thus, no illuminated fragments of service-books are currently recognized among the Manichaean book fragments. Yet due to the fragmentary character of the evidence, it is certainly possible that some of the hymn sets and individual hymns listed in Table 6/2 may have been identified as parts of service-books if the rest of their manuscripts had been preserved. The pustaka folio (MIK III 8260, Figure 5/28) is the first page from an illuminated anthology of religious literature, which originally contained a minimum of 12 texts on its 50 or so leaves, as suggested by the numerous fragments identified as belonging to this book.[10] Such an anthology can be distinguished from a hymnbook by the fact that it contains literature in various genres, including prose texts, without any specific thematic organization.

The existence of Manichaean illuminated hymnbooks in Turfan is also documented through a couple of textual pieces of evidence. The illuminated leaf with the hymn index (M 576)[11] retains a list of hymns contained in a lost hymnbook, listing hymn titles under categories written in red ink—"Hymns of Light," "Monday-Hymns," "Hymns of the Living Self."[12] With the list on its illuminated recto, continuing (and perhaps concluding) on its illuminated verso, this page could represent the last or one of the last pages of the manuscript, with the "table of contents" (in the back of the book, in the French fashion) of a hymnbook, exactly as in the case of the Coptic Manichaean psalm-book edited by Charles R. C. Allberry.[13] Another well-known fragment from a lost Middle Persian hymnbook is a bifolio that preserves a colophon, actually mentioning the book being a hymnbook: "it was in the year 546 after the birth of the Apostle of Light … that this hymnbook (M. Persian *mahrnâmag*), full of living words and beautiful hymns, was begun" (MIK III 203, Figure 3/5).[14] Although the carefully written and well-preserved bifolio with this colophon is not illuminated, already F.W.K. Müller had suggested that previous pages were likely to be illuminated. Müller's idea is supported not only by the content of the pages, which includes a subject often accompanied with illumination (i.e., a benediction on the members of the Uygur ruling family), but also by the scribal decoration on this page. The scribe created a checkered pattern within the lines of the three columns by writing them in blocks of red and black ink. As we shall see, this feature is often seen on other examples of illuminated benedictions that can be part of service-books.

---

[8] Of the 12 fragments, one (M 797) is a bifolio of a codex with part of a hymn on each of its four pages, five (M 23, M 576, M 730, MIK III 4970, and MIK III 4983) are double-sided folia of codices, four (M 223, MIK III 4981 a & f, M 559, and MIK III 8259 folio 1) are found on only one side of a codex folio, and one (MIK III 8260) is a pustaka page.

[9] For an illustration see Gulácsi 2001a, No. 4.

[10] Clark 1982, 146–147.

[11] For an iullustration see Gulácsi 2001a, No. 1.

[12] BeDuhn 2001, 210.

[13] Allberry, 1938a, xxii.

[14] Klimkeit 1993, 274.

Table 6/3. Religious Prose Preserved from Manichaean Illuminated Books (8 examples)

NARRATIVE (2)	TREATIES (2)
Narrative of Unidentifiable Content (2)	*"On the Origin of the World" (1)*
M 694 recto	MIK III 8259 folio 2(?) recto & verso
M 694 verso	*"On the Development of the Human Fetus" (1)*
	So 18700 & M 501 e recto & verso
PARABLE (2)	
"Parable of Bashandad" (1)	SERMON or TREATISE (2)
MIK III 8259 folio 1(?) recto	*"On Adopting Convoluted Rules" (1)*
"Parables of the Five Limbs" (1)	MIK III 6368 recto
MIK III 4981 b (silk)	*"On the Seven Kinds of Auditor" (1)*
	M 171 folio 1 verso & folio 2 recto

Regarding the illumination of the manuscripts in which these 21 hymns were featured, the majority of these texts (19 examples) were adorned solely with decorative designs. In addition, a small number of hymn-pages are accompanied with figural scenes (two examples), and one hymn is decorated with both a figural scene and a decorative design on its page. The folio with the hymn index (M 576) contains a floral decoration on its recto, while on its verso remnants of an intracolumnar book painting are preserved in addition to the floral decoration. All in all this survey confirms the existence of illuminated hymnbooks (M576, M 233, M 797) and illuminated anthologies of religious literature (MIK III 8260) in Manichaean Turfan.

Religious Prose

Religious prose constitutes a larger category of pietistic literature that includes narratives (accounts of usually religious mythology), treatises (systematic discussions of facts or principles), parables (an instructional comparison or simile), and sermons (religious instruction). Narratives, treatises, and parables form standard parts of religious literature that were meant to be read alone or in groups. Sermons, composed originally for oral delivery, are often written down for future reference. The performative nature of the latter is indicated by the use of the plural second person as the preacher addresses the audience. Characteristics of these genres are recognizable on the illuminated remains of Turfan Manichaean books, as seen in the three examples below: the first one is a treatise on the development of the human fetus, the second one is a parable-like passage used to characterize one of the five limbs of perfection, and the third one is a sermon:

> Then as much as [ ] limbs of the body [are grow]ing and so much the soul with (skill) [ ] in the body becomes more visible. [ ] if it is a son he turns his face to the mother's [back]. And if it is a daughter she turns her face to the mother's belly. [And] it has both hands together toward the face and [the knees] toward the chin. And inside the [mother's] womb it stays so in [ ] difficulty (So 18700 & M 501 e recto).[15]

> And the sign of the limb of perfection: it is like a tower, which is full of weapons (and) equipment, and like a man who between a mountain and deep waters proceeds without fear; and furthermore it is like a fully armed knight (MIK III 4981 b).[16]

> … if one hold. If one believes in adopting convoluted rules, if there be a non-believing *kunichi* or an ordinary *tiligchi* [among you], it is necessary to recognize … him (MIK III 6368 recto).[17]

---

[15] Reck 2005.
[16] BeDuhn 2001, 241.
[17] The meaning of *kunichi* and *tiligchi* remains unclear (BeDuhn 2001, 231).

Eight Manichaean illuminated texts can be identified as religious prose (Table 6/3). Of these, two fragments (MIK III 8259 and MIK III 6368) contain texts of several genres, and therefore must have belonged to two illuminated anthologies. The additional six folia contain solely religious prose, which could have been parts of either illuminated anthologies or service-books. The types of illumination accompanying these prose texts are surveyed in Table 6/1. Most of them (six texts) are accompanied solely with decorative designs, including the verso of the folio with the treatise discussing "Development of the Human Fetus" (So 18700 & M501 e). The recto of this treatise, just as the page with the "Parable of Bashandad" (MIK III 8259 folio 1 recto), is found on both pages illuminated with figural scenes.

Benedictions

Benediction, a minor genre of religious literature, is characterized by the invocation of a divine blessing on an actual member of the community. Blessings are often performed at the end of religious services. If the liturgy is written down in a service-book, the benediction becomes literature. Benedictions are always contemporaneous with the use of the manuscript and thus are most likely to contain historical data. The listing of Uygur names and titles form a distinctive characteristic of this genre in Turfan.

The best-preserved benediction from a Turfan Manichaean manuscript is found on the non-illuminated bifolio surviving from the Middle Persian hymnbook known as the *Mahrnamag* (MIK III 203). On one of its folia, the listing of the male members of the Uygur court is followed by the roll of the female members of the Uygur court. This enumeration takes up at least one and a half pages from the codex. Benedictions surviving on other Manichaean illuminated folia are more fragmentary. The best-preserved of them blesses (lit. asks for the protection of) the male members of the Uygur court:

> Truly may they protect and guard the whole family of auditors: Foremost, the great king, the great, glorious, valiant, blessed, worthy of both happinesses, both lives, both kingdoms, in body and in soul, king of the Easterners, keeper of the religion, marshal of the righteous, splendid auditor, diademed king, (of) praised and blessed name: **Ulug Elig Tängritä Kut Bulmish Ärdämin El Tutmish Alp Kutlug Külüg Bilgä Uygur Khagan**, the child of **Mani**, … he whose name and … Four-**Tugristan** (?) (MIK III 36 recto).[18]

In light of such relatively well-preserved examples of benedictions, when Uygur names and titles are recognized in more fragmentary illuminated texts, they are interpreted as parts of benedictions, as seen in the example below that contains the epithet of an Uygur ruler:

> The charismatic king, (He) who Obtained Charisma from the Moon God, (He) who is Imbued with Charisma, (He) who Maintained the Realm with Courage and Valor (lit.: **Ay Tängritä Kut Bulmish Kut Ornanmish Alpin Ärdämin El Tutmish** (MIK III 6368 verso, start of column 2).[19]

Altogether, six illuminated texts can be identified as benedictions (Table 6/4). One (MIK III 8259) is a bifolio that seems to derive from a service-book, from which four texts are retained: on the illuminated folio 1(?) we find a parable, a benediction, and a hymn to Mani, whereas on the non-illuminated folio 2(?) there is a cosmological treatise. The other fragments with benedictions do not contain enough data for further identification. They could have been parts of hymnbooks or service-books. Regarding the types of illuminations used together with these texts, Table 6/1 shows that among the benedictions identified on illuminated codex fragments, most (five texts) are accompanied with figural scenes. Only one page with a section from a "Benediction on the Sacred Meal" is decorated with solely floral decoration, and even this text is accompanied by a complex figural scene on its recto.

---

[18] BeDuhn 2001, 232–234.
[19] BeDuhn 2001, 232.

Table 6/4. Benedictions Preserved from Manichaean Illuminated Books (6 examples)

Benediction on Sacred Meal & Leaders (1)	_Benediction on the Uygur Court (3)_	_Benediction on an Uygur Ruler (1)_
MIK III 4974 recto and verso	MIK III 36 recto	MIK III 6368 verso
	MIK III 4979 recto	
Benediction on Religious & Secular Leaders (1)	Or. 8212-1692 recto	
MIK III 8259 folio 1(?) recto		

Colophons

Colophons are texts at the end of the books with remarks about the circumstances of their creation. They may refer to the patron and the authorities organizing the commission, as well as the scribes and illuminators who worked on the project. Often, they contain a date. The most complete Manichaean colophon from Turfan is found on the bifolio of the _Mahrnamag_ (MIK III 203). It includes a date (762 CE) together with other useful information regarding the unusual circumstances of the creation of its book. The section preserved from the colophon reads as follows:

> (It was) in the year 546 after the birth of the Apostle of Light, (that is) now in the year ... , when He (Mani) was raised up in might, and in the year 162 after raising (death) of the beneficient Shad Ohrmizd, that this hymnbook full of living words and beautiful hymns, was begun.
>
> The scribe who had started to write it at the commands of the spiritual leaders was not able to finish it. As he could not devote himself to it, and because he had no time, he wrote (only) a little, and did not complete it. It remained in its incomplete form at this place for many years. It lay around and was deposited in the monastery of Argi (Karashahr).
>
> When I, Yazadamand, the preacher, saw this hymnbook lying around, incomplete and useless, I ordered my beloved child, (my) dear son, Naxurigroshn ("the first born of the Lights"), to complete it, so that it might serve to increase the faith, so that (it might become) a (useful) hymnbook in the hands of the children of faith, the new pupils, so that souls would be purified and doctrine, wisdom, and with the blessing of Mar Doshist, the bishop, and the fine leadership of Mar Yisho Aryaman ("Jesus the Friend"), the presbyter, and through the diligence of the wise preacher Yazad-amad, and furthermore through the zeal and efforts of Naxurigroshn, who together with other scribes worked toward that end with warm heart and a loving mind and who transcribed them day and night until everything was finished and completed ...
>
> And I, Naxurigroshn, the servant and scribe, in (making) preparation and arrangements in writing for the sake of this book ... (MIK III 203).[20]

Blessings similar to the ones seen in benedictions may also be incorporated into the dedication (beginning) or into the colophon (at the end) of a religious book. Two Manichaean illuminated texts preserve colophons with fragmentary blessings and, in one case, a merit transfer:

> An auditor, Alp Singqur Tegin, begged and implored to His Majesty My Lord the Bishop (_aftadan_): "Please let [a scribe] quietly write a sacred book in the name of myself." [So], I Uzurk Puhr, whose writing is unskillful, had written [this sacred book] for Alp Singqur Tegin. Being with joy together all his relatives, for the house of the auditors ... (Or. 8212-1692 recto).[21]

---

[20] Klimkeit 1993, 274–275.
[21] Moriyasu 1997, 47.

Table 6/5. Colophons Preserved from Manichaean Illuminated Books (2 examples)

Colophon fragment with name of patron (1)	_Colophon with merit transfer (1)_
Or. 8212-1692 recto	MIK III 4959 recto

… these noble benefactors and others whose name I have not remembered: may they all live in body and soul; may they receive from this book the portion of benefits. Amen (MIK III 4959 recto).[22]

Only two illuminated texts can be identified as colophons (Table 6/5). One (Or. 8212-1692) directly follows a benediction, just as seen on the non-illuminated _Mahrnamag_ fragment, suggesting that the benedictions were placed at the very end of these illuminated books, just before they concluded with a colophon. Regarding the types of illuminations, both colophons are found on pages with decorative designs (Table 6/1), which most likely resulted from having benedictions on the same pages.

Omen Texts

Omen texts forecast good or evil outcomes of the future. They form a marginal group of Manichaean religious literature, for this prognosticating genre belongs to popular religious practice that may cross the boundaries of separate religious communities. Although there could have been non-illuminated omen texts, the one surviving Manichaean example of this genre is illuminated. Its text reads as follows:

> The tenth sign: the earth becomes agitated, or the sun and moon on "_Gozihr_."
> The eleventh sign: if filth comes forth from a silken garment.
> The twelfth sign: if a strange steppe- or seabird sits before one's face.
> The thirteenth sign: if a lamp goes out without cause (M 556).[23]

This text is found on a one-sided paper fragment (M 556) that contains parts of at least six omens.[24] Unfortunately, the text does not retain enough from the original composition to decipher whether these named signs connote positive or negative outcomes, nor even any clue regarding the issue/question to be determined. Since the back of the sheet is blank, it is possible that this fragment derives from an individual sheet of paper used as a personal reference, or from a scroll-formatted book. It is less likely that this fragment is from a codex, since its page arrangement does not accord with the pattern observed on illuminated codex fragments. Nevertheless, each omen is accompanied with a figural scene (see Table 6/1).

Letters

Letters, illuminated for special occasion, were written between distinguished members of the community. The best-preserved Manichaean illuminated manuscript known today is a Sogdian language letter in scroll format (81 TB: 65:01) written between church officials. It was sent from the bishop (_aftadan_) named Shahyar Zadag to the teacher (_mozhak_) Aryaman Puhr on the occasion of celebrating the lunar New Year.[25] As pointed out by Yutaka Yoshida, this 135-line scroll consists of epistolary formulas in the following sequence:

Lines 1–25:   Addressee's name accompanied by expressions of greeting and praise, followed by the mentioning of the mozhak's associates

---

[22] BeDuhn 2001, 228.
[23] Reck and Sundermann 1997.
[24] Reck and Sundermann 1997.
[25] Personal communication with Yutaka Yoshida.

Book painting inserted between lines 25 and 26.

Lines 26–30:	Sender's name prefaced by adjectives expressing his humble feeling toward the addressee
Lines 31–37:	Expression of respect and homage followed by confession of sins and wish for atonement
Lines 37–51:	Sender's concern about the health and welfare of the addressee and his congregation, including the Uygur khagan and his court
Lines 51–55:	Health and safety enjoyed by the sender and his congregation
Lines 55–69:	Statement that thereby begins the main body of the letter, together with the sender's excuses not to come see the *mozhak* in person
Lines 70–109:	Sender wishes happy and prosperous New Year for the addressee, his church, and the Uygur khagan and his family
Lines 109–112:	Reference to the caravan that will bring the letter
Lines 112–129:	Sender and his colleagues send their greetings to the laypeople living with the addressee and the lay communities of both parties are mentioned
Lines 130–131:	Date
Lines 132–135:	Names of the sender and the addressee (81 TB 65:01).[26]

Yutaka Yoshida also noted that the phraseology of this letter is strikingly similar to Manichaean hymns in honor of church leaders, patrons, and the Manichaean church in general. In light of this recognition, Yoshida raised the possibility that "New Year hymns" may have been ritually performed to the Uygur khagan on the occasion of this event.[27] The similarity between the genres of letters and hymns draws attention to the varied function of Manichaean scriptoria, indicating that this office or workshop of the church fulfilled a highly active and visible role that finds its presence in multiple facets of Manichaean community life. Furthermore, it is also likely that letters of similar greetings, with illuminated inserts, were sent regularly from the office of the bishop to other distinguished members of the Manichaean community, including the khagan and other high-ranking members of the court. Although only one text can be identified as an illuminated letter (see Table 6/1), as we shall see, another illuminated scroll fragment that retains only bits from its text nevertheless documents the practice of letter illumination in Manichaean Turfan.

***

In summary, the above survey revealed that hymns and benedictions are the most frequently illuminated genres in the surviving folia of Turfan Manichaean religious literature. Regarding types of illumination, hymns and religious prose are accompanied with decorative designs. Benedictions, however, are always adorned with figural scenes, even on pages where they conclude followed by a colophon. Regarding the types of manuscripts to which these illuminated folia belonged, we learn that certain official letters were illuminated, just as were anthologies. One illuminated fragment seems to be from a service-book. The folia of illuminated hymns could have been parts of illuminated hymnbooks, but just like texts of religious prose, they might have belonged to illuminated anthologies or even service-books.

Survey of Identifiable Figural Scenes

On the surviving 89 fragments of Manichaean illuminated manuscripts, the subjects of 26 figural compositions can be identified because they retain large enough sections of visual information to recognize their contents. A significant group of paintings in Manichaean manuscripts are marginal floral decorations. These surround the texts with mainly vegetal motifs, occasionally incorporating scarves, plates of food, or musi-

---

[26] The summary was provided by Yutaka Yoshida.

[27] Yutaka Yoshida kindly provided a copy of his paper discussing the illuminated Sogdian letter for the first time that was delivered at the Third European Conference of Iranian Studies, 1995, Cambridge, England.

Table 6/6. Overview of Pictorial Subjects in Identifiable Figural Scenes of Manichaean Illuminated Book Fragments (26 examples)

THEOLOGY (3 scenes)	DOCTRINE (5 scenes)	RITUALS (12 scenes)	INSTITUTION (3 scenes)	PATRONS (1 scene)	OTHER (2 scenes)
Third Messenger (1) MIK III 4965 recto	Primary Prophets (1) MIK III 4947 & III 5 d (scroll)	Alms Service (3) *M 559 recto* M 6290 b recto MIK III 6376 recto	Headgear of Officials w/ Decorative Figures (2) MIK III 4614 (scroll) *80 TB 65:01 (scroll)*	Ruler with Military Elite (1) *MIK III 36 verso*	Omens (2) *M 556 recto* *M 556 recto*
Unidentifiable Mythological Figure (2) MIK III 4965 verso MIK III 7283 recto	Work of the Religion (1) *MIK III 4974 recto*	Sermon (2) MIK III 6265 & III 4966 c recto *MIK III 8259 f 1(?) recto*	Elects in Scribal Duty (1) *MIK III 6368 recto*		
	Judgment after Death (2) MIK III 4959 verso MIK III 6258 a recto	Hymnody (1) *MIK III 6368 verso*			
	Elect in Paradise (1) *MIK III 8260 recto*	Bema Celebration (3) *MIK III 4979 a, b verso* *Or. 8212-1692 verso* MIK III 6257 verso			
		Conversion (2) *MIK III 4979 a, b recto* MIK III 6626 & III 6379 c recto			

Italics indicates associated identifiable text.

cians. Since their primary function is to embellish the manuscript, they are referred to here as decorative designs. Due to their marginal location and dominant floral motifs, it is relatively easy to recognize fragments with decorative designs. Other identifiable illuminations contain more complex visual information, depicting varied subjects. Such scenes may be spread out on the entire page, inserted into the text areas as columnar scenes, or placed along the outer margins. They are referred to here as figural scenes. Their subject matter can be determined only if most of the painting, or at least a significant portion of the central area survives. The identifications of the pictorial subjects (just like the elements of their iconography) are not argued here, but are drawn from previous studies by Albert von Le Coq, Hans-Joachim Klimkeit, Jorinde Ebert, Larry Clark, and myself. Table 6/6 provides an overview of these book paintings, listing them in columns under general subject categories such as theology, doctrine, ritual, institution, patrons, and other. Supplementing their listings are examples of the images from within each thematic categories.

Images with theological themes (Table 6/6 and Plate 7a, b) are centered around figures from Manichaean theology. Three book paintings portray such subjects. All are fragments of full-page compositions that show the main figure in the center of a symmetrically arranged setting. One of them (MIK III 4965 recto[?], Plate 7a) arguably depicts the *Third Messenger*, identified on the basis of his multi-layered halo, which incorporates 12 female heads that are possibly symbols of "Light Maidens."[28] Another fragment

---

[28] Gulácsi 2001a, 104.

retains an image (MIK III 4965 verso [?]) of a so far *unidentified mythological figure*, standing under a crowned arch decorated with a female head (MIK III 4965 verso[?], Plate 7b).The third painting (MIK III 7283 recto) also shows a yet-unidentified male mythological figure. His image is enclosed in a mandorla, and is surrounded by a dozen or so gilded plates with female heads on them.[29]

Images with doctrinal themes (Table 6/6 and Plate 7c, d) portray principle religious tenets. Five book paintings depict four such tenets from the core of Manichaean teachings. One of the most important Manichaean teachings is that all religions are part of a universal faith and that the messengers of this faith prior to Mani (Zoroaster, Buddha, and Jesus) were all true prophets. Most likely, these *Primary Prophets* were the subject of a now fragmentary scene (MIK III 4947 & III 5 d, see Plate 7c) that retains a named image of the Buddha positioned in one of the four corners around a large central figure, now lost.[30] Another core Manichaean teaching explains the goal of being Manichaean on a mythological scale. *The Work of the Religion*, as it is called in Manichaean texts, is being part of the process of re-separation of light from darkness and sending the light back to the Father of Greatness, to the Realm of Light. The stages of this process are represented on one of the only intact Manichaean book paintings (MIK III 4974 recto).[31] A third important teaching relates to *Judgment After Death*, which determines the afterlife of a person. On one fragment (MIK III 4959 verso, Plate 7d), a man dressed in a loincloth is standing before a judge. A goat-head hanging on his neck seems to symbolize his sin of consuming or killing animals.[32] In the other possible judgment scene (MIK III 6258 a recto) a man in a loincloth is standing with a golden bowl in his hands.[33] The fourth identifiable doctrinal subject relates to the teaching on the afterlife of a righteous elect, who will not reincarnate, but will depart to Paradise, i.e., the Realm of Light. The scene identified here as an *Elect in Paradise Scene* (MIK III 8260 recto, Plate 6d) shows a male elect under a tree, from which his headgear hangs suspended. The elect is looking down onto a realm where two kneeling elects flank a fire-altar.[34]

Scenes that portray rituals (Table 6/6 and Plate 7e, f) show elements from prescribed procedures of religious rites. Five Manichaean rituals can be recognized on 11 book paintings. (1) *Alms Service* was the most important daily duty of the laity. The best-preserved depiction of such a ritual (M 559 recto, Figure 5/8) shows laywomen holding plates of food, facing at least one female elect. In another scene (M 6290 b recto) lay-people stand with plates of food in their hands behind a row of seated elects. On a smaller fragment (MIK III 6376 recto), two laymen kneel next to a bowl.[35] (2) *Sermons* are captured in images that portray seated elects, with their hands in communicative gestures, surrounded by laity. In one of the most complete Manichaean paintings (MIK III 8259 f1[?] recto) we find two elects, one with gesturing hands and another holding a book, and a group of lay people seated on rugs. A more fragmentary image of this subject also survives (MIK III 6265 & III 4966 c recto). (3) *Hymnody* representations have sermon-like iconography, except that the laity plays musical instruments. One such image can be identified (MIK III 6863 recto). (4) The most important Manichaean ritual, which commemorated Mani's death and celebrated the hope for his second coming, is often referred to as the *Bema Celebration* in scholarly writings, after an empty throne (Gr. *bēma*), described by Augustine of Hippo as part of the ceremonial setup. The largest Manichaean book painting (MIK III 4979 verso) portrays this festival,[36] as do two more fragmen-

---

[29] Gulácsi 2001, No. 48.
[30] Jorinde Ebert presented a paper on the reconstruction of the fragment, arguing for the presence of four figures surrounding the main image in 2001 during the 5th International Congress on Manichaean Studies.
[31] Gulácsi 2001a, 83–86.
[32] Le Coq 1923, 61; Klimkeit 1982, 37.
[33] Gulácsi 2001a, 82.
[34] Gulácsi 2001a, 152–154.
[35] For an illustration see Gulácsi 2001a, No. 38.
[36] Klimkeit 1982, 16, 34; Ebert, 1994, 5.

tary images (Or. 8212-1692 verso and MIK III 6257 verso).[37] (5) Finally, *a Conversion* ritual is shown in a painting where the right hand of a high-ranking elect clasps both hands of a ruler. In one scene, this act is witnessed by groups of heavenly beings and members of the Manichaean community (MIK III 4979 a, b recto, Plate 7f).[38] The same hand-gesture and sections from the two main figures are also retained on a badly damaged originally full-page book painting (MIK III 6626 & III 6379 c recto).[39]

Pictorial themes that relate to the church institution (Table 6/6 and Plate 8a, b) regard the organization of the religious community. Three book paintings belong to this category. Two show the *Headgear of Church Officials with Decorative Figures* (MIK III 4614, Plate 8a; and 81 TB 65:01, Figure 6/5a), where the headgear of a high-ranking elect is incorporated into a decorative pictorial arrangement created around an inscription.[40] The one other scene that may be interpreted as belonging to this category shows Elects in *Scribal Duty* (MIK III 6368 recto, Plate 7b).[41]

The patrons of the Manichaean church (Table 6/6 and Plate 7c, d), the *Ruler and His Military Elite*, are the subjects of one book painting (MIK III 36 verso, Plate 7c). On this symmetrically arranged representation, armored military officials surround the large figure of an enthroned ruler. Although the body position of the ruler, as well as details of his throne, resemble images of rulers in Sassanian and Sogdian works of art, the armor of the generals accords with the depiction of armor in East and East Central Asian art. The military leaders are shown on a smaller scale, standing in the two rows of five on both sides of the ruler.

Finally, the category "other" is introduced here for the *Omens* (Table 6/6 and Plate 8d, e). These scenes depict events that are considered to be signs upon the sight of which the outcome of the future can be foretold. Two paintings are retained, with recognizable content on one page (M 559 recto) that originally contained at least six such scenes. The first image shows a house and two birds—one in a window and the other on the roof (Plate 8d). The second image is that of a candleholder with three flickering lights (Plate 8e).[42]

This overview reveals that the subject matter of figural scenes in Manichaean illuminated books is not exclusively religious in nature. A few non-religious themes include the depiction of a ruler and his warriors, as well as omen illustrations. Among the religious images, representations of rituals are the most frequent. They are found on about half of the recognizable miniatures. Book paintings with theological and doctrinal subjects also form a notable group. They are seen on about a third of the fragments, and may be considered together, since both concern depictions of core Manichaean teachings.

IDENTIFIABLE TEXTS AND THEIR ILLUMINATIONS

Random chances of survival, discovery, and rescue have sadly narrowed the group of objects to be considered in the final phase of this survey. There are 14 (3+11) cases when an identifiable figural scene is preserved together with an identifiable text. In addition, there are 20 cases when floral decorative designs are seen with identifiable texts. There are thus 34 examples of recognizable texts and recognizable illuminations from Manichaean illuminated books.

Using a table format we are able to survey which identifiable figural scene accompanies which identifiable text (Table 6/7). Between the two images with doctrinal subjects, the *Work of the Religion Scene*

---

[37] For a study of the subject, see Gulácsi 2004.
[38] Klimkeit 1982, 34.
[39] Personal communication with Dr. Clark (see Gulácsi 2001a, 108–110).
[40] Gulácsi 2001a, 144–146.
[41] Le Coq 1923, 56; Klimkeit 1982, 38.
[42] Gulácsi 2001a, 126–127.

Table 6/7. Degrees of Contextual Cohesion between Identifiable Texts and Identifiable Illuminations (34 examples)

Relationship	PAGE OF FRAGMENT	SUBJECT OF ILLUMINATION	SUBJECT OF TEXT
INTERRELATED			
Figural Scene & Text	M 556 recto	Omen	Omen
(3 example)	M 556 recto	Omen	Omen
	MIK III 36 r & v	Ruler with Military Elite	Benediction on Ruler & Milit. Elite
UNRELATED			
Figural Scene & Text	M 559 verso	Alms Service	Hymn to the Father of Greatness
(11 examples)	MIK III 4974 recto	Work of Religion	Benediction on the Sacred Meal
	MIK III 4979 verso	Conversion	Benediction on the Royal Court
	MIK III 4979 r & v	Bema Celebration	Benediction on the Royal Court
	MIK III 6368 verso	Hymnody	Benediction on the Ruler
	MIK III 6368 verso	Elects in Scribal Duty	Prose on Convoluted Rules
	MIK III 8259 fl [?] recto	Sermon	Parable of Bashandad
	MIK III 8259 fl [?] recto	Sermon	Benediction on the Leaders
	MIK III 8260 r & v	Elect in Paradise	Hymn to Mani
	Or. 8212-1692 r & v	Bema Celebration	Benediction on the Royal Court
	81 TB 65:1 (scroll)	Headgear of Church Official	Letter between Church Officials
Decorative Design &	M 23 recto	Floral Motifs with Food	Hymn to the Prophets
Text (20 examples)	M 23 verso	Floral Motifs with Scarves	Hymn to the Prophets
	M 171 f 1 verso	Floral Motifs with Food	Prose on the Auditors
	M 171 f 2 recto	Floral Motifs with Scarves	Prose on the Auditors
	M 233 recto	Floral Motifs with Food	Hymn
	M 576 recto	Floral Motifs	Hymn
	M 694 recto	Floral Motifs	Narrative
	M 730 recto	Floral Motifs with Scarves	Hymn to the Father of Greatness
	M 730 verso	Floral Motifs with Scarves	Hymn to the Father of Greatness
	M 797 f 1[?] recto	Floral Motifs	Hymn index
	MIK III 4970 b recto	Floral Motifs	Hymn
	MIK III 4970 b verso	Floral Motifs	Hymn
	MIK III 4974 verso	Floral Motifs	Benediction
	MIK III 4976 a, b recto	Floral Motifs	Sermon or Hymn
	MIK III 4976 a, b verso	Floral Motifs	Sermon or Hymn
	MIK III 4981a (silk)	Floral Motifs with Food	Hymn to Mani
	MIK III 4981 f (silk)	Floral Motifs	Hymn to Mani
	MIK III 4983 recto	Floral Motifs	Hymn to the Third Messenger
	MIK III 8259 fl(?) v	Floral Motifs with Victories	Hymn
	So 18700 & M 501 e v	Floral Motifs with Musician	Hymn

illuminates a benediction on the sacred meal and the leaders of the community (MIK III 4974 recto and verso), and the *Elect in Paradise Scene* adorns a hymn to Mani (MIIK III 8260 recto and verso). Among the six paintings with ritual themes, the *Alms Service Scene* is seen with a hymn to the Father of Great-ness (M 559 recto & verso); the *Sermon Scene* illuminates two texts on the same page—a parable and a benediction on the religious and secular leaders of the community (both on MIK III 8259 fl [?] recto); the *Hymnody Scene* accompanies a benediction (MIK III 6368 verso); the two scenes of the *Bema Celebration* are painted next to benedictions on both fragments (Or. 8212-1692 recto & verso, and MIK III 4979 a, b, recto & verso); and the *Conversion Scene* illuminates a benediction (MIK III 4979 a, b recto). Between the two images that relate to the church institution, the *Headgear of a Church Official* and Musicians adorns a letter between church officials (80 TB 65:01) and the *Elects in Scribal Duty Scene* is painted together with a sermon on rules (MIK III 6368 recto). Regarding the patron theme, one miniature that depicts a *Ruler and Military Elite* is located next to a benediction on the Uygur khagan and his military officials (MIK III 36 recto & verso). Finally, the two omen texts are preserved with identifiable *Omen Scenes* (M 559 recto).

Based on this information, we are in a good position to judge how closely these images relate to their texts. By searching for shared elements of content between the painted and the written messages, three different degrees of relatedness can be discovered: (1) interrelated text and figural scene, (2) unrelated text and figural scene, and (3) unrelated text and decorative design.

Interrelated Text and Figural Scene

Interrelatedness is seen between the text and the image when the general subject of the text is identical with the general subject of the book painting. In such cases, the illumination is an illustration of the text. All in all, two instances of this type of contextual cohesion are retained within the corpus of Manichaean book art (Table 6/8).

The paper piece with the omens (M 556, Figure 6/1 and Plate 8d, e) shows a full connection between the texts and their illuminations. When the sun and the moon are mentioned in the text, the damaged image contains a moon crescent; when washing of silk is discussed, the squeezing of cloth is shown; when birds are mentioned, two birds are featured in the composition; when a lamp with extinguished flame is discussed, the lantern is shown with flickering flames. One by one, the omens in the text are illustrated in their adjacent images. It is important to note, however, that this illustrated omen fragment represents an unusual case within the corpus of Manichaean book art. Curiously, the page arrangement of this fragment does not accord with the rest of the surviving examples. The list of omens not only has a blank back side, but also an unprecedented page layout, which nevertheless accords with the standard sideways orientation of figures in relation to the direction of the writing. It is possible that this paper piece did not belong to a codex-formatted bound book, but was a loose sheet used for personal reference, or part of a longer manuscript in a scroll format.

The only other example for interrelated text and illumination seen on a codex folio that fully accords with the rest of the Manichaean illuminated corpus is the fragment on which the patrons of the Manichaean church are the subject of both the image and its associated text (MIK III 36, Figure 6/2 and Plate 8c). The painting on the verso depicts a large figure of a ruler seated on an elaborate throne with his knees spread in a fashion often seen in Sassanian royal imagery. The ruler is surrounded by figures in tightly spaced rows wearing military armor, which can best be interpreted as a visual reference to the Uygur ruling elite. The text on the recto offers a benediction on these patrons. It names the khagan and the military leaders, listing their functions and ranks:

> Truly may they protect and guard the whole family of auditors: Foremost, the great king, the great, glorious, valiant, blessed, worthy of both happinesses, both lives, both kingdoms, in body and in soul, king of the Easterners, keeper of the religion, marshal of the righteous, splendid auditor, diademed king, (of) praised and blessed name: **Ulug Elig Tängritä Kut Bulmish Ärdämin El Tutmish Alp Kutlug Külüg Bilgä Uygur Khagan**, the child of **Mani**, ... he whose name and ... Four-**Tugristan** (?) ...

> And also ... the great protectors and generals of the fortunate king: Foremost, **El Ögäsi Nigoshakpat, El Ögäsi Yägän Säväg Totok, El Ögäsi Ötür Boyla Tarkhan**; and also *Totoks* (military governors): **Tapmish Kutlug Totok, Chik Totok**; and the *Chigshis* (district magistrates): **Baga Chigshi, Yägän Öz Chigshi, Tudun Chigshi; Batga Changshi** (keeper of the annals, [Chin. *ch'ang shih*]), **Köl Sangun Tiräk, Inanchu Bilgä Tiräk**; and also the *Boylas* (meaning unclear) **Tapmish Boyla, Tarkhan Ishpara Boyla**. May they

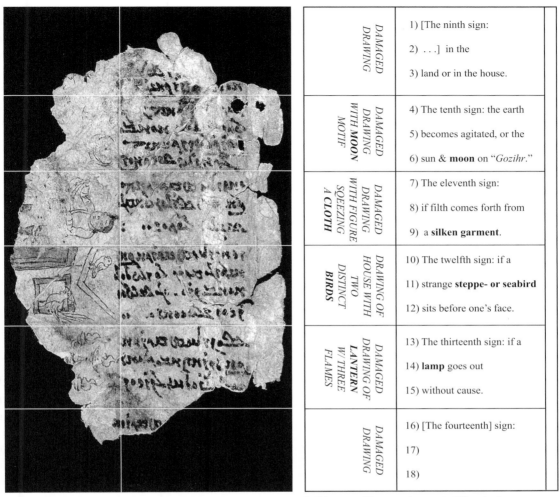

DAMAGED DRAWING		1) [The ninth sign: 2) . . .] in the 3) land or in the house.
*DAMAGED DRAWING WITH **MOON** MOTIF*		4) The tenth sign: the earth 5) becomes agitated, or the 6) sun & **moon** on "*Gozihr*."
*DAMAGED DRAWING WITH FIGURE SQEEZING A **CLOTH***		7) The eleventh sign: 8) if filth comes forth from 9) a **silken garment**.
*DRAWING OF HOUSE WITH TWO DISTINCT **BIRDS***		10) The twelfth sign: if a 11) strange **steppe- or seabird** 12) sits before one's face.
*DAMAGED DRAWING OF **LANTERN** W/ THREE FLAMES*		13) The thirteenth sign: if a 14) **lamp** goes out 15) without cause.
DAMAGED DRAWING		16) [The fourteenth] sign: 17) 18)

a: M 556 verso(?)   b: Diagram with text and content of illumination

Figure 6/1. Example of Interrelated Text and Illumination (M 556 verso[?])
(SBPK, Berlin-Brandenburgische Akademie der Wissenschaften, Turfanforschung, Berlin)

all live in invulnerability, and in the end receive a fortunate reward forever. Let it be so!

And also the renowned *Ichräkis* (chamberlains) who serve before the fortunate king: Foremost … **Ötür Boyla Tarkhan … Kutlug Ichräki, … Tapmish Ichräki, … Kutlug T** … (MIK III 36).[43]

As the reconstruction of this fragment confirms, this benediction must have started already on the previous folio and continued on the subsequent folia. Only two lines are missing from the first column on the recto. The second column on this page still lists the male members of the court. In light of the benediction preserved on the *Marhnamag* (MIK III 203, Figure 3/6a), it is most likely that the listing of the women of

---

[43] After BeDuhn 2001, 232–234.

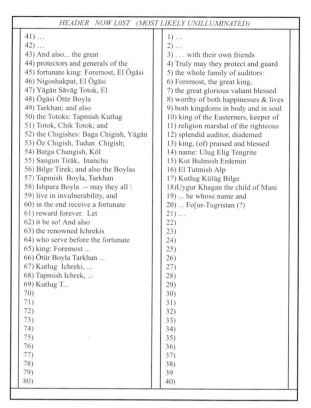

41) ...
42) ...
43) And also... the great
44) protectors and generals of the
45) fortunate king: Foremost, El Ögäsi
46) Nigoshakpat, El Ögäsi
47) Yägän Säväg Totok, El
48) Ögäsi Ötür Boyla
49) Tarkhan; and also
50) the Totoks: Tapmish Kutlug
51) Totok, Chik Totok; and
52) the Chigishes: Baga Chigish, Yägän
53) Öz Chigish, Tudun Chigish;
54) Batga Changish, Köl
55) Sangun Tiräk, Inanchu
56) Bilge Tirek; and also the Boylas
57) Tapmish Boyla, Tarkhan
58) Ishpara Boyla -- may they all \
59) live in invulnerability, and
60) in the end receive a fortunate
61) reward forever. Let
62) it be so! And also
63) the renowned Ichrekis
64) who serve before the fortunate
65) king: Foremost ...
66) Ötür Boyla Tarkhan ...
67) Kutlug Ichreki, ...
68) Tapmish Ichrek, ...
69) Kutlug T...
70)
71)
72)
73)
74)
75)
76)
77)
78)
79)
80)

1) ...
2) ...
3) . . . with their own friends
4) Truly may they protect and guard
5) the whole family of auditors:
6) Foremost, the great king,
7) the great glorious valiant blessed
8) worthy of both happinesses & lives
9) both kingdoms in body and in soul
10) king of the Easterners, keeper of
11) religion marshal of the righteous
12) splendid auditor, diademed
13) king, (of) praised and blessed
14) name: Ulug Elig Tengrite
15) Kut Bulmish Erdemin
16) El Tutmish Alp
17) Kutlug Külüg Bilge
18) Uygur Khagan the child of Mani
19) ... he whose name and
20) ... Fo[ur-Tugristan (?)
21) ...
22)
23)
24)
25)
26)
27)
28)
29)
30)
31)
32)
33)
34)
35)
36)
37)
38)
39
40)

FULL-PAGE BOOK PAINTING
RULER AND HIS MILITARY ELITE

a: Diagram with text and content of illumination, recto

b: Diagram with content of illumination, verso

c: MIK III 36 recto

d: MIK III 36 verso

Figure 6/2. Example of Interrelated Text and Illumination (MIK III 36)
(SMPK, Museum für Indische Kunst, Berlin)

the court followed after the surviving full-page painting on the verso. This indicates that several subsequent folia in this illuminated book were devoted to the benediction on the Uygur court illustrated at least by one full-page image.

Unrelated Text and Figural Scene

The pictorial and textual components of the manuscript are considered unrelated when the subject of the writing and the painting does not correspond on the same page or associated pages. All together 11 cases of this type of integration are documented within the corpus of Manichaean book illumination (Table 6/8). Although none of them can be interpreted as "illustrations" of their texts, they accord with the general context of their texts by representing scenes from the religious life of the church. From among these 11 cases, two representative examples are discussed below in greater detail. The first is characteristic to illuminated books, and the second relates to illuminated letters.

A complex program of illumination is found on the relatively well-preserved codex folio that most likely derived from an illuminated anthology or service-book (MIK III 4974, Figure 6/3). Besides the columns of the text, the recto contains a large intracolumnar scene flanked by a pair of putto on lotus flowers, as well as an illuminated header. The intracolumnar painting depicts the Work of the Religion. In four stages, this composition represents the journey of the light particles to the Realm of Light: (1) the food donated by the laity, (2) the elects' bodies, (3) the "vessels of light" (waxing moon touching the sun), and (4) the right hand of God—a symbol for the ultimate destination, the Realm of Light.[44] This scene is enclosed in a text that started already on the now-lost previous folio of the book and ran through both sides of the surviving two pages, concluding on the subsequent folio, now lost. Unlike the image, the text does not relate to the subject of the Work of the Religion. Instead, it contains a benediction on the Sacred Meal and the religious leaders of the community by associating each ecclesiastical rank with a member of the Manichaean pantheon and one of the 12 virtues (*shardarift*):[45]

> (recto) ... with good omen and good premonition(?),
> and may he establish [it] over the entire holy religion,
> and over the meal of **Aryaman Roshn**
> and over you, praised leader who stands [as] a banner of the gods of light,
> and over the whole election of light.
>
> First Sovereignty: You, our highest deity, are likened to **Zurvan**,
> who [with] rulership [is] crowned (verso) [at] the banquet,
> who with ... -lessness and love nurtures all the gods and **Mahraspandan**.
> From him they receive the gift of godliness, light, beauty, and
> fragrance, pleasant song, and evoked spirit;
> and happy and fortunate they become forever.
> So you also, loving and compassionate father, nurture and enlighten the elect and
> the auditors with greater zeal and they are connected with the wisdom of the gods.
>
> Second Wisdom: You good teacher, our compassionate mother,
> are like in sagacity to the Mother of the Living,
> the dearest of all the gods,
> the one from whom went forth all instruction of piety.
> So you also are a loving mother,
> who [with] evoked wisdom bears children by speech,

[44] For an article on the subject, see Gulácsi 2001b.
[45] BeDuhn 2001, 228–230.

HEADER SURROUNDED WITH FLORAL AND SCARF DECORATION		
POTTO ON LOTUS FLOWER	12) banner of the gods 13) of light, and 14) over the whole 15) election of 16) light. First 17) Authority: You,	1) with good omen and 2) good premonition, 3) and may he 4) establish [it] over 5) the entire holy 6) religion, and
GOD'S HAND REACHING INTO THE SCENE	*WORK OF THE RELIGION SCENE*	
POTTO ON LOTUS FLOWER	18) our highest deity, 19) are likened 20) to Zurvan, who 21) [with] rulership 22) [is] crowned	7) over the meal of 8) Aryaman Roshn 9) and over you, 10) praised leader 11) who stands
		POOL OF WATER WITH LOTUS PLANT

a: Diagram w/ text and content of illumination, recto

HEADER SURROUNDED WITH FLORAL AND SCARF DECORATION	
26) and they are connected 27) with the wisdom 28) of the gods. 29) Second Wisdom: You 30) good teacher, 31) our compassionate mother 32) are like in 33) sagacity to the Mother 34) of the Living, 35) the dearest of 36) all the gods, 37) the one from whom went 38) forth all instruction 39) of piety. 40) So you also are 41) a loving mother, 42) who [with] evoked 43) wisdom bears 44) children by speech, 45) and nurtures them 46) with spiritual milk, 47) and leads them forward 48) to the stature of 49) godliness. 50) Third Victory: [. . .]	1) at the banquet who with 2) ... -lessness 3) and love 4) nurtures 5) all the gods and 6) Mahraspandan. 7) And from him 8) they receive the gift 9) of godliness, 10) light, 11) beauty, and 12) fragrance, pleasant 13) song, and evoked 14) spirit; and 15) happy and fortunate 16) they become forever. 17) So you also, 18) loving and 19) compassionate father, 20) nurture and 21) enlighten 22) the elect and 23) the auditors with 24) greater zeal 25) [. . .]

b: Diagram w/ text and content of illumination, verso

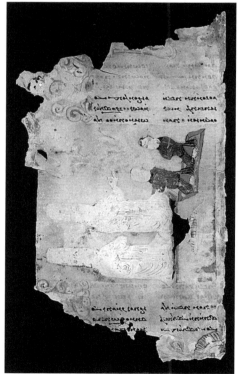

c: MIK III 4974 recto

d: MIK III 4974 verso

Figure 6/3. Example of Unrelated Text and Illumination (MIK III 4974)
(SMPK, Museum für Indische Kunst, Berlin)

A characteristic example of an illuminated page with decorative designs can be seen on the back of the folio with the Work of the Religion Scene that derived from an illuminated hymnbook or service-book (MIK III 4974 verso, Figure 6/3). Just as on the recto of the folio, wide margins surround the area of the text. The header is almost completely lost, but its original existence is indicated through the surrounding decorative design, only faint traces of which remain. Scarf motifs on the left and intertwined flower buds on the right indicate that the decorative design on this page densely filled out the upper margin and stopped relatively high on the page, at the third line of the text.

Occasionally, musicians and victories are integrated into the marginal decoration of the page, an example of which is preserved on a torn paper piece with the Treatise on the Development of the Human Fetus that once belonged to an illuminated anthology or service-book (So 18700 & M 501e, Figure 6/4). Retaining most of the upper half of a folio, this fragment includes delicate line drawings on the upper and outer margins around a treatise on the development of the human fetus. While the recto is adorned solely with a decorative design along what is left from the upper margin, on the verso a marginal figural scene accompanies the continuation of the text.

(recto)   and into limbs he divides and distributes and makes visible. Then as much as [ ] limbs of the body [are grow]ing and so much the soul with (skill) [ ] in the body becomes more visible. [ ] if it is a son he turns his face to the mother's [back]. And if it is a daughter she turns her face to the mother's belly. [And] it has both hands together toward the face and [the knees] toward the chin. And inside the [mother's] womb it stays so in [ ]difficulty. [ ] [ ] in [ ] [ ] this [ ]

(verso)   it is difficult and cruel, so that inside there it moves very much. If into this pla[ce] the wind in the mother's womb gathers. And this ch[ild] turns away from this place and his head is turned upside down. And he makes to this [ ] and dirty place, [ ] out of which he wants to be born. And in that place, so much [ ] difficulties and miseries [he has seen?] as if somebody [ ] him [ ]. And furthermore as [ ] [ ] and … [ ].[50]

Next to the text, along the outer margin, a musician can be seen among the remnants of at least three figures. Parts of two scarves indicate the previous figure, and a tiny part from a rounded carpet signals the subsequent figure, suggesting a row of figures seated on carpets with scarves blown around their upper bodies. The use of scarves seems to be a continuation of the decorative program illuminating the header, since above the first line of the text similar scarves are seen in a rhythmical distribution. The illumination on these pages does not illustrate the subject of the text. Just like the scarves around the header, the musicians along the outer margin form a decorative addition that adorns these pages. The text, mentioning no musicians and no scarves, keeps its focus on the human fetus.

Table 6/8 allows us to systematically survey the correlation and degree of relatedness of text and image in Turfan Manichaean book art. On the 89 fragments, 34 examples retain identifiable illumination together with an identifiable text. Of these, less then 3 percent (two examples) show close contextual relationship between the text and the image. It is interesting that all three miniatures are non-religious in their pictorial subjects (two omen scenes, and one scene with a ruler and his generals). The rest, 97 percent of the examples, document no shared subjects between the texts and their illuminations.

---

[50] Reck 2005.

Conclusion

The area of the Turfan region yielded the only group of illuminated Manichaean manuscripts known to us today. This corpus of 89 fragments derived from books made and used from around the tenth century. In order to understand what kind of contextual cohesion characterized the text and illumination of these books, this survey has analyzed the painted and written contents of the remains and, on the basis of numerical data, revealed a variety of facts that were previously unknown about Turfan Manichaean book art. Most important, it has become clear that complex figural compositions of these pages do not fulfill any illustrative role, but similarly to the floral and vegetal motifs of the decorative designs, they play a decorative function.

Regarding the types of manuscripts, we learned that most of the 89 fragments are torn folia from illuminated religious books. Since a significant number of texts (39) can be identified in these fragments, it is clear that many of them are from hymnbooks, service-books, and anthologies. Furthermore, illuminated official letters and an omen book are also documented. This proves that Manichaean liturgical books and letters were made in luxurious editions in the Turfan region, and that certain official church documents were also equipped with exquisite decorations. Regarding the distribution of text and illumination, this information suggests that the pictorial program varied within these manuscripts. Circa half of the fragments, especially pages with hymns, were adorned solely with decorative designs painted along the margins. The benedictory sections, especially the texts that addressed the secular leaders of the Turfan Manichaean community, were accompanied by complex, full-page figural scenes.

Regarding the subjects of illumination, our survey confirms that complex pictorial representations with religious themes were contained in Turfan Manichaean illuminated books. Twenty-five scenes are identifiable, indicating that rituals (11 scenes) as well as theological and doctrinal subjects (8 scenes) were depicted most frequently. Ritual scenes always show lay people, dressed in Uygur elite garments, sometimes named as members of the royal clan. In addition to such a local element the frequent use of lotus flowers in these paintings suggests the possibility that they were developed locally and thus employed as decorations of illuminated text-books. In contrast, scenes with theological and doctrinal subjects must have derived from a pre-Turfan layer of Manichaean book art, as suggested by their use of West Asian iconography. Many such scenes most certainly originated in Mani's *Picture-Book*, from where they were copied into the illuminated text-books. These ideas are supported by the lack of contextual cohesion between the paintings and the text of Turfan Manichaean books.

Regarding the issue of how well paired the illuminations and the texts were in terms of their subjects, the above survey proves that the vast majority of scenes were not used as "illustrations"—that is, these paintings did not reflect the content of their associated texts. Many texts were accompanied by floral decorations, whereas others were accompanied by depictions of generic events from the life or the teaching of the Manichaean church. Only rarely, in just a few cases, did the pictorial subjects match the textual subject of the page.

These findings allow us to judge the function of illumination in this book art. In light of the above four points, I suggest that the vast majority of figural scenes play primarily a decorative role that is analogous to the role of marginal floral illuminations in these manuscripts: both exalt the text with images pleasant to Manichaean eyes without remarking on the writing. This decorative role, however, does not mean that the figural scenes cannot occasionally show closer connection to the content of their texts, but *they do not have to visually interpret them*. In other words, the illustrative/interpretive quality of the image is a possibility at best, but not a requirement on the remains of Turfan Manichaean book art.

Attributing a decorative function to illumination in mediaeval religious books is not exclusive to Central

Asian Manichaean book art. A similar claim in connection with Byzantine service-books was presented recently by Nancy Patterson Ševčenko in her 1998 essay on the subject.

> Rarely do the illustrations in liturgical manuscripts develop or comment in any significant way upon the content of the text they accompany.... The illustration of these manuscripts serves mainly to facilitate their use in the performance of the liturgy; it enhances their value as precious vessels and acts as a guide into the intricate scheduling of the text.[51]

Already in 1986 John Lowden suggested a new way to think about the reasons why such manuscripts are illuminated, in his "Luxury and Liturgy" article on the issue of function of illumination in Byzantine service-books. Recognizing that the illustrations not only rarely illustrated the texts, but also that the reader could not "look at" the paintings within the context of use, Lowden wrote:

> It could be argued that illustrations were included *despite* the fact that these books were liturgical and not *because* of it.... In the middle and late periods, the Byzantines seem to have had a clear idea of what luxury in a book meant, and it included illustrations, often with much use of gold leaf and pigment to imitate solid metal and enamel. Perhaps there was less concern about who would look at the illustrations in a liturgical book and when, than about satisfying a public expectation of what a luxury book ought to look like.[52]

The Manichaeans in Turfan seem to have had a similar attitude toward the role of illumination in their religious books. They created exquisite works of art around the tenth century by uniting texts and pictorial scenes in their manuscripts. The pictures and the texts in these books were not "matched" to one another according to our twenty-first century sense of what illustrated books ought to look like. Their book paintings were not "aligned" with the direction of the texts, since they were oriented sideways within the manuscripts. At the same time, these paintings did not capture the contents of the writings. As we learned from the analyses above, these illuminations depicted general scenes from the life and teaching of the community and did not visually comment upon their associated texts. Thus, it seems that just as the Christians in Byzantium, the Manichaeans in Turfan were also keen on introducing "luxury" to the religious life of mediaeval Central Asia.

---

[51] Ševčenko 1998, 223.
[52] Lowden 1986, 287.

POSTSCRIPT

A sound methodology is key to the success of any scholarship. Art history is no exception. Only through methodologically defined research can this discipline meaningfully contribute to our understanding of the past. Especially in mediaeval Central Asia, from where relatively few historical sources survive and archaeological data are limited, works of art are important visual sources of information for a range of subjects researched by a variety of historical disciplines—cultural history, social history, political history, religious history, as well as art history. Art historians, however, do have a responsibility in obtaining and disseminating a basic body of knowledge about the works of art themselves before interpreting them, and/or excluding certain parts of them to suit the scope of a specific project.

To have to make due with just fragments as primary sources is one particular challenge that must be met by historians of Central Asian art. Starting with the very basics, first one must know how to orient the illuminated fragments correctly, what kind of manuscript they derive from, and what any writing on them says. In addition, it is also essential to know what materials they were made of, and how they were made, with special attention to the stages of the artist's work often left exposed from beneath the damaged original layer of the finished book painting. Only after such an elementary comprehension—taken for granted in other areas of art history—can scholarly research set out to successfully contemplate the contents of these works of art, the history behind their development, and their role within their immediate and broader contexts, including their cultural, religious, artistic, political, social, and economic settings.

Mediaeval Manichaean Book Art is designed to provide a basic understanding about a specific group of illuminated manuscript fragments created during the ca. 300-year-long Turfan epoch of Manichaean activities. The conclusions reached here have immediate implications for how distinct painting traditions and styles are defined, for how subjective judgments of stylistic development are tested, and for how different painting media are to be considered in comparative analysis. They raise questions about unstated assumptions in the field about the function of illumination in books, and the presumed relation and coherence between text and image in terms of both their orientation and content. Due to the much-needed attention to the sources themselves, this study represents only a foundation for the subsequent exploration of these implications and of a variety of other important aspects of this corpus. Each subject discussed in the six chapters can be and should be taken further, involving not only the research of Manichaean book art itself, but also opening up the study of the remains for comparative research. The task for such future projects will be relating this corpus to its immediate Central Asian setting with Buddhist, Nestorian, and secular artistic components, as well as incorporating it into the study of a broader art historical context that considers this art's cultural ties with and contribution to the formation of other artistic traditions in West, Central, and East Asia during late antique and mediaeval times.

BIBLIOGRAPHY

Abe, Takeo
    1954   "Where Was the Capital of the West Uighurs?" *Silver Jubilee Volume of the Zinbun-Kagaku-Kenkyusyo Kyoto University*, 435–450. Kyoto: Kyoto University Press.

Alexander, Jonathan J. G.
    1992   *Medieval Illuminators and their Methods of Work.* New Haven: Yale University Press.

Allberry, Charles R. C.
    1938a   *A Manichaean Psalm-Book. Part 2.* Manichaean Manuscripts in the Chester Beatty Collection 2. Stuttgart: W. Kohlhammer.
    1938b   "Das manichäische Bema-Fest." *Zeitschrift für die neutestamentliche Wissenschaft und die Kunde der älteren Kirche.* 37: 2–10.
    1938c   "Manichaean Studies." *The Journal of Theological Studies* 39: 337–349.

Allen, Terry
    1985   "Byzantine Sources for the Jâmi' al-Tawârîkh of Rashîd al-Dîn." *Ars Orientalis* 15: 121–136.

Andreas, F. C., and W. B. Henning
    1933   "Mitteliranische Manichaica aus Chinesisch-Turkestan II." *Sitzungsberichte der Preussischen Akademie der Wissenschaften*, Philosophisch-historische Klasse 17: 294–363.

Arnold, Sir Thomas W.
    1924   *Survivals of Sasanian and Manichaean Art in Persian Painting.* Oxford: Clarendon Press.
    1938   "Book Painting: A. The Origins." *A Survey of Persian Art from Prehistoric Time to the Present*, edited by A. U. Pope and P. Ackerman, vol. 5: 1808–1819. London: Oxford University Press. Reprinted in 1964. Tokyo: Meiji Shobo.

Arnold-Döben, Victoria
    1978   *Der Bildersprache des Manichäismus.* Arbeitsmaterial zur Religionsgeschichte 3. Köln: E. J. Brill.

Asmussen, Jes P.
    1965   *X^{u}āstvānīft: Studies in Manichaeism.* Acta Theologica Danica 7. Copenhagen: Prostant Apud Munksgaard.
    1975   *Manichaean Literature: Representative Texts, Chiefly from Middle Persian and Parthian Writings.* Persian Heritage Series 22. New York: Scholars' Facsimiles & Reprints.

Badiee, Julie
    1996   "Painting during the reign of Ahmad Jalayir (reg 1382–1410)." *Dictionary of Art*, edited by Jane Turner, vol. 16, 320. New York: Grove's Dictionaries.

Beckwith, Christopher
    1987   *The Tibetan Empire in Central Asia.* Princeton: Princeton University Press.

Banerjee, P.
    1970   "Hindu Trinity from Central Asia." *Bulletin, National Museum, New Delhi* 1970/2: 17–20.

Bang, W.
    1924   "Manichaeische Miniaturen." *Le Muséon* 37: 109–115.

BeDuhn, Jason David
    1995   "Magical Bowls and Manichaeans." *Ancient Magic and Ritual Power*, edited by Marvin Meyer and Paul Mirecki, 419–434. Leiden: E. J. Brill.
    1996   "The Manichaean Sacred Meal." *Turfan, Khotan und Dunhuang: Vorträge der Tagung "A. V. Gabain und die Turfanforschung", veranstaltet von der Berlin-Brandenburgischen Akademie der Wissenschaften in Berlin (9.–12. 12. 1994)*, edited by Ronald E. Emmerick, Werner Sundermann, Ingrid Warnke, and Peter Zieme, 1–16. Berlin: Akademie Verlag.
    2000a   *The Manichaean Body in Discipline and Ritual.* Baltimore: Johns Hopkins University Press.
    2000b   "Eucharist or Yasna?: Antecedents of Manichaean Food Ritual." *Studia Manichaica: IV Internationaler Kongreß zum Manichäismus, Berlin 14–18 Juli 1997*, edited by Ronald E. Emmerick, Werner Sundermann, and Peter Zieme, 14–36. Berlin: Akademie Verlag.
    2001   "Middle Iranian & Turkic Texts Associated with Manichaean Art from Turfan." *Manichaean Art In Berlin Collections* by Zs. Gulácsi, 203–238. Turnhout: Brepols.

Behzad, Taherzade
    1938   "Book Painting: H. The Preparation of the Miniaturist's Materials." *A Survey of Persian Art from Prehistoric Time to the Present*, edited by A. U. Pope and P. Ackerman, vol. 5: 1921–1927. London: Oxford University Press. (Reprinted in 1964. Tokyo: Meiji Shobo).

Bhattacharya-Haesner, Chayya
    2003   *Central Asian Temple Banners in the Turfan Collection of the Museum für Indishce Kunst, Berlin.* Berlin: Dietrich Reimer Verlag.
    2004   "Buddhist and Manichaean Banners: A Comparative Study." *Silk Road: Trade Travel, War, and Faith*, edited by S. Whitfield with U. Sims-Williams, 313–315. London: The British Library.

Blair, Sheila S. & Bloom, Jonathan M.
    1994   *Art and Architecture of Islam*. New Haven: Yale University Press.
Bowman, Sheridan
    1990   *Radiocarbon Dating*. London: British Museum Press.
Boyce, Mary
    1954   *The Manichaean Hymn-Cycles in Parthian*. London Oriental Series 3. London: Oxford University Press.
    1960   *A Catalogue of the Iranian Manuscripts in Manichaean Script in the Berlin Turfan Collection*. Berlin: Akademie Verlag.
    1975   *A Reader in Manichaean Middle Persian and Parthian: Texts with Notes*. Acta Iranica 9. Leiden: E. J. Brill and Téhéran-Liège:
                    Bibliothèque Pahlavi.
Brown, Michelle P.
    1994   *Understanding Illuminated Manuscripts: A Guide to Technical Terms*. Malibu, California: The J. Paul Getty Museum in associa-
                    tion with The British Library.
Brunner, Christopher J.
    1980   "Liturgical Chant and Hymnody among the Manichaeans of Central Asia." *Zeitschrift der Deutschen Morgenländischen
                    Gesellschaft* 130: 342–368.
Bryder, Peter
    1985   *The Chinese Transformation of Manichaeism: A Study of Chinese Manichaean Terminology*. Löberöd: Bokförlaget Plus Ultra.
    1988   "Where the Faint Traces of Manichaeism Disappear." *Altorientalische Forschungen* 15: 201–208.
    1991   "Cao'an Revisited." *Manichaica Selecta: Studies Presented to Professor Julien Ries on Occasion of His Seventieth Birthday*, edited
                    by Aloïs van Tongerloo and Søren Giversen, 35–42. Lovanii: Drukkerij Foerts.
Bussagli, Mario
    1963   *Painting of Central Asia*. Geneva: Skira.
Cahill, James
    1980   *An Index of Early Chinese Painters and Paintings*. Berkeley: University of California Press.
Calkins, Robert, G.
    1984   *Programs of Mediaeval Book Illumination*. Lawrence: University of Kansas.
Cameron, Ron and Arthur J. Dewey (trs.)
    1979   *Cologne Mani Codex: English and Greek*. Missoula: Scholars Press.
Carboni Stefano, see Petrosyan *et al.*, 1995.
Chao Huashan,
    1993   "Investigation of Manichaean Cave Temples in Turfan." *Iranian Journal of Archaeology and History* 8/4: 3–10.
    1993b   "Chuxun Gaochang Moni si de zongji." *Kaogu yu wenwu* 1993/1: 84–93.
    1996   "New Evidence of Manichaeism in Asia: Description of Some Recently Discovered Manichaean Temples in Turfan."
                    Monumenta Serica 44: 267–315.
Chavannes, Eduard, and Paul Pelliot
    1911–13   "Un traité manichéen retrouvé en Chine: traduit et annoté." *Journal asiatique* 1911: 499–617, and 1913: 99–394.
Chen Yuan
    1923a   Monijiao ru Zhunggub kao = A Study of the entry of Manichaeism into China. *Guoxue jiakan* 1/2: 203–240.
    1923b   Monijiao ts'an-ching (= Fragmentary Manichaean Sutra). *Guoxue jiakan* 1/2: 531–544.
Clark, Larry V.
    1975   *Introduction to the Uyghur Civil Documents of East Turkestan (13th–14th cc.)*. Ph. D. diss., Indiana University, Bloomington.
    1982   "The Manichaean Turkic *Pothi-Book*." *Altorientalische Forschungen* 9: 145–218.
    1992   "Portraits of Mani in the Turfan Paintings." Paper presented at the Third International Conference on Manichaeism,
                    London, July, 1992. Unpublished.
    1997   "The Turkic Manichaean Literature." In *Emerging from Darkness: Studies in the Recovery of Manichaean Sources*, edited by
                    Paul Mirecki and Jason BeDuhn, 89–142. Leiden: E. J. Brill.
    2000   "The Conversion of Bügü Khan." In *Studia Manichaica: IV Internationaler Kongreß zum Manichäismus, Berlin 14–18 Juli
                    1997*, edited by Ronald E. Emmerick, Werner Sundermann, and Peter Zieme, 83–123. Berlin: Akademie Verlag.
    2005   *Turkic Manichaean Texts*. Corpus Fontium Manichaeorum. Turnhout: Brepols (in press).
Clauson, Sir Gerard
    1972   *Etymological Dictionary of Pre-Thirteenth Century Turkish*. Oxford: Clarendon Press.
Coakley, J. F.
    1992   *The Church of the East and the Church of England*. Oxford: Clarendon Press.
Crum, W. E.
    1919   "A 'Manichaean' Fragment from Egypt." *Journal of the Royal Asiatic Society* 1919: 206–208.
Cumont, Franz V. M.
    1908   *Recherches sur le Manichéisme I: La Cosmogonie manichéennes d'après Théodore bar Khôni*. Bruxelles: H. Lamertin.
    1913   "Mani et les origines de la miniature persane." *Revue archéologique* 22/4: 82–86.
Czeglédy, Károly
    1973   "Gardizi on the History of Central Asia (746–780 A.D.)." *Acta Orientalia Academiae Scientarum Hungaricae* 27/3: 257–
                    267.

1984   "The Foundation of the Turfan Uyghur Kingdom." *Tibetan and Buddhist Studies. Commemorating the 200th Anniversary of the Birth of A. Csoma De Körös*, edited by Lajos Ligeti, vol.1, 159–163. Budapest: Akadémiai Kiadó.

Delaissé, L. M. J.
1976   "Towards a History of the Medieval Book." *Codicologica I: Théories et principes*, edited by A. Gruys, 75–83. Leiden: E. J. Brill.

Dictionary of Art
1996   *Dictionary of Art*, edited by Jane Turner. New York: Grove's Dictionaries.

Doresse, Jean
1972   *The Secret Books of the Egyptian Gnostics: An Introduction to the Gnostic Coptic manuscripts discovered at Chenoboskion*. New York: AMS Press.

Drége, Jean-Pierre
1979   "Les Cahiers des Manuscrits de Touan-houng." *Contributions aux Études sur Touen-houang*, edited by Michel Soymié, 17–37. Genève-Paris: Librairie Droz.

Ebert, Jorinde
1992   "Die 'Vier licht Götterkönige' als Schutzgottheiten in einen Manichäischen Seidenbildfragment." *Künstlerischer Austausch / Artistic Exchange. Akten des XXVIII. Internationalen Kongress für Kunstgeschichte, Berlin 15–20 Juli 1992*, edited by T. W. Gaehtgens, 489–512. Berlin: Akademie Verlag.
1994   "Darstellungen der Passion Manis in bekannten und unbekannten Bildfragmenten des Bema-Fest aus der Turfan-Sammlung." *Memoriae Munusculum: Gedenkband für Annemarie v. Gabain*, edited by Klaus Röhrborn and Wolfgang Veenker, 1–28. Veröffentlichungen der Societas Uralo-Altaica 39. Wiesbaden: Otto Harrassowitz.
2004   "*Segmentun* and *Clavus* in Manichaean Garments of the Turfan Oasis," in M. Yaldiz and P. Zieme (eds.), *Turfan Revisited. The First Century of Research into the Arts and Cultures of the Silk Road*, 72–83. Berlin: Reimer Verlag.

Elverskog, Johan
1997   *Uygur Buddhist Literature*. Silk Road Studies 1. Turnhout: Brepols.

Encyclopedia Britannica
1987   *Encyclopedia Britannica*. 15th edition, Chicago: Encyclopedia Britannica Inc.

Encyclopedia of World Art
1964   *Encyclopedia of World Art*. New York: McGraw-Hill.

Esin, Emel
1972   "Notes on the Manichaean Paintings of East Turkistan" in *Memorial Volume of the VIth International Congress of Iranian Art and Archaeology: Oxford, September 11–16th, 1972*, Teheran, Iranian Center for Archaeological Research, 49–80.

Ettinghausen, Richard
1938   "Manuscript Illumination." *Survey of Persian Art from Prehistoric Time to the Present*, edited by A. U. Pope and P. Ackerman, vol. 5, 1937–1974. London: Oxford University Press (Reprinted in 1964. Tokyo: Meiji Shobo).
1962   *Arab Painting*. New York: Skira.

Farrer Anne
1993   "Calligraphy and Painting for Official Life." *The British Museum Book of Chinese Art*, edited by Jessica Rawson, 84–132. London: Thames & Hudson.

Forte, Antonino
1973   "Deux études sur le manichéisme chinois." *T'oung Pao* 59: 220–253.
1993   "A New Study on Manichaeism in Central Asia." *Orientalistische Literaturzeitung* 88/2: 117–124.

Fraser Sarah E.
1999a   "A Reconsideration of Archaeological Finds from the Turfan Region." *Dunhuang Tulufan yanjiu*, Peking: Peking University Press, vol. 4, 375–418.
1999b   "The Manuals and Drawings of Artists, Calligraphers, and Other Specialists in Dunhuang." *L'art de Dunhuang à la Bibliothèque nationale de France*, edited by J.-P. Drège, 55–104. Paris: École française d'Extrême-Orient.

Gabain, Annemarie von
1964   "Alttürkische Schreibkultur und Druckerei." *Philologiae Turcicae Fundamenta*, edited by Louis Bazin, et al., vol. 2, 171–190. Wiesbaden: Franz Steiner Verlag.
1973a   "Kshitigarbha-Kult in Zentralasien: Buchillustrationen aus den Turfan-Funden." *Indologen-Tagung 1971*, edited by Herbert Härtel and V. Moeller, 47–71. Wiesbaden: Otto Harrassowitz.
1973b   *Das Leben im uigurischen Königreich von Qocho (850–1259)*. Veröffentlichungen der Societas Uralo-Altaica 6. Wiesbaden: Otto Harrassowitz.

Gabain, Annemarie von, and Werner Winter
1958   *Ein Hymnan an den Vater Mani auf "tocharisch B" mit alttürkischer Übersetzung*. Türkische Turfantexte 9. Berlin: Akademie Verlag.

Gardner, Iain
1995   *The Kephalaia of the Teacher: The Edited Coptic Manichaean Texts in Translation with Commentary*. Nag Hammadi and Manichaean Studies 37. Leiden: E. J. Brill.

Geng Shimin, and Hans-Joachim Klimkeit
1985   "Zerstörung manichäischer Klöster in Turfan." *Zentralasiatische Studien* 18: 7–11.

Ghilain, A.
  1939   *Essai sur la langue Parthe*. Louvain: Bureaux du Muséon.
Giès, Jacques, and Moniq Cohen, eds.
  1995   *Sérinde, Terre de Buddha: Dix siècles d'art sur la Route de la Soie*. Paris: Réunion des Musées Nationaux.
Grabar, Oleg
  1984   *The Illustrations of the Maqamat of the Thirteen Century: The Bourgeoisie and the Arts*. Chicago: Chicago University Press.
  1992   *The Mediation of Ornament*. Bollingen Series XXXV, 38. Princeton: Princeton University Press.
Grohman, A. and Thomas W. Arnold
  1929   *Denkmäler islamischer Buchkunst*. München: Kurt Wolff Verlag.
Gratzl, Emil
  1938   "Book Covers." In *A Survey of Persian Art from Prehistoric Time to the Present*, edited by A. U. Pope and P. Ackerman, vol. 5,
              1975–1994. London: Oxford University Press (Reprinted in 1964. Tokyo: Meiji Shobo).
Gray, Basil
  1977   *Persian Painting*. New York: Skira-Rizzoli.
Grünwedel, Albert
  1906   "Bericht über archäologische Arbeiten in Idikutschari und Umgebung im Winter 1902–1903." *Abhandlungen der König-
              lich Preussischen Akademie der Wissenschaften*, 1906–1909, I. Abteilung, 1–196.
  1912   *Altbuddhistische Kultstätten in Chinesisch-Turkistan*. Berlin: Georg Reimer.
Gulácsi, Zsuzsanna
  1996   "The Textile Furnishings of Uyghur Manichaean Miniatures." *Turfan, Khotan und Dunhuang: Vorträge der Tagung "A. V.
              Gabain und die Turfanforschung", veransteltet von der Berlin-Brandenburgischen Akademie der Wissenschaften in Berlin (9.–12. 12.
              1994)*, edited by Ronald E. Emmerick, Werner Sundermann, Ingrid Warnke, and Peter Zieme, 101–134. Berlin:
              Akademie Verlag.
  1997   "Identifying the Corpus of Manichaean Art among the Turfan Remains." *Emerging from Darkness: Studies in the Recovery
              of Manichaean Sources*, edited by Paul Mirecki and Jason BeDuhn, 177–215. Leiden: E. J. Brill.
  1998   *Mediaeval Manichaean Book Art: A Study of Design, Function, and Origin of Manichaean Book Illumination*. Ph. D. diss., Indiana
              University, Bloomington.
  2000   "Rules of Page Arrangement on Manichaean Illuminated Book Fragments." *Studia Manichaica: IV Internationaler Kongreß
              zum Manichäismus, Berlin 14–18 Juli 1997*, edited by Ronald E. Emmerick, Werner Sundermann, and Peter Zieme,
              270–307. Berlin: Akademie Verlag.
  2001a   *Manichaean Art In Berlin Collections*. Turnhout: Brepols.
  2001b   "Reconstructing Manichaean Book Paintings through the techniques of their Makers." *The Light and the Darkness:
              Studies in Manichaeism and its World*, edited by Paul Mirecki and Jason BeDuhn, 105–128. Leiden: E. J. Brill.
  2003   "Dating the 'Persian' and Chinese Style Remains of Uygur Manichean Art: A New Radiocarbon Date and Its Impli-
              cations for Central Asian Art History." *Ars Asiatiques* 58: 5–33.
  2004a   "Text and Image in Manichaean Book Art: A Study of Contextual Cohesion." *Turfan Revisited: The First Century of
              Research into the Arts and Cultures of the Silk Road*, edited by M. Yaldiz and P. Zieme, 100–115. Berlin: Reimer Verlag.
  2004b   "Manichaean Book Art." *Silk Road: Trade Travel, War, and Faith*, edited by S. Whitfield with U. Sims-Williams, 121–123
              and 289. London: The British Library.
  2005   "Mani's *Picture-Box*? A Study of a New Textual Reference and its Supposed Pictorial Analogy in the British Library
              (Or. 8212-1692)." *Studia Manichaica: V. International Congress of Manichaean Studies, Sept. 2001 Naples*, edited by L. Cirillo
              and A. v. Tonderloo. Turnhout: Brepols (in press).
Haloun G. and Henning W.B.,
  1952–53   "The Compendium of the Doctrines and Styles of the Teaching of Mani, the Buddha of Light", *Asia Major*, N.S. III:
              184–212.
Hambis, Louis
  1963   "Manichaean Art." *Encyclopedia of World Art*, vol. 9, 433–443. New York: McGraw-Hill.
Hamilton, James
  1986   *Manuscrits ouïgours du IX⁵-X⁵ siècle de Touen-Houang*, Paris: Peeters, vol. 1–2.
  1992   "Calendriers manichéens ouïgours de 988, 989 et 1003" in J.-L. Bacqué-Grammont, et al. *Mélanges offers à Louis Bazin
              par ses disciples, collègues at amis*. Varia Turcica 19, 7–23. Paris: L'Harmattan.
Hamilton, James and Nui Ru-Ji
  1994   "Deux inscriptions funéraires turques nestoriennes de la Chine Orientale." *Journal asiatique* 282/1: 147–164.
The Harper Collins Dictionary of Art Terms and Techniques.
  1991   *The Harper Collins Dictionary of Art Terms and Techniques*. Second edition. New York: Harper Perennial.
Härtel, Herbert
  1957   "Über das Schicksal der Turfansammlungen." *Orientalistische Literaturzeitung* 52: 5–12.
  1982   "Introduction." *Along the Ancient Silk Routes: Central Asian Art from the West Berlin State Museums*, by Herbert Härtel and
              Marianne Yaldiz, 13–55. New York: Metropolitan Museum of Art.

Härtel, Herbert, and Marianne Yaldiz
1982   *Along the Ancient Silk Routes: Central Asian Art from the West Berlin State Museums.* New York: Metropolitan Museum of Art.
1987   *Die Seidenstraße: Malereien und Plastiken aus buddhistischen Höhlentempeln. Ausstellung des Museums für Indische Kunst Berlin.* Berlin: Staatliche Museen Preußischer Kulturbesitz, Museum für Indische Kunst, Berlin.
Härtel, Herbert, et al.
1980   *Die Meisterwerke aus dem Museum für Indische Kunst Berlin.* Belser Kunstbibliothek. Stuttgart: Belser.
Henning, Walter Bruno
1934   "Zum zentralasiatische Manichäismus." *Orientalistische Literaturzeitung* 37: 1–11.
1937   *Ein manichäisches Bet- und Beichtbuch.* Abhandlungen der Koniglich Preussischen Akademie der Wissenschaften 1936, Philosophisch-historische Klasse 10.
1943   "The Book of the Giants." *Bulletin of the School of Oriental and African Studies* 11: 52–74.
1945   "The Manichaean Fasts." *Journal of the Royal Asiatic Society* 1945: 145–164.
Henrichs, Albert
1973   "Mani and the Babylonian Baptists: A Historical Confrontation." *Harvard Studies in Classical Philosophy* 77: 29–59.
Huntington, John C.
1986   "A Note on Dunhuang Cave 17, 'the Library' or Hong Bian's Reliquary Chamber." *Ars Orientalis* 16: 93–102.
Huntington, Susan
1993   *The Art of Ancient India: Buddhist, Hindu, Jain.* Second Printing. New York: Weatherhill.
Ibn al-Jawzi, Abu al-Faraj 'Abd al-Rahman ibn 'Ali
1992   *al-Muntazam fi tarikh al-muluk wa-al-umam*, Vol.13. Bayrut: Dar al-Kutub al-'Ilmiyah.
Ibn Miskawayh Ahmad Ibm Muhammad,
1914   *Kitab tajarib al-umam*, edited by H. F. Amedroz. Baghdad: Yutlab min Maktabat al-Muthanna.
Jackson, A. V. Williams
1938   "The Personality of Mani." *Journal of the American Oriental Society* 58: 235–240.
Kalter, Johannes, and Margareta Pavaloi, eds.
1995   *Erben der Seidenstraße: Uzbekistan.* Stuttgart: Hansjörg Mayer in Zusammenarbeit mit dem Linden-Museum Stuttgart und dem Museum für Völkerkunde, Berlin.
Kara, György and Peter Zieme
1979   *Ein uigurisches Totenbuch: Nāropas Lehre in uigurischer Übersetzung von vier tibetischen Traktaten nach der Sammelhandschrift aus Dunhuang* British Museum Or. 8212 [109]. Wiesbaden: Otto Harrassowitz.
Kerstein, P.
1914   "Die Durchbrucharbeit." *Archiv für Buchbinderei* 14: 8–11.
Kessler, Konrad
1889   *Mani: Forschungen über die manichaische Religion.* Berlin: G. Reimer.
Kitzinger, Ernst
1980   *Byzantine Art in the Making: Main Lines of Stylistic Development in Mediterranean Art 3rd–7th Century.* Cambridge: Harvard University Press.
Khalidov B., see Petrosyan et al., 1995.
Klimkeit, Hans-Joachim
1980   "Hindu Deities in Manichaean Art." *Zentralasiatische Studien* 14: 179–199.
1982a   *Manichaean Art and Calligraphy.* Iconography of Religions Section 20. Leiden: E. J. Brill.
1982b   "Vom Wesen manichäischer Kunst." *Zeitschrift für Religions- und Geistesgeschichte* 34: 195–219.
1990   "The Donor at Turfan." *Silk Road Art and Archaeology: Journal of the Institute of Silk Road Studies (Kamakura)* 1: 177–201.
1993   *Gnosis on the Silk Road: Gnostic Texts from Central Asia.* San Francisco: Harper-Collins.
1996   *Manichäische Kunst an der Seidenstraße. Alte und Neue Funde*, Opladen, Westdeutscher Verlag—Revised version in English: "Manichaean Art on the Silk Road: Old and New Discoveries." *Studies in Manichaean Literature and Art*, edited by M. Heuser and H.-J. Klimkeit, 300–313. Leiden: E. J. Brill.
1998   "On the Nature of Manichaean Art." *Studies in Manichaean Literature and Art*, edited by M. Heuser and H.-J. Klimkeit, 270–290. Leiden: E. J. Brill.
Klyashtorny, S. G.
1988   "East Turkestan and the Kaghans of Ordubalïq." *Acta Orientalia Academiae Scientiarum Hungaricae* 42: 227–280.
Koenen, Ludwig and Cornelia Römer
1985   *Der Kölner Mani-Kodex.* Bonn: Rudolf Habelt GMBH.
Kudara, Kogi, Werner Sundermann, and Yutaka Yoshida
1997   *Iranian Fragments from the Ōtani Collection: Iranian Fragments Unearthed in Central Asia by the the Ōtani Mission and Kept in the Library of the Ryukoku University.* Facsimile Series of Rare texts in the Library of the Ryukoku University 17. Kyoto: Ryukoku University.
Le Coq, Albert von
1909a   "Köktürkisches aus Turfan." *Sitzungsberichte der Königlich Preussischen Akademie der Wissenschaften* 1909: 1047–1061. (Reprinted 1972 in *Sprachwissenschaftliche Ergebnisse der deutschen Turfan-Forschung*, edited by György Hazai, vol. 1, 532–546. Leipzig: Zentralantiquariat der Deutschen Demokratischen Republic).

1909b   "Ein christliches und ein manichäisches Manuskriptfragment in türkischer Sprache aus Turfan (Chinesisch-Turkistan)."
         Sitzungsberichte der Königlich Preussischen Akademie der Wissenschaften 1909,1202–1218. (Reprinted 1972 in *Sprachwissenschaft-
         liche Ergebnisse der deutschen Turfan-Forschung,* edited by György Hazai, vol. 1, 547–563. Leipzig: Zentralantiquariat der
         Deutschen Demokratischen Republik).

1913   *Chotscho: Facsimile-Wiedergabe der Wichtigeren Funde der ersten Königlich Preussischen Expedition nach Turfan in Ost-Turkistan.*
         Berlin: Dietrich Reimer. (Reprinted 1973. Gratz: Akademie Druck).

1922   *Türkische Manichaica aus Chotscho III.* Abhandlungen der Königlich Preussischen Akademie der Wissenschaften 1922,
         Philosophisch-historische Klasse 2. (Reprinted 1972 in *Sprachwissenschaftliche Ergebnisse der deutschen Turfan-Forschung,*
         edited by György Hazai, vol. 1, 452–464. Leipzig: Zentralantiquariat der Deutschen Demokratischen Republic).

1923   *Die manichäischen Miniaturen.* Die buddhistische Spätantike in Mittelasien 2. Berlin: Dietrich Reimer. (Reprinted 1973.
         Gratz: Akademie Druck).

1925   *Bilderatlas zur Kunst und Kulturgeschichte Mittel-Asiens.* Berlin: Dietrich Reimer and Ernst Vohsen. (Reprinted 1973. Gratz:
         Akademie Druck).

Lee, Marshal
1965   *Book Making: The Illustrated Guide to Design and Production.* New York: Bower.

Lee, Sherman E.
1994   *History of Far Eastern Art.* Fifth edition. New York: Prentice Hall and Harry N. Abrams.

Lieu, Samuel N. C.
1992   *Manichaeism in the Later Roman Empire and Medieval China.* Second edition. Tübingen: J. C. B. Mohr (Paul Siebeck).
1994   *Manichaeism in Mesopotamia and the Roman East.* Leiden: E. J. Brill.
1997   "Manichaean Art and Text from the Silk Road." *Studies in Silk Road Coins and Culture: Papers in Honour of Professor Ikuo
         Hirayama on His 65th Birthday,* edited by K. Tanabe, J. Cribb & H. Wang, 262–312. Kamakura: Institute of Silk Road
         Studies.

Liu Ts'un-yan,
1976   "Traces of Zoroastrian and Manichaean Activities in Pre-Tang China." *Selected Papers from the Hall of Harmonious Wind,*
         edited by Liu Ts'un-yan, 3–55. Leiden: E. J. Brill.

Losty, Jeremiah P.
1982   *The Art of the Book in India.* London: British Library.

Loubier, J.
1910   "Orientalische Einbandkunst." *Archiv für Buchbinderei* 10: 33–43.

Lowden, John
1986   "Luxury and Liturgy: The Function of Books." *Church and People in Byzantium,* edited by R. Morris, 263–279. Birming-
         ham: Birmingham University Press.
1992   *The Octateuchs: A Study in Byzantine Manuscript Illumination.* University Park: Pennsylvania State University Press.
1997   *Early Christian and Byzantine Art.* London: Phaidon Press.

Mackerras, Colin
1968   *The Uighur Empire According to T'ang Dynastic Histories: A Study in Sino-Uighur Relations 744–840,* Camberra, Australian
         National University Press.
1973   *The Uighur Empire According to T'ang Dynastic Histories: A Study in Sino-Uighur Relations 744–840.* Columbia: University of
         South Carolina Press.
1990   "The Uighurs." *The Cambridge History of Early Inner Asia,* edited by Denis Sinor, 317–342. Cambridge: Cambridge
         University Press.

Mason, Penelope
1993   *History of Japanese Art.* New York: Harry N. Adrams.

Martinez, A. P.
1982   "Gardīzī's two Chapters on the Turks." *Archivum Eurasiae Medii Aevi* 2: 109–219.

Mayer, Ralph
1991   *The HarperCollins Dictionary of Art Terms and Techniques.* New York: Harper Perennial.

McGraw-Hill Dictionary of Art
1969   *McGraw-Hill Dictionary of Art.* Edited by B.S. Myers. New York: McGraw-Hill.

Mez, Adam
1922   *Die Renaissance des Islams.* Heidelberg: C. Winter.
1939   *The Renaissance of Islam.* Pathna: Jubilee Printing and Publishing House.

Minorsky V.
1948   "Tamim ibn Bahr's Journey to the Uyghurs." *Bulletin of the School of Oriental and African Studies* 12/2: 275–305.

Mikkelsen Gunner B.
1997   *Bibliographia Manichaica: A Comprehensive Bibliography of Manichaeism Through 1996,* Turnhout: Brepols.
2003   "The Fragments of Chinese Manichaean Texts from the Turfan Region" *Turfan Revisited: The First Century of Research
         into the Arts and Cultures of the Silk Road,* edited by M. Yaldiz and P. Zieme, 213-220.

Monneret de Villard, Ugo
1938   "Book Painting: B. The Relations of Manichaean Art to Iranian Art." *Survey of Persian Art from Prehistoric Time to the*

Present, edited by A. U. Pope and P. Ackerman, vol. 5: 1820–1828. London: Oxford University Press. (Reprinted 1964. Tokyo: Meiji Shobo).

Moriyasu Takao,

1980   "Uiguru to Tonkô" ["The Uygurs and Dunhuang"] in K. Enoki (ed.), *Tonkô no rekishi*, Tokyo, Daitô shuppansha, (Kôza Tonkô/Collected papers on Tun-huang, vol. 2), 297–338.

1991   *Uiguru Mani-kyô-shi no kenkyû / A Study on the History of Uighur Manichaeism: Research on Some Manichaean Materials and Their Historical Background*, Toyonaka-shi, (Ôsaka Daigaku Bungakubu kiyô, vols. 31-32).

1997   "Daiei-Toshokan shozô Run moji Mani-kyô bunsho monjo Kao. 0107 no shin kenkyû" [A Manichaean Runic Manuscript with Miniature (Kao. 0107) Housed in the British Library], *Nairiku Ajia gengo no kenkyû* [Studies on Inner Asian Languages], vol. 12, 41–73.

1999   "Provisional Report of Researches on Historical Sites and Inscriptions in Mongolia from 1996 to 1998." *Toyonaka [Osaka], Osaka Daigaku Bungakubu, The Society of Central Asian Studies*, 123–125 and 209–226.

2000   "The Western Uighur Kingdom and Tun-huang around the 10th–11th Centuries." *Sonderdruck aus Berlin-Brandenburgische Akademie der Wissenschaften: Berichte und Abhandunglen der Berlin-Brandenburgische Akademie der Wissenschaften* vol. 8, 337–368. Berlin: Akademie Verlag.

2001   "Uighur Buddhist Stake Inscriptions from Turfan." *Silk Road Studies V: De Dunhuang à Istanbul*, edited by L. Bazin and P. Zieme. Turnhout: Brepols.

2003   "IV. Decline of Manichaeism and the Rise of Buddhism among the Uighurs with a Discussion on the Origin of Uighur Buddhism: Four lectures at the College de France, May 2003, on the History of Manichaeism among the Uighurs from the 8th to the 11th centuries in Central Asia." *World History Reconsidered Through the Silk Road*. Osaka University the 21st Century COE Program: Interface Humanities research Activities 2002–2003. Group 3, 84–112. Osaka: Osaka University.

2005   *Die Geschichte des uigurischen Manichäismus an der Seidenstrasse*. Berlin: Reimer Verlag.

Morony, Michael G.

1984   *Iraq after the Muslim Conquest*. Princeton: Princeton University Press.

Müller, Friedrich Wilhelm Karl

1904a   "Handschriften-reste in Estrangelo-schrift aus Turfan, Chinesisch-Turkistan I." Abhandlungen der Königlich Preussischen Akademie der Wissenschaften, Sitzungsberichte 1904, 348–352.

1904b   *Handschriften-reste in Estrangelo-schrift aus Turfan, Chinesisch-Turkistan II*. Anhang zum den Abhandlungen der Königlich Preussischen Akademie der Wissenschaften 1904.

1912a   *Ein Doppelblatt aus einem manichäischen Hymnenbuch (Mahrnmag)*, Abhandlungen der Königlich Preussischen Akademie der Wissenschaften 1912, Philosophisch-historische Klasse 5.

1912b   Der Hofstaat eines Uiguren-Königs. In *Festschrift Vilhelm Thomsen zur Vollendung des siebzigsten Lebensjahres am 25. Januar 1912*, 207–213. Leipzig: Otto Harrassowitz.

1915   *Zwei Pfahlinschriften aus den Turfanfunden*. Abhandlungen der Königlichen Preussischen Akademia der Wissenschaften 1915, Philologisch-historische Klasse 3.

Museum für Indische Kunst, ed.

1986   *Museum für Indische Kunst, Berlin: Katalog 1986, Ausgestellte Werke*. Berlin: Staatliche Museen Preußische Kulturbesitz.

Osgood, Cornelius

1951   *The Koreans and Their Culture*. New York: Roland Press.

Oxford Dictionary of Byzantium

1991   *Oxford Dictionary of Byzantium*. New York: Oxford University Press.

The Oxford Companion to Art

1996   *The Oxford Companion to Art*. 17th impression. Oxford: Oxford University Press.

Pelliot, Paul

1973   *Recherches sur les Chrétiens d'Asie Centrale et d'Extrême-Orient*. Paris: Impr. nationale.

Petrosyan Yuri *et al.*

1995   *Pages of Perfection: Islamic Paintings and Calligraphy from the Russian Academy of Sciences, St. Petersburg*. Lugano: ARCH Foundation.

Polotsky, H. J.

1934   *Manichäische Homilien*. Stuttgart: W. Kohlhammer Verlag.

Puech, Henri-Charles

1972   "Le Manichéisme." *Historie des Religions II*, edited by Henri-Charles Puech, 523–645. Encyclopédie de la Pléiade 34. Bruxelles: Édition Gallimard.

1979   *Sur la Manichéisme et autres essais*. Paris: Flammarion.

Reck, Christiane

1992   *Mitteliranische manichäische Montags- und Bēmahymnen: Edition und Kommentar*. Ph. D. diss., Humboldt-Universität zu Berlin.

2004   *Gesegnet sei dieser Tag. Manichaeische Festtagshymnen. Edition der mittelpersischen und parthischen Sonntags-, Montags- und Bemahymnen*. Berliner Turfantexte 22. Turnhout: Brepols.

2005   "The Tribulation of Human Experience: A Sogdian Fragment Corresponding to a passage of Burzoy's preface to
               Kalilah wa Dimnah?" Studia Manichaica: V. International Congress of Manichaean Studies, Sept. 2001 Naples, edited by L. Cirillo
               and A. v. Tongerloo. Turnhout: Brepols (in press).

Reck, Christiane and Werner Sundermann
1997   "Ein illustrierter mittelpersischer Manichäischer Omen-Text aus Turfan." *Zentralasiatische Studien* 27: 7–23.

Reeves, John C.
1997   "Manichaean Citations from the *Prose Refutations* of Ephrem." In *Emerging from Darkness: Studies in the Recovery of Man-
               ichaean Sources*, edited by Paul Mirecki and Jason BeDuhn, 217–288. Leiden: E. J. Brill.

Reischauer, Edwin O.
1955   *Ennin's Travel in T'ang China.* New York: Ronald Press.

Richardson, H. E.
1985   *A Corpus of Early Tibetan Inscriptions.* Royal Asiatic Society. Hertford: Stephen Austin and Sons.

Riederer, Josef
1977   "Technik und Farbstoffe der frühmittelalterlichen Wandmalereien Ostturkistans." *Beiträge zur Indenforschung: Ernst
               Waldschmidt zum 80. Geburstag gewidmet*, edited by Museum für Indische Kust, Berlin, 353–423. Berlin: Museum für
               Indische Kunst, SMPK.

Ries, Julien
1976   "La fête de Bêma dans l'église de Mani." *Revue des Études Augustiniennes* 22: 218–233.
1988   *Les études manicheennes: Des controverses de la Réforme aux Découveres du XXᵉ siècle.* Louvain-la-Neuve: Centre d'histoire des
               religions.

Robinson, Basil W.
1965   *Persian Drawings from the 14th through the 19th century.* New York: Shorewood Publishers.

Rogers, J.M. (ed.)
1986   *The Topkapi Saray Museum: The Albums and Illustrated Manuscripts.* Boston: Little, Brown, and Company.

Rong Xinjiang,
1996   "Dunhuang zangjingku de xingzhi jiqi fengbi yuanyin." *Dunhuang Tulufan Yanjin* vol. 2, 23–40. Peking: Peking Univer-
               sity Press.

Rosenfield, John M.
1967   *The Dynastic Arts of the Kushans.* Berkeley: University of California Press.

Ross, Denison E.
1972   "Introduction" to *A History of the Moghuls of Central Asia: Tharikh–i–Rashidi*, 1-128. London: Curzon Press.

Rowland, Benjamin
1970   *The Art of Central Asia.* New York: Crown.

Rudolph, Kurt
1983   *Gnosis: The Nature and History of Gnosticism.* San Francisco: Harper and Row Publishers.

Salmony, Alfred
1922   *Die chinesische Steinplastik.* Berlin: Verlag für Kunstwissenschaft.

Sander, Lore
1968   *Paläographisches zu den Sanskrithandschriften der berliner Turfansammlung.* Wiesbaden: Franz Steiner Verlag.

Schaff, Philip (ed.)
1956   *Selected Library of the Nicene and Post-Nicene Fathers of the Christian Church.* Vol. 4. *St. Augustin: Writings against the Manichaeans
               and the Donatists.* Grand Rapid: W. R. Eerdmans.

Schlegel, Gustav
1896   *Die chinesische Inschrift auf dem uigurischen Denkmal in Kara Balgassun*, Helsingfors, La Société Finno–Ougrienne.

Schröter, Barbara
1996   "Gewebetechnische Untersuchung an manichäische Gewebe der Turfan-Sammlung des Museum für Indische Kunst
               in Berlin." A study commissioned by the Museum für Indische Kunst, Berlin, SMPK. Unpublished.
2003   "Techniques of Production, Ornamentation, and Embroidery." *Central Asian Temple Banners in the Turfan Collection of the
               Museum für Indische Kunst, Berlin*, by Ch. Bhattacharya-Haesner, 477–489. Berlin: Dietrich Reimer Verlag.

Seckel, Dietrich
1993   "Rise of Portraiture in Chinese Art." *Artibus Asiae* 53: 7–26.

Seiler-Baldinger, Annemarie
1994   *Textiles: A Classification of Techniques.* Washington, D.C.: Smithsonian Institution Press.

Šavčenko, Nancy P.
1998   "Illuminating the Liturgy: Illuminated Service Books in Byzantium." *Heaven on Earth: Art and Church in Byzantium*, edited
               by L. Safran, 186–228. Park: Pennsylvania State University Press.

Shailor, Barbara A.
1994   *The Medieval Book.* Toronto: University of Toronto Press.

Shiruku Rodo to Bukkyo bunka: Otani tankentai no kiseki
  1991   *Shiruku Rodo to Bukkyo bunka: Otani tankentai no kiseki*. Kanazawa-shi: Oshikawa Kenritsu Rekishi Hakubutsukan.
Shôsô-in Office,
  1989   *Treasures of the Shôsô-in: The South Section*. Tokyo: Asahi Shinbun Publishing Company.
Sickman, Laurence, and Alexander Soper
  1988   *Art and Architecture of China*. London: Penguin Books.
Sildergeld, Jerome
  1982   *Chinese Painting Style: Media, Methods, and Principles of Form*. Seattle: University of Washington Press.
Simms, George
  1993   *The Book of Kells*. Scribes, Scholars and Saints: The Art of Celtic Manuscript Series. Video recording. Ulster Video
               Production (1987). Princeton: Films for the Humanities, Inc.
Sims-Williams, Nicholas and James Hamilton
  1990   *Documents turco-sogdiens du IXe-Xe siècles du Touen-houang*. London: School of Oriental and African Studies.
Snellgrove, David, and Hugh Richardson
  1980   *A Cultural History of Tibet*. Boulder: Prajna Press.
Stanley-Baker Joan,
  1996   "Wu Daozi." *Dictionary of Art*, edited by Jane Turner, vol. 33, 422–424. New York: Grove's Dictionaries.
Stein, Aurel
  1912   *Ruins of Cathay: Personal Narrative of Explorations in Central Asia and Westernmost China*, I–II. London: Macmillan. (Reprinted
               1987. New York: Dover Publications).
  1921   *Serendia: Detailed Report of Explorations in Central Asia and Westernmost China*, I–V. Oxford: Oxford University Press.
               (Reprinted 1980. Delhi: Motilal Banarsidass).
  1928   *Innermost Asia: Detailed Report of Explorations in Central Asia, Kan-su and Eastern Iran*, I–V. Oxford: Oxford University Press.
               (Reprinted 1981. New Delhi: Cosmo Publications).
Su Bai
  1998   "Origins and Trends in the Depiction of Human Figures in China of the Fifth and Six Centuries." *China: 5000 Years
               of Innovation and Transformation of the Arts*, edited by S. Lee, 132–143. New York: Guggenheim Museum Publications.
Sullivan, Michael
  1984   *The Arts Of China*. Third edition. Berkeley: University of California Press.
Sundermann, Werner
  1973   *Mittelpersische und parthische kosmogonische und Parabeltexte der Manichäer*. Berliner Turfantexte 4. Berlin: Akademie Verlag.
  1981   *Mitteliranische manichäische Texte kirchengeschichtlichen Inhalts*. Berliner Turfantexte 11. Berlin: Akademie Verlag.
  1985a   *Ein manichäisch-sogdisch Parabelbuch*. Berliner Turfantexte 15. Berlin: Akademie Verlag.
  1985b   "Ein übersehenes Bild Manis." *Altorientalische Forschungen* 12: 172–174.
  1990   *The Manichaean Hymn Cycles Huyadagmān and Angad Rōšnān in Parthian and Sogdian*. Corpus Inscriptionum Iranicarum,
               Supplementary Series 2. London: School of Oriental and African Studies.
  1991a   "Manichaean Traditions on the Date of the Historical Buddha." *The Dating of the Historical Buddha (= Die Datierung des
               Historischen Buddha, I Symposien zur Buddhismusforschung) 4/1*, edited by Heinz Bechert, 426–438. Göttingen: Vanden-
               hoeck and Ruprecht.
  1991b   "Probleme der Edition iranisch-manichäischer Texte." In *Ägypten, Vorderasien,Turfan: Probleme der Edition und Bearbeitung
               altorientalischer Handschriften*, Schriften zur Geschichte und Kultur des alten Orients 23. Edited by Horst Klengel and
               Werner Sundermann, 106–112. Berlin: Akademie Verlag.
  1992a   "Iranian Manichaean Turfan Texts Concerning the Turfan Region." In *Turfan and Tun-huang: The Texts: Encounter of
               Civilizations on the Silk Route*, Orientalia Venetiana 4. Edited by Alfredo Cadonna, 63–84. Firenze: Leo S. Olschki.
  1992b   *Der Sermon vom Licht-Nous: Eine Lehrschrift des östlichen Manichäismus, Edition der parthischen und sogdischen Version*. Berliner
               Turfantexte 17. Berlin: Akademie Verlag.
  1994   "Iranische Personennamen der Manichäer." *Die Sprache: Zeitschrift für Sprachwissenschaft* 36/2: 244–270.
  1996   "Three Fragments of Sogdian Letters and Documents." *La Persia e l'Asia Centrale da Alessandro al X secolo*, Atti Dei Con-
               vegni Lincei 127. 99–111. Roma: Accademia Nazionale dei Lincei.
  1999   *Der Sermon von der Seele*. Berliner Turfantexte 19. Berlin: Akademie Verlag.
Sundermann, Werner, ed.
  1996b   *Iranian Manichaean Turfan Texts in Early Publications (1904–1934)*. Corpus Inscriptionum Iranicarum, Supplementary
               Series 3. London: School of Oriental and African Studies.
Tardieu, Michel
  1981   *Manichéisme*. Que sais-je? MCMXL. Paris: Presses Universitaires de France.
Tekin, Sinasi
  1980   *Buddhistische Uigurica aus der Yüan-zeit*. Wiesbaden: Otto Harrassowitz.
  1993   *Eski Türklerde Yazı, Kagit, Kitap ve kagit Damgaları*. Istanbul: Eren.

Thilo, Thomas
    1991   "Einige Bemerkungen zu zwei chinesisch-manichäischen Textfragmenten der Berliner Turfan-Sammlung." *Ägypten Vorderasien Turfan*, edited by H. Kleigel and W. Sundermann, 161–170. Berlin: Akademie Verlag.

Tokyo Kokuritsu Hakubutsukan, Kyoto Kokuritsu Hakubutsukan, Asahi Shinbunsha (=Tokyo National Museum, Kyoto National Museum, and Asahi Shinbunsha), (eds).
    1991   *Doitsu Tūrufan tankentai Seiiki bijutsuten* (= *Central Asian Art from the Museum of Indian Art, Berlin, SMPK*). Tokyo: Asahi Shinbunsha.

Tokyo National Museum and NHK and NHK Promotions
    2002   *Brocade and Gold from the Silk Road: In Commemoration of the 30th Anniversary of the Normalization of Diplomatic Relations between Japan and China.* Tokyo: NHK and NHK Promotions.

Tongerloo, Aloïs van
    1982   "La structure de la communauté manichéenne dans le Turkestan chinois à la lumière des emprunts moyen-iraniens en ouigour." *Central Asiatic Journal* 26: 262–288.

Tulufan diqu wenwu guanlisuo
    1985   "Bozikelike qianfodong yizhi qingli jianji." *Wen Wu* 8: 49–65.

Turfan Museum, ed.
    1992   *Turfan Museum.* Urumqi: Xinjiang Fine Arts and Photo Publishing House.

Waldschmidt, Ernst, and Wolfgang Lentz
    1933   "Manichäische Dogmatik aus chinesischen und iranischen Texten." *Sitzungsberichte der Preussischen Akademie der Wissenschaften* 13: 480–607.

Weitzmann, Kurt
    1959   *Ancient Book Illumination.* Cambridge: Cambridge University Press.

Weitzmann, Kurt, and Herbert L. Kessler
    1990   *The Frescoes of the Dura Synagogue and Christian Art.* Dumbarton Oaks Studies 28. Washington, D.C.: Dumbarton Oaks Research Library and Collection.

Whitfield, Roderick, and Anne Farrer, eds.
    1990   *Caves of the Thousand Buddhas: Chinese Art from the Silk Route.* New York: George Braziller.

Whitfield, Susan
    1998   "Count Otani's Central Asian Expeditions." *International Dunhuang Project News* 10: 1–2.

Whitfield, Susan (ed. With Ursula Sims-Williams)
    2004   *Silk Road: Trade Travel, War, and Faith.* London: The British Library.

Wilkens, Jens
    2000   *Manichäisch-türkische Texte der Berliner Turfansammlung.* Alttürkische Handschriften Tiel VIII. Stuttgart: Franz Steiner Verlag.

Wright, David H.
    1992   *Codicological Notes on the Vergilius Romanus (Vat. lat. 3867).* Studi e Testi 345. Vatican: Biblioteca Apostolica Vaticana.

Wurst, Gregor
    1995   *Das Bemafest der ägyptischen Manichäer.* Arbeiten zum spätantiken und koptischen Ägypten 8. Altenberge: Oros Verlag.

Yaldiz, Marianne
    1987   *Archäologie und Kunstgeschichte Chinesisch-Zentralasiens (Xinjiang).* Leiden: E. J. Brill.

Yamabe, Nobuyoshi
    1998   "The Implications of the 'Manichaean' Caves at Toyok, Turfan, for the Origin of *Guan wuliangshou jing.*" *Rennyo Shônin no sôgôteki kenkyû*, edited by Tokunaga Daishin, 280–250. Kyoto: Nagata Bunshôdô.

Yamada Nobuo
    1993   *Sammlung uigurischer Kontrakte 1–3*, edited by Juten Oda, et al. Osaka: Osaka University Press.

Yoshida Yutaka
    1990   "Some New Readings of the Sogdian Version of the Inscription." *Documents et archives provenant de l'Asie Centrale*, edited by A. Haneda, 117-123. Kyoto.
    2002   "Manichaean Sogdian Letters Discovered in Bezeklik." *Annuaire de la Section des Sciences Religieuses de l'École Pratiques des Hautes Études*, tom 19 (2000-2001), 233-236.

Yoshida Yutaka et al.
    2000   *Studies in the New Manichaean texts Recovered in Turfan.* Beijing. (In Chinese).

Zhongguo meishu quanji. Diaosubian 6: Yuan Ming Qing diaosu
    1988   Zhongguo meishu quanji. Diaosubian 6: Yuan Ming Qing diaosu. Beijing: Renmin Meishu Chucanshe.

Zieme, Peter
    1975   *Manichäisch-türkische Texte.* Berliner Turfantexte 5. Berlin: Akademie Verlag.
    1991   *Die Stabreimtexte der Uiguren von Turfan und Dunhuang: Studien zur alttürlischen Dichtung.* Budapest: Akadémiai Kiadó.

1992a   *Gesellschaft im Uigurischen Königreich von Qoco. Kolophone und Stifter des altturkischen buddhistischen Schrifttums aus Zentralasien,* Opladen, Westdeutscher Verlag.

1992b   "Manichäische Kolophone und Könige." *Studia Manichaica. II. Internationaler Kongreß zum Manichäismus,* edited by Gernot Wießner and Hans-Joachim Klimkeit, 319–328. Wiesbaden: Otto Harrassowitz.

1996   "Old Turkish Version of the *Scripture on the Ten Kings." Proceedings of the 38th Permanent International Altaistic Conference (PIAC). Kawasaki, Japan, August 7–12, 1995,* edited by Giovanni Stary, 401–425. Wiesbaden: Otto Harrassowitz.

INDEX

81 TB 65:01   22-24, 29, 37, 38, 56, 89, 90-92, 110, 112, 130, 135, 178, 180, 181, 186, 187, 188, 197, 202, 203, 206, 207, 213, 215, 216, Tab. 1/3, Tab. 1/4, Tab. 1/12, Tab. 4/1, Tab. 5/13, Tab. 6/1, Tab. 6/6, Tab. 6/7, **Fig. 3/15c, Fig. 4/2g, Fig. 5/23, Fig. 6/5a**

Abe, Takeo   4, 223
Allberry, Charles R. C.   7, 198, 223
Allen, Terry   122, 223
Anthology (of Religious Literature)   45, 54, 93, 190, 198, 211, 217
Armenian   193
Arnold, Sir Thomas W.   6, 8, 18, 59, 85, 103, 114, 116, 223, 226
Arnold-Döben, Victoria   7, 223
Asmussen, Jes P.   1, 3, 90, 223
Auditor   3, 25, 199, 200, 201, 207, 208, 210, 211, 212
Augustine (of Hippo)   30, 59, 206

Babylon   1, 2
Badiee, Julie   121, 122, 223
BeDuhn, Jason David   xvi, 3, 12, 22, 28, 43, 46, 48, 98, 103, 114, 127, 196, 198, 199, 200, 209, 211, 213, 223
Banerjee, P.   7, 223
Bang, W.   7, 223
Beckwith, Christopher   xv, 41, 223
Behzad, Taherzade   6, 223
Beinecke Library   86, **Fig. 3/13c**
Bema   7, 48, 61, 63, 98, 149, 204, 205, 207, 213; *Bema Festival*: 7, 29, 30, 48, 51, 61
Benediction   196-198, 200-203, 207-209, 211, 213
Beshbalik   2, 4, 41, 58
Bhattacharya-Haesner, Chayya   xv, 25, 223
Binding structure (silk)   74, 75, 85
Bishop (Parthian *aftadan*)   26, 56, 88, 121, 122, 201, 202, 203, 213, 216
Blair, Sheila S. & Bloom, Jonathan M.   122, 224
Blue Background   4, 13, 27, 28, 29, 46, 99, 107, 109, 111, 137, 148, 153, 155, 157, 165, 169, 171, 183, 186
Bodleian Library   115, 192, 193, **Fig. 4/3a, Fig, 5/29**
Book Binding   12, 13, 30, 31, 59, 60, 64-69, 71, 73, 76, 86, 91, 103, 137, 138, 141, 142, 144, 178, 190, 193; *Strengthened binding*: 67-69; *Coptic binding*: 31
Book Cover   6, 8, 30, 31, 32, 36, 37, 83-88, 90, 91, 93
Bookmakers   11, 59, 60, 103, 104
Bowman, Sheridan   45, 224
Boyce, Mary   7, 16, 17, 18, 20, 54, 64, 80, 103, 224
British Library   xv, 6, 7, 19, 36, 37, 121, 122, Fig. 4/7a, **Fig. 4/10a, 4/10b**
Brown, Michelle P.   97, 116, 121, 224
Bryder, Peter   8, 40, 224
Buddha   25, 28, 91, 186, 188, 205

Buddhist   xv, 3, 4, 8, 15, 18, 20, 22-26, 28, 39, 40, 42-45, 58, 74, 93, 94, 106, 109, 111-114, 125, 129, 130, 131, 132, 177, 188, 221
Bussagli, Mario   116, 224

Cahill, James   130, 224
Calkins, Robert, G.   9, 224
Calligraphy   1, 18, 22, 43, 59, 60, 61, 66, 67, 76, 93, 97, 99, 100, 101, 103, 133, 138, 169
Cameron, Ron – Arthur J. Dewey (trs.)   1, 3, 61, 224
Carboni Stefano   see under Petrosyan *et al.*,
Central Asia   1, 3, 4, 5, 12, 15, 18, 24-26, 36, 39, 43, 44, 59, 60, 64, 88, 93, 104, 105, 111, 112, 114, 116, 121, 122, 127, 131, 188, 206, 219, 221
Ch. 0015   6, 22, 36, 89, 90, 92, 178, 186, Tab. 1/3, Tab. 1/4, Tab. 1/12, Tab. 5/13, **Fig. 3/15a, Fig. 5/22**
Chao Huashan,   8, 39, 224
Chavannes, Edward, and Paul Pelliot   8, 39, 40, 42, 224
China   *Song China*:19, 44, 55, 106, 129, 130; *Tang China*: 4, 8, 26, 106, 114, 127-130
Christian   xvi, 3, 5, 15, 22, 25-27, 30, 44, 59, 67, 85, 104, 114, 116, 193, 196, 219
Clark, Larry V.   xv, xvi, 4, 6, 28, 38, 40, 41, 42, 43, 54, 69, 93, 96, 190, 196, 198, 204, 206, 224
Coakley, J. F.   26, 224
Codex   1-3, 7-9, 11-13, 26-31, 35-38, 45-48, 52, 55-57, 60, 61, 64, 66, 67, 69, 71, 74-78, 80, 81, 83, 88, 89, 93, 94, 98, 99, 103, 105-107, 111, 112, 117, 121, 127, 133, 135-138, 141, 142, 144, 146, 148, 151, 155, 158, 161, 162, 163, 165, 167, 169, 173-178, 186, 188, 191, 193, 195, 200, 202, 208, 211; *Codex Cover*: 37, 81, 84-86, 88; *Horizontal codex* 193; *Silk Codex* (see under silk); *Vertical codex*: 77, 1933
Codicology   8, 9, 10, 12, 98, 105
Cologne Mani Codex   1, 3, 61, 78, 224
Color Repertoire   85, 123
Coptic   6, 31, 61, 64, 67, 85, 114, 198, 225, 226
Crum, W. E.   22, 224
Czeglédy, Károly   4, 42, 224

D 258, 18   190, Tab. 5/14
Dating   xv, 56, 58, 111, 113, 121, 127, 130, 226, 231; Scientific dating: 11; Carbon-dating (radiocarbon dating): 129, 224; Stylistic dating: 11, 131
Delaissé, L. M. J.   8, 9, 10, 225
Dictionary of Art   91, 225
Doresse, Jean   87, 225
Drége, Jean-Pierre   26, 225
Dunhuang   xv, 2, 4, 5, 8, 21, 22, 24, 26, 36, 90, 106, 128, 129, 131

East Asia   4, 19, 22, 26, 39, 76, 104, 106, 116, 125, 127, 132,

221
Ebert, Jorinde   6, 7, 16, 18, 25, 29, 48, 167, 186, 204, 205, 225
Elect   3, 7, 24, 25, 27, 28, 31, 63, 85, 104, 105, 108, 116, 123,
    124, 125, 130, 205, 206, 211, 212, 213, Color Plate 3; Elect
    in Paradise: 204, 205, 207; Female elect: 31, 123, 124, 205,
    213
Encyclopedia Britannica   45, 225
Encyclopedia of World Art   5, 7, 44, 133, 225
Ephrem (the Syriac)   3, 88, 230
Esin, Emel   6, 225
Ettinghausen, Richard   115, 225
Exhibition   5, 6, 7, 80, 133, 146
Expeditions   4, 5, 6, 20, 21, 36, 38, 67, 90

Farrer, Anne   26, 130, 131, 225
Fraser Sarah E.   41, 127, 131, 225
Freer Gallery of Art   122, **Fig. 4/7b**
Fukien   1, 8, 43

Gabain, Annemarie von   5, 26, 43, 54, 93, 127, 167, 196, 225
Gansu   4, 8, 129
Gardner, Iain   22, 188, 226
Geng Shimin, and Hans-Joachim Klimkeit   4, 226
Giès, Jacques, and Moniq Cohen, eds.   90, 226
Gold   25, 28, 29, 10, 31, 44, 56, 85, 86, 88, 97, 104, 105, 107,
    109, 117, 120, 121, 131, 165, 186, 188, 205, 219, Color Plate
    4; Gilding: 12, 26, 28, 29, 30, 31, 56, 69, 71, 73, 85, 87, 88,
    97, 98, 107, 109, 116, 117, 118, 123, 180, 186, 205, 213, 215;
    Gold ink: 97, 98, 104, Color Plate 4
Graffito   36, 89, 90, 92, 178
Grabar, Oleg   18, 115, 226
Gratzl, Emil   6, 85, 226
Gray, Basil   121, 226
Grohman, A. and Thomas W. Arnold   85, 226
Gulácsi, Zsuzsanna   6, 11, 16-19, 23, 27-30, 32, 36, 39-44, 48,
    69, 73, 74, 82, 89, 94, 96, 97, 99, 109, 111, 114, 117, 121,
    123, 125, 148, 149, 186, 188, 198, 204-206, 211, 218, 226
Grünwedel, Albert   3, 6, 20, 42, 226

Haloun G. and Henning W.B.,   25, 114, 226
Hambis, Louis   5, 7, 18, 44, 116, 133, 226
Hamilton, James   27, 42, 43, 55, 226
Härtel, Herbert   4, 5, 6, 7, 20, 124, 133, 227
Henning, Walter Bruno   25, 31, 61, 62, 63, 64, 97, 98, 114,
    196, 223, 226, 227
Henrichs, Albert   1, 227
Homilies   81
Huntington, John C.   131, 227
Huntington, Susan   xvi, 227
Hymnbook   41, 56, 61, 96, 113, 198-203, 217, 218

Ibn al-Jawzi, Abu al-Faraj 'Abd al-Rahman ibn 'Ali   30, 227
Ibn Miskawayh Ahmad Ibm Muhammad,   30, 227
Ink   59, 61, 66, 67, 74, 76, 94, 97, 98, 99, 103, 014, 107, 116,
    121, 122, 123, 125, 130, 137, 138, 142, 149, 157, 165, 180,
    198, Color Plates 3 and 4; *Gold ink*: see under "gold"
Islamic   xvi, 4, 5, 30, 44, 85-87, 104, 106, 113, 114, 116, 121,
    193

Jesus   188, 201, 205

Kara, György and Peter Zieme   26, 227
Karabalgasun   2, 4, 40, 41, 113, 129
Kephalaia   61, 64, 188, 226
Käd Ogul Koshtir Memoir   4, 42
Kocho   1, 4, 5, 6, 15, 20, 21, 24, 27, 36, 38, 41, 42, 43, 56, 58,
    85, 111, 124, 126
Kerstein, P.   6, 227
Kessler, Konrad   227, 232
Khalidov B.,   see Petrosyan
Klimkeit, Hans-Joachim   4, 5, 6, 7, 8, 16, 17, 18, 38, 39, 41, 89,
    93, 112, 113, 116, 133, 195, 196, 198, 201, 204, 205, 206,
    226, 227
Klyashtorny, S. G.   41, 114, 227
Kudara, Kogi and Werner Sundermann and Yutaka Yoshida
    28, 60, 227

Le Coq, Albert von   5, 6, 7, 15, 16, 17, 18, 20, 24, 26, 27, 31,
    40, 42, 43, 44, 69, 85, 98, 93, 113, 114, 125, 133, 135, 196,
    204, 206, 228
Letter of the Seal   61, 63
Lieu, Samuel N. C.   1, 3, 4, 6, 8, 24, 30, 41, 42, 114, 129, 228
Liu Ts'un-yan,   40, 228
Losty, Jeremiah P.   91, 228
Loubier, J.   6, 87, 228
Lowden, John   xvi, 9, 10, 27, 113, 219, 228

M 1 (MIK III 203)   See under MIK III 203
M 2   114
M 4a   100, 101, 102, 103, **Fig. 3/17d, Fig. 3/18e**
M 4b   102, 103, Fig. 3/18f
M 10   67, 68, 69, Fig. 3/4a
M 23   16, 21, 24, 28, 37, 82, 117-120, 171, 197, 198, 207, Tab.
    1/1, Tab. 1/2, Tab. 1/4, Tab. 1/11, Tab. 3/7, Tab. 4/2, Tab.
    5/5, Tab. 6/1, Tab. 6/2, Tab. 6/7, **Fig. 4/3, Fig. 4/5b,
    Fig. 4/6c, Fig. 4/6d**
M 36   67, Tab. 3/3
M 37   80, 81, Tab. 3/5, **Fig. 3/11a**
M 168   16, 24, 37, Tab. 1/1, Tab. 1/4, Tab. 1/11
M 171   16, 21, 24, 37, 67, 69, 72, 73, 81, 82, 103, 117, 137,
    138, 139, 171, 197, 199, 207, Tab. 1/1, Tab. 1/2, Tab. 1/4,
    Tab. 1/11, Tab. 3/3, Tab. 3/7, Tab. 4/2, Tab. 5/1, Tab. 5/5,
    Tab. 6/1, Tab. 6/3, Tab. 6/7, **Fig. 3/6c & d, Fig. 3/11b,
    Fig. 5/5**
M 178 (MIK III 4990)   See under MIK III 4990
M 233   16, 21, 24, 37, 171, 100, 197, 198, 199, 207, Tab. 1/1,
    Tab. 1/2, Tab. 1/4, Tab. 1/11, Tab. 3/8, Tab. 4/2, Tab. 5/5,
    Tab. 6/1, Tab. 6/2, Tab. 6/7
M 267a   80, 81, Tab. 3/5, **Fig. 3/11a**
M 279   102, **Fig. 3/18b**
M 322   80, 81, Fig. 3/11a, Tab. 3/5
M 380 a, b   16, 24, 37, Tab. 1/1 Tab. 1/2, Tab. 1/4, Tab.
    1/11
M 403   102, 103, Fig. 3/18c
M 411   102, 103, Fig. 3/18d
M 501 e   16, 21, 23, 24, 28, 34, 37, 81, 83, 96, 117, 125, 159,
    171, 175, 197, 199, 207, 214, 217, Tab. 1/1, Tab. 1/2, Tab.
    1/9, **Color Plate 6a**

M 501 f   16, 21, 37, 177, Tab. 1/10, Tab. 5/12

M 508   16, 24, 37, Tab. 1/1, Tab. 1/4, Tab. 1/11

M 556   16, 21, 24, 37, 176, 197, 202, 207, 208, 209, Fig. 6/1, Tab. 1/1, Tab. 1/2, Tab. 1/4, Tab. 1/11, Tab. 5/10, Tab. 6/1, Tab. 6/6, Tab. 6/7, **Color Plates 8 e and 8f**

M 559   16, 21, 24, 37, 78, 82, 94, 108, 112, 175, 197, 198, 204-208, 213, Tab. 1/1, Tab. 1/2, Tab. 1/4, Tab. 1/11, Tab. 3/7, Tab. 4/1, Tab. 5/8, Tab. 6/1, Tab. 6/2, Tab. 6/6, Tab. 6/7, **Fig. 3/8, Fig. 4/1e, Fig. 5/18**

M 569 a-f   176, Tab. 5/10

M 576   16, 21, 24, 37, 81, 82, 100, 117, 141, 142, 153, 154, 155, 169, 171, 197, 198, 199, 207, Tab. 1/1, Tab. 1/2, Tab. 1/4, Tab. 1/11, Tab. 3/7, Tab. 4/2, Tab. 5/2, Tab. 5/4, Tab. 5/5, Tab. 6/1, Tab. 6/2, Tab. 6/7, **Fig. 3/11b, Fig. 5/12**

M 596 a-f   16, 21, 24, 28, 37, 171, 173, Tab. 1/1, Tab. 1/2, Tab. 1/4, Tab. 1/11, Tab. 5/4, Tab. 5/7

M 660 a, b   16, 21, 34, Tab. 1/1, Tab. 1/2, Tab. 1/9

M 694   16, 21, 24, 37, 171, 197, 199, 207, Tab. 1/1, Tab. 1/2, Tab. 1/4, Tab. 1/11, Tab. 5/5, Tab. 6/1, Tab. 6/3, Tab. 6/7

M 730   7, 16, 24, 37, 83, 117, 171, 196, 197, 198, 207, Tab. 1/1, Tab. 1/4, Tab. 1/10, Tab. 3/8, Tab. 4/2, Tab. 5/4, Tab. 6/1, Tab. 6/2, Tab. 6/7

M 797   16, 21, 24, 37, 66, 81, 83, 96, 100, 102, 120, 140, 171, 197-199, 207, Tab. 1/1, Tab. 1/2, Tab. 1/4, Tab. 1/11, Tab. 3/3, Tab. 3/8, Tab. 5/1, Tab. 5/5, Tab. 6/1, Tab. 6/2, Tab. 6/7, **Fig. 3/11c, Fig. 3/18a, Fig. 4/6b, Fig. 5/6**

M 801 (MIK III 53)   See under MIK III 53

M 810a   27, Tab. 1/6

M 817a   21, 28, 173, Tab. 1/2, Tab. 5/7

M 857   16, 24, 27, 28, 37, 99, Tab. 1/1, Tab. 1/4, Tab. 1/11, **Color Plate 4f**

M 871 a   16, 37, 117, Tab. 1/1, Tab. 1/11, Tab. 4/2

M 1002, 1006, 1007, 1023, 1028, & 9000   80, Tab. 3/6

M 1156   16, 21, 27, 37, 112, 171, Tab. 1/1, Tab. 1/2, Tab. 1/6, Tab. 1/11, Tab. 4/1, Tab. 5/4

M 1881   24, Tab. 1/4

M 1886   16, 21, 34, Tab. 1/1, Tab. 1/2, Tab. 1/9

M 1887   16, 21, 34, 37, 99, 117, 171, Tab. 1/1, Tab. 1/2, Tab. 1/9, Tab. 1/11, Tab. 4/2, Tab. 5/4

M 4831   16, 21 24, 37, 112, 117, 118, 120, Tab. 1/1, Tab. 1/2, Tab. 1/4, Tab. 1/11, Tab. 4/1, Tab. 4/2, Tab. 5/6, **Fig. 4/6b**

M 6020   70, 71, **Fig. 3/5a**

M 6290 b   16, 24, 25, 37, 117, 176, 204, 205, Tab. 1/1, Tab. 1/2, Tab. 1/4, Tab. 1/11, Tab. 4/2, Tab. 5/10, Tab. 6/6

M 7981   100, 101, **Fig. 3/17b**

M 7984   100, 101, **Fig. 3/17c**

M 8113 (MIK III 103)   See under MIK III 103

M 8200   16, 21, 24, 37, 117, 176, Tab. 1/1, Tab. 1/2, Tab. 1/4, Tab. 1/11, Tab. 4/2, Tab. 5/9

Mackerras, Colin   4, 39, 128, 129, 228

Mani   1, 3, 4, 7, 25, 30, 41, 54, 61, 78, 88, 89, 106, 114, 121, 196, 197, 198, 200, 201, 205, 207, 208, 210, 218

Martinez, A. P.   41, 228

Mayer, Ralph   98, 228

McGraw-Hill Dictionary of Art   106, 228

Mediterranean   2, 3, 19, 61, 64, 121

Mesopotamia   1, 3, 22, 44, 45, 106, 114, 127

Mez, Adam   4, 30, 228

Middle Persian   3, 22, 41, 43, 46, 55, 56, 61, 69, 94, 96, 106, 114, 127, 133, 178, 198, 200

MIK III 5 a-d   16, 21, 34, Tab. 1/1, Tab. 1/9, also see under MIK III 1947 & III 5 d

MIK III 36   16, 17, 21, 24, 29, 37, 41, 70, 71, 81, 82, 98, 112, 157, 167, 176, 197, 200, 201, 204, 206-210, Tab. 1/1, Tab. 1/2, Tab. 1/4, Tab. 1/10, Tab. 3/7, Tab. 4/1, Tab. 5/2, Tab. 5/11, Tab. 6/1, Tab. 6/4, Tab. 6/6, Tab. 6/7, **Color Plate 8c and 8d, Fig. 3/5c & b, Fig. 3/11b, Fig. 5/11, Fig. 6/2**

MIK III 38   80, 81, Tab. 3/6, **Fig. 3/11e**

MIK III 53 (M 801)   61-64, 66, 78, 80, 81, 97, 98, 198, Tab. 3/1, Tab. 3/5, **Fig. 3/1, Fig. 3/2, Fig. 3/11b**

MIK III 101   66, Tab. 3/1

MIK III 103 (M 8113)   64-66, 78, 80, 81, Tab. 3/1, Tab. 3/5, **Fig. 3/3, Fig. 3/11a**

MIK III 104   16, 17, 21, 24, 37, 94, 177, Tab. 1/1, Tab. 1/2, Tab. 1/4, Tab. 1/10, Tab. 5/12

MIK III 134   16, 21, 28, 29, 37, 112, 177, 188, Tab. 1/1, Tab. 1/2, Tab. 1/7, Tab. 1/10, Tab. 4/1, Tab. 5/12

MIK III 141 a   25, 123, Tab. 4/3

III 141 c   See under MIK III 4815 & III 141 c

MIK III 151   16, 21, 24, 25, 27, 37, 74, 76, 94, 96, 108, 112, Tab. 1/1, Tab. 1/2, Tab. 1/4, Tab. 1/5, Tab. 1/10, Tab. 4/1, **Fig. 3/16c, Fig. 4/1a**

MIK III 164   25, 127, Tab. 4/4

MIK III 189   190, Tab. 5/14

MIK III 203 (M 1)   41, 56, 66, 72, 73, Tab. 2/3, Tab. 3/1, **Fig. 3/6a**

MIK III 4614   16, 21, 23, 25, 37, 90, 91, 125, 127, 182, 204, 206, 215, 216, 218, Tab. 1/1, Tab. 1/2, Tab. 1/10, Tab. 4/4, Tab. 6/6, **Color Plates 6c and 8a, Fig. 5/24, Fig. 6/5c & d**

MIK III 4624   42, 123, 125, 130, Tab. 4/3

MIK III 4815 & III 141 c   25, 123, 125, Tab. 4/3, **Fig. 4/8b**

MIK III 4937   16, 21, 37, Tab. 1/1, Tab. 1/2, Tab. 1/10

MIK III 4943   16, 28, 29, 37, 177, Tab. 1/1, Tab. 1/7, Tab. 1/10, Tab. 5/12

MIK III 4947 & III 5 d   16, 21, 28, 34, 37, 44, 91, 108, 112, 120, 178, 185, 186, 204, 205, Tab. 1/1, Tab. 1/2, Tab. 1/7, Tab. 1/9, Tab. 1/10, Tab. 4/1, Tab. 5/13, Tab. 6/6, **Color Plate 7c, Fig. 4/1c, Fig. 4/1d, Fig. 4/6d, Fig. 5/26**

MIK III 4956 a-d   16, 21, 24, 27, 34, 37, 112, 120, 171, 173, 175, 176, 177, Tab. 1/1, Tab. 1/2, Tab. 1/4, Tab. 1/6, Tab. 1/9, Tab. 1/10, Tab. 4/1, Tab. 5/5, Tab. 5/7, Tab. 5/8, Tab. 5/11, Tab. 5/12, **Fig. 4/6a**

MIK III 4957   16, 21, 37, Tab. 1/1, Tab. 1/2, Tab. 1/10

MIK III 4958   16, 21, 24, 34, 37, 73, 83, 110, 112, 148, 171, 176, 188, Tab. 1/1, Tab. 1/2, Tab. 1/4, Tab. 1/9, Tab. 1/10, Tab. 3/9, Tab. 4/1, Tab. 5/9, Tab. 5/10

MIK III 4959   7, 16, 21, 24, 37, 44, 81-83, 108, 112, 133, 134, 163, 164, 175, 176, 178, 186, 197, 202, 204, 205, Tab. 1/1, Tab. 1/2, Tab. 1/4, Tab. 1/10, Tab. 3/9, Tab. 4/1, Tab. 5/9, Tab. 5/11, Tab. 6/1, Tab. 6/5, Tab. 6/6, **Color Plate 7d, Fig. 3/11d, Fig. 4/1d, Fig. 5/1, Fig. 5/16**

MIK III 4960   16, 21, 24, 37, 110, 112, 205, Tab. 1/1, Tab. 1/2, Tab. 1/4, Tab. 1/10, Tab. 4/1, Tab. 5/10, **Fig. 4/2d**

MIK III 4962 a-c   16, 21, 24, 27, 34, 37, 112, 173, 177, Tab.

1/1, Tab. 1/2, Tab. 1/4, Tab. 1/6, Tab. 1/9, Tab. 1/10, Tab. 4/1, Tab. 5/7, Tab. 5/12

MIK III 4964   16, 21, 24, 25, 37, 82, 110, 112, 118, 120, 176, 188, Tab. 1/1, Tab. 1/2, Tab. 1/4, Tab. 1/10, Tab. 4/1, Tab. 5/10, **Fig. 4/1b, Fig. 4/2a, Fig. 4/6c**

MIK III 4965   16, 21, 28, 29, 37, 110, 112, 113, 117, 119, 120, 193, 204, 205, Tab. 1/1, Tab. 1/2, Tab. 1/ 7, Tab. 1/10, Tab. 4/1, Tab. 6/6, Color Plate 7a & b, Fig. 4/2a, Fig. 4/5a, Fig. 4/6d

MIK III 4966 a-c   16, 21, 24, 25, 34, 37, 52, 57, 69, 73, 82, 171, Tab. 1/1, Tab. 1/2, Tab. 1/4, Tab. 1/9, Tab. 1/10, Tab. 5/4, also see under MIK III 6265 & III 4966 c

MIK III 4967 a-c   16, 21, 24, 37, 96, 112, 117, 118, 120, 171, 176, 186, Tab. 1/1, Tab. 1/2, Tab. 1/2, Tab. 1/4, Tab. 1/10, Tab. 4/1, Tab. 4/2, Fig. 4/6a, Tab. 5/5, Tab. 5/10, Tab. 5/11

MIK III 4968   16, 21, Tab. 1/1, Tab. 1/2

MIK III 4969   16, 21, 24, 28, 37, 83, 98, 99, 112, 118, 120, 171, Tab. 1/1, Tab. 1/2, Tab. 1/4, Tab. 1/10, Tab. 3/8, Tab. 4/1, Tab. 5/4, **Color Plate 4a & e, Fig. 4/6a, Fig. 4/6c**

MIK III 4970 b-c   16, 17, 21, 24, 37, 82, 99, 117, 118, 120, 171, 176, 197, 198, 207, Tab. 1/1, Tab. 1/2, Tab. 1/4, Tab. 1/10, Tab. 3/7, Tab. 4/2, Tab. 5/4, Tab. 5/5, Tab. 5/8, Tab. 5/10, Tab. 6/1, Tab. 6/2, Tab. 6/7 **Color Plate 4d, Fig. 4/6a**

MIK III 4971 a-d   16, 21, 24, 25, 28, 37, 82, 111, 117, 120, 165, 166, 167, 175, 176, 177, Tab. 1/1, Tab. 1/2, Tab. 1/4, Tab. 1/10, Tab. 3/7, Tab. 4/2, Tab. 5/10, Tab. 5/12, **Fig. 5/17**

MIK III 4972 a-d   16, 17, 21, 24, 29, 37, 96, 112, 171, 173, 175, 188, Tab. 1/1, Tab. 1/2, Tab. 1/4, Tab. 1/10, Tab. 4/1, Tab. 5/4, Tab. 5/7, Tab. 5/8

MIK III 4973 a   16, 21, 37, Tab. 1/1, Tab. 1/2, Tab. 1/10

MIK III 4974   7, 16, 20, 21, 24, 25, 28, 29, 37, 81, 82, 96, 98, 110, 112, 141, 142, 144, 145, 146, 148, 155, 161, 165, 167, 171, 175, 176, 197, 201, 204, 205, 207, 211, 212, 213, 217, Tab. 1/1, Tab. 1/2, Tab. 1/4, Tab. 1/10, Tab. 3/7, Tab. 4/1, Tab. 5/2, Tab. 5/4, Tab. 5/8, Tab. 5/9, Tab. 5/10, Tab. 6/1, Tab. 6/4, Tab. 6/7, Tab. 6/7, **Fig. 3/11b, Fig. 4/2g, Fig. 5/8, Fig. 6/3**

MIK III 4975   16, 18, 21, 37, 90, 91, 112, 178, 183, 184, Tab. 1/1, Tab. 1/2, Tab. 1/5, Tab. 1/10, Tab. 4/1, Tab. 5/13, **Fig. 3/15b, Fig. 5/25**

MIK III 4976 a, b & S 49   16, 21, 24, 27, 34, 37, 38, 82, 83, 94, 96, 112, 172, 173, 197, 207, Tab. 1/1, Tab. 1/2, Tab. 1/4, Tab. 1/9, Tab. 1/10, Tab. 4/1, Tab. 3/9, Tab. 5/6, Tab. 6/1, Tab. 6/7, **Fig. 5/20**

MIK III 4979
16, 20, 21, 23-25, 29, 30, 37, 41, 48, 51-53, 55, 83, 98, 105, 106, 108, 110-112, 141, 142, 146-149, 157, 161, 165, 171, 176, 188, 197, 201, 204-07, 213, Tab. 1/1, Tab. 1/2, Tab. 1/4, Tab. 1/10, Tab. 3/8, Tab. 4/1, Tab. 5/2, Tab. 5/3, Tab. 5/4, Tab. 5/10, Tab. 6/1, Tab. 6/4, Tab. 6/6, Tab. 6/7, **Color Plates 5, 6b, and 7f, Fig. 2/5, Fig. 2/6, Fig. 2/7, Fig. 4/1a, Fig. 4/1b, Fig. 4/1c, Fig. 4/1e, Fig. 4/2a, Fig. 4/2b, Fig. 4/2c, Fig. 4/2d, Fig. 4/2e, Fig. 4/2f, Fig. 5/9**

MIK III 4981 a-f   7, 16, 21, 23, 24, 28, 34, 37, 65, 66, 74-76, 100, 117, 171, 197-199, 207, Tab. 1/1, Tab. 1/2, Tab. 1/4,

Tab. 1/9, Tab. 1/10, Tab. 4/2, Tab. 6/1, Tab. 6/2, Tab. 6/3, Tab. 6/7, **Color Plate 2, Fig. 3/3c, Fig. 3/7a**

MIK III 4983   17, 21, 24, 27, 37, 65, 66, 67, 69, 73, 83, 98, 100, 107, 110, 112, 118, 120, 171, 197, 198, 207, Tab. 1/1, Tab. 1/2, Tab. 1/4, Tab. 1/10, Tab. 3/3, Tab. 3/8, Tab. 4/1, Tab. 5/4, Tab. 6/1, Tab. 6/2, Tab. 6/7, **Color Plate 4b, Fig. 3/3b, Fig. 4/2f, Fig. 4/6a**

MIK III 4984   17, 21, 37, Tab. 1/1, Tab. 1/2, Tab. 1/10

MIK III 4990 (M 172)   64, 66, 98, 100, 101, 103, Tab. 3/1, **Color Plate 1, Fig. 3/17a**

MIK III 6252 a-c   17, 21, Tab. 1/1, Tab. 1/2

MIK III 6254   17, 21, Tab. 1/1, Tab. 1/2

MIK III 6255   17, 21, Tab. 1/1, Tab. 1/2

MIK III 6257   17, 21, 25, 27, 37, 108, 112, 176, 204, 206, Tab. 1/1, Tab. 1/2, Tab. 1/5, Tab. 1/10, Tab. 4/1, Tab. 5/11, Tab. 6/6, **Fig. 4/1a**

MIK III 6258 a, b   17, 21, 24, 48, 34, 37, 98, 107, 110, 112, 171, 176, 204, 205, Tab. 1/1, Tab. 1/2, Tab. 1/4, Tab. 1/9, Tab. 1/10, Tab. 4/1, Tab. 5/4, Tab. 5/10, Tab. 6/6, **Fig. 4/2f**

MIK III 6261   17, 21, 27, 37, 117, 171, Tab. 1/1, Tab. 1/6, Tab. 1/10, Tab. 4/2, Tab. 5/4

MIK III 6265 & III 4966 c   17, 21, 24, 29, 34, 37, 48, 49, 52, 52, 22, 83, 94, 95, 108, 110, 171, 175, 188, 204, 205, Tab. 1/1, Tab. 1/2, Tab. 1/4, Tab. 1/9, Tab. 1/10, Tab. 3/8, Tab. 4/1, Tab. 5/5, Tab. 5/8, Tab. 6/6, **Color Plate 7e, Fig. 2/3b, Fig. 2/4, Fig. 2/6, Fig. 2/7, Fig. 3/16a, Fig. 4/1b, Fig. 4/1e, Fig. 4/2c, Fig. 4/2e, Fig. 4/2g**

MIK III 6267   17, 21, 31, 32, 37, 83, 86-88, Tab. 1/2, Tab. 1/8, Tab. 1/10, **Fig. 3/14b**

MIK III 6268   44, 83-88, Tab. 1/1, Tab. 1/8, Tab. 1/10, Tab. 4/1, **Fig. 3/12, Fig. 3/14a**

MIK III 6270   25, 31, 127, Tab. 4/4

MIK III 6274   21, 25, Tab. 1/2

MIK III 6275   25, 89, 110, **Fig. 4/2b**

MIK III 6278   28, 112, 183, Tab. 4/1

MIK III 6279 a-i   24, Tab. 1/4

MIK III 6283   25, 45, 83, 123, Tab. 4/3

MIK III 6284   Tab. 1/1, Tab. 1/2, Tab. 1/7, Tab. 1/10, Tab. 4/1, Tab. 5/12, **Fig. 2/3c, Fig. 2/4**

MIK III 6286   21, 25, 30, 31, 45, 85, 123, Tab. 1/2, Tab. 4/3, **Fig. 1/2**

MIK III 6368   Tab. 1/1, Tab. 1/2, Tab. 1/5, Tab. 1/10, Tab. 2/1, Tab. 3/3, Tab. 3/8, Tab. 4/1, Tab. 5/2, Tab. 5/5, Tab. 5/8, Tab. 5/11, Tab. 6/1, Tab. 6/3, Tab. 6/4, Tab. 6/6, Tab. 6/7, **Color Plates 3 and 8b, Fig. 3/11c, Fig. 4/1a, Fig. 4/1b, Fig. 4/1e, Fig. 4/2c, Fig. 4/2d, Fig. 5/2, Fig. 5/3, Fig. 5/13**

MIK III 6374   17, 21, 27, 37, 82, 173, Tab. 1/1, Tab. 1/2, Tab. 1/6, Tab. 1/10, Tab. 5/7, Tab. 6/1

MIK III 6376   17, 21, 28, 29, 37, 177, 204, 205, Tab. 1/1, Tab. 1/2, Tab. 1/7, Tab. 1/10, Tab. 5/12

MIK III 6377 a b d f & III 6990 a   17, 21, 24, 28, 34, 37, 81, 82, 83, 99, 112, 171, Tab. 1/1, Tab. 1/2, Tab. 1/4, Tab. 1/9, Tab. 1/10, Tab. 3/9, Tab. 4/1, Tab. 5/4, **Color Plate 4g, Fig. 3/11d**

MIK III 6378 a-h   17, 21, 24, 28, 29, 34, 37, 176, 177, Tab. 1/1, Tab. 1/2, Tab. 1/4, Tab. 1/7, Tab. 1/9, Tab. 1/10, Tab. 5/10, Tab. 5/12

MIK III 6379 a-h   17, 21, 27, 34, 37, 112, 173, 176, Tab. 1/1,

Tab. 1/6, Tab. 1/9, Tab. 1/10, Tab. 4/1, Tab. 5/7, Tab. 5/10

MIK III 6379 c   See under MIK III 6626 & III 6379 c

MIK III 6388a   25, 111, 112, Tab. 4/1

MIK III 6626 & III 6379 c   17, 21, 28, 29, 34, 37, 112, 171, 204, 206, Tab. 1/1, Tab. 1/2, Tab. 1/7, Tab. 1/9, Tab. 1/10, Tab. 4/1, Tab. 5/5, Tab. 5/12, Tab. 6/6

MIK III 6915 a, b   25, 123, Tab. 4/3

MIK III 6916   108, 111, 112, Tab. 4/1, **Fig. 4/1c**

MIK III 6917   123, Tab. 4/3

MIK III 6918   25, 123, 130, 216, Tab. 4/3

MIK III 6953 a-n   25, 123, Tab. 4/3

MIK III 6981   124, **Fig. 4/8a**

MIK III 6989 a-d   17, 21, 28, 29, 34, 37, 91, 110, 112, 178, 187, 188, Tab. 1/1, Tab. 1/2, Tab. 1/7, Tab. 1/9, Tab. 1/10, Tab. 4/1, Tab. 5/13, **Fig. 4/2a, Fig. 4/2g, Fig. 5/27**

MIK III 7048   17, 21, 32, 37, 83, 87, 88, Tab. 1/1, Tab. 1/2, Tab. 1/8, Tab. 1/10

MIK III 7060   21, 25, Tab. 1/2

MIK III 7068   31, 32, 68, **Fig. 3/14c**

MIK III 7251   7, 17, 21, 24, 28, 37, 117, 118, 120, 171, Tab. 1/1, Tab. 1/2, Tab. 1/4, Tab. 1/10, Tab. 4/2, Tab. 5/4, **Fig. 4/6c, Fig. 4/6d**

MIK III 7266   17, 21, 27, 37, 112, 173, Tab. 1/1, Tab. 1/2, Tab. 1/6, Tab. 1/10, Tab. 4/1, Tab. 5/7

MIK III 7283   17, 21, 37, 112, 177, 186, 204, 205, Tab. 1/1, Tab. 1/2, Tab. 1/10, Tab. 4/1, Tab. 5/12, Tab. 6/6

MIK III 7285   17, 21, 24, 25, 37, 94, 95, 108, 112, 176, Tab. 1/1, Tab. 1/2, Tab. 1/4, Tab. 1/10, Tab. 4/1, Tab. 5/10, **Fig. 3/16b, Fig. 4/1c**

MIK III 8259   Tab. 1/1, Tab. 1/2, Tab. 1/4, Tab. 1/10, Tab. 2/1, Tab. 3/3, Tab. 3/8, Tab. 4/1, Tab. 5/2, Tab. 5/3, Tab. 5/5, Tab. 5/8, Tab. 5/10, Tab. 6/1, Tab. 6/2, Tab. 6/3, Tab. 6/4, Tab. 6/6, Tab. 6/7, **Fig. 2/1, Fig. 2/2, Fig. 2/3a, Fig. 2/4, Fig. 2/4, Fig. 2/7, Fig. 3/4b & c, Fig. 3/11c, Fig. 4/1d, Fig. 4/2c, Fig. 4/2e, Fig. 4/6b, Fig. 5/7**

MIK III 8260   Tab. 1/1, Tab. 1/2, Tab. 1/4, Tab. 1/10, Tab. 4/3, Tab. 5/14, Tab. 6/1, Tab. 6/2, Tab. 6/6, Tab. 6/7, **Color Plate 6d, Fig. 5/28**

Mikkelsen Gunner B.   5, 39, 127, 229

Minorsky V.   40, 228

Monneret de Villard, Ugo   6, 18, 229

Moriyasu Takao,   xvi, 4, 7, 38, 41, 42, 43, 55, 56, 114, 196, 201, 229

Morony, Michael G.   42, 114, 229

Museum für Indische Kunst   xv, 5, 7, 26, 80, 93, 98, 229

Museum of Fine Arts, Boston   126, 139, **Fig. 4/9a**

Müller, Friedrich Wilhelm Karl   4, 5, 22, 26, 41, 42, 196, 198, 229

No. 11074   21, 24, 37, 38, 112, Tab. 1/3, Tab. 1/4, Tab. 1/12, Tab. 4/1, **Fig. 1/4**

North Africa   6, 22, 59, 114

Or. 12452/3   21, 24, 33, 36, 37, 112, 141, 158, 160, Tab. 1/3, Tab. 1/4, Tab. 1/12, Tab. 4/1, Tab. 5/2, **Fig. 1/3, Fig. 5/15**

Or. 8212-1692   83, 112, 141, 142, 149, 150, 157, 167, 176, 197, 201, 202, 204, 206, 207, 226, Tab. 1/3, Tab. 1/4, Tab. 1/12,

Tab. 3/8, Tab. 4/1, Tab. 5/2, Tab. 5/11, Tab. 6/1, Tab. 6/4, Tab. 6/5, Tab. 6/6, Tab. 6/7, **Fig. 5/10**

Oxford Dictionary of Byzantium   8, 229

Paint   74, 86, 88, 97, 105, 107, 115, 117, 131, 162; *Gold paint*: 131

Parchment   9, 30, 33, 36, 37, 59, 60, 64, 65, 70, 76, 78, 88, 89, 98, 100, 103, 111, 121, 158, 161, Color Plate 1

Paper   4, 10, 13, 27, 30, 36-38, 43, 45, 46, 48, 55, 59-61, 64, 66, 67, 69, 71-76, 80, 85, 88-90, 93, 94, 97, 98, 100, 103, 104, 111, 120, 126, 127, 133, 146, 148, 151, 153, 155, 163, 165, 167, 177, 178, 180, 183, 186, 188, 190, 193, 198, 202, 203, 206, 208, 213, 217; *Chinese paper*: 30

Parthian   1, 3, 22, 44, 46, 61, 63, 94, 106, 113, 127

Pelliot, Paul   8, 26, 39, 40, 42, 224, 229

Persia   3; *Sasanian Persia*: 113; *Abbasid Persia*: 19, 30

Petrosyan Yuri *et al.*   115, 229

Picture-Book   106, 113, 114, 178, 191, 193, 218

Psalm-Book   81, 84

Punctuation Decoration   12, 22, 43, 61, 66, 67, 73, 76, 97, 98, 100, 138, 141

Pustaka   21, 26, 36, 37, 43, 54, 57, 60, 88, 91, 93, 124, 126, 135, 136, 177, 188, 189, 190, 191, 193, 195, 198

Reck, Christiane   xv, 155, 158, 196, 199, 202, 217, 230

Reeves, John C.   3, 88, 114, 230

Reischauer, Edwin O.   24, 230

Riederer, Josef   107, 230

Ries, Julien   5, 230

Robinson, Basil W.   121, 230

Rogers J.M.   212, 230

Roman Empire   3, 30

Rong Xinjiang,   131, 230

Ross, Denison E.   4, 230

Rowland, Benjamin   230

Rudolph, Kurt   87, 230

Russian Academy   36, 115, 229, **Fig. 4/3b**

S 23   115, **Fig. 4/3b**

S 30   7, 21, 24, 36, 37, 112, Tab. 1/3, Tab. 1/4, Tab. 1/12, Tab. 4/1

S 42   21, 24, 36, 37, 112, Tab. 1/3, Tab. 1/4, Tab. 1/12, Tab. 4/1

S 49 a, b   7, 21, 24, 27, 34, 36, 37, 38, 82, 83, 94, 112, 171, 172, 173, Tab. 1/3, Tab. 1/4, Tab. 1/9, Tab. 1/12, Tab. 4/1 Tab. 4/1

S 50   7, 21, 36, 37, Tab. 1/3, Tab. 1/12

Salmony, Alfred   230

Sander, Lore   xv, 17, 230

Schaff Philip (ed.)   30, 59, 230

Schlegel, Gustav   40, 230

Schröter, Barbara   74, 80, 230

Scribes   3, 10, 11, 12, 22, 43, 59, 60, 93, 94, 96, 97, 99, 100, 103, 104, 114, 165, 201

Scribal Decoration   22, 23, 43, 60, 66, 73, 88, 93, 96-98, 100-104, 163, 198

Scroll   5, 8, 22, 26, 28, 29, 36, 37, 38, 40, 55, 56, 58, 60, 88, 89, 90, 91, 92, 94, 103, 111, 125, 127, 130, 135, 136, 177-183, 186, 188, 191, 193, 197, 202, 203, 204, 208, 213, 216; Pictorial Scroll: 90, 91, 130, 184, 185, 186, 187, 188; *The 13*

Emperors Scroll: 130; Horizontal Scroll: 178, 180, 183, 186, 193; Vertical Scroll: 178, 180, 193
Seal   7, 61, 63, 89, 90, 180
Seckel, Dietrich   130, 231
Service-book   98, 198, 200, 203, 211, 217-219
Shoso-in Office   130, 230, **Fig. 4/9b**
Sickman, Laurence, and Alexander Soper   130, 231
Sideways   10, 11, 27, 46, 54, 76, 115, 121, 178, 180, 183, 190, 191, 192, 193, 195, 208, 219, Color Plate 5
Silk   30, 39, 60, 66, 74, 75, 76, 89, 90, 94, 96, 97, 103, 104, 111, 112, 117, 121, 123, 124, 126, 128, 131, 132, 171, 183, 197, 198, 199, 207, 208; *Silk Codex*: 7, 20, 25, 96, 97, Color Plate 2; *Silk Road*: 1, 2, 4, 7, 96, 133
Silk Road   1, 2, 4, 7, 36, 128, 133
Simms, George   97, 231
Sims-Williams, Nicholas   178, 231
So 18700 & M 501 e   16, 21, 23, 24, 25, 34, 37, 81, 96, 117, 125, 141, 142, 158, 159, 171, 175, 197, 199, 200, 207, 214, 217, Tab. 1/1, Tab. 1/2, Tab. 1/11, Tab. 3/8, Tab. 4/2, Tab. 5/2, Tab. 5/4, Tab. 5/8, Tab. 6/1, Tab. 6/3, Tab. 6/7, **Color Plate 6a, Fig. 3/11c, Fig. 5/14, Fig. 6/4**
Splicing   61, 70-73, 90
Stanley-Baker, Joan,   130, 231
Stein, Aurel   12, 36, 231
Su Bai   130, 231
Sundermann, Werner   xv, xvi, 7, 12, 26, 38, 55, 60, 80, 89, 127, 133, 190, 196, 202, 231
Synaxeis   81
Syriac   3, 5, 22, 27, 44, 114, 115, 116, 121, 122, 192, 193
Śavčenko, Nancy P.   219, 231

Tamim ibn Bahr   40, 228
Tarim Basin   4, 41, 113
Teacher (M. Persian. *mozhak*)   42, 56, 202, 211, 212, 213, 216
Thilo, Thomas   127, 232
T.M. 332   16, 21, 23, 24, 28, 37, 171, Tab. 1/1, Tab. 1/4, Tab. 4/2, Tab. 5/4
Tokyo Kokuritsu Hakubutsukan, Kyoto Kokuritsu Hakubutsukan, Asahi Shinbunsha (=Tokyo National Museum, Kyoto National Museum, and Asahi Shinbunsha), (eds).   7, 232
Tokyo National Museum and NHK and NHK Promotions   180, 232
Tulufan diqu wenwu guanlisuo   8, 38, 232
Turfan Museum   xv, 8. 37, 38, 232

U 75   190, Tab. 5/14
U 76   190, Tab. 5/14
U 77   190, Tab. 5/14
U 79   190, Tab. 5/14
U 80   190, Tab. 5/14
U 81   190, Tab. 5/14
U 82   190, **Fig. 5/28, Tab. 5/14**
U 83   190 Tab. 5/14
U 84   190 Tab. 5/14
U 85   190, Tab. 5/14

U 86   190, Tab. 5/14
U 87   190, Tab. 5/14
U 88   190, Tab. 5/14
U 89   190, Tab. 5/14
U 90   190, Tab. 5/14
U 91   190, Tab. 5/14
U 92   190, Tab. 5/14
U 93   190, Tab. 5/14
U 94   190, Tab. 5/14
U 95   190, Tab. 5/14
U 96   190, Tab. 5/14
U 97   190, Tab. 5/14
U 98   190, Tab. 5/14
U 99   190, Tab. 5/14
U 100   190, Tab. 5/14
U 101   190, Tab. 5/14
U 102   190, Tab. 5/14
U 103   190, Tab. 5/14
U 104   190, Tab. 5/14
U 106   190, Tab. 5/14
U 107   190, Tab. 5/14
U 108   190, Tab. 5/14
U 109   190, Tab. 5/14
U 110   190, Tab. 5/14
U 246   16, 24, Tab. 1/1, Tab. 1/4
U 2972   26
Underdrawing   86, 99, 107, 115, 117, 118, 123, 125
Uygur   4, 7, 12, 16, 22, 26, 29, 36, 40-46, 52, 54-59, 90, 94, 103, 105-117, 121-132, 178, 190, 198, 200, 201, 203, 208, 210, 211, 213
Uygur Steppe Empire   4, 41, 42, 58, 106, 114, 128

Waldschmidt, Ernst, and Wolfgang Lentz   196, 230, 232
Weitzmann, Kurt   196, 232
West Asia   1, 6, 22, 26, 27, 44-46, 76, 85, 87-89, 100, 103-106, 108, 110, 112-125, 127, 129, 130, 132, 178, 193, 218, **Color Plate 6**
Wilkens, Jens   17, 232
Winter, Werner   54, 127, 225
Whitfield, Roderick, and Anne Farrer, eds.   28, 131, 232
Whitfield, Susan   xv, 7, 38, 97, 232
Wright, David H.   9, 10, 232
Wu Daozi   126, 130, **Fig. 4/9b**
Wurst, Gregor   7, 232

Yaldiz, Marianne   v, xv, 4, 5, 7, 70, 42, 43, 97, 124, 232
Yamabe, Nobuyoshi   39, 232
Yan Liben   126, 130, **Fig. 4/9a**
Yoshida, Yutaka   xvi, 38, 40, 56, 60, 180, 196, 202, 203, 216, 227, 232

Xinjiang   xv, 5, 8, 18, 38, 39, 130

Zieme, Peter   xv, 26, 43, 54, 55, 111, 112, 127, 232
Zoroastrian   3, 205
Zoroaster   205